Chivalry and Exploration

_____ 1298–1630 _____

Chivalry and Exploration

_____ 1298–1630 _____

Jennifer R. Goodman

THE BOYDELL PRESS

First published 1998
The Boydell Press, Woodbridge

ISBN 0 85115 700 9

910·9   Goo

The Boydell Press is an imprint of Boydell & Brewer Ltd
PO Box 9, Woodbridge, Suffolk IP12 3DF, UK
and of Boydell & Brewer Inc.
PO Box 41026, Rochester, NY 14604–4126, USA

A catalogue record for this book is available
from the British Library

Library of Congress Cataloging-in-Publication Data
Goodman, Jennifer R. (Jennifer Robin), 1953–
   Chivalry and exploration, 1298–1630 / Jennifer R. Goodman.
      p. cm.
   Includes bibliographical references and index.
   ISBN 0–85115–700–9 (hardback : alk. paper) : £45.00 ($81.00 US)
   1. Discoveries in geography. 2. Geography, Medieval.
3. Civilization, Medieval – Romances. I. Title.
G89.5.G66 1998
910'.9 – dc21   97–40076

This publication is printed on acid-free paper

Printed in Great Britain by
St Edmundsbury Press Ltd, Bury St Edmunds, Suffolk

CONTENTS

ILLUSTRATIONS

ACKNOWLEDGEMENTS

To list the scholars who contributed time, encouragement, ideas, and criticism to this project boggles the mind. I should first thank my teachers, living and dead, who directed my interest towards the later Middle Ages and Renaissance. Larry Benson has advised, inspired, and sympathized with me ever since his seminar on Chivalric Romances. Alan Heimert, for whom I wrote the paper that became this book, merits my special thanks for his good counsel. The late Franco Simone drew my attention to French fifteenth-century literature and the theme of *translatio studii*. B. J. Whiting first suggested I work on Caxton and printing history, and explained that the pun is the highest form of humor, especially when you make it yourself.

This book could never have been completed without my colleagues and students at Texas A&M. Nancy Joe Dyer, Zoltan Kosztolnyik, Harrison T. Meserole, Bedford Clark, and Vivian Paul have listened to me talk about it and offered many useful suggestions. I owe a debt of gratitude to a number of friendly and patient Hispanists, and historians of things Iberian, foremost among them Alan Deyermond and Jim Muldoon.

In 1991 I was able to undertake a research trip to Spain and England, thanks to a Summer Stipend from the Columbian Quincentenary Initiative of the National Endowment for the Humanities. During that period, I profited from the chance to consult Dr Lotte Hellinga at the British Library and the staff of the Biblioteca Nacional in Madrid and the Archivio de la Corona de Aragon and the Biblioteca de Catalunya in Barcelona. I also want to thank Karen Birkner, who served as my initial research assistant on this project; and the staff of Houghton Library at Harvard and the University of Minnesota Libraries, with special thanks to Carol Urness, Curator of the James Ford Bell Collection, for her help with the illustrations.

My parents are to be thanked for seeing me through to the end of this branch of my *chemin de longue étude*. My Bernese Mountain Dogs Garbo and Kilroy also deserve credit – Garbo for starting me off in grand style, and Kilroy for insisting that I sit at the computer. Last but not least, my thanks to Hzik-Leyb.

Jennifer R. Goodman
College Station, Texas
August 1996

INTRODUCTION

> *"The age of chivalry is past," said Mary Dacre. "Bores have succeeded to dragons."*[1]

> *What people believe to be true about their past is usually more important in determining their behavior and responses than truth itself.*[2]

LIFE IS A WORK OF the imagination.[3] This is the first premise on which this study rests. Or, as Montaigne put it, *"fortis imaginatio generat casum:* A strong imagination begetteth chance."* Over the past few years, scholars have been rediscovering the human imagination as a force in history. This, perhaps, comes as a reaction to the dominance of what Samuel Johnson would have called "systematic" explanations in late-nineteenth- and twentieth-century historical studies: the overwhelming stress on economic, political, social, and biological constraints on human behavior.[4] (Imagination plays a little acknowledged role in these areas of human experience, too.) Human beings make themselves in the image of their beliefs. Throughout our lives, we struggle to enact our fantasies. An idealized world of the imagination colors our perceptions and shapes our decisions. The young Jewish Londoner of 1913 who read Zane Grey and set out to homestead in the Peace River Country reflects a human tendency that can be traced back through the earliest annals of human consciousness.[5] It is true that sad experience tends to check imaginative aspiration. The haberdasher may not be able to reinvent himself as a wilderness fisherman fast enough to feed his wife and child. All too often, translating the wilder flights of

---

1   Benjamin Disraeli, *The Young Duke*, bk 2, ch. 5, in his *Works* (New York, 1904), III.101.
2   Michael Kammen, *Mystic Chords of Memory: The Transformation of Tradition in American Culture* (New York, 1991), pp. 38–39.
3   My first line is inspired by and responds to Robert Hughes, *Culture of Complaint: The Fraying of America* (New York, 1993), p. 13.
4   "Of Dr. Hurd, bishop of Worcester, Johnson said to a friend, 'Hurd, Sir, is one of a set of men who account for every thing systematically; for instance, it has been a fashion to wear scarlet breeches; these men would tell you, that according to causes and effects, no other wear could at that time have been chosen.' " James Boswell, *Life of Johnson*, ed. George Birkbeck Hill (Oxford, 1887), IV.189. The quotation from Michel de Montaigne is from his essay, "Of the force of imagination," *Essays*, trans. John Florio, ed. J. I. M. Stewart (London, 1931), I.83. For the French text of the essay, see Michel de Montaigne, *Essais*, ed. Maurice Rat (Paris, 1962), I.100ff.
5   The Londoner in question was my grandfather, Harry Lewis (1882–1946); his intellectual life and experiences are detailed in my article in progress, "Harry Lewis and Jewish Life in Medicine Hat, 1917–1942."

1

the imagination into practice leads to humiliation or destruction. It can also lead to forms of extreme behavior, and of recognition or notoriety, that forever elude the prudent.

If imagination shapes human life, what, then, shapes the imagination? The question has long preoccupied philosophers. One contributing element is art. Many artists of our own day debate or deny their own function as shapers of the imaginations and the lives of their contemporaries. They prefer the classical formula that "art imitates life" to Oscar Wilde's subversive inversion, "Life imitates Art."[6] They depict themselves as reporters, keen-eyed observers, or perhaps aloof Olympian commentators on civilization, not its designers. Artists still want to be gods, but they prefer Marcion's Greek ideal of a remote, totally apathetic divine being to the emotionally engaged God of the Hebrew Bible.[7] Such artists still create worlds that reflect the world of their own experience, with varying degrees of distortion. At the same time, they resist the idea that members of their audiences might choose to take up mental residence in the worlds of their making. Yet that is what auditors in fact do. The second premise underlying this study, then, is that art – in this case, imaginative literature – does indeed shape human self-perception, vision and behavior.

If, as Robert Hughes observed, America is a collective work of the imagination, where does this imaginative vision originate? What are the sources that inspire it? Again, the question has been asked before, and can be answered in many different ways. A myriad visions, native and imported, ancient and modern, play their part in shaping our "America." Some of the deepest roots of this idea and of the American experience are only now beginning to be traced by specialists in Native American cultures. Others have been long recognized, but are today discounted or gone out of fashion. Of these elements in the imaginative creation of America, perhaps the most often misunderstood is the

6   The debate over "imitation" began for Auerbach with Plato's *Republic*, bk 10. Cf. Erich Auerbach, *Mimesis: The Representation of Reality in Western Literature*, trans. Willard R. Trask (Princeton, 1953), pp. 554–55. See Allan Bloom, trans., *The Republic of Plato* (New York, 1968), pp. 277–90. For Wilde, see "The Decay of Lying" (1889), rpt. in *Literary Criticism of Oscar Wilde*, ed. Stanley Weintraub (Lincoln, 1968), p. 182.

7   For a discussion of Marcion's conception of God as a being "incapable of anger, entirely apathetic, free from all emotions," and for the Biblical prophets' opposing vision, see Abraham J. Heschel, *The Prophets* (1962; rpt. New York, 1975), II.79–80. See also Jaroslav Pelikan, *The Christian Tradition: A History of the Development of Doctrine*, I: *The Emergence of the Catholic Tradition (100–600)* (Chicago, 1971), pp. 53–54. Also pertinent as background to this study are pp. 71–81. The ongoing influence of Marcion's contributions to Western thought, through his efforts to separate Judaism and Christianity, law and gospel, a cruel Creator and a true God of redemption, is still little appreciated. As a thinker he attracted both Luther and Barth. His radical dualist solution to the mystery of how evil can emerge from good still claims many adherents. This is the underlying problem posed by a study of chivalry and exploration. For Robert Hughes' comment, see *Culture of Complaint*, p. 13.

role of late medieval European chivalric ideals in the era of European expansion – the Age of Discovery, as it used to be called.

It was not always thus. From the fourteenth to the twentieth century, European adventurers and their historians were much given to identifying the deeds of explorers and conquerors with the exploits of the knights errant of medieval chivalric mythology. Herbert E. Bolton's *Coronado: Knight of Pueblos and Plains* was published as recently as 1949.[8] With the rise of modern economic history this connection was to be increasingly rejected as naive, triumphalist or imperialistic. The language of chivalry has faded from American studies, except where it might apply to the exploits of indigenous peoples against European intruders.[9] Few if any of the remarkable works of scholarship inspired by the 1992 Columbian Quincentenary choose to involve themselves with chivalry.[10]

The early link between chivalry and exploration is difficult for the contemporary scholar to ignore entirely, given its presence in certain essential primary

---

[8] Bolton, *Coronado: Knight of Pueblos and Plains* (1949; rpt. Albuquerque, 1990), was published as vol. 1 of the Coronado Cuarto Centennial Publications, 1540–1940, in a series edited by George P. Hammond. Washington Irving and Prescott should also be cited as notable contributors to the annals of chivalric writing about exploration.

[9] For instances of this application of chivalric vocabulary to Native American warriors, while denying it to their European opponents, see John Hemming, *Red Gold: The Conquest of the Brazilian Indians, 1500–1760* (Cambridge, Mass., 1978), p. 96: "These Aimoré were very different from the Tupi, who went into battle gaudily plumed, in a phalanx and shouting defiantly. The Tupi had refined their inter-tribal wars to such an extent that their fighting became almost chivalrous, with elaborate rituals and rules of conduct. For all its barbarity there was something elegant about Tupi warfare, and this made them easy victims of ruthless Europeans." Francis Jennings, *The Invasion of America* (1975; rpt. New York, 1976), pp. 168–70. Here, in his comparison of seventeenth-century Indian and European modes of warfare, Jennings finds that "Only a few generations before the invasion of America, Europeans had conducted war according to feudal rules very different from those of the nation-state but startlingly similar in many respects to the practices of Indian war." Jennings proceeds to draw a detailed comparison between chivalric practice and Native American tribal conduct. The element of European chivalry he discusses at greatest length is "the sparing of women and children," the aspect of the chivalric code that was emphasized in the nineteenth century. Jennings suggests that this forbearance might have some biological rationale, as it might have served to rebuild declining populations. In this respect he sees the Indians as "more chivalrous" than the European knight. Parallels have also been adduced between Aztec military traditions and European chivalric institutions. See M. D. Coe, "The Aztec Empire: Realm of the Smoking Mirror," in *Circa 1492: Art in the Age of Exploration*, ed. Jay A. Levenson (New Haven, 1991), pp. 504–05, and Ross Hassig, *Aztec Warfare* (Norman, 1988). Discussions of this type underline the need for a systematic program of comparative chivalric studies. See J. R. Goodman, "European Chivalry in the 1490s," *Comparative Civilizations Review* 26 (Spring 1992), pp. 43–72.

[10] Among the works that have reshaped the field in recent years, Stephen Greenblatt's *Marvellous Possessions: The Wonders of the New World* (Chicago, 1992) and William D. Phillips, Jr. and Carla Rahn Phillips' *The Worlds of Christopher Columbus* (Cambridge, 1992) have been of special importance for English-speaking readers.

sources. It stands fast in Bernal Diaz del Castillo's identification of Tenochtitlan as something out of *Amadís*, the naming of California after an imaginary island of Amazons from *Las Sergas de Esplandián*, and many other instances.[11] Meanwhile extensive developments in the study of medieval literature and chivalry, as well as fresh approaches to late medieval chivalry and its literature, demand a reopening of the discussion.

> Human beings are what they understand themselves to be; they are composed entirely of beliefs about themselves and about the world they inhabit . . . A human life is composed of performances, and each performance is a disclosure of a man's belief about himself and the world and an exploit in self-enactment.[12]

In 1933 Irving Leonard investigated the role of popular European literature, notably Renaissance chivalric literature, in the Americas. His *Books of the Brave* is now an indispensable work in its field. *Books of the Brave* documents in detail the book trade between Spain and its American colonies. It explores the reading habits of the *conquistadores* and their successors in Mexico and Latin America, with special attention to the dissemination of the sixteenth-century Spanish chivalresque romances – *Amadís*, *Palmerin*, and their offspring.[13] In this study I am returning to the same field, gleaned so memorably by Professor Leonard. But I am approaching it from a different direction. For me the subject begins earlier in history – as early as the conjunction of Marco Polo and the Rustichello (or Rusticiano) da Pisa who was his cellmate. Rustichello is known to literary history as the compiler both of Polo's adventures in Cathay, and of an influential Arthurian prose romance, the *Compilation of Rusticiano da Pisa*. The interplay between the chivalric imagination and the European narrative of exploration can be established this early. My discussion continues through the attempted conquest of the Canaries in 1402 by the knight errant Gadifer de la Salle and

---

11 Many of these examples are discussed in Irving Leonard's *Books of the Brave* (1949; rpt. Berkeley and Los Angeles, 1992). But, as the 1992 reprinting of *Books of the Brave* acknowledges, Professor Leonard's pioneering work has not been supplemented by later studies in English.

12 Michael Oakeshott, "Education: The Engagement and its Frustration," in *The Voice of Liberal Learning: Michael Oakeshott on Education*, ed. Timothy Fuller (New Haven, 1989), p. 64.

13 Professor Leonard's documentation of the longterm history of this literature as it infiltrated American cultures has been pursued in different directions by such scholars as Peter Burke, Juan Gil, and Luis Weckmann. See Peter Burke, "Chivalry in the New World," in *Chivalry in the Renaissance*, ed. Sydney Anglo (Woodbridge, 1990), pp. 253–62. Juan Gil, *Mitos y utopías del descubrimiento*, vol. 1: *Colón y su tiempo*; vol. 2: *El Pacífico*; vol. 3: *El Dorado* (Madrid, 1989); Luis Weckmann, *La herencia medieval de México* (3 vols., Mexico City, 1984). For more specialized studies that extend the work of Irving Leonard, see Rolena Adorno's introduction to the 1992 edition of *Books of the Brave*, in particular pp. xxviii–xl.

his cohorts, into the worlds of Henry the Navigator, Cortes and Cabeza de Vaca, Ralegh and Captain John Smith.[14] Chronologically, then, the field takes a different shape in this investigation.

This volume also reflects an altered perspective on the nature of late medieval chivalry, and a new vision of the later history of chivalric literature. My discussion emphasizes the international character of European chivalry and the body of writings that supported it. The phenomenon of chivalry as it intersects exploration will be my principal concern here, rather than the subsequent literary histories of Spain and the Americas.

This book is, then, conceived as a comparative analysis. It reinterprets two literatures, the chivalric literature of the fourteenth through the sixteenth century, and the exploration narratives of the same era. My immediate goal is to show how a new appreciation of the chivalric literature sheds light on tales of exploration. As twentieth-century readers revisit the imaginative fiction of this period, they experience the fantasies of the age. They can then hope to understand the era's actions, reactions, insights, limitations, enterprises, and crimes in a new way. The ultimate goal of this project is to explore the role of the imagination in human experience and in the records of that experience.

Any student of that pair of loaded terms, chivalry and exploration, risks classification as a reactionary celebrant of the murderers and tyrants of the past. Only a perverse being would attempt to rescue Cortes and company by reasserting their status as moral paragons in shining armor. Without question, the safest course is to classify the matter as a subject for students of historical writing. The chivalric language employed by such major writers as Irving, Prescott and Parkman certainly merits intelligent attention within the context of the chivalric revival of the nineteenth century.[15] But the connection of chivalry and exploration runs deeper in this literature. Chivalry and exploration have been comrades since at least the days of Marco Polo, if not since the days of the First Crusade. To regard their conjunction as a problem of style, of nineteenth- and twentieth-century historiography, protects the chivalry of the Middle Ages from critical scrutiny, in part by negating its longterm influence. The scholars who refuse to see any chivalry in exploration seem to cherish a fonder view of chivalry than do those who admit its presence. They also find

---

[14] Felipe Fernández-Armesto, *Before Columbus: Exploration and Colonisation from the Mediterrranean to the Atlantic 1229–1492* (Basingstoke and London, 1987); M. Keen, "Gadifer de la Salle: A Late Medieval Knight Errant," in *The Ideals and Practice of Medieval Knighthood: Papers from the First and Second Strawberry Hill Conferences*, ed. Christopher Harper-Bill and Ruth Harvey (Woodbridge, 1986), pp. 74–85.

[15] Such a study of the chivalric language of nineteenth-century historians would draw on the substantial investigations of nineteenth-century medievalism already in existence. Mark Girouard's *The Return to Camelot: Chivalry and the English Gentleman* (New Haven, 1981) offers much useful background material for such a discussion. An equivalent volume dealing with the nineteenth-century American chivalric revival does not immediately come to mind.

themselves in opposition to specialists in chivalry who recognize exploration as a natural outgrowth of the medieval "cult of knight-errantry."[16]

The assumption that any identification of the conquistadores and their contemporaries as chivalric figures must constitute an attempt at rehabilitation is interesting in itself. This supposition reveals how positive the image of medieval chivalry remains among even the most advanced Western thinkers. Emblematic of this persistent admiration of the European chivalric ideal is Francis Jennings' discussion of the true chivalry of the indigenous peoples of the Americas. In Jennings' assessment, the medieval knight exemplified many attractive qualities that were still better represented by the Native American warrior: training from youth in martial arts, sports, and the hunt, the experience of a ritual of initiation, voluntary service of a chieftain rather than paid or conscripted participation in combat, and a primary loyalty to his family. The seventeenth-century European invader, by contrast, is only a cruel agent of nationalism and intolerance. Interestingly, Jennings classifies the crusade as a nationalist phenomenon, rather than a chivalric one. Chivalry, in his analysis, is reduced to one essential feature: the concern to spare women and children in warfare. Without question, this somewhat Victorian characterization of chivalry regrettably oversimplifies an elaborate and sophisticated code of conduct and mythology of warfare.[17]

Historians, most of all historians of culture and of literature, need to recognize the role of the imagination in history. When it is attentively reconsidered, it can prove as powerful in its own way as the body, restored to historical prominence by Foucault, or the higher intellect, the usual province of the "historian of ideas." Against the modern enterprise of "demythologizing" the past, an overwhelming number of primary sources assert the central importance of myth, then and now. If we are to understand our ancestors, or ourselves, we need to understand our common fantasies.

This project cuts against entrenched academic practice in two additional ways. First, it takes issue with the devaluation of the romance as a form of literature. Secondly, it questions the long-accepted belief in a "decadence" or "death" of European chivalry in the fourteenth and fifteenth centuries. Both of these issues deter any study of chivalry or chivalric romance as a factor in the imaginative world of the period 1298–1630, or any later era. Ultimately, both debates spring from a larger problem, which is our organization of history by periods – the idea of a Middle Age and a Renaissance.

In the minds of students of literature today few genres rank lower than the romance. In spite of the late Northrop Frye's gallant attempt to rehabilitate it in *The Secular Scripture*, the genre still poses a challenge to scholarship, in part because of its size, the length of its history, and the contrast between the works

---

[16] Maurice Keen, *Chivalry* (New Haven, 1984), p. 250.
[17] Jennings, *The Invasion of America*, pp. 169–70.

it contains. Even when the viewer's focus is restricted to romances of the period traditionally considered the Middle Ages, the variety of narratives that are called romances remains startling. Medieval romances may be stylized or minutely detailed in their level of verisimilitude: the range is broad. They may employ verse or prose. They do share certain thematic concerns, such as a preoccupation with the exploration or discovery of individual identity. They also share a looser type of plot construction than that preferred by mainstream novelists up to the twentieth century. Their narrative logic or illogic is often diametrically opposed to the incremental, carefully explained and motivated movement we associate with the standard novel.

As Northrop Frye observed, the stock-in-trade of the romance is most often the wish-fulfillment fantasies of its audiences. Georges Duby and, for a later period, Daniel Eisenberg argue that these seem primarily, but not exclusively, to have been younger or perhaps socially unsettled audiences, readers and hearers in search of patterns of conduct and aspirations on which to model their own lives. Duby argues in a celebrated essay that the original chivalric romance of the twelfth century was designed for the *iuvenes*, younger sons of knightly families with no expectation of inheritance in the form of land.[18] The element of social uncertainty may be more important to stress than the issue of age, since the term *iuvenes* was applied to young men as old as forty. Still, this feature – the romance's appeal to the young – may account for the strong didactic element in certain specialized romances: *Le Roi Ponthus et la belle Sidoine*, *Cleriadus et Meliadice*, and *Amadís de Gaula* itself come to mind in this context. They become "courtesy books," used to teach proper modes of conduct to young readers and hearers. This aspect of their vogue may also help to explain why the romances were attacked by sixteenth-century humanist educators like Juan Luis Vives and Roger Ascham.[19] These concerned intellectuals express

---

[18] Northrop Frye, *Anatomy of Criticism: Four Essays* (Princeton, 1957), p. 383, where the romance is identified as "the nearest of all literary forms to the wish–fulfillment dream"; Frye elaborated his ideas about the romance in *The Secular Scripture: A Study of the Structure of Romance* (Cambridge, Mass., 1976); G. Duby, "Dans la France du Nord-Ouest. Au XIIe siècle: les 'jeunes' dans la société aristocratique," *Annales, Economies–Sociétés–Civilisations* 19 (1964), pp. 835–46. A translation of this article by Fredric L. Cheyette, "In Northwestern France: The 'Youth' in Twelfth-Century Aristocratic Society," appears in Cheyette's anthology, *Lordship and Community in Medieval Europe: Selected Readings* (New York, 1968), pp. 198–209. Daniel Eisenberg, *Romances of Chivalry in the Spanish Golden Age* (Newark, 1982), pp. 89–90, 93–97.

[19] Juan Luis Vives, *De Institutione Feminae Christianae*, in *Opera Omnia* (1783; rpt. London, 1964), IV.65–301; Roger Ascham, *The Scholemaster*, in *Whole Works*, ed. J. A. Giles (London, 1864), bk 1, p. 159. For other critics, especially in Spain, see Eisenberg, *Romances of Chivalry*, pp. 10–12, and 47. Other humanist educators were not above adapting the romance to their own educational programs: cf. Jean du Pin, Bishop of Rieux, and his Allobrogian Tale of 1516, which turns out to be the romance of *Paris and Vienne* in Latin. This may have been the *Winnie ille Pu* of its day. See Robert Kaltenbacher, ed., "Der altfranzösische Roman *Paris et Vienne*," *Romanische Forschungen* XV (1904), pp. 350–51.

horror at the seductive immorality of long lists of successful romances. They sound rather like a contemporary American school board.

The evil psychological effects of the romance on its readers have been debated in every generation since the thirteenth.[20] For every author who rants against the injurious effects of such reading on a young person's later career, another rushes up to report the beneficial moral import of these apparently frivolous works. By the eighteenth century, Samuel Johnson was even willing to bear witness to both possibilities. Generally, though, the strength of the genre does not lie in any overt didactic tendency. The romance was, first of all, written and read as entertainment. This play element only strengthens its impact on the imagination.

The identity of the audience of romance has been much debated, and is discussed below in the next chapter. On close examination, these audiences resist restriction by gender or social position. The long-entrenched assumption that the romances began to lose their aristocratic audiences in the sixteenth century has recently been challenged, but it is debatable whether they became the property of the ignorant lower classes.[21] The exclusively aristocratic

---

20 The discussion of the psychological effect of reading romances runs at least from Dante's Francesca da Rimini (*Inferno* II:137; "Galeotto fu il libro e che lo scrisse." "A Galehaut was the book and he who wrote it." This is the prose *Lancelot* as an irresistible incitement to adultery). The same concern preoccupies Samuel Johnson and, later, Louisa May Alcott. According to Bishop Percy, Johnson attributed to his lifelong fondness for romances of chivalry "that unsettled turn of mind which prevented his ever fixing in any profession." See Walter Jackson Bate, *Samuel Johnson* (New York, 1975), p. 26. See also James Boswell, *Life of Johnson*, IV.16–17; cf. IV.3, n. 8, where Mrs. Piozzi reports Johnson's comment on the rise of didactic children's literature: " 'Babies do not want,' said he, 'to hear about babies; they like to be told of giants and castles, and of somewhat which can stretch and stimulate their little minds.' When I would urge the numerous editions of *Tommy Prudent* or *Goody Two Shoes*, 'Remember always,' said he, 'that the parents buy the books and that the children never read them.' " For Louisa May Alcott's view of fantasy literature as harmful to young readers, see *Little Men* (1871; rpt. Boston, 1890), pp. 46–47. In *Little Women* and *Jo's Boys* she objects to the sort of gothic romance she had been known to write herself, and to risqué French novels. Positive views of the romance appear in William Caxton's prefaces and epilogues, notably his preface to his 1485 edition of Malory, and to his *Blanchardyn and Eglantine* of 1489, in Sir Philip Sidney's *Apology for Poetry*, and in many other sources. For all this, see Jennifer R. Goodman, *Malory and William Caxton's Prose Romances of 1485* (New York, 1987), pp. 14–27.

21 Eisenberg, *Romances of Chivalry*, pp. 90–110; Albrecht Classen, *The German Volksbuch: A Critical History of Late-Medieval Genre* (Lewiston, 1995), and Professor Classen's personal communication during a discussion at the special session on *Mélusine* at the 1993 MLA conference in Toronto. Clive Griffin, *The Crombergers of Seville: The History of a Printing and Merchant Dynasty* (Oxford, 1988), p. 153. Earlier in his book, Griffin argues against the belief that printing broadened the reading public or lowered the price of books (pp. 6–7). See also Adorno's introduction to Leonard, pp. xx, xxxviii. Joan Ferrante, "Whose Voice? The Influence of Women Patrons on Courtly Romances," in *Literary Aspects of Courtly Culture*, ed. Donald Maddox and Sara Sturm-Maddox (Cambridge, 1994), pp. 3–18. See also J. R. Goodman, " 'That Wommen holde in ful greet

character of the readership of such fictions remains unproven. Without question, certain romances were aimed at particular audiences. Joan Ferrante has discussed the special characteristics of a group of works written for female patrons, as, for instance, *Guillaume de Palerne* was in the late twelfth century. The typical reader of the sixteenth-century Spanish chivalric romances may have been a young gentleman, judging by dedications of particular works to elegant young patrons. The audience identified by Duby as the original targets of the romance in the twelfth century, the landless younger sons of knightly houses, clearly continued to maintain their interest in these heroic volumes for generations. They were also to provide a surplus of volunteers to European expeditions of exploration and conquest. Specific cases can be found to demonstrate that mothers and their male and female children, soldiers, clerics, and teachers might all be caught reading romances throughout the period to be discussed in this volume. The romances have always attracted a wider range of readers than is generally supposed.[22]

A second factor that has impeded the study of the romance is the scholarly neglect of a crucial segment of its history. That is the prose romance of the fifteenth century, a category of works much beloved of early European printers and too often neglected by academic specialists at large. As a result of this neglect, the literary history and status of the romance between about 1450 and 1600 are still misunderstood. This study reconsiders the influential works of this period in relation to their more familiar relatives, and in the process revises the history of the genre. The rediscovery of these later prose romances is indispensable to understanding the role of chivalry at this period and its relation to the phenomenon of European exploration. This widely disseminated chivalric fiction should also be recognized as a key factor in the "civilizing process" described by Norbert Elias, and now receiving new attention from social science historians. Throughout the sixteenth century this literature worked alongside the courtesy books studied by Elias to bring courtly manners and attitudes to a wider public. Historians need to re-examine this chivalric inheritance if they are to understand the fall in European homicide rates during this period, set alongside the violence Europeans plunged into all across the globe at the same time.[23]

---

reverence': Mothers and Daughters reading Chivalric Romances," in *Women, The Book, and the Worldly*, ed. Lesley Smith and Jane H. M. Taylor (Cambridge, 1995), pp. 25–30.

[22] Eisenberg, *Romances of Chivalry*, pp. 93–97; Adorno's introduction to Leonard, *Books of the Brave*, p. xx; Bolton, *Coronado*, pp. 19–20, 52–53, 55, 60–61 on the youth and social background of Coronado and his recruits. This class represented a serious unemployment problem for the Mexican authorities around 1539. Coronado and his subordinate García López de Cárdenas were both second sons of Spanish noblemen, left without fortunes by the laws of primogeniture. Bolton estimates the ages of Coronado's men as "mostly in the twenties, with many still younger, and very few above thirty" (Bolton, *Coronado*, p. 60).

[23] See Norbert Elias, *The Civilizing Process: The History of Manners*, trans. Edmund Jephcott

The only fifteenth-century prose romance of any kind that remains familiar to English-speaking readers today may be Malory's *Morte Darthur*. That work tends to be viewed by readers and critics as a sort of solitary monster, rather than as a member of a boisterous extended family. Malory's masterpiece is at once an abridged translation from thirteenth-century prose and a *mise en prose* of certain sources in verse. It is also a profoundly idiosyncratic and influential text.

Prose romances in their own right originated long before the Middle Ages. Many of the Greek "novels" or "romances" are prose works. Apuleius's tale of Cupid and Psyche, if not the entire frame story of the *Golden Ass*, might be classified as a sort of prose romance. The prose narrative of adventure returned to fashion in the thirteenth century with the great French Arthurian cycles, like the *Lancelot-Grail* cycle, or the Prose *Tristan* and its appendages, which include the *Compilation of Rusticiano da Pisa*. Through to the sixteenth century, prose held its own alongside verse as a medium for tales of love and war. Indeed, the fifteenth century has been recognized as one of the most active eras for the production of romances in prose. The range of sizes and styles represented among the narratives of this era is dazzling. Perhaps at no other period was the literature of chivalry as rich, as varied, or as accessible as it was between 1480 and 1580, precisely during the age of European expansion. Early printers were able to reproduce the classic chivalric works of earlier periods, going back as far as the thirteenth century. They could disseminate the chivalric compositions of their contemporaries, bringing traditional chivalric myth out in new forms – whether the fifteenth-century prose redaction of a verse original, a substantially new prose work like *Tirant lo Blanch* or a "sentimental romance" like San Pedro's *Cárcel de Amor*, a traditional verse romance such as *Bevis of Hampton*, or *Sir Isumbras*, or a romance epic in the new Italianate mode like those of Pulci, Boiardo, or Ariosto. They could even commission new translations or illustrations. Meanwhile, the manuscript tradition continued to flourish alongside the technological innovations of the early printers. Scribes, too, continued to supply the market with chivalric volumes.

Specific chivalric works will be discussed in more detail below, in chapters one and two. It has always proven difficult to characterize the stars of such an eclectic galaxy without reducing them to uniformity. The presence of chivalric motifs in a broad range of texts in circulation at this period bears witness, by itself, to continuing interest in the subject. Medieval chivalry was to remain a commodity in demand long after scholarship had pronounced it dead. Some

(New York, 1978). (First published as *Uber den Prozess der Zivilisation* (Basel, 1939).) The ongoing research of the historians Barbara Hanawalt, Eric H. Monkkonen, Pieter Spierenburg, and Lawrence Stone is pertinent here. For a brief suggestion of their findings, presented at the Social Science History Association conference of 1994, see Fox Butterfield, "A History of Homicide Surprises the Experts," *New York Times*, Sunday, 23 October 1994, p. 10.

chivalric authors and their works did attain canonical status, and are much studied to this day. Ariosto, Boiardo, Spenser, and Tasso still reign as creators of Renaissance romance-epics, and no one questions the importance of *Amadís* and the Hispanic chivalresque romance of the sixteenth century. The large-scale thirteenth-century prose romances survive, some in "modernized" editions of the late fifteenth and sixteenth centuries, and in translations of that period, others in new editions and recent translations. In other cases, single volumes are all that linger in twentieth-century consciousness of what had been a mighty host. Although Sir Thomas Malory's *Morte Darthur* ranks as the crowning masterpiece of medieval English Arthurian literature, few specialists in Malory recognize that his book belongs to a class of fifteenth-century works, now too often neglected, a fair number of which do still exist in English translation as well as in many European languages.

The relatively concise fifteenth-century prose romance sometimes offered a new story. More often, it was a reworking in prose of an earlier verse romance or epic. Equally often, it might be a translation. Malory's *Morte Darthur* is both a *mise en prose* of the Alliterative and Stanzaic *Mortes Darthur* and a translation of a "French book" or books. At the same time, it remains an original work of startling power and idiosyncrasy. The celebrated Catalan romance, Joannot Martorell and Martí Joan de Galba's *Tirant lo Blanch*, exemplifies a second, related type of fifteenth-century chivalric fiction: the new story taking as its starting-point older materials, in this case Ramon Lull's *Libre del orde de cavayleria (Book of the Ordre of Chyualry)* and the hoary old romance of *Guy of Warwick*. While not many other fifteenth-century prose romances have been permitted to stand beside Malory – *Tirant lo Blanch* may be the only other work accorded the same respect – this neglected group of romances remains a literature of great charm, entertainment, and importance for the history of Western culture. It by no means merits the level of neglect to which it has sunk. In fact, I contend that this neglect warps the history of literature in serious ways.

The extensive nonfictional literature of late medieval and Renaissance chivalry is probably even less known today than the late medieval *mise en prose*. The theory and mythology that were once at the fingertips of every person with pretensions to social status are now the preserve of a few dusty specialists. What has been lost? Certainly, we know too little of a world of stories and characters that entranced our ancestors from the Middle Ages through the eighteenth century, in English, French, German, Greek, Hebrew, Icelandic, Italian, Ladino, Latin, Norwegian, Portuguese, Russian, Spanish, Yiddish, and any number of other languages. We barely recall the tribulations of the twin heroes Valentine and his twin, the wild man Orson. We are no longer conversant with the adventures of the knight Arthur of Algarve among the savages and monsters of darkest Ireland, the travels of Charlemagne's knights to the Fountain of Youth, nor Huon of Bordeaux's granddaughter's experience as a woman warrior who ultimately becomes a man. These works recorded the familiar adventures of King Arthur and his knights, but also the exploits of earlier and later generations, going back to the days of Alexander the Great forward from the end of the Round Table. All of known history could be and indeed was visualized in this body of narrative as an extended chivalric romance. These characters were once domestic figures as familiar as Robin Hood, or Batman. To us they remain, at best, vaguely familiar names. Yet if we are to understand even in part the imagination of Marco Polo's day, or of Cortes', we must try to refamiliarize ourselves with this world of fantasy. The rewards are great.

Two elements of this neglected subgenre deserve further introductory comment here. Both hinder its acceptance in the canon of Western literature. The first impediment is the question of the proper literary classification of the *mise en prose*. The second is the literary status of translation. Both of these problematic issues have been used to dislodge these works from consideration as true "prose romances," or, indeed, as literature *per se*.

These limiting factors must be related to the current ideal of "originality" – the set of blinkers we all wear as twentieth-century readers. Translations are routinely demoted from the front ranks of literature, if not from classification as literature at all, because they are by definition "not original." In the same way, specialists have long regarded the prose reworking of a text first written in verse as a distinctly lesser art form, if it is an art form at all. The terms used to describe such works vary. Georges Doutrepont called them, gracefully at least, *mises en prose*. Today Norris J. Lacy prefers the term "prosification" (after "versification") to differentiate such derivative compositions from the "prose romance" proper. These works should not be classified with romances originally written in prose, presumably because they are "too slavishly" derivative of some superior poetic original. Curiously enough, the Lancelot-Grail cycle is never seen as a "prosification" of Chrétien or any other precursor, any more than one sees the horse as a mere Eohippus writ large: the expansion or alteration of style is too great.

For the first generation of scholars to reinvestigate medieval English literature in the later eighteenth and early nineteenth centuries, any metrical romance took precedence over any prose romance, Malory perhaps excepted. Poetry was the higher art form. After all, any *bourgeois gentilhomme* might speak in prose. The image of the early romance sung by wandering minstrels to harps in halls, as in *Sir Orfeo*, consorted better with a poetic text – though chronologically the vernacular prose romance does not lag far behind the verse romance. If classical and Celtic romances are taken into account the gap narrows still further, to the point of invisibility.[24]

The *mise en prose* is in fact a species of translation, not from another tongue, but from one mode of discourse to another within the same source language. As such it suffers from the same lack of literary appreciation as does the translation. It is rarely given the chance to be assessed on its own terms. But in its own day, this variety of romance did stand clear of its verse predecessors. Its

---

[24] See J. R. Goodman, *Malory and William Caxton's Prose Romances*, pp. 22–23.

audiences read, often without any knowledge of a previous verse text, without the ability to lay hands on the verse original, and, it sometimes seems, without any desire to do so. The fact that such books were written at all, and that they were written in quantity, bears witness to a powerful desire for prose narratives in preference to stories told in rhyme. The proliferation of these prose versions of verse romances in the fifteenth century reveals that, for that era, prose was the fashionable medium. Georges Doutrepont, who remains the chief authority on the phenomenon, associates it with the influential court of Philip the Good of Burgundy.[25]

Another element that influenced the later history of the *mise en prose* and that merits more detailed study is the early printer. The printer's most obvious impact may be on the scale of the prose romance. He or she selected from among available manuscript versions of a text, often preferring abridged texts that could be published more cheaply. Many long prose romances, new and old, were also printed, but they could prove expensive, risky ventures. In too many cases the publication of a large book precipitated the bankruptcy and flight of the printer, as happened with Colard Mansion's *Ovide Moralisé* of 1484.[26] The art of the *metteur en prose* was honorable in its time. Such writers regarded themselves as modernizers, organizers, commentators on a chaotic legacy. They were right. The effect of casting a verse text into prose, giving it a new structure and new words, is critical to the character of the work. The resulting composition is a new thing, and not always a lesser thing than its verse predecessor. Again, it is our criteria for the evaluation of literature that need to be reconsidered as we reconsider these texts.

Those fifteenth-century romances that cannot be denigrated as "mere prosifications" because they appear to be independent of any single verse original have been disqualified from critical consideration in another way. They are for the most part "composite romances", new compositions that recycle motifs from earlier narratives. (Some benighted works manage to qualify as both prosification and composite romance.) The energy and inventiveness of the authors of the later Middle Ages in breeding these hybrids has never been much appreciated by scholarship. Indeed, such works annoy specialists in Arthurian literature by demanding a knowledge of Charlemagne, or irk scholars of the *roman d'antiquité* by employing elements of Celtic mythology. *Ogier le Danois*, in which Charlemagne's peer has an affair with King Arthur's notorious half-sister Morgan la Fée, exemplifies the problem. This work was successful enough to be reprinted sixteen times in the sixteenth century. *Huon de Bordeaux*, which John Bourchier, Lord Berners, translated into English in the days of Henry VIII, a primary source of Shakespeare's Oberon, is an even more elaborate compos-

---

25 Georges Doutrepont, *Les Mises en prose des épopées et des romans chevaleresques du XIVe au XVIe siècle. Mémoires de l'Académie Royale de Belgique. Classe des lettres, series 2, vol. 40 (Brussels, 1939).

26 *William Caxton: An Exhibition* (London, 1976), p. 47.

ite. In fact, the process of conflation of disparate materials is not much different in these works than it is in Boiardo, who presented Charlemagne's knights perhaps most successfully as Arthurian knights errant and lovers. Montalvo, in creating his *Amadís,* and Martorell in *Tirant lo Blanch* work in the same way – as, indeed, did the creators of much of traditional literature, from Homer through Shakespeare. Boiardo's and Ariosto's works, the admired classics of Renaissance imaginative literature, are only the most prominent of a much larger range of such "composite romances," but, of course, one hardly ever thinks of *Orlando Innamorato* and *Generides* as in the same league. The fact that such works are not often considered together exemplifies the scholarly tendency to segregate what it perceives to be "elite" from "popular" art, often with no solid historical rationale.

Such alchemies as those practiced by the creators of the composite romances are hazardous. The ingredients prove volatile, and liable to explode on contact. The experimenters were reckless, and their results are more than a little erratic. In the hands of a refined genius, the effects are quite different from those achieved by a hack. Still, the wide diffusion of this method of composition needs to be better recognized. Whether they were geniuses or not, this is how many imaginative artists of this period worked to build an heroic narrative. They assembled their fictions out of prefabricated parts – literary components, now, rather than the oral formulae their ancestors had recombined to create their epics.

What vogue did this literature retain in the sixteenth century? And how long did it go on? These questions remain to be answered. As statistically oriented, supposedly computer-literate folk, we want to count numbers of books, sales, and reprintings as statements of longterm audience interest or market appeal, and estimate the percentage of the book trade that such work represents. Statistics are difficult to come by, in part because these works have been purposely excluded from primary studies, and in part because such evidence no longer exists, if it was ever collected. The structure of existing catalogues and even the newest computerized databases reflect traditional categories of scholarship. This approach impedes the tracking of any work over time. Incunabula (fifteenth-century printed books) are rigorously segregated from early printed books of the sixteenth century and later eras. As a result, both the wide international dissemination and the longterm popularity of this literature still escape full appreciation. Bibliographic studies of single works do document an astonishing longevity. The cumulative effect of many such individual studies has not as yet been pointed out. Editors, working in isolation, naturally tend to see the work they are studying as exceptional, a singular masterpiece. Yet, when the history of these late medieval romances is viewed collectively, the record of publication becomes still more impressive. This medieval chivalric fiction in many cases outlasts the vogue of *Amadís* by two or three hundred years, at a conservative estimate. It was still easily available to the romantic mythographers of the nineteenth century like Scott, Morris, and Dumas, who used it to create a new popular literature of quest, mystery, conquest, passion and fantasy. Of twentieth-century critics perhaps only Northrop Frye appreciated the continuity of this narrative tradition. As we disinter this forgotten layer of chivalric narrative, we recognize the roots of twentieth-century popular culture – the modern fantasy novel, science fiction, the thriller, the gothic romance, even the detective story. Its roots run this deep. The link is direct and unsevered. It travels through the American romance of Hawthorne and the Gothic fiction of the romantic period, and on to most of the prose fiction we read for entertainment today.[27]

This is a heterodox notion. The split between popular and high cultures has been generally viewed as a development of the nineteenth century. In fact, a fissure between two modes of writing began to yawn in the sixteenth century, or even earlier, as the humanists campaigned to remake literature, Latin and vernacular, after the image of Cicero. The courtly vernacular fiction of previous generations, still beloved of their more conservative contemporaries, they singled out for vituperation; a less "classical" literature would be difficult to find. In the competition for affluent secular patrons, the humanist scholar and artist jousted against King Arthur and Blanchardyn with weapons of war. This literature was not merely unlearned – that is, not in Latin or Greek – it was uncouth according to all the best Roman stylistic criteria. It was also historically (and no doubt politically) incorrect. This comes across clearly in the humanist reaction against the surviving *romans d'antiquité*. In the prologue to his 1513 translation of the *Aeneid*, Gavin Douglas' harshest critique is reserved for the prose descendant of the *Roman d'Eneas* translated and published by William Caxton as his *Eneydos*, as recently as 1490. The Portuguese scholar Vasco da Lucena advertised his new translation and completion of Quintus Curtius' life of Alexander to his patron Charles the Bold of Burgundy as a demythologized narrative. Earlier histories were "plaines de évidens mensonges," but this one will present an Alexander who effects his conquests "without flying in the air, without going underwater, without spells, without giants, and without being as strong as Renaut of Montauban, as Lancelot, as Tristan, as Raynard who used

---

[27] Gail Orgelfinger, ed., *The Hystorye of Olyuer of Castylle*, trans. Henry Watson (New York and London, 1988), pp. 247–58. Some sense of the manuscript and publication history of other romances can be obtained from the bibliographic section of the romance volume of J. Burke Severs, gen. ed., *A Manual of the Writings in Middle English 1050–1500* (New Haven, 1967). For sixteenth-century France in particular, see Richard Cooper, " 'Nostre histoire renouvelée': the Reception of the Romances of Chivalry in Renaissance France (with bibliography)," in *Chivalry in the Renaissance*, ed. Anglo, pp. 175–238. For German editions, see Paul Heitz, *Versuch einer zusammenstellung der deutschen volksbucher des 15 und 16 jahrhunderts nebst deren spateren ausgaben und literatur* (Strassburg, 1924). For critical attitudes, see Northrop Frye, *The Anatomy of Criticism* and *The Secular Scripture*; Mikhail Bakhtin grapples with the romance in *The Dialogic Imagination* (Austin, 1981), but sees it as a phase in the evolution of the novel, rather than as a distinct, ongoing current of narrative art.

to kill fifty men pell-mell, one after another." This is all a slap at the ancient *Roman d'Alexandre* tradition, as well as other super-heros of romance.[28]

Michel de Montaigne's declaration of his own ignorance of chivalric fiction is too often cited as representative of his generation, and, indeed, as an infallible token of the death of romance. "For of King *Arthur*, of *Lancelot du Lake*, of *Amadis*, of *Huon of Burdeaux*, and such idle time consuming, and wit-besotting trash of bookes wherein youth doth commonly ammuse it selfe, I was not so much as acquainted with their names, and to this day know not their bodies, nor what they containe: So exact was my discipline."[29] In fact this statement bears witness, as Montaigne says himself, mainly to the prejudices of his tutors. He was, after all, the shining product of a rigorous experimental program of intensive classical learning. It is a mistake to proffer him as a kind of Renaissance Everyman, when he is in fact a quite distinctive individual. Montaigne's remark also reflects the national biases affecting the survival of different romances in different countries, as a widely disseminated international literature was parceled out into separate national canons. English humanists of Montaigne's day could still betray a *tendre* for King Arthur, as Sidney does in his *Apology for Poetry*. Even Ascham is willing to concede that the *Morte Darthur's* "open manslaughter and bold bawdry" might be less pernicious to English youth than the contents of certain Italian volumes. Montaigne may disclaim knowledge of Arthur and Amadis, two foreign heroes, but he reveals elsewhere that like a good Frenchman he knows his Froissart and reveres the exploits of Charlemagne. This same nationalism still impedes the study of what was for centuries an international literature. Perhaps, in this era of European Community, scholars may be better equipped, and permitted, to appreciate both the international vogue of chivalric literature and the barriers that have blocked its recognition.

Most teachers of literature specialize in a single linguistic tradition, most often their own. Even comparatists tend to favor one language above the rest. A primary criterion for a work's admission into the canon of a national

---

28 For an important phase of the debate, see Giraldi Cinthio, *Discorso intorno al comporre dei romanzi* (Venice, 1554), written in 1549, in defence of Ariosto and the romance aesthetic. (In *Scritti Estetici di Giambattista Giraldi Cintio*, ed. Giulio Antimaco (1864).) For an English translation, see Giraldi Cinthio, *On Romances*, trans. Henry L. Snuggs (Lexington, 1968). For the quotation from Vasco de Lucena, "sans voler en l'air, sans aler soubs mer, sans enchantemens, sans gayans, et sans estre si fort comme Regnauld de Montalban, comme Lanselot, comme Tristan, comme Raynouard qui tuoit cinquante hommes cop-à-cop," see Georges Doutrepont, *La littérature française à la cour de Bourgogne* (Paris, 1909), p. 183. The translation is mine.

29 Michel de Montaigne, *Essays*, trans. John Florio, ed. J. I. M. Stewart (London, 1931), I.177. Montaigne describes the method by which his father arranged for him to learn Latin as his first language earlier in the essay, pp. 174–75. Earlier still in his essay, he recommends that a young gentleman "survay what-soever is rare and singular about him: a building, a fountaine, a man, a place where any batell hath been fought, or the passages of *Caesar* or *Charlemaine*" (p. 153). For the French text see "De l'institution des enfans," bk 1, ch. 26, *Essais*, ed. Maurice Rat (Paris, 1962), I.190, 187–88, 167.

literature is that is should have been first written in that language. Rabelais' *Pantagruel* stands fast in the French literary canon; Urquhart's inspired English translation of Rabelais is only a second-class item as a work of English literature. Twentieth-century scholars are only now beginning to accord medieval translators some respect, attempting to appreciate their methods and standards rather than apologizing for their failure to live up to modern criteria.[30] The disdain expressed in Gavin Douglas' demolition of Caxton's *Eneydos* echoes in the editors' prefaces to most translated romances. The humanist biblical criticism of Petrarch, Erasmus, and their contemporaries who attacked Jerome's Vulgate as an inept and inaccurate translation also did much to shape our received ideas about translators and translation. The "new learning" remains, for most twentieth-century scholars, both a lodestar and a shackle.[31] The limitations of its vision of the world are only belatedly becoming apparent.

The medieval translator of romance, like virtually every other medieval author, was almost always an adaptor. The less skillful or adventurous, or perhaps more conscientious writers might clutch at the original language of the text with what we would now regard as a deathgrip. William Caxton does this; a fair percentage of the French vocabulary is imported into English along with the story. In the same work, he or she may cut, paste, intrude and invent with shocking freedom, drawing on extraneous sources or on original impulses. When any romance and its translations are examined side by side, the distinctive character of each version emerges clearly. Nicholas de Lange's elegant model of the translator as a performing musician, interpreting someone else's composition for a new audience, responsible both to the composer and to his listeners, can help us to appreciate this predicament.[32]

At their best, medieval translations, like good modern translations, stand on their own. These are works that enrich their adopted language, as Malory's

---

[30] The pioneers in this field include Jeannette Beer and Roger Ellis, together with the many scholars they have encouraged.

[31] C. S. Lewis' *English Literature in the Sixteenth Century* (Oxford, 1954) should be mentioned as an exception.

[32] Nicholas de Lange, "Reflections of a Translator," The Sixteenth Annual Rabbi Louis Feinberg Memorial Lecture in Judaic Studies, Judaic Studies Program, University of Cincinnati, 18 March 1993, p. 6. The earliest translator of a French prose romance into German was Countess Elizabeth of Nassau–Sarrebrück c.1434; Eleanor of Scotland translated *Ponthus* into German; Margaret Tyler published her translation of the first part of the *Espejo de Principes y Cavalleros* (*The Mirrour of Princely deedes and Knighthood*) in 1578. See Sir Henry Thomas, *Spanish and Portuguese Romances of Chivalry* (Cambridge, 1920; rpt. New York, 1969), pp. 242–37. Thomas quotes the translator's apology for her own undertaking. Thomas points out (p. 244) that a number of the Spanish chivalresque romances had been ascribed to female authors, with varying degrees of accuracy. The future St Teresa of Avila confessed that she had written one. See also Daniel Eisenberg, *Castilian Romances of Chivalry in the Sixteenth Century: A Bibliography* (London, 1979), pp. 27, 60, 77–78. Elizabeth Spearing's forthcoming book focuses on the essential role of women in the world of the sixteenth-century Spanish prose romance.

Morte Darthur enriches English and Herberay's *Amadís de Gaule* did French.[33]
If we neglect them because they are immigrants rather than native born texts,
we lop off a vital branch of any national literature. We also make nonsense of
literary history, because these works do become part of the language and the
literature into which they are introduced. They are read and assimilated by
audiences who may go on to write new works under their influence, as *Amadís*
assimilated the French Arthurian tradition. Until specialists in national literatures reread these books, their true impact cannot be fully assessed. The
problem is artificial, an artifact of academic culture and pedagogy. Readers of
these works did not reject them because they were translations. If the truth be
told, they may have read them more avidly, as exotic imports from distant,
prestigious centers of civilization.

Irving Leonard at one point puzzles over why a late sixteenth-century
Spaniard would bother to lug not *Amadís* but *Oliveros de Castilla* and the
Historia del Emperador Carlo Magno y de los doce pares de Francia out to the
Philippines in his trunk. These short prose romances are, he remarks, "hardly
representative of this literary fashion at its prime."[34] To the traveler, their scale
must, again, have weighed in their favor. *Oliveros* and the *Historia del Emperador
Carlo Magno* are relatively concise books. Some of the major volumes of the
sixteenth century test the scholarly reader's weight-lifting ability when she tries
to carry them from the librarian's desk to her reading table. The Elizabethan
satirist Martin Marprelate's characterization of his opponent's tome, "a port-
able book, if your horse be strong enough," could well apply to certain romances. There were other attractions as well, which may be rediscovered by
reading the books themselves. Part I of this book discusses the appeal of late
medieval chivalric narratives of precisely this kind.

The scepticism, and indeed the hostility with which Renaissance chivalry has
been evaluated over the past century, bear witness to an apparent need among
scholars to proclaim the death of chivalry. This is analogous to the desire to
certify the death of romance, a need often satisfied by Don Quixote, who is
supposed to nail down the coffin. What motivates this chivalric eschatology? It
requires the scholar to ignore or dispose of a great deal of primary evidence to
the contrary, supporting the survival of chivalric mythology and idealism at
least as late as the sixteenth and seventeenth centuries. Surely the underlying
problem has to do with the way historians subdivide the past into discrete
periods. Chivalry and romance must die because they are "medieval" and do
not belong in the Renaissance, except as grotesque fossils. The struggle to split
off a "Renaissance" from a "Middle Age" began as early as Petrarch's invention

---

[33] See A. D. Deyermond, "The Lost Genre of Medieval Spanish Literature," *Hispanic Review*
43 (1975), pp. 231–59, esp. p. 246; A. D. Deyermond, "*La historia de la linda Melosina*:
Two Spanish Versions of a French Romance," in *Medieval Hispanic Studies Presented to
Rita Hamilton*, ed. A. D. Deyermond (London, 1976), pp. 57–65.

[34] Leonard, *Books of the Brave*, pp. 228–29.

of the latter term. Denys Hay is perhaps the most eminent twentieth-century specialist to point out how many continuities connect the era from 1300 to 1700. The specialized professional training of both medieval and Renaissance scholars promotes a division that runs counter to the nature of human experience.

In general, historians tend to overstress the new, because it is history's business to chart the rise of new ideas, as well as to chronicle events in series. To be a historian of conservative forces in any form, the continuing presence of traditional beliefs, may seem a little like being a historian of inertia. Major continuities are too often underrated or ignored, when they are not argued out of existence as inconvenient to the narrative. Somehow this satisfies a psychological hunger to escape from our own past, possibly from our parents. We need to believe we can escape, if only through ignorance. Yet much energy in recent years has been devoted to recovering neglected histories, many of them displaying patterns of continuity and change at odds with established ideas of periodization. Within Western European history, women, peasants, Jews, animals, and the physical environment all offer different experiences of life. As their divergent stories are incorporated in the main narrative, they exert stresses upon the rigid framework of accepted historical fact. All this should push us towards a more delicate sense of the variable tempo of change from one mode of life to another. Along with this, it might be wise to cultivate a greater respect for the tenacity of certain long-standing traditions within any culture. Failure to develop this respect leaves us prey to constant astonishment as ancient beliefs reappear without warning to disrupt our contemporary world. In particular, we underestimate the strength of traditional elements in Western culture, while celebrating them elsewhere. Part of the myth of modern Western civilization is, after all, that it has discarded myth.

In certain fields the "new learning" of the Renaissance did break dramatically with the past – in art, historiography, education, classical studies – though even there, conservative thinkers might impede the march of "progress." In other areas alteration came slowly, if at all. The gradual geographic spread of Italian humanist ideas northward has long been recognized. Modes of thought and behavior changed at different rates in different places. Franco Simone once advocated a painstaking re-examination of the fifteenth century, decade by decade, as the only sound way to arrive at an understanding of the period. It is fair to say that present academic institutions, the organization of the profession, and tools of research all combine to mask the element of continuity from one period to another. The operative model that lies behind Petrarch's concept of Middle Ages and Renaissance, it might be argued, is the Christian history of the world as formulated in the Gospels. The Middle Ages are characterized much as Christianity characterizes Judaism. The older covenant must be declared dead to make room for its divinely appointed successor. After an era of "prolonged intellectual lethargy" or "stagnation," there is a return of divine inspiration in a glorious new birth. The Renaissance becomes the Christ of historical eras, and indeed retains all the prestige that such an analogy implies. In arguing for a strong element of continuity from the Middle Ages through the Renaissance, I am advocating a linear view of time more consistent with Jewish tradition.

Huizinga found that the death of chivalry was essential to his concept of the "waning (or autumn) of the Middle Ages." There is a clear, symbiotic relationship between these two ideas. If chivalry does not die on schedule, how is the Renaissance to differ from the Middle Ages? It becomes that much more difficult to draw a sharp distinction between the two periods. To study this era intelligently, scholars need to resist the long-standing tendency to portray these two ages as adversaries. By reconsidering exploration as a product of the late medieval chivalric imagination, I hope to demonstrate one potential advantage of such a long-range historical perspective.

What of chivalric practice in the Renaissance? Here, the problem is not to document all the panoply of knightly actions in the sixteenth century and beyond. The problem lies in how to interpet this primary evidence. Is it qualitatively different from earlier evidence? Does this difference, if any, reflect creativity or decadence? The problem is analogous to the difficulty of evaluating Renaissance Latin. My colleagues of the American Association for Neo-Latin Studies assess the Ciceronian language of the Humanists in largely positive terms; C. S. Lewis once denounced it as a tongue regulated out of existence by the reapplication of outdated laws. Does Renaissance chivalry remain a living language, or is it dead on arrival?

The tournament has certainly been seen as a quintessential chivalric event, a good point at which to test the pulse of chivalry. The history of the tournament as a form of medieval military game for knights extends without a break from the twelfth to the seventeenth century in England, disregarding its continuations in the Americas and its nineteenth-century and ongoing twentieth-century revivals. Within that span of time the character of the event alters radically in England alone, from the first brutal mass combats in the fields to the elaborately symbolic "barriers" and "Accession Day tilts" of the Tudors and Stuarts. That such events had changed a great deal in their later phases goes without saying. The question is, to what extent change constitutes decadence.[35]

One measure of decay is divergence from the original form. The tournament had diverged, without a doubt, though not out of all recognition. It retained its character as a venue for military practice and public display of knightly skills and equipment into the sixteenth century. There was some shift of emphasis from practice with lance and sword or battleaxe towards virtuoso equestrian display. One enterprising sixteenth-century French tournament, that of

---

[35] See Richard Barber and Juliet Barker, *Tournaments: Jousts, Chivalry, and Pageantry in the Middle Ages* (Woodbridge, 1989); for later events, see also Alan Young, *Tudor and Jacobean Tournaments* (London, 1987).

Nozeroy (1519–20), incorporated what appears to be a cannon.[36] The tournament can be seen accommodating new military developments while it preserves some old ones. It is by no means an unchanging anachronism.

The tournament needs to be considered in two ways, as a pragmatic military exercise, but also as courtly performance, a character it had developed as early as the end of the thirteenth century. Do the elaborate allegorical devices of Sir Philip Sidney and his contemporaries reflect the sterility of an outworn medium, or Renaissance vitality? At the end of the sixteenth century, as a later chapter of this book will demonstrate, Captain John Smith still found the tournament essential to his military career. A hundred years earlier, the Chevalier Bayard had shared his sentiments.

The problem, then, is not to document chivalric events of the era of exploration – there is no shortage – but to rate the level of "sincerity" of the participants, always a hazardous task. Samuel Johnson once said, "We cannot prove any man's intention to be bad."[37] Every era has its idealists and its cynics. The scholar decides who will be allowed to speak for the period, which voices are to be singled out as "representative," based on his or her preconceived image of the age. Even the creation of anti-chivalric stereotypes like Don Quixote, who is much more than this, may be open to challenge as a sign of the end. After all, the thirteenth century had Sir Dinadan of the prose *Tristan* and the author of the *Queste del Saint Graal*, two equally acid critics of chivalry. The *Queste* castigates the moral bankruptcy of worldly knights in vigorous terms; Dinadan undermines the Arthurian universe from within by his exposure of the many ludicrous aspects of the conventions that govern the behavior of the knight errant. Yet neither of these well-aimed attacks is now imagined to have toppled chivalry as a secular system of values. The human practitioners of chivalry marched on to new eras of exuberant self-expression. Cervantes' masterpiece is better positioned in history to be hailed as the slayer of both chivalry and chivalric fiction, but on closer examination its title should also be questioned. Plenty of evidence points to the survival of the chivalric idealist.

As one infallible signal of the decay of chivalry in the Renaissance, Sydney Anglo discusses the rise of the duel, a cult of personal honor and revenge that he sees as replacing a broader, public-spirited medieval ideal of loyalty to a lord, family, or a larger cause.[38] Here, as in our own day, we are dealing with an escalation of violence and of the technology of violence. How such threats to social stability relate to a sense that traditional values have failed deserves careful examination in both historical contexts. Certainly, in the American

---

[36] B. Prost, ed., *Traités du Duel Judiciale: relations de Pas d'armes et Tournois* (Paris, 1872), pp. 235–59. Malcolm Vale defends the later tournaments as military practice in *War and Chivalry* (London, 1981), pp. 62–87. On this see also J. R. Goodman, "European Chivalry in the 1490s," *Comparative Civilizations Review* 26 (1992), pp. 43–72, at pp. 47–56.

[37] James Boswell, *Life of Johnson*, I.12

[38] *Chivalry in the Renaissance*, pp. xiii–xiv.

South as late as the 1800s, the cult of the duel was regarded by its practitioners as a sign that the chivalry of old was alive and well in their quarter of the globe.

The conjunction of chivalry and exploration is only another instance of this larger pattern. Their most obvious point of intersection has already been mentioned: the two meet in the chivalric language used by the historians of European exploration and conquest, from the fifteenth century onwards. This has been discussed for the most part as a repellent feature of these histories, springing from a regrettable desire to glorify the oppressors of indigenous peoples. A detailed historiographical study of this matter needs to be undertaken. But this is a secondary issue.

The immediate task remains to examine the primary evidence that underlies and supports this trend in historical writing. The chivalric vocabulary of later historians draws on the language and the attitudes of the European adventurers themselves, of their courtly patrons, and of the first generation of writers who described these events for their own times. Drawn in many cases from the classes for whom the chivalric romances were first designed, volunteers for such missions could see themselves as knights errant venturing into the unknown and obtaining enhanced social status as a result of their prowess. Gomes Eanes de Zurara depicts Prince Henry the Navigator and his brothers planning the first Portuguese foray into North Africa as a crusading exploit to prove their fitness for knighthood. Cortes describes his expedition to find Montezuma (Mocteçucoma) as a quest. The second part of this book discusses these cases and others. In this pilot study, limited by constraints of time and space, I focus on six of the most striking and influential conjunctions of chivalry and exploration. Many more could have been added.

These cases and their evidence might all be dismissed by a sceptical audience as "mere propaganda." Such a dismissal brands both writers and explorers as hypocrites rather than unconscious deceivers of themselves or misguided idealists. It requires an assessment of sincerity. By the same token, propaganda, displaying an attractive image in order to gain or retain power, must rank as an important force in history. Whatever the reader's view of the writer's or traveler's motives, the phenomenon reveals much about the human mind. The fact that a sixteenth-century adventurer, or his prince, would wish others to see him as a knight-errant on a quest, or as a crusader, tells us that these were still glamorous pictures. The continuing prestige of medieval chivalry might be used to cloak a host of sordid deeds. It might also exert control over patterns of perception, shaping responses to affect the way an event might be judged. The power of the chivalric ideal in this context may perhaps be suggested by two further items of evidence. The first is Bartolomé de las Casas' proposal of a new chivalric order, the Knights of the Golden Spur, dedicated to reforming the abuses of the conquistadores in Latin America.[39] Here the arch-critic of his contemporaries' conduct draws on the grand tradition of chivalry itself to

[39] Leonard, *Books of the Brave*, p. 55.

redress the balance. The second is "el Inca" Garcilaso de la Vega's description of Inca warriors in explicitly chivalric terms. To enhance the status of his maternal ancestors in the eyes of a Spanish adudience, he translates their warrior culture into European terms. This instance reflects the persistent attraction of chivalry even in the era of Don Quixote. It also suggests that chivalry itself would benefit from comparative study, especially at this point in history. The European chivalry of the later Middle Ages and Renaissance was only one of many competing warrior codes still practiced all across the planet. This was the moment when warriors trained in many of these codes came into contact with one another for the first time. In the case of Christian and Islamic warrior cultures, the conflict went back many generations. In other cases – in Africa, India, the Americas, China, Japan, and Southeast Asia – exponents of European chivalry encountered warriors trained in other codes of honor. The way these global "chivalries" or warrior systems react to one another should be recognized as a key aspect of the history of the era. Comparative chivalric studies need to play an active role in the reevaluation of the period.[40]

Even within the confines of Europe, late medieval chivalry remained an international preoccupation. The cosmopolitan quality of the chivalric culture at this period has in fact impeded its study, just as it impedes the study of chivalric literature. Too often, historians play down the chivalric element in their national history, fearing that their ancestors may appear backward, unenlightened, still medieval while the rest of the world had discarded the Middle Ages. Yet all over Europe – in Portugal, Spain, France, Italy, England, Scotland, the Holy Roman Empire, Eastern Europe, Scandinavia – sixteenth-century princes, and even seventeenth-century ones, reveled in chivalric pageantry and courtly games. They hankered after new crusades and sometimes even went on them, as did King Sebastian of Portugal, who was killed in North Africa in 1578, generating legends of his possible return that parallel those of the return of King Arthur.[41] They patronized tournaments and orders of knighthood, or retired to hermitages in the manner of Ramon Lull's model knight of the *Book of the Ordre of Chyualry* or Lancelot du Lac, or as the Emperor Charles V did in 1558.

Investigations such as this one must deal with the interplay between fiction and historical narrative. Grappling with this problem can help us to understand

---

[40] This theme, which I began to discuss in "European Chivalry in the 1490s," continues in "The Image of the Knight in Ibero-American Cultures," forthcoming in the proceedings of the Inter-American Institute's inaugural conference on Cultural Transmission and Transformation in the Ibero-American World, 1200–1800. This continuing program of research leads toward a book in this area.

[41] "Sebastianists" held that the king was hidden (a *rei encuberto*) on an enchanted island, or on pilgrimage. In this belief they supported four pretenders to the Portuguese throne between 1584 and 1603. "Sebastianism" remained a political force into the nineteenth century, and was reported to have adherents as late as the early twentieth century and as far afield as rural Brazil. Cf. "Sebastian," *Encyclopedia Britannica* (11th edn, New York, 1910–11), 24.566.

the relationship between action and imagination, myth and human behavior. This book studies the way men and women imagined themselves, and how they presented themselves to one another. The focus is on human motivations, in certain cases self-deceptions or rationalizations – on the psychology of exploration and conquest. In the process, the analysis exposes the strengths and the limitations of our ancestral heroic codes, both of the invaders and the invaded. It suggests, again, that the West knows less than it should about its own history.

One of the major flaws of modern philosophy has been its zeal to "demythologize" the world at large.[42] As self-proclaimed twentieth-century rationalists, too many intellectuals find it difficult to believe in belief. The belief in question may be that of our ancestors, or of our contemporaries. In either case, our education equips us badly to understand it, or even to accept its existence. The resurgence of old patterns – of feudal relationships, of cults of personal honor and vengeance, of holy wars – strikes the modern sceptic as inconceivable. If such a thinker had only paid due attention to the history of Western vernacular literature, he or she might have seen how deep such currents run in civilizations all across the globe. All this territory of the mind cries out to be rediscovered.

---

[42] See Iris Murdoch, "Fact and Value," in *Metaphysics as a Guide to Morals* (New York, 1993), pp. 47–48. "Historical change is (in part and fundamentally) change of imagery. This is often prompted by scientific discovery. Think how our idea of our home planet has altered, both as we look back over hundreds of years, and over scores of years; Earth, now, as a travelling spaceship, seen from the outside, vulnerable, lonely, precious. Technological progress can deeply affect our sense of ourselves, as Marxists tried to explain. The agency can be mysterious, darkness moving upon darkness. We are at present involved in deep thought-changes, of which the unattractive word 'demythologization' names some." The powerful reaction – the backlash – against "demythologization" now in progress deserves more discussion than it has received. Few periods in history cling with more tenacity to their myths, or have been more prolific in creating new ones, than the final decades of the twentieth century.

PART ONE

Chivalric Literature in
an Age of Exploration

CHAPTER ONE

Towards the Rediscovery of a Literature

Rede Froissart: there shall ye see manhode, curtosy and gentilesse.
. . .
*And syth the incarnacion of Oure Lord byhold that noble Kyng
of Brytayne, Kyng Arthur, with al the noble knyghtes of the
Round Table, whos noble actes and noble chyvalry of his
knyghtes occupye soo many large volumes, that [it] is a world,
or a thyng incredyble to byleve.*[1]

THE TRUE MEASURE OF the chivalry of the fifteenth and sixteenth centuries
cannot be taken without rediscovering an essentially lost literature. Two key
elements in the galaxy of chivalric fiction of that age have received extensive
treatment: the romance epics of Pulci, Boiardo, Ariosto, and Spenser, and the
Hispanic chivalresque romances of Garci Rodriguez de Montalvo and his
followers. But a broad range of material remains too often excluded from
consideration. Later medieval chivalric literature continued to be printed,
translated, read and reprinted across Europe throughout the sixteenth century
and in some cases well beyond. This category of work comprises a wide variety
of material: chivalric histories and fictions of differing genres and origins,
chivalric manuals and biographies, tournament records and heraldic studies.
Until this literature is better appreciated, it will remain impossible to comprehend the chivalry of this era.

The main point to emphasize in this initial overview of the subject is the
quantity, diversity, and vitality of the chivalric literature available to European
readers and hearers between 1400 and 1600. Spurred on by princely chivalric
enthusiasts, writers reshaped much of the extensive medieval literature of
knighthood. Traditional heroic poems became prose texts. Major bodies of
legends inherited from the early Middle Ages were grafted upon one another,
with Charlemagne's knights patterning themselves upon the Knights of the
Round Table. New verse forms and new patterns of organization altered the old
stories. From the 1470s onward, printers all across Europe seized upon this mass

---

[1] Ramon Lull, *Boke of the Ordre of Chyualry*, trans. William Caxton. This excerpt (from the
epilogue) is edited in N. F. Blake, ed., *Caxton's Own Prose* (London, 1973), p. 126.

27

of new and old chivalric literature and proceeded to translate, publish, and disseminate it to a broadened range of readers and hearers.

The idea of the "printing press as an agent of change," the harbinger of the Renaissance and publicist of the New Learning, remains well-entrenched among twentieth-century students. New technology and new ideas would seem to accord elegantly with one another. Yet the printing press also served as an agent of continuity throughout this era, to such an extent that the intransigent conservatism of the sixteenth-century reading public often baffles scholarship. The presses spread new ideas, without question: they also spread hoary old ones. They extended the lifespan of innumerable medieval texts well beyond the Middle Ages, and put them in the hands of unexpected audiences.[2]

A quick spot check of a few better-known or representative chivalric publications may shed light on this paradox. In 1485, the year of Hernan Cortes' birth, the English printer William Caxton published Sir Thomas Malory's *Morte Darthur* for the first time: it was reprinted in 1498, 1529, 1527, 1578, and 1634.[3] Malory had finished his distinctive adaptation of French and English Arthurian romances in 1469–70. His book was to dominate all later English-language Arthurian literature. This idiosyncratic masterpiece reflects many lively trends in the fifteenth-century reshaping of romance. Malory's book is at once a prose rendering of the Middle English alliterative and stanzaic *Mortes Darthur*, a translation from the French, an abridgement, a cycle of connected romances, and a one-volume biography of Arthur and his knights. While it reflects many of the most recent trends in fifteenth-century fictional technique, it remains quite distinct in form from the Arthurian volumes that were soon to be published in Europe, with the *Lancelot du Lac* of 1488 being the earliest to appear.[4]

Later in 1485 Caxton's press issued the publisher's own translations of two complementary chivalric texts. *The Lyf of the Noble and Crysten Prynce Charles the Grete* is the only known English version of Jean Bagnyon's prose *Histoire de Charlemagne* (also known as *Fierabras*). Here, too, Caxton had chosen an authoritative volume. The French text of Bagnyon's compact version of the life

---

2   See Elizabeth L. Eisenstein, *The Printing Press as an Agent of Change* (2 vols., Cambridge, 1979) which discusses the problem in detail, but without much reference to the printing of chivalric literature.

3   Cf. Barry Gaines, *Sir Thomas Malory: An Anecdotal Bibliography of Editions, 1485–1985* (New York, 1990). The hiatus in the publication of Malory's work between 1634 and 1816 has been associated with a loss of interest in King Arthur, but see Roberta F. Brinkley, *The Arthurian Legend in the Seventeenth Century* (Baltimore, 1932). For more discussion of the publication context of Malory's *Morte Darthur*, see Jennifer R. Goodman, *Malory and Caxton's Prose Romances of 1485* (New York, 1987). For some afterthoughts, see my two later articles on this subject, "Malory and Caxton's Chivalric Series, 1481–85," in *Studies in Malory*, ed. James W. Spisak (Kalamazoo, Michigan, 1985), pp. 257–74, and "Caxton's Chivalric Series, 1480–85," in *The Study of Chivalry*, ed. Howell P. Chickering and Thomas H. Seiler (Kalamazoo, 1988), pp. 645–62.

4   *Lancelot* was first published at Rouen by J. Le Bourgeois and at Paris by J. du Pré.

of Charlemagne and deeds of his knights was written in Switzerland around the same time as Malory's work. It had already been printed in Geneva, in 1478, and twice reprinted; a Lyons edition also appeared in 1485. There were twenty-six reprintings of Bagnyon's text before 1600.[5] As the *Historia del Emperador Carlo Magno y de los doce pares de Francia,* in Nicolás de Piemonte's translation, this version of Charlemagne's deeds remained in print in Spain from at least 1521 to the twentieth century. Its special influence on Spanish and Latin American culture has been noted by many scholars, from Irving Leonard to Luis Weckmann. Bagnyon's volume also had a German vogue, in an abbreviated translation by Jean II, duke of Palatinat-Simmern (1486–1557) that dispensed with the history to concentrate on the romance. His *Fierrabras* of 1533 was printed a second time in 1594.[6] This important book is little read today, even by specialists. It incorporates a prose version of one of the most popular Charlemagne poems within a compact legendary biography of that emperor. The *Historia del Emperador Carlo Magno,* as it relates to Charles V and to Cortes, is discussed below (chapter six).

The third chivalric work Caxton published in 1485 was *Paris and Vienne,* whose French text of about 1432 is ascribed to a Pierre de la Cypede. This is a romance of a different kind, and on a different scale. Caxton printed *Paris and Vienne* on thirty-five double-columned pages, while the only complete copy of his Malory volume to survive, in the Pierpont Morgan Library, requires 432 leaves in the same typeface. *Paris and Vienne,* a concise narrative of love and knightly achievement, betrays no connection to any body of national chivalric mythology. The young knight, Paris, loves and wins his liege lord's daughter, Vienne, in a classic plot involving courtship through musical entertainment and chivalric display, an unsuccessful elopement, the lovers' geographical separation and tests of loyalty and resourcefulness for both partners, ending in their reunion. MacEdward Leach identified the work as one of a new class of late medieval romances, "more realistic, more local, more circumstantial in detail,

---

5   See Jean Bagnyon, *L'Histoire de Charlemagne (parfois dite Roman de Fierabras),* ed. Hans-Erich Keller, Textes littéraires français (Geneva, 1992). See also Hans-Erich Keller, *Autour de Roland: Recherches sur la chanson de geste* (Paris and Geneva, 1989); André de Mandach, *Naissance et développement de la chanson de geste en europe. V. La geste de Fierabras: Le jeu du réel et de l'invraisemblable, avec des textes inédits.* Publications romanes ct françaises, CLXXVII (Geneva, 1987), pp. 150–52; Jean Bagnyon, *The Lyf of the Noble and Crysten Prynce Charles the Grete,* trans. William Caxton, ed. Sidney J. Herrtage, EETS e.s. 36–37 (London, 1881). R. Cooper, " 'Nostre histoire renouvelée:' The Reception of the Romances of Chivalry in Renaissance France (with bibliography)," in *Chivalry in the Renaissance,* ed. Sydney Anglo (Woodbridge, 1990), pp. 206–07.

6   On the Spanish and Latin American fortune of Bagnyon, see André de Mandach, *Naissance et développement;* P. Burke, "Chivalry in the New World," in *Chivalry in the Renaissance,* ed. Anglo, pp. 257–58, 261; Irving A. Leonard, *Books of the Brave* (1949; rpt. Berkeley and Los Angeles, 1992), p. 55; Luis Weckmann, *The Medieval Heritage of Mexico,* trans. Frances M. López-Morillas (New York, 1992), pp. 142–43. For the German *Fierrabras,* see Keller, *Autour de Roland,* pp. 293–95.

and closer to actual life." The bibliographical history of *Paris and Vienne* in England, France, Italy, Germany, Sweden, and the Iberian peninsula runs from 1487 to the mid-nineteenth century.[7]

Caxton was by no means the only printer of 1485 at work disseminating vernacular chivalric fiction. In the same year, A. Neyret issued *Baudoin conte de Flandres* at Chambéry, the second of ten editions of this *chanson de geste* in French before 1600. Alongside Bagnyon's *Fierabras*, Guillaume Le Roy at Lyons reprinted *Pierre de Provence et la Belle Maguelonne*, a disarming little volume of the same sort as *Paris and Vienne*, and one with an even more extensive appeal for European printers of the sixteenth century and later.[8] The Crombergers of Seville issued *La historia de la linda Magalona y del muy esforzado caballero Pierres de Provenza* in 1519 and again in 1533. Whether *para niños* – for children – or for some older audience, ten thousand copies of *Pierres y Magalona* were imported into Mexico in the year 1600 alone.[9] A striking feature of both *Paris et Vienne* and *Pierre de Provence* is the balance maintained in the plot between the male and female main characters. Vienne and Maguelonne emerge triumphant from a series of independent trials. They become fully-developed characters in their own right, quite different from one another. In many ways these ladies display more resourceful personalities than their suitors. Their adventures contradict the received idea of the typical heroine of romance as a passive, colorless being.

As the dates of his 1485 prose romances indicate, Caxton seemed to be busy making recent French chivalric texts available to readers of English who were no longer bilingual: he has been described as the supplier of Burgundian best-sellers to the English market. Caxton had begun his literary career by translating a new Burgundian romance of antiquity, Raoul Le Fèvre's *Recueil des histoires de Troye*, as his *Recuyell of the Histories of Troy* in 1471. He kept up his preference for late medieval prose versions of chivalric narratives to the end, as his *Four Sonnes of Aymon* (1488), *Blanchardyn and Eglantine* (1489) and *Eneydos* (1490) suggest. Later printers were in no hurry to discard this vintage

---

7   MacEdward Leach, ed., preface to *Paris and Vienne*, trans. William Caxton, EETS o.s. 234 (London, 1957 for 1951), p. v. For bibliographical descriptions of these volumes, see Leach's preface, pp. xi–xii, and James W. Spisak, ed. introduction to *Caxton's Malory* (Berkeley and Los Angeles,1983), II.612–16. The English, Spanish, and German texts are discussed in my 1993 paper, "A Saracen Princess in Three Translations," in *The Medieval Translator* 5 (1996), pp. 432–48. Cooper records nine editions of the French text before 1600. See Leach, *Paris and Vienne*, pp. 118–20; Cooper, "Nostre histoire", p. 218.

8   Sixteen pre-1600 printings of the French are listed in Cooper's bibliography, "Nostre histoire", pp. 218–19.

9   Clive Griffin, *The Crombergers of Seville: The History of a Printing and Merchant Dynasty* (Oxford, 1988), p. 250. Burke, "Chivalry in the New World," p. 257. *Pierre de Provence* is one of the books Juan Luis Vives condemned in 1524, alongside *Amadís* and *Lancelot*. See Burke, "Chivalry in the New World," p. 253, n. 2. The realistic depiction of Maguelonne's elopement from her father's palace may have distressed the educator of Christian women in particular.

of chivalric narrative. In 1522, when Jacobo Cromberger of Seville was printing the second of Cortes' *cartas de relaciones* describing his expedition in search of "a great lord called Mutezuma," the printers of Paris were issuing such volumes as *Ogier le dannoys* and *Ysaïe le Triste.*[10] This *Ogier* is, again, a prose version of a verse text, the *Roman d'Ogier* in alexandrines of about 1335. Georges Doutrepont described the prose reworking as an attempt to give the effect of a "semi-historical compilation," and Knud Togeby concurs that the fifteenth-century prose writer's goal was to make the wildly fantastic adventures of Charlemagne's knight Ogier sound as much as possible like sober historical fact.[11] This goal explains much about its direct prose style and that of other fifteenth-century prose narratives of this kind. *Ysaïe le Triste* is a late-fourteenth- or early-fifteenth-century sequel to the prose *Tristan*, relating the adventures of a son of Tristan and Isolde in the ruinous landscape of post-Arthurian Britain. For Jane Taylor, this is "one of the most interesting of the late Arthurian romances."[12] The situation shows no sign of disentangling itself even towards the end of the sixteenth century. In 1587, the year that Sir Walter Ralegh established his second Virginia colony, the third book of *L'histoire de Primaleon de Grece* (trans. G. Chapuis) was printed in Lyons for the second time, and *Olivier de Castille et Artus d'Algarbe*, a short Burgundian prose romance of about 1455, was reprinted in Paris by N. Bonfons, one of five known editions of this French text before 1600. *Primaléon* is the second book of *Palmerin de Oliva*, the great rival of *Amadís* as what might be called a serial chivalric romance of the sixteenth century. Perhaps written by Francisco Vázquez, and first printed in Salamanca in 1512, it has nine later editions up to 1598 listed in Daniel Eisenberg's bibliography of Castilian romances of chivalry. *Primaléon* was not to appear in English until Anthony Munday began publishing his translation in three installments, beginning in 1589. In fact, the 1580s saw the beginning of the taste for the sixteenth-century Hispanic chivalric romances in England, just as it was fading out in Europe. *The Mirrour of Princely Deedes and Knighthood* (the *Espejo de Principes y Cavalleros* of Diego Ortuñez de Calahorra), the earliest of the new Hispanic chivalresque romances to be translated into English, only came out in 1580 or so. As Thomas notes, the English vogue

[10] Hernan Cortes, *Letters from Mexico*, ed. and trans. Anthony Pagden (New Haven, 1986), p. 50. Griffin, *The Crombergers of Seville*, pp. 57, 237. Cooper, "Nostre histoire," pp. 210, 215. *Ogier le dannoys* (Paris, s.d. (c.1522)), was first printed in Lyons, in 1496; *Ysaie le Triste* (Paris, s.d. (c.1522)).

[11] Knud Togeby, *Ogier le Danois dans les littératures européennes* (Munksgaard, 1969), pp. 221, 148, 223.

[12] J. H. M. Taylor, "Ysaïe le Triste," in *The New Arthurian Encyclopedia*, ed. Norris J. Lacy (Chicago and London, 1991), p. 530. Cf. André Giacchetti, ed., *Ysaÿe le Triste: roman arthurien du moyen âge tardif* (Rouen, 1989). There were four sixteenth-century printings in France; this is the earliest extant. See Cooper, "Nostre histoire," p. 215.

for this literature was belated and subdued by comparison to its Continental success.[13]

Gail Orgelfinger has documented the fortune of *Olivier de Castille* among French, English, Flemish, German, Spanish, and Italian printers. The Spanish translation of this Burgundian "romance of friendship" that updates the tale of *Amis and Amiloun* with elegant fifteenth-century chivalric protocol and adventures in the wilds of Ireland went on being republished at regular intervals from 1499 to 1943, when it was reissued in Argentina. In England it had been available since 1518.[14]

When Captain John Smith's *Generall Historie of Virginia* was published in 1624, it might have shared a shelf in the bookstalls of London with Matthew Mainwaringe's retelling of *Paris and Vienne*, in MacEdward Leach's description, "a highly fantastic, verbose, sentimental, and impossible story, full of verbal gymnastics."[15] The earliest extant edition is that of 1618 (London: Richard Hawkins): there seem to have been eight reprints of Mainwaringe's confection up through 1650. Far from valuing the "believable" approach that the fifteenth-century author of the French *Paris et Vienne* had championed in his preface, seventeenth-century readers apparently preferred to have their blood curdled by ghosts, avengers, and theatrical tirades. This is *Paris and Vienne* as rewritten for the admirers of the *Duchess of Malfi.* Other fifteenth-century romances persisted as well, and not in England alone.[16]

This spot check of chivalric publications against some major landmarks of the history of exploration, although unsystematic, does bring out the curious persistence of concise fifteenth-century prose narratives of chivalry all across Europe. Many belong to the class associated with the Burgundian court of Philip the Good (1419–67), though a number of the great thirteenth-century prose and verse romances were also printed and translated. These perennial favorites coexisted amicably with the grand vogue of *Amadís* and *Palmerín*, which ran its course in Castile from about 1510 to 1590, and in France from 1540 to about 1580, dominating the book trade in vernacular fiction and stimulating numerous emulators. In England, as we have seen, the period of their popularity comes later, from roughly 1580 to 1620, with a revival of interest around 1650.[17] This tidal wave of elaborate chivalric prose naturally

13 Daniel Eisenberg, *Castilian Romances of Chivalry in the Sixteenth Century: a bibliography* (London, 1979), pp. 79–80. Cf. Sir Henry Thomas, *Spanish and Portuguese Romances of Chivalry* (Cambridge, 1920; rpt. New York, 1969), pp. 92–100, 250–52.

14 Cooper, "Nostre histoire," p. 218; Gail Orgelfinger, ed., *The Hystorye of Olyuer of Castylle,* trans. Henry Watson (New York and London, 1988), pp. 247ff.

15 Leach, *Paris and Vienne,* p. 117.

16 Orgelfinger assigns a tentative date of 1625 to the final French edition of *Olivier de Castille* on her list. An Italian translation of 1552 had been reprinted in Venice in 1592, and again in 1622. See Orgelfinger, *The Hystorye,* pp. 248, 252–53.

17 Cooper, "Nostre histoire," p. 191; Daniel Eisenberg, *Romances of Chivalry in the Spanish Golden Age* (Newark, 1982), p. 90; Thomas, *Spanish and Portuguese,* pp. 242–63. Samuel

distracts the critic's attention from earlier, deliberately understated forms of chivalric literature.

Something similar might be said about Castiglione's *Il Cortegiano*, published in Venice in 1528, and first translated into Spanish by the courtly poet Juan Boscán in 1540, and into English by Thomas Hoby in 1561. Students of chivalry differ on the extent to which Castiglione's book represents a major shift of values from the medieval knight to the cultivated Renaissance gentleman. To this reader's eye, Castiglione proffers an elegant combination of new and old elements; he stresses learning, but also courtesy, temperance, the love of a courtly lady, and the duty of princes to lead crusades. His ideals still overlap to some extent with those of Ramon Lull.[18]

The celebrated Hispanic chivalric romances and Castiglione's courtesy book did not offer the only model of knighthood available to *aficionados* of the sixteenth century and beyond. Nor are they of much use, for chronological reasons, as guides to the chivalric world in which Columbus and his patrons grew up. We must look to still earlier works to shed light on the chivalry of Henry the Navigator and Ferdinand and Isabella. Later, these fifteenth-century romances complement sixteenth-century chivalric texts in critical ways. In manuscript and in printed editions, medieval knightly literature continued to hold audiences before, during, and after the age of *Amadís* – even, in certain surprising cases, well after the age of Don Quixote. They need to be stressed here as a much underread and misunderstood literature, the foundation upon which the fantastic palaces of Amadís were built. The effort to include them once again should foster our sense of the multiple dimensions of late medieval and Renaissance chivalric literature.

It remains difficult to obtain a clear picture of the situation because, to my knowledge, no single bibliographical work or database covers all this territory. The student must fish for chivalric texts in a series of individual studies and

Johnson and Edmund Burke were still reading *Palmerin of England*, *Florismarte de Hircania*, and *Don Belianis of Greece* in the late eighteenth century. Bishop Percy recalled of Johnson, that " 'when a boy he was immoderately fond of reading romances of chivalry, and he retained his fondness for them through life; so that (adds his Lordship) spending part of a summer [the summer of 1764] at my parsonage-house in the country, he chose for his regular reading the old Spanish romance of *Felixmarte of Hircania* in folio, which he read quite through. Yet I have heard him attribute to these extravagant fictions that unsettled turn of mind which prevented his ever fixing in any profession.' " In 1776 Johnson was reading *Il Palmerino de Inghilterra*. Burke admitted his fondness for *Palmerin of England* and *Don Belianis of Greece*, at one point in the House of Commons. See James Boswell, *Life of Johnson*, ed. George Birkbeck Hill (Oxford, 1887) I.49, and n. 2.

18 See Barber, *The Knight and Chivalry* (rev. edn, Woodbridge, 1995), pp. 392–93; Keen, *Chivalry*, p. 249; Castiglione, *Il Cortegiano*, ed. Ettore Bonora (Milan, 1972), pp. 317–18. The effect when Castiglione praises the future kings of France and England and the future emperor Charles V while advocating a crusade is rather reminiscent of *Les Trois fils du Roi*.

disparate indices, organized by century, collection, or nationality. Remarkable gaps in scholarship still frustrate students, or stimulate them.[19]

What audiences did this late medieval chivalric literature hold? In the beginning, as its authors make clear, this was a literature written for courtly patrons, for affluent princes with strong pretensions to chivalric prowess. In the sixteenth century, Daniel Eisenberg argues, the picture must have changed. He suggests that those shorter late medieval chivalric stories that remained in print might have survived as children's literature. For that reason, and because they were in most cases translated from languages other than Castilian, he does not evaluate them in his studies of the sixteenth-century chivalresque romance.[20]

Without question, evidence can be marshalled to support this contention. An appeal to younger audiences would not be a development altogether at odds with the character of the original medieval chivalric romance. Georges Duby identified the target group for whom romances were first written as the *juvenes*, who were not children at all, but young, landless knights buzzing round the twelfth-century castle, hungry for land, glory, riches, marriage, and social stability. In the world of the romance, all their dreams are fulfilled. By military prowess and personal charm, the hero wins a position in feudal society, if not a kingdom of his own.[21] This literature would seem to have been designed to fulfil the fantasies of young audiences with knightly aspirations, and could have become schools of behavior for the aspiring young, holding up often contradictory models of conduct for emulation. Was Roland the warrior to imitate? Or would Galahad be a surer guide to renown? As for women who read romances, with which figures would they identify? Passionate queens like Guinevere and Isolde, or two-fisted Saracen princesses like Floripas, ingenious and outspoken guides like Lyonet, or abused and imprisoned maidens who ultimately marry their true loves? Would they, instead, feel free to imagine themselves as knights? In some cases, historical testimony or bibliographical

---

[19] The first detailed study of a Spanish printing house, Clive Griffin's book on the Crombergers, was published as recently as 1988. Daniel Eisenberg's *Castilian Romances* excludes all translations, in and out of Castilian, and all Hispano-Arthurian material, though the Hispano-Arthurian works are expertly covered in Harvey L. Sharrer's bibliography. Georges Doutrepont's study remains the principal work on the fifteenth-century prose versions of chivalric romances. Gail Orgelfinger's salient comment on the need for additional work on late medieval romance remains as true in 1993 as it was in 1988 (Orgelfinger, *The Hystorye*, p. xxv). Modern editions of many texts are still needed; besides that, the nature and the historical importance of this body of material needs to be better recognized.

[20] Eisenberg, *Romances of Chivalry*, p. 90, n. 2; *Castilian Romances*, p. 7.

[21] G. Duby, "In Northwestern France: The 'Youth' in Twelfth-Century Aristocratic Society," in *Lordship and Community in Medieval Europe: Selected Readings*, ed. Frederick L. Cheyette (New York, 1968), pp. 198–209, the editor's translation of "Dans la France du Nord-Ouest: Au XIIe siècle: les 'jeunes' dans la société aristocratique," *Annales, Economies-Sociétés-Civilisations* 19 (1964), pp. 835–46.

evidence can give us a sense of how medieval audiences reacted, but often we are left wondering.

One recurrent feature that might suggest the writers were aware of a young audience is the attention devoted to specific ingredients of the hero's training. The making of the young knight, from boyhood to chivalric renown – and, often, the complementary social training of the maiden – preoccupy many romances. The detailed description of Lancelot's chivalric education by the Lady of the Lake in the prose *Lancelot* is only the best-known of these set pieces. In such tales of the protagonist's youth before he attains knighthood, authors seem impelled to elaborate their own ideals of aristocratic education and child development.[22]

With or without this didactic trend, the young probably enjoyed romances of chivalry from the start. That they continued to enjoy them throughout the fifteenth and sixteenth centuries, and long beyond that, is also not difficult to prove. In the 1470s and 1480s Edward IV's male and female children were exposed to chivalric reading by both of their parents, in different ways. During the period when his household ordinances provided that the Prince of Wales should listen to unspecified "noble stories" at mealtimes, his sisters seem to have been poring over their mother's manuscript of the *Mort Artu* (MS British Library Royal 14. E. III). The eldest, Elizabeth of York, may even have received a pointed message from her future mother-in-law by way of a copy of *Blanchardyn and Eglantine*. In the sixteenth century even children locked into a stringent program of classical education by humanist tutors somehow managed to lay hold of King Arthur, as Lady Jane Grey's signature in the same *Mort Artu* manuscript and Roger Ascham's lament in *The Scholemaster* both indicate. Montaigne tells us he was not so lucky. Indeed, the sixteenth-century humanist denigrators of romance complain precisely that this literature erodes the morals of the young and the female audiences who read it. "Yet I know, when Gods Bible was banished the Court, and Morte Arthure receiued into the Princes chamber. What toyes, the dayly readyng of such a booke, may worke in the will of a yong ientleman, or a yong mayde, that liueth welthelie and idlelie, wise men can iudge, and honest men do pitie." This passage suggests that such "toys" were indeed being read.[23]

---

22 For varying examples of the education of the knight in romances of different vintages, see *Lancelot do Lac*, ed. Elspeth Kennedy (Oxford, 1980), I.38–48, 138–48; *The Hystorye of Olyuer of Castylle*, ed. Gail Orgelfinger, pp. 20–24; *Paris and Vienne*, ed. Leach, pp. 2–3; Joanot Martorell and Martí Joan de Galba, *Tirant lo Blanc*, trans. David H. Rosenthal (London and New York, 1984), pp. 42-56; *Amadis of Gaul*, books I and II, trans. Edwin B. Place and Herbert C. Behm (Lexington, 1974–75), pp. 49–50, 56–63. A counter-theme, that of the youth sheltered from any knowledge of knighthood who nevertheless proves to have chivalry in his blood, recurs in the Perceval romances from Chrétien on.

23 Roger Ascham, *The Scholemaster* (London, 1570) cited in Thomas, *Spanish and Portuguese*, p. 264, n. 1. For the reading of "noble stories" at mealtimes in the household of the future Edward IV, see Nicholas Orme, *From Childhood to Chivalry* (London, 1984), p. 183. For Elizabeth Woodville's ownership of MS BL Royal 14. E. III, and its association

Whether younger readers devoured medieval texts, while older youths read *Amadís,* may be more difficult to establish. It could be argued that the more sexually explicit Renaissance narratives might be more often withheld by concerned parents, or that the stylistic elaboration of the later works made them less accessible to the very young than the stripped-down, pseudo-historical prose of many fifteenth-century texts. Eisenberg considers that *Amadís* and its progeny also appealed to a youthful readership, though, again, not to the exclusion of adults.[24] The future saint, Teresa of Avila, depicts herself as a twelve-year-old reading unspecified books of chivalry with her mother, when they stimulated her interest in such vanities as clothes and cosmetics. Before that she recalls enjoying saints' lives of the more bloodcurdling sort.

Before accepting the suggestive idea that the late medieval prose romances became the children's literature of the Renaissance, two perhaps contradictory points should be noted – one of qualification, and another of interpretation. The first point is that, where information is available, it seems clear that medieval texts of this basic type, books like *Mélusine* and *L'Histoire de Charlemagne,* were directed to adult patrons themselves, not to their offspring. There were pragmatic reasons for this. The adult patron could pay the writer. In certain cases this was a literature written by and for the knights themselves, and sometimes by their ladies. Among the knights should be numbered Joannot Martorell, the author of *Tirant lo Blanch,* as well as Sir Thomas Malory, and, later still, Sir Philip Sidney. There seems to have been a certain vogue for the translation of French prose romances into German among the ladies of the Holy Roman Empire, started by Countess Elisabeth of Nassau-Sarrebrück, and continued by Eleanor of Scotland.[25] In other cases, the author or translator might be an aristocratic courtier and administrator, like Matteo Maria Boiardo (1440–92) or John Bourchier, Lord Berners (1469–1533). Countess Elizabeth's grandson, the duke of Palatinat-Simmern (1446–1557), was to produce German translations of both Bagnyon and *Les Quatre fils Aymon* (as *Haymonskinder*). The clerk writing in a prince's service, like David Aubert or Raoul Le Fèvre for Philip the Good of Burgundy, can also be held responsible for contributions to the stock of chivalric narrative. Few verifiable instances of monastic authorship can be cited, though Roger Ascham liked to insist that chivalric romances "were made in Monasteries, by idle Monks, or wanton Chanons."[26] In the sixteenth century and beyond, these medieval books never seem to have been

with her daughters Elizabeth of York and Cicely, and for the connections between Elizabeth of York and Caxton's *Blanchardyn and Eglantine,* see J. R. Goodman, " 'That wommen holde in ful greet reverence': Mothers and Daughters reading chivalric romances," in *Women, The Book, and the Worldly,* ed. Lesley Smith and Jane H. M. Taylor (Cambridge, 1995), pp. 25–30.

24 Eisenberg, *Romances of Chivalry,* pp. 93–95.

25 Elisabeth of Nassau-Sarrebrück, trans., *Lohier et Maller,* 1437; see Keller, *Autour de Roland,* p. 287.

26 See Thomas, *Spanish and Portuguese,* pp. 263–64.

read by children to the exclusion of an adult audience. "Honest King Arthur may never displease a soldier," Sir Philip Sidney remarked. The booksellers' dispatches that label the shorter medieval chivalric romances being exported to the Americas as "for children," "para niños," date from 1599 and 1605.[27] Even if this label can be accepted as accurate, a century earlier the case may well have been different. As adults were more likely to buy the books than their children, and as we have difficulty determining for what readership the purchased volume was intended, the hypothesis still resists proof. There are certainly notable instances of purchases of such romances by childless bibliophiles like Columbus' son Fernando, though it should be noted that don Fernando began his collection as a very young man. To assume that such a reader could hardly be purchasing any book of this sort for his own reading reveals more about twentieth-century cynicism than sixteenth-century intentions. Evidence of this kind suggests that the notion of an exclusive "children's literature" at this period may well be anachronistic.

The second observation is that, as a children's literature – if it was any such thing – this late medieval chivalric fiction needs to be recognized as a key influence on its readers' adult behavior. The books that children read may shape their perceptions, their self-images, often their lives, to a much greater extent than the books they amuse themselves with as adults. Long before young men about the court were modeling themselves on the elegant Amadís and the virtuous Esplandián, they were playing at Galahad and Roland, and their sisters were playing along with them. If Professor Eisenberg is correct in identifying these volumes as children's books, then it is to these often neglected, late medieval *mises en prose* that we should look for primary images of chivalry underlying all too many exploits of the fifteenth and sixteenth centuries.

A related question concerns evidence of the declining prestige of this literature. In the past, students of the subject detected and lamented a distinct decline in the production standards of later editions of chivalric works. The grand folio volumes of the Parisian master Antoine Vérard, sometimes printed on vellum and supplied with hand-colored illustrations, vie with the glories of the fifteenth-century display manuscript. From there it seems to have been all downhill, as later printers, driven by the economics of their profession, sought out less expensive materials and techniques, and experimented with smaller type-faces. By the end of the sixteenth century, a tightly packed pocket edition on comparatively flimsy paper, something resembling the mass-market paperback of today, had been achieved. This decline in the size and splendor of the physical book irresistibly suggests a corresponding loss of status. When expensive editions no longer repay the printer's investment, does this mean that the book's content is no longer of any interest to affluent readers? The logic is suspect. One might with equal propriety assume that modern millionaires never buy super-market paperbacks. It is no doubt true that the cheaper books of chivalry

---

[27] Eisenberg, *Romances of Chivalry*, p. 90, n. 2.

became, the more accessible they were to a younger, lower-class audience. It is more dubious to argue that such a broadening of the readership would cause courtly readers to abandon such works as beneath their notice, or that the failure to produce sumptuous display copies meant that printers had given up the thought of attracting a few wealthy purchasers in favor of an aspiring underclass.

Where it can be discerned, evidence of book ownership or reading of these books would seem to be the best guide to the chivalric audiences of the period. Evidence of reading is of course preferable: as Jeanne Krochalis astutely observes, knowing what books people owned has never been quite the same thing as knowing what they read. Royal libraries, with their accumulations of presentation copies, can be especially misleading on this subject. From the fifteenth century all through the sixteenth century European monarchs continued to be chivalric enthusiasts, with Charles VIII and François I of France, Henry VIII of England, James IV of Scotland, the Holy Roman Emperors Maximilian I and Charles V, and Sebastian of Portugal almost falling over themselves in the effort to appear more chivalrous than one another. Even Philip II of Spain, remembered today for the asceticism of his later years, appeared in tournaments and pronounced chivalric vows under stress, as in his enterprise against the England of Elizabeth I. Fashions in royal reading changed as the century wore on. Where Charles VIII seems to have admired *Les trois fils du roi* and wanted to name his son Roland, François I would become an admirer of *Amadís* and the monarch to whom Castiglione first dedicated his *Cortegiano*. Maximilian went so far as to concoct three autobiographical chivalric romances of his own, *Der Weisskunig, Theuerdank,* and *Freydal.* His grandson, Charles V, preferred Olivier de la Marche's Burgundian chivalric allegory, *Le chevalier délibéré.* In England, Edward IV and Henry VII both had their eldest sons christened Arthur. In 1503, Queen Isabella was well supplied with Hispanic Arthurian reading, some of which she may have inherited. Merlin, Joseph of Arimathea, the third part of the *Demanda del Santo Grial,* and Lancelot all find mention in the catalogues of her library. She has been identified as an admirer of *Tirant lo Blanch,* like Cervantes a century later, and her husband Ferdinand was known as an early enthusiast of *Amadís.*[28]

---

28 For Isabella's booklist of 1503, see I. Michael, " 'From Her Shall Read the Perfect Ways of Honour': Isabel of Castile and Chivalric Romance," in *The Age of the Catholic Monarchs, 1474–1516: Literary Studies in Memory of Keith Whinnom,* ed. Alan Deyermond and Ian MacPherson, *Bulletin of Hispanic Studies,* Special Issue (Liverpool, 1989), pp. 103–112; and Francisco Javier Sánchez Cantón, *Libros, Tapices y Cuadros que Coleccionó Isabel la Católica* (Madrid, 1950). For a lucid account of aristocratic English readers of the late fourteenth and early fifteenth centuries, see Jeanne E. Krochalis, "The Books and Reading of Henry V and his Circle," *Chaucer Review* 23 (1988), pp. 50–77. For Charles VIII's reading and the controversy over his son's name, see Yvonne Labande-Mailfert, *Charles VIII et son milieu: 1470–1498: la jeunesse au pouvoir* (Paris, 1975).

Where reading cannot be documented, public display can. The chivalric performances of Maximilian I, and of his grandson Charles V as a "new Charlemagne," both drew on the elaborate knightly rituals of the fifteenth-century dukes of Burgundy. Philip II of Spain took part in a series of jousts at Whitehall in 1554–55, and a major tournament in 1557, as gestures towards Anglo-Iberian chivalric reconciliation.[29] Royal sponsorship of tournaments continued into the seventeenth century in England with the "chivalric cult" surrounding James I's elder son, Prince Henry (1595–1612).[30]

In his prefaces and epilogues, written between 1471 and 1490, William Caxton stressed the importance of chivalric literature for an audience of noble ladies and gentlemen, though certain of his chivalric publications are also presented as appealing to all estates: Malory's *Morte Darthur* was one such work. The notion of a lower-class readership for the sixteenth-century Hispanic chivalresque romances has been discounted, on the grounds of expense, and the concomitant lack of free time and light to read them by, but it is not clear that such volumes were indeed comparatively expensive, and it is difficult to establish either levels of mass literacy or book prices in sixteenth-century Spain. Much the same thing can be said about the problem elsewhere in Europe. It does seem clear that the courtly prestige of many chivalric works might well attract the social climbers of the day, anxious to use such books as a "school of chivalry," as the French translation of *Amadís* was identified. In some cases, the text itself might even welcome such a readership. *Valentine et Orson* includes a stirring role for the virtuous merchant who achieves knightly status defending a sexually harassed empress.[31]

Most of all, the evidence supports the idea that these chivalric works con-

---

29 Alan Young, *Tudor and Jacobean Tournaments* (London, 1987), pp. 30–32. For Maximilian, see Richard Barber and Juliet Barker, *Tournaments: Jousts, Chivalry, and Pageantry in the Middle Ages* (Woodbridge, 1989), pp. 67–70.

30 Young, *Tudor and Jacobean Tournaments*, pp. 37–40. James I recommended jousting to his son in his manual of princely education, *Basilikon Doron*, and it was for Henry's passage of arms at Whitehall on Twelfth Night, 1610 that Ben Jonson wrote his Arthurian *Speeches at Prince Henries Barriers*.

31 Eisenberg, *Romances of Chivalry*, pp. 99–100; Michael, "From Her Shall Read"; Griffin, *The Crombergers of Seville*, pp. 137–39. For Caxton's prologues and epilogues, see *The Prologues and Epilogues of William Caxton*, ed. W. J. B. Crotch, EETS o.s. 176 (London, 1928). See also Henry Watson, trans., *Valentine and Orson*, ed. Arthur Dickson, EETS o.s. 204 (London, 1937; rpt. New York, 1971). The English text of the romance was translated by Wynkyn de Worde's assistant or apprentice Henry Watson from the fifteenth-century French. Douglas Gray suggests that he may have used the 1489 Lyons edition of *L'histoire des deux vaillans chavaliers Valentin et Orson* printed by J. Maillet, for which see Cooper, "Nostre histoire," p. 221. Only a fragment survives of de Worde's edition of about 1510. The English romance was reprinted in 1555 by W. Copland as *The hystory of the two valyaunte brethren Valentyne and Orson*; cf. Douglas Gray, ed., *The Oxford Book of Late Medieval Verse and Prose* (Oxford, 1985), p. 463. Gray points out the notable longevity of this romance in England (p. 213). In France, Cooper lists eleven reprintings of *Valentin et Orson* up to about 1600, the date at which his bibliography ends.

tinued to satisfy audiences like those for whom they were first written. Throughout the period, young aristocrats can be observed leafing through the pages of the *Morte Darthur,* or of the *Quatre fils Aymon,* or of *Amadís.* St Theresa and her brother Roderigo enjoyed books of chivalry so much that they composed one of their own. Five of the seven younger sons of the family, who may well have encountered this literature at their mother's knee alongside the future saint, would embark on military careers in Latin America, and two would die there in battle.[32]

While Fernandez-Armesto tells his readers that Prince Henry the Navigator was given to sensational reading, he does not specify the source of his comment. "The sort of reading matter Henrique favoured might have inspired a taste for 'mirabilia' – sensational tales of the fabulous and exotic."[33] We can assume that the Portuguese prince had access to the royal library, compiled in part by his father Dom João I, and his mother Philippa. His eldest brother Dom Duarte certainly used it for source material in the composition of his *Leal Conseilheiro,* and J. I. Roquete publishes a catalogue of Duarte's books in his edition of that work. Among the items listed are three Arthurian volumes, a *Livro de Tristam* (item 29), a *Merli(n)* (item 32), and most significantly perhaps in view of the Portuguese chivalric attraction to its hero, a *Livro de Galaaz* (item 35). Duarte possessed a copy of a *Conquista dultra mar* (item 54), perhaps a version of the late thirteenth-century Hispanic compendium of crusader history and romance better known as the *Gran Conquista de Ultramar.* This work might well prove a powerful source of crusading inspiration. The catalogue does not

---

32 For the aristocratic readership of the *Morte Darthur,* besides evidence cited earlier in this chapter, see Goodman, "That wommen holde in ful greet reverence." Caxton and Wynkyn de Worde both address aristocratic readers in their editions of Malory; see Barry Gaines, *Sir Thomas Malory,* p. 9 for de Worde's remarks of 1498 to "ye mighty and pompous lordes," and p. 11 for Sir Philip Sidney's tutor's complaints of 1578 on the "reading of vile and blasphemous, or at least prophane and frivolous bokes, such as are that infamous K. Arthur." See also Teresa of Avila, *The Book of Her Life,* in *Collected Works,* trans. Kieran Kavanaugh, O. C. D. and Otilio Rodriguez, O. C. D., Institute of Carmelite Studies, vol. I (Washington, D.C., 1976). The "books of chivalry" may have had some impact on Teresa's brothers' careers. The brother who wrote a chivalric romance with Teresa, Roderigo de Cepeda (b. 1511), sought his fortune in Latin America, like his younger brother Agustín de Ahumada (b. 1527), later governor of Tacuman in Argentina. Agustín went out to Peru and Chile in 1544 at the age of seventeen, and did not return in Teresa's lifetime; though their brothers Lorenzo (1519–?) and Pedro (1521–?) returned in 1575. A younger brother, Antonio (1530–46), died from his wounds after fighting in the battle of Iñaquito. Roderigo had sailed for the Americas in 1535, when he was twenty-four, and was also killed in combat there. At least five of the seven younger sons of the family, then, went as young men to South America.

33 Felipe Fernández-Armesto, *Before Columbus: Exploration and Colonisation from the Mediterranean to the Atlantic, 1229–1492* (Basingstoke and London, 1987), p. 188; Duarte, *Leal Conseilheiro,* ed. J. I. Roquete, pp. xx–xxii. See Harvey L. Sharrer, *A Critical Bibliography of Hispanic Arthurian Material,* vol. I: *Texts: The Prose Romance Cycles* (London, 1977), pp. 26–27, 37–40, 43–46.

identify the texts too specifically, nor the language in which they were written – they might be in Portuguese, or just as easily in Castilian or French.[34] These are at any rate some possible connections. The prince's mother, Queen Philippa, was known to be fond of John Gower's *Confessio Amantis*, which she brought with her from England to Portugal, and had translated into Portuguese. That massive compendium of stories conveyed, among others, new English versions of tales of the wanderings of Constance, Apollonius of Tyre, and Alexander to the Portuguese court.[35]

The Spanish royal library, as represented in Queen Isabella's booklist of 1503, offers some instructive parallels. Many of the almost four hundred books listed must have been inherited from her father, Juan II of Castile. Stability is plausible in royal libraries, but so is accretion. A similar but not identical trio of Arthurian volumes appears in the middle of Isabella's catalogue: "qui se dice de Merlin e habla de Josepe ab Arimathia" (item 142); "la tercera parte de la demanda del Santo Grial" (item 143), and "historia de Lanzarote" (item 144). These do sound like Castilian titles, which suggest Castilian translations, corresponding approximately to some version of the *Baladro del Sabio Merlin* with Joseph of Arimathea attached (parts one and two of the Grail story); the *Demanda del Santo Grial*, which would be the Quest of the Holy Grail proper, with Galahad. It seems as though both Portuguese and Spanish royal libraries included three-volume Arthurian histories, and that in both cases the Grail story was prominent. Isabella's list does not include a *Gran conquista*, though the crusade must have figured in some of the other historical compendia on the royal bookshelves. The collection did include some technical chivalric works (a *Dotrinal de Caballeros*) as well as a Trojan history in two volumes, the *Libro de Buen Amor* of the Archpriest of Hita, devotional and classical works, and a mirror for princes. There is no mention of *Amadís*, a favorite of her husband Ferdinand, or of *Tirant*; we know of the royal interest in these works from other sources.[36]

Arthurian prose romances and the *roman d'antiquité* seem to be the major common denominator uniting these two Iberian royal booklists. Isabella seemed more attached to her many tapestries, a number of them representing scenes from romances, than to her books. Arthur and Galahad figured among

---

34 Harvey Sharrer's indispensable bibliography of Spanish and Portuguese Arthurian texts identifies surviving Portuguese manuscript texts of a *Historia da mesa redonda e da demanda do Santo Grial* (Sharrer Ae6; Vienna, Osterreichische Nationalbibliothek, 2594), which is the third branch of the post-Vulgate *Roman du Graal*, taking the story from Galahad's arrival at court to the deaths of Arthur, Guinevere, Lancelot, and King Mark; two folios of a Portuguese *Livro de Tristàn* (Sharrer Ad3) and a Torre do Tombo MS *Libro de Josep Abaramatia*, subtitled *Primeira parte da Demanda do Santo Grial* (Sharrer Ae3).

35 For Philippa of Lancaster, see W. J. Entwistle and P. E. Russell, "A reinha D. Felipa y sua côrte," in *Congressso do mundo português – publicações* 11 (Lisbon, 1940), pp. 319–46.

36 See I. Michael, "From Her Shall Read"; Peggy K. Liss, *Isabel the Queen: Life and Times* (Oxford and New York, 1992).

the subjects. Again, these might have been inherited from earlier generations. We cannot tell who read the books from the booklist, or if they were read. By contrast, in the England of the 1480s we can be somewhat surer that Elizabeth Woodville and her daughters glanced at a version of the French *Morte Artu,* because the manuscript survives, and they took the trouble to write their names in it. Evidence of the content of the court pageants in which Isabel participated might be useful here. In Portugal we do know of a tournament in which João II appeared as the Knight of the Swan, a character familiar from crusader romances, including the *Gran Conquista de Ultramar.*[37] In all these cases, the royal personages involved have been accused by their biographers of modeling their behavior on chivalric romance – Edward IV and Isabella in their marital exploits, Henry the Navigator and the *Reyes católicos* in their crusading aspirations.

What of the reading of the explorers, Christopher Columbus, for example? As it is presently reconstructed Columbus' booklist is mostly technical. He tended to rely heavily on Pierre d'Ailly's *Imago Mundi* and on Cardinal d'Ailly's theologico-astrological discussions bound in the same volume. It was Cardinal d'Ailly who cited Roger Bacon's reference to the Prophecies of Merlin as a key to God's plan for the universe, in a passage Columbus selected for inclusion in the *Libro de las Profecías.* In Columbus' case scholars are not sure they have identified all his books among the massive collection his son developed. We know his son Fernando acquired a copy of the *Historia de la linda Melosina* in 1514, and of the French text in 1535, as well as a variety of other romances. Columbus' readings in the classics of medieval travel literature – *The Book of Marco Polo,* among others – led him to expect to find an island populated by Amazons in the East Indies, and to look for traces of the Terrestrial Paradise. Both of these geographical marvels appeared in *Las Sergas de Esplandián* early in the sixteenth century, bringing the later history of *Amadís* into line with the latest discoveries. These were also commonplaces of medieval romance geography, especially tales of Alexander's adventures in India, and the wanderings of those intrepid explorers Ogier the Dane, Huon of Bordeaux, and Bevis of Hampton. (This point will be explored in detail later in this study.) In those instances where Columbus annotated a volume, though, we are given proof that he actually read the work – a distinct advantage not shared by students of Isabella's library. After the d'Ailly volume the work he annotated most copiously seems to have been the *Historia Rerum Ubique Gestarum* of Aeneas Sylvius Piccolomini in a 1477 edition.[38] In this historical work of Aeneas Sylvius

---

[37] Garcia de Resende, *Chronica dos valerosos e insignes feitas del rey dom Ioa II de gloriosa memoria* (Lisbon, 1622), pp. 79–84. For an overview of Spanish and Portuguese tournaments in the later Middle Ages, see Barber and Barker, *Tournaments,* ch. 4.

[38] A collection of Columbus' marginal notes is reproduced in the *Raccolta Colombina* I, part ii, 289–525. For Fernando Columbus' *Melusine,* see Alan Deyermond, "*La historia de la linda Melosina*: Two Spanish Versions of a French romance," in *Medieval Hispanic Studies*

Piccolomini, later Pope Pius II, Columbus confronted the writing of a distinguished humanist author who was also an impassioned advocate of the crusade, and who died in 1464 at the western Italian port of Ancona after taking the Cross himself in a vain attempt to motivate the princes of Europe. The thirteen-year-old Christopher Columbus, whether still in Genoa or anywhere else in the Christian world, could hardly have failed to be impressed by the event.

A wide variety of chivalric romances contributed heroic motifs and images on which military or mercantile adventurers of the era of European expansion might model their lives. Many of the early Portuguese and Castilian explorers were drawn from the minor nobility, or in Columbus' case, aspired to become members of the aristocracy. These were the readers and hearers to whom these romances had always appealed. The second division of this study will discuss specific connections between the chivalric literature of the period and particular exploration narratives.

One reason scholars are reluctant to read such books is that they have acquired a reputation for low aesthetic quality. Among the most consistent themes in the history of literature is the insistence that the chivalric fiction of the later Middle Ages lacks any discernible literary merit. This aesthetic disdain differs notably from the moral, often clerical, criticism of secular literature that surfaced early in the Middle Ages. As already mentioned, Dante provided the most famous example of this line of thought in Francesca da Rimini's indictment of the Prose Lancelot as an incitement to adultery: "Galeotto fu il libro e che lo scrisse." Into the seventeenth century, a succession of these moral critics pay homage to the attractive power of secular chivalric literature. If it were not so seductive, it would not endanger the souls of its readers. The humanist educators Juan Luis Vives and Roger Ascham were excited because they knew the books they deplored as incitements to "open manslaughter and bold bawdry" were being read and admired, often by the impressionable young or by women. They were hazardous to their readers because they were attractive. By contrast, later aesthetic critics – the historians of literature – find it difficult to believe that such a literature can or should have found an audience at all,

Presented to Rita Hamilton, ed. A. D. Deyermond (London, 1977), pp. 57–65, at p. 62. The records indicate that Fernando Columbus bought a copy of a 1512 Valencia edition of *Melosina* in Valladolid in 1514, but it is no longer to be found in his collection. His copy of the 1528 Lyons edition of Jean d'Arras' *Roman de Mélusine* published by Olivier Arnoullet was purchased at Montpellier in 1535 for 30 *dineros*. See Jean Babelon, *La Bibliothèque Française de Fernand Colomb* (Paris, 1913), pp. 8–9. This volume was still in the Biblioteca Colombina at the time when Babelon conducted his researches. Fernando Columbus' records of book purchases are of great value to the student of the European book trade in the earlier sixteenth century. Recently the Fundacion Mapfre America has undertaken to publish a new facsimile of Fernando Columbus' catalogue of his library. This supercedes the previous facsmile edition, Archer M. Huntington, ed., *Catalogue of the Library of Ferdinand Columbus* (New York, 1905). In this connection I am grateful to Professor Charles Faulhaber for supplying me with much helpful information and good advice.

certainly never an audience with any pretensions to taste. This aesthetic con-demnation reflects the changing tastes of new generations of writers. The authors of the prose reworkings of medieval verse romances had their own linguistic or stylistic objections to the poems they revised. Jean Bagnyon, for instance, thought the verse *Fierabras* was disorganized. Frequently prefaces complain that the work's language was out of date. As classical literature became the standard of excellence for the learned, defenders of the romance in its new or old forms, like Giraldi Cinthio, took to the barriers to support the conflicting aesthetic ideal of variety against neo-Aristotelian unity.

Both of these bands of critics, the moralists and the aesthetes, signal how far from being an official "canonical" literature this massive body of chivalric writing was at any time. Its astonishing longevity depended on its continuing appeal to new generations of readers and hearers. This is a literature that can be described as resolutely extra-canonical, or perhaps even anti-canonical. Official literary history has never found a place for it. It does recognize the literary ancestors of this body of texts, the epics of the ancient world and the *chansons de geste* of the earlier Middle Ages, and its heirs, the romance epics, the Hispanic chivalric romances, and the "folk-books." While later medieval chiv-alric literature fails to fit into established literary hierarchies, it can claim recognition as a force in history, if only as a vehicle for the transmission of medieval ideals into the future. This literature demands to be read on its own terms, not as a tin can tied to the hearse of the Middle Ages, nor a cul-de-sac leading away from the high road to the Renaissance. It has a crucial role to play, one well worth exploring.

What is this much-abused body of literature, too often summarized out of existence? In its rehabilitation the first qualities to emphasize are the variety and attractiveness of the chivalric material available to customers of the early printshops. In fact, the literature of late medieval chivalry resists categorization. This cannot be the full-scale study of late medieval chivalric literature that the subject deserves – an enterprise well beyond the scope of this work. But some introductory description is essential before moving on to the larger problem, with stress on those works and themes of greatest significance for an under-standing of the intersection of chivalry and exploration.

CHAPTER TWO

The Romance as an Imaginative Literature of Travel

MANY THEMES, motifs and preoccupations link the literature of late medieval chivalry with factual narratives of exploration. Some preliminary account of these common interests is needed. A descriptive survey becomes more necessary since late medieval chivalric romances are little read today even by specialists in the period. The exploratory discussion offered in this study has been subdivided. This chapter analyzes the geographic span and the exotic scenery of the later chivalric romance – the way these narratives see, or perhaps reinvent the world. Other key chivalric issues, like chivalric morality and its limits in these texts, the crusade and conversion, and plot structures that recur throughout this literature, will be examined later, as they become useful for the interpretation of specific exploration narratives.

The moral or psychological effect of reading chivalric romances, if any, proves to be a matter of continuing debate. In his publisher's preface, Caxton advised the readers of Malory's *Morte Darthur* to "do after the good and leave the evil, and it shall bring you to good fame and renommee." He wrote as a reader well aware of the moral complexities that characterize this celebrated Arthurian work. For Samuel Johnson, early reading in Hispanic books of chivalry eroded his ability to concentrate. The discussion continues down to the present-day controversy over children's exposure to sex and violence onscreen – "open manslaughter and bold bawdry" revisited. Before any discussion of their applications in the fifteenth and sixteenth centuries can be attempted, the student needs to look at the world through the lenses of these works.

Sir John Mandeville and Marco Polo presented themselves to their contemporaries as true travelers undertaking real journeys. The chivalric romances of the fifteenth and sixteenth centuries depict journeys of the imagination. Some of them may draw on personal experience or solid recent information. At least two enterprising writers in the early part of the fourteenth century, the authors of *Baudouin de Sebourc* and *Perceforest*, seem to have adapted *The Book of Marco Polo* into chivalric fiction, while in the mid-fifteenth century the Catalan author Martí Joan de Galba used Mandeville in his conclusion to *Tirant lo Blanch*.[1]

---

[1] For *Baudouin de Sebourc*, see Edmond René Labande, *Etude sur Baudouin de Sebourc, chanson de geste* (Paris, 1940); for *Perceforest*, see J. H. M. Taylor, "Aroés the Enchanter – an episode in the *Roman de Perceforest* and its source," *Medium Aevum* 47 (1978), pp.

Some narratives depend on the authority of ancient science, as do certain of Alexander's adventures. These works should be read as the grandparents of our science fiction. Other romances are absolute fantasies, independent and so far untraceable. Often multiple sources of inspiration mingle inextricably in a single work.

It would be a mistake to attempt to specify which species of fictional journeys sheds the most light on exploration literature. Each contributes to our understanding of the problem in its own way. The chivalric narratives of the later Middle Ages and Renaissance need to be seen as an imaginative literature of travel, quite as much as they are fictions of war and love. They should be recognized as a too often neglected resource for understanding attitudes to travel, travellers' tales, and the conduct of Europeans abroad.

Travel is a staple of the romance as far back in history as romances can be identified. If the *Odyssey* is seen as the first romance, it must also be seen as an early instance of the adventurous journey. Jason's voyage to find the Golden Fleece has been identified as the first quest narrative. Alexander the Great's expeditions to the exotic East may have given a renewed impetus to this narrative tradition. Tales of the travels of geographically separated families, husbands and wives, parents and children, divided lovers and parted friends seeking reunions were numerous in antiquity.[2] This, too, is the stuff of romance. What with "exile and return," pilgrimages, quests of miscellaneous knights errant and their ladies, crusades and conquests, almost no form of journey remains unattempted in chivalric narrative. There are journeys to the center of the earth, journeys under the sea, journeys to outer space, journeys to the Other World or to undiscovered new lands. Knights travel by preference on horseback, but also on foot, or by ship. To fill the chronological gap between Pegasus and the Wright brothers, they may also make use of magic horses (as in *Cleomadés*, *Richard Coeur de Lion* and *Valentine and Orson*), gigantic birds, griffons, demons, clouds, or other devices to fly from one end of the earth to the other. Indeed, they may simply will themselves and their friends to appear in a distant location, as Oberon the dwarf king of the Fairies does in *Huon of Bordeaux* or as Morgue (Morgan le Fay) does in *Ogier le Danois*.[3] The later romances proffer

---

30–39; cf. Joanot Martorell and Martí Joan de Galba, *Tirant lo Blanc*, ed. Martí de Riquer (Barcelona, 1979), Introduction. Galba in particular seems to have depended on Mandeville as he completed the North African section of the narrative. It seems quite possible that as the later prose romances are studied more attentively, additional borrowings from Polo may be detected. There is also evidence that Polo's book borrows from the romances. For some discussion of this point, see below, ch. 5.

2 Cf. B. P. Reardon, ed., *Collected Ancient Greek Novels* (Berkeley, 1989).

3 *Huon of Bordeaux*, ed. S. L. Lee, EETS e.s. 40, 41, 43, 50 (London, 1882–87). *Ogier le Danois: Roman en Prose du XVIᵉ siècle*. Facsimile reproduction of Antoine Vérard's Paris edition of 1498, from the copy in the Biblioteca Nazionale Universitaria de Turin, ed. Knud Togeby (Munksgaard, 1967), p. 282. Ogier asks Lady Morgue to wish them somewhere in France: "Ma dame ie vous prie tant humblement comme ie puis quil vous

a treasure trove of convincingly described voyages with all their attendant mishaps, and of the wildest fantasies of travel, of well-informed observations and of imaginative expectations. They also supply models of behavior for their readers to emulate, suggesting how to act or not to act in a wide range of bizarre emergencies and commonplace predicaments of the voyager.

In these tales of travel, each period displays its own preoccupations. For the ancient Greek novelists or romancers, shipwreck, pirates and slavery, occult practices, hazardous religious cults, sexual molestation, execution and human sacrifice all imperil the wanderer. The late medieval knight is more likely to be imprisoned, impoverished, held up or hanged than he is to be enslaved or threatened with rape. Where the Greek prose romances depict the heterogeneous religious landscape of the ancient Mediterranean, the later medieval and Renaissance texts focus almost exclusively on the confrontation of Christianity and Islam.

The geographic range of particular chivalric voyages is worth noting. This element tends to reveal the terrestrial preoccupations of the writers and their audiences. With its help we can map the expanding universe of the chivalric imagination. The full symbolic effect of the geography of these romances, with all its political and religious resonances, has yet to be recovered. Notwithstanding many attractive individual variations from the pattern, the reader can observe that three geographical registers recur throughout this literature. Arthurian romances tend to deploy their heroes across a fictionalized British Isles and France that include such imaginary or semi-imaginary locations as the kingdoms of Logres, Gorre, Norgales, Sorelois, Norhombeland, Benoïc and Gaunes in Gaul, Camelot (equated by Malory at one point with Winchester), Corbenic the Grail Castle, and numerous other castles, fountains, forests, passages, and islands distinguished by their various perils. There are fountains of the Hermit, of Fairies, of the Giant, of the Lion, of Knights, of Shepherds, of True Lovers, an Adventurous fountain, the fountain Brahaigne, the fountain of Guiron the Courtois, of the Sapynoie, of the Virgin, of the Pine, of the Shadow, of Tears, of the Two Sycamores, of Marvels, of the Stag, of the Valley of Tears, later renamed the Valley of Joy, of Galahad, and of Lancelot. As G. D. West and other scholars testify, Arthurian geography is a frustrating, contradictory field of inquiry, only now beginning to receive the systematic research that it demands for proper understanding.[4]

Other romances look to the East, sending European heroes out on the trails of Alexander and of the crusaders. There is, again, a mixture of real places and

---

plaise nous souhaitier quelque part en France." Then a cloud transports him, his enchanted horse Papillon, and his comrade Benoit to Montpellier.

4   G. D. West, *An Index of Proper Names in French Arthurian Prose Romances*, University of Toronto Romance Series 35 (Toronto, 1978), p. xiii. All of the place names cited have entries in the index. Cf. G. D. West, *An Index of Proper Names in French Arthurian Verse Romances, 1150–1300*, University of Toronto Romance Series 15 (Toronto, 1969).

imaginative inventions. Both the imaginary and the actual location can be loaded with significance for a contemporary audience. Especially after its fall to the Turks in 1453, Constantinople became a center of attention, almost displacing Jerusalem as the chief object of Christian chivalric interest. Babylon and Damascus, Cairo and Alexandria are mentioned often. Spain and North Africa become key battlegrounds in these works, thanks to the Reconquest, but later texts may shift the scene of the action to Cyprus and Rhodes.

Some narratives unroll themselves against a factual map of the world. Their knights have their feet planted firmly on the same ground that their readers tread. The dynastic romance of *Mélusine* is peppered with the names of French towns, castles, and monasteries supposedly founded by that enterprising fairy. When her sons leave home to seek their fortunes, they go to identifiable locations: Cyprus and Armenia, Luxembourg and, again, wildest Ireland. Raimondin of Lusignan ends his days a hermit in Aragon, perched high on the cliffs of Montserrat. This factual geography furthers the romance's aims as a dynastic legend, dramatizing the rise of the Lusignans. Other kinds of romances also tie their stories to the map of Europe. The recently edited Castilian romance of about 1492, *La Corónica de Adramón*, sets its events in Poland, England, and Italy, incorporating a detailed account of a pilgrimage through a series of fifteenth-century Italian cities.[5]

Stories notable for the amount and eclectic variety of ground their heroes cover are, first, by right of antiquity, the Alexander romances, then those somewhat interdependent narratives *Bevis of Hampton* (*Beufves d'Anthonne,*) *Huon de Bordeaux,* and *Ogier le Danois*. All of these medieval tales of travel were well known and beloved of sixteenth-century printers in France. Some, but not all of them attained readers and printers in other languages as well.[6] These

---

5   Jean d'Arras, *Mélusine*, nouvelle édition, conforme à celle de 1478, revue et corrigée, ed. Charles Brunet (Paris, 1854). Gunnar Anderson, ed., *La Corónica de Adramón* (2 vols., Newark, 1992).

6   R. Cooper, " 'Nostre histoire renouvelée': The Reception of Romances of Chivalry in Renaissance France (with bibliography)," in *Chivalry in the Renaissance*, ed. Sydney Anglo (Woodbridge, 1990), pp. 221–22, cites ten French Alexander romances printed between 1506 and 1584, with titles that escalate from Michel le Noir's *Alixandre le Grant* to *L'hystoire du très-vaillant, noble, preux et hardy roy Alixandre le grant.* Two Alexander romances in verse are known to have been printed in the British Isles, the fourteenth-century *Lyfe of Alisaunder* (c.1525) and the Scottish *Alexander Buik* (ca.1580). Cf. R. M. Lumiansky, in *A Manual of the Writings in Middle English 1050–1500*, gen. ed. J. Burke Severs (New Haven, 1967), pp. 105, 272. Cooper lists five editions of *Beufves d'Anthonne* ("Nostre histoire," p. 205), beginning with Vérard's undated folio volume and ending with an undated quarto published by J. Bonfons, also in Paris. In addition to seven entire or fragmentary manuscripts of two English versions of the romance, three early printed editions of the English text survive at least in part, the first published by Wynkyn de Worde at Westminster in 1500, the second by Richard Pynson (London, 1503), and the third by William Copland around 1565 (STC nos. 1987–89). See Charles Dunn, *A Manual of the Writings in Middle English: Romances*, p. 215. In England *Huon de Bordeaux* is best known through Lord Berners' translation, *The Boke of Duke Huon of*

elaborate journeys resist summarization. A sketch of Huon's fantastic voyages may perhaps give a pale reflection of the nature of such trips.

In his earliest series of adventures, Huon of Bordeaux travels from France to Jerusalem, then on through a magical wood and then by sea (aboard the sea monster Mallabron) to Babylon. He and his fiancée, the Saracen Princess Esclarmonde, are shipwrecked on a desert island. She is later taken by pirates to the city of Mombrant. The reunited couple return by way of Rome, are married there, and then fall into the hands of Huon's wicked brother Gerard, who imprisons them at Bordeaux. In the later, second round of adventures, Huon sets off for a tournament at Maience. The romance propels him from there to Cologne. Later, on the high seas, he encounters the soul of Judas in the Perilous Gulf. His ship is wrecked at the Castle of the Adamant, an event that also figures in the prose version of *Ogier le Danois*. Eventually, Huon is carried off by a griffin to the Earthly Paradise, where he finds both the fountain and the apple tree of youth. He emerges in Persia, converts and rejuvenates the "Admiral" (Emir) with the help of the apples, and sets off for home by way of the City of Angory, fighting alongside his converted Saracen allies for the recovery of the Holy Land. He must circle back to France to save his wife from the emperor of Germany. At the conclusion of the story, Huon succeeds to Oberon's fairy realm. His travels end in the Other World.

This concatenation of real and imaginary places, the known and the fantastic or mythical, gives this particular romance and its imitators an eclectic quality. The effect that might be compared to twentieth-century Latin American "magic realism." Or is it? The fifteenth- and sixteenth-century writer and his or her audience may not have been altogether certain which of the places described were actual and which were well beyond the realm of possibility. This uncertainty could well blur any reader's sense of a juxtaposition of styles. A barrage of "travellers' tales" was expanding the known world at a disconcerting rate. On Shakespeare's testimony, the colorful experiences of the European princes and adventurers of the fifteenth and sixteenth centuries encouraged readers to believe again in the fantasies of the authors of the romances. The case histories discussed in the second part of this study may cast some light on the locations beloved of the romances and their degree of probability for their medieval and Renaissance readers.

In the midst of so much competitive effort, borrowing, and piling on of new special effects, the ultimate fantasy may be difficult to identify. *Partonopeus de*

Burdeux (London: Wynkyn de Worde?, c.1534), while in France nine sixteenth-century editions of *Les prouesses du noble Huon de Bordeaulx* have been detected by Cooper, "Nostre histoire," p. 217, beginning in 1513 with Michel Le Noir; later printers elaborate on the title in different ways, for instance *Les prouesses et faictz merveilleux du noble Huon de Bordeaulx; Les prouesses et faictz du tres preulx, noble et vaillant Huon de Bordeaulx.* Cooper has fourteen editions of the prose *Ogier le Danoys* between 1496 and 1583; there is no English edition. Knud Togeby gives an exhaustive discussion of the *Ogier* tradition in his study of the romance.

Blois (in its Castilian translation *El libro del conde Partinuplés*) should certainly be in the running. This fifteenth-century prose romance, available in six manuscript versions in verse but never printed in England until the nineteenth century, ran through numerous editions in Spanish prose. Leonard ranks it second in popularity among sixteenth-century readers in the Spanish colonies of Latin America, based on his study of export records. It has been called "one of the best narratives of its kind, one of the most rationally composed, and one of the most ingenious in its details although, perhaps, not one of the most refined." In a reversal of Apuleius' tale of Cupid and Psyche, it is the knight Partonope, led astray by a magic boar, who travels to a magic castle by means of a magic ship, where he finds himself in bed with an invisible but most seductive lady.[7] She declares herself to be Melior, empress of Byzantium, and forbids him to try to see her. When he does, on his mother's advice, he loses her, and must undergo a period of penance and despair in the forest before he can win her back by his knightly prowess. In the end, Partonope attains the lady and the throne of Constantinople.

This conclusion brings together two grand fantasies of the world of chivalric romance – the love of an all-powerful fairy mistress who can endow her knight with unlimited wealth, and the idea of becoming the Byzantine emperor. These motifs occur separately with some frequency: Morgan le Fay and Mélusine are both fairy mistresses, as is Generides' mother. Tirant lo Blanch does not quite attain the imperial crown, since he dies just before he can marry his princess, but his friend Hippolytus becomes emperor by marrying the princess's widowed mother. Amadís's son Esplandián does become emperor, however, at the end of *Las Sergas de Esplandián*, Montalvo's fifth book. So does Palmerin de Oliva, progenitor of the rival series of chivalresque romances, and Gadifer, son of Theseus of Cologne in the romance *Theseus de Cologne*.[8] Valentine and Orson are lost twin heirs to the empire. This particular fantasy may have gripped the knights of Europe with special force after the fall of Constantinople in 1453.

[7] For *Partonope de Blois*, see L. H. Hornstein, in *A Manual of the Writings in Middle English*, pp. 304–07, where some basic references to the German *Partonopier und Melior* of Conrad of Wurzburg, and to the Icelandic and Danish versions of the romance are also to be found; Cooper does not list any early French editions of *Partonopeus*. The Spanish *Libro del conde Partinuplés* was printed in Alcalá de Henares in 1513, and reprinted in Seville by Jacobo Cromberger in 1519; see Clive Griffin, *The Crombergers of Seville: The History of a Printing and Merchant Dynasty* (Oxford, 1988), p. 249 and no. 192 of his bibliographical appendix. The *Manual* classifies *Partonope* as a "miscellaneous romance." For Menéndez y Pelayo's description of *Partinuplés*, see Irving A. Leonard, *Books of the Brave* (1949; rpt. Berkeley and Los Angeles, 1992), p. 109.

[8] For *Theseus de Cologne*, see Margaret Schlauch, *Chaucer's Constance and Accused Queens* (New York, 1927), where she describes it as "a late composite of elements from several such tales," and "a highly diverting tale, well worth rescuing from the obscurity in which it at present reposes." pp. 82–83, 102–03, 107. On pp. 122–26 she gives a partial summary of the narrative. Cooper's bibliography lists two mid-sixteenth-century Parisian editions of the *Hystoire des faictz & gestes du chevalier Theseus de Coulogne*, p. 220.

Taking a different tack, *Olivier de Castille et Artus de Algarbe* (a Burgundian work of c.1455) sets its folkloric plot in a plausible contemporary scene. It does have its wilderness – the wilds of Ireland, well stocked with fearsome forest creatures and vengeful local kings. The natives, one presumes Gaelic speakers, attempt to communicate with the questing Portuguese knight Artus by sign language. "And whan he wolde haue ony thynge he muste make some sygne / or elles they coude not vnderstande hym."[9] This feature is not mere local color. It heightens the suspense of the narrative as Artus forges his way through the Irish shrubbery. "He wente on fote / and soo longe he wente that on a daye he founde hymselfe in a thycke forest / in the whiche dyuers wylde beestes dydde remayne. They had wel made hym sygne that he sholde not entre in to that forest but he had not vnderstonden them" (Orgelfinger, pp. 149–50). Artus' ordeal in the Irish forest extends to combat against a somewhat misplaced lion and another unidentified but marvellous beast that whistles hideously as it approaches (Orgelfinger, p. 151). Between these combats, without the benefit of horse or armor, the starving Artus grubs for roots and leaves to eat, inspired by the legend of John the Baptist. "And whan the nyghte came he put hym on a lytell tree / for drede of dombe beestes" (Orgelfinger, p. 151). Here the mid-fifteenth-century Burgundian author depicts a form of heroic endurance in an alien landscape, based on biblical tradition and on his sense of Ireland as a place at once foreign and accessible. His England, where Artus' stepbrother Oliver wins the princess in the three-day tournament, supplies both the most elegant fifteenth-century chivalric spectacle and quite different perils of the forest. In England, the hazards are robbers, not monsters. The imaginary Ireland of *Olivier de Castille* tests the knight errant's ingenuity in novel and notably inelegant ways. The episodes of insanity of Yvain, Lancelot, and Tristan in the Arthurian romances also reduce their heroes to the bare essentials, stripping them of their armor and their ability to communicate with their fellow humans, and sending them out to contend with the forces of the wilderness.[10] By contrast, Artus of Algarbe retains his sanity, while losing everything else. Episodes like these cry out to be set beside the narratives of benighted,

---

9   Gail Orgelfinger, ed., *The Hystorye of Olyuer of Castylle*, trans. Henry Watson (New York and London, 1988), p. 149. Appendix A of this edition details printed editions of this romance: ten French printings (1482–c.1625), twenty-six in Spanish (1499–1943), two in Flemish (c.1510 and c.1550), six in English (1518–1903), four German editions (1521–1928), and three Italian editions (1552–1622). The earliest edition of the German text pairs *Olwyuer* with *Valentino und Orto* (*Valentine and Orson*). For its frequent appearance on lists of books exported to the Spanish colonies in the sixteenth century, see Leonard, *Books of the Brave*, pp. 109–10. Griffin discusses the four Cromberger printings of this romance (1507, 1509, 1510, and 1535) in more detail, *The Crombergers of Seville*, p. 248 and in the appendix, nos. 29, 41, 50, 390.

10 Cf. Elspeth Kennedy, "*Tristan forsene*: the episode of the hero's madness in the prose *Tristan*," in *The Changing Face of Arthurian Romance: Essays on Arthurian Prose Romances in Memory of Cedric E. Pickford*, ed. Alison Adams, Armel H. Diverres, Karen Stern, and Kenneth Varty (Cambridge, 1986).

wandering Europeans like Cabeza de Vaca. Leonard suggests that the piety of *Olivier de Castilla* might have appeased the clerical censors who eyed shipping lists with suspicion; it also seems to have been among the volumes most frequently imported for sale in New Spain.

A similar test is imposed on Maguelonne of *Pierre de Provence et la Belle Maguelonne* in an Italian forest, in a book Leonard regards as the third most often shipped for sale in the Indies.[11] Here, Maguelonne reverses the stereotype of the fair lady who waits around to be rescued. Like Artus, she climbs trees, to escape wild beasts, and also in the hope of catching sight of her lost love. Indeed, she shouts for him until she becomes "toute rauque," altogether hoarse. When this fails, she makes her way to the high road to Rome. There she persuades a passing female pilgrim to change clothes with her. She smears her face with dirt mixed with saliva, effacing her identity as a glamorous Neapolitan princess. In this disguise Maguelonne is able to plod to Rome, where she prays at St Peter's, then back to Genoa, and on by sea to Pierre's homeland of Provence, where she founds her own church of St Peter and hospital near Aigues-Mortes. The author assures the reader that these edifices still exist. Meanwhile, her beloved Pierre has been rescued at sea by Saracen pirates – by no means an imaginary peril in the fifteenth century. The Egyptian court where Pierre serves the sultan is not described in any degree of detail; still, it would have been regarded as a "real place." Only the desert island where he is inadvertently marooned, rather in the manner of the Count of Monte Cristo but without the treasure, seems an altogether imaginary, or conventional, location.

Paris et Vienne likewise tries to situate its adventures within an up-to-date geography, in both Europe and the Near East. The cities of Vienne and Paris figure as key sites. There is a "particular and realistic picture of the city of Vienne and its surroundings," extending to architectural details of the Dauphin's palace and its site, Messire Bertrand's bank, "the boatman and his craft, . . . the road and posting stations to Aigues-Mortes . . ."[12] The story recognizes the

---

11 *Pierre de Provence et la Belle Maguelonne*; this concise romance does not seem to have been translated into English, but was most successful in Europe; Cooper lists sixteen French editions of this volume, the earliest dating to the 1470s. *Pedro Provenzal y Magalona* is one of the works castigated by Vives in his *Instruction of the Christian Woman*; Irving Leonard, in *Books of the Brave*, p. 109, is one of few twentieth-century scholars to have read or appreciated this attractive romance, which he describes as one that was "written in Provençal or Latin by Bernardo de Treviez, and had enjoyed high favor with Petrarch, who is said to have spent some time in his youth correcting and polishing its style." For the two Cromberger editions of *La historia de la linda Magalona y del muy esforzado caballero Pierres de Provenza*, of 1519 and 1533, see Griffin, *The Crombergers of Seville*, p. 250, and nos. 193 and 352 of his appendix.

12 MacEdward Leach, ed., *Paris and Vienne*, EETS o.s. 234 (London, 1957), p. xix. Caxton based his edition on the shorter of two French versions of the romance, surviving in MS BN français 20044, and several Italian copies. Gherard Leeu of Antwerp printed this French text in 1487. He also reprinted Caxton's English text in 1492. Wynkyn de Worde (1502) and Pynson (1510) reprinted it. For additional information on the English vogue

renewed importance of Burgundy and the Burgundian Netherlands in the fifteenth century. The hero and his best friend take an excursion to Brabant to attend tournaments there, and, later, the earl of Flanders contrives a match for Vienne with the son of the duke of Burgundy, a magnificent but unwanted suitor. *Paris and Vienne* also looks towards England and Italy, by introducing an English Prince Edward and a son of the marquis of Saluzzo as supernumerary figures. Paris' exile begins with a pilgrimage to Jerusalem, starting by ship from Venice. He writes his best friend from Genoa "how for veray dysplaysyr and melancolye he wold goo into somme straunge contreye / And that fro than forth on he shold sende to hym noo moo letters / And that he neuer retche for to here moo tydynges fro hym / nomore than of a deed persone" (Leach, p. 58). Paris' expedition is better planned than most: "tofore or he took his waye / he lerned for to speke the langage of moores" in Alexandria (Leach, p. 59). Once fluent in Arabic, Paris and his servant proceed towards India, arriving in the "land of Prester John," where Paris grows a long beard, adopts Moorish dress, and learns "alle the custommes and maners of the contree," though the author insists that he remains a steadfast Christian. Paris' studies enable him to assist the falconers of the sultan of Babylon back in Egypt, and attain a position at court. This itinerary is not portrayed in lines that throb with local color, but it does offer greater plausibility than the travels of Pierre of Provence. The author knows enough to identify falconry as a common interest of European and Arab gentlemen. The heroine's tyrannical father is given an equally believable errand into the East when he is assigned to travel through Syria, Damascus, and the Holy Land, ostensibly as a pilgrim, but in reality as a spy for a projected crusade. He is arrested at Ramallah on the information of "somme euyl crysten men for to gete money," and imprisoned at Alexandria. This event represents poetic justice, since the Dauphin had earlier imprisoned his daughter Vienne to make her agree to marry the man of his choice. It also makes it possible for Paris to win Vienne by extricating her father from the sultan's "hard and stronge toure"

of *Paris and Vienne*, and some reference to the seventeenth-century version of this romance by Matthew Mainwaringe, see Jennifer R. Goodman, *Malory and William Caxton's Prose Romances of 1485* (New York, 1987), pp. 72–73, and Leach's bibliographical note. For the French text, see R. Kaltenbacher, "Der altfranzösische Roman *Paris et Vienne*," *Romanische Forschungen* XV (1904), pp. 321–695; A. Galmes de Fuentes, ed., *Historia de los Amores de París y Viana* (Reproduccion fotografica del MS – Texto en caracteres árabes – Texto en caracteres latinos), Colleccion de litteratura española aljamiado-morisca, 1 (Madrid, 1970). Cooper lists nine French printings between 1487 and the end of the sixteenth century; Kaltenbacher and Leach have ten. There was also a Latin translation by Jean Du Pin, bishop of Rieux, printed in 1516. The Spanish *Paris y Viana* appears on Vives' list of objectionable romances in the *Instruction of a Christian Woman* of 1524. Kaltenbacher and Leach also cite fifteenth- and sixteenth-century printings of the shorter *Paris et Vienne* in Italian, Flemish, Spanish, Catalan, German, Russian, and Swedish. The longer version, represented in six fifteenth-century manuscripts, seems not to have interested the early printers; for this text, see Kaltenbacher's 1904 edition. See also Goodman, *Malory and William Caxton's Prose Romances*, p. 68.

(Leach, p. 62). The element of chivalric prowess in these tales of travel is kept to a pragmatic minimum. This is not a flamboyant story of clashing Christian and Moslem armies, as supplied by *Tirant lo Blanch* or *Mélusine*. The plot manages to remain adventurous while also remaining on a human scale.

Even more impressive for its geographic specificity is the late fifteenth-century Italian pilgrimage described in *La Corónica de Adramón*, a text of about 1492. The author of this Castilian romance of chivalry narrates a tour of notable churches, hospitals, and palaces, from Asti to Agrigento in Sicily, in all probability from personal experience.[13] The writer's chivalric universe takes in Poland, Bohemia, Santiago de Compostela, Avignon, and England. The characters know of the Portuguese expeditions to Guinea, and speculate on yet unnavigated sectors of the planet (Anderson, pp. l–li). As more research is devoted to later romances like this one, their value as narratives of travel may be better recognized. More instances of these romances' dependence on travellers accounts are also likely to surface. The two genres prove to be interdependent in many ways.

Aside from prolonging the plot and entertaining the audience, the chief purpose of the journey in the chivalric romances is to try the mettle of the main characters. The tests may be physical or psychological, spiritual or material. The stresses the authors impose reveal their own ideas about travel as a human activity, and the qualities they value in their principal characters. *Olivier de Castille* and *Pierre de Provence et la Belle Maguelonne* are only two of many romances to explore the notion of travel as an ordeal. This is, after all, one of the most ancient components of the romance. The "hero's journey" has received much attention from Joseph Campbell and other students of world mythology. The idea of the journey as a test of character, or as a symbol for life itself, has always been appreciated, as far back as the history of literature can be traced. The human race has been so much given to wandering across the face of the earth for so long that few cultures retain no tradition of a testing journey. The chivalric fictions of the age of exploration are not exceptional in this regard. Few romances of this era manage to do without a journey of some sort, whether it is an exile and return of the hero, a quest, a pilgrimage, a crusade, or some other form of expedition. Some of these journeys are voluntary, undertaken as the fulfillment of a vow or to carry out a mission of some kind: these are the quests, pilgrimages, and crusades. Other plots force the protagonist to travel, whether as a form of execution or ordeal at sea in the "rudderless boat," or by accident, as when Ogier and Pierre de Provence are blown off course by storms. Bad fortune or divine displeasure often motivate travel.

The element of volition in these plots transmutes the enterprise. The leader of a crusade – Charlemagne, Enrique fi de Oliva, Godefroy de Bouillon, Richard the Lion-Hearted – may differ significantly in his chivalric identity from the

---

[13] Gunnar Anderson, ed., *La Corónica de Adramón* (Newark, 1992), pp. xxi–xxxiii. The only surviving copy of this romance is BN 191 Espagnol; there are no known printings before 1992.

victim of a shipwreck. For one thing, he usually leads an army. Few female protagonists are given the chance to lead armies, although the Amazon queen of California who comes to the siege of Constantinople with her air force of man-eating griffins in Montalvo's *Las Sergas de Esplandián* does come to mind, as should Joan of Arc. In considering travel as an ordeal, we approach the concept of the hero as victim, a theme as dear to writers today as it was to Homer and Virgil. Heroic status is tested by placing the central figure under extreme stress to see how much punishment he or she can tolerate while retaining a sense of purpose or identity or, indeed, while surviving at all. The hard-boiled detective who is perpetually being beaten up falls into this category.

The saint's life, no less than the romance, found the journey a useful plot element. No one can read these two genres without appreciating the links between them. Since both are heroic narratives, sharing many of the same religious and social values, it should come as no surprise that both sides might resort to the same tactics. The missions of Paul, Mary Magdalene's legend of travel across the Mediterranean, St Thomas' voyage to India, and the voyage of St Brendan all depict the Christian saint as unfortunate traveller. These are only the most celebrated of many possible examples. Elements drawn from this tradition surface in a number of romances, especially towards the end, as writers are tempted to provide their characters with edifying deaths. A fair number promote their fictional heroes to sainthood. Renaut de Montauban of the *Quatre fils Aymon* (*Four Sonnes of Aymon*) is martyred in a "union dispute" while building a cathedral.[14] Guy of Warwick and Valentine and Orson all undertake penitential exiles that culminate in their deaths. Mélusine's husband Raimondin atones for his betrayal of her by becoming a hermit on the cliffs of Montserrat. Charlemagne's peers all become martyrs for their faith at Roncesvaux in book three of Jean Bagnyon's *Fierabras*, while Charlemagne winds up in a kind of reliquary tomb, and Malory has Arthur's remaining knights travel to the Holy Land to die in combat against the Turks on Good Friday. The penitential journey or exile remains a vital element of such programs of spiritual elevation.

As in several of the instances just mentioned, a character's exile may be mandated as a divinely ordained expiation of sin. Medea in Raoul LeFèvre's

---

[14] The *Quatre fils Aymon* was another favorite of fifteenth- and sixteenth-century printers. Cooper ("Nostre histoire") has twenty-eight editions of the French text in his bibliography, dating from about 1480 to c.1600. Caxton published his translation, *The Four Sonnes of Aymon*, in 1488, at the request of John de Vere, earl of Oxford. In German this romance appeared as *Haymonskinder*, translated by the same duke of Palatinat-Simmern (Jean II, 1486–1557) who translated Jean Bagnyon's *Fierabras*. According to Leonard, *El libro . . . del noble y esforzado caballero Reinaldos de Montalbán* came into Spanish from Italian, and also figured among the favorite chivalric works exported to New Spain, along with *La trapesonda que es tercero libro de Don Reinaldos*; cf. *Books of the Brave*, p. 110. For four printings of *La trapesonda* (1533, c.1541, 1545, and 1548) see Griffin, *The Crombergers of Seville*, pp. 152, 251.

Histoire de Jason, that notable Burgundian *roman d'antiquité* of the 1460s, becomes a kind of penitential Magdalen in the wilderness.[15] Pierre de Provence's separation from his Maguelonne is brought on by an understandable moment of voyeurism. Penitential exile can also be imposed by religous authorities, as in *Valentine and Orson,* where the pope decrees it in a case of involuntary parricide.

In the travels of most protagonists of romance, the misfortunes inherent in any voyage by land or sea are evoked, often in their most elementary shape, and sometimes elaborated into grotesque forms. Everyday misadventures can be described in graphic terms. Knights may encounter the most prosaic sort of highway robbery, as Oliver does in *Olivier de Castille.* The non-swimming Pierre de Provence (no Beowulf he) flounders out to sea in a rotten skiff. The experience of being lost in a forest may also be believably described, or it may be elaborated with the addition of lions, tigers, bears, fairy kings, and unidentified monsters *ad infinitum.* Also on the grotesque or elaborate side should be counted perils like the Castle of the Adamant, where the ships of both Ogier the Dane and Huon of Bordeaux stick fast, the Amazon Island of California in *Las Sergas de Esplandián,* and the Sinbadlike experience of being carried off by a giant bird or griffin. One of the joys of reading these romances is that one can never be too sure which way the author is going to jump – towards the quotidian, or off into the wildest of fantastic voyages. For every romance like *Paris and Vienne* that claims to admit only plausible events, ten cherish the option of charging off in either direction. This flexibility has not endeared the genre to critics over the centuries, but it persistently entrances readers. The broad range of possibilities, the license to wed the credible to the incredible in the same story, gives the romance a large part of its fascination.

How is any of this pertinent to the factual narrative of exploration? First, and foremost, it can be argued, these fictional travels color their readers' perceptions and interpretations of their own journeys and those of others. Indeed, they suggest approaches to describing actual journeys. The chivalric romances introduce an important vocabulary of travel, at least as important as that supplied by the narratives of Mandeville and Marco Polo, two works not untouched by romance themselves. These descriptive strategies become all the more attractive because they present travel as a heroic experience, and travelers as sympathetic, noble figures.

One of the most hazardous aspects of travel, in reality and in narrative, is the way it changes the traveler's social status or identity. Physical hardship, immer-

---

15 Caxton translated Le Fèvre's *Histoire de Jason* into English as *The History of Jason,* and printed it in 1477. Cooper lists six French editions of *Les fais et prouesses du chevalier Jason,* beginning with the 1477 Bruges edition of Colard Mansion, Caxton's partner, and culminating in 1530 (Cooper, "Nostre histoire," pp. 222–23). Le Fèvre's later work, the *Recueil des histoires de Troye,* had inspired Caxton's first attempt at translation, completed 19 September 1471. This volume had twelve French printings between 1476, when Caxton and Mansion published it, and 1544 (Cooper, "Nostre histoire," p. 224).

sion in alien cultures, and insufficient funds all contribute to achieve this effect. In the romance this risk of travel can become a heroic opportunity. In hagiography, it can also become penitential, one of the routes to sainthood. Both of these viewpoints can prove distinctly consoling for the unlucky traveler, as they were for Cabeza de Vaca.

The Fairy Mélusine's eldest son Urian articulates the proper attitude of the late-fourteenth-century knight as he sets off on his maiden voyage. In the language of the 1478 edition of Jean d'Arras' prose romance:

> "My lady, may it please you, it would seem about time for us to go on a journey to acquaint ourselves with lands, countries, and foreign territories, in order to gain honor and good fame in alien lands; in this way we will begin to know how to speak different languages with the good folk, and will find out many curious things in those alien parts that are not known hereabouts; and also, if fortune or good adventure be our friend, we have the will to conquer lands and countries."[16]

Because they are eight brothers, Urian goes on to say, they realize that the paternal heritage cannot be split between them without diminishing the family's status. He and his brother will give up their share and seek their fortune elsewhere. Their mother responds that this proposal reflects her son's "grant vaillance de coeur." Among the notable features of the passage are Urian's ideas about travel as a form of education as well as a prelude to knighthood. One of his goals is to find a figure of established prowess to make him a knight, since the repute of the man who knights him by tradition extends to the new knight.[17] In the event, Urian is knighted by the dying king of Cyprus after proving himself in combat against the Turks. At the end of his tale, Jean d'Arras returns to the idea, promoted earlier in his narrative, that travel "broadens the mind." Those

---

[16] *Mélusine*, p. 121. "Ma dame, se il vous plaist, il seroit bien temps que nous allissions voyager pour congnoistre les terres, les contrées et les pays estranges, affin d'acquerir honneur et bonne nommée ès estranges marches, par quoy nous fussions introduictz de sçavoir parler diverses langues avecq les bons, et de diverses choses qui sont par les estranges marches et pays qui ne sont pas communes par decha; et aussi, se fortune ou bonne adventure nous vouloit estre amie, nous avons bien volenté de conquerir terres et pays…" The translation is mine, for lack of a better. For a list of sixteen editions of the French *Mélusine*, dating from 1478 to 1597, see Cooper, "Nostre histoire," pp. 217–18. For the two Spanish translations of the *Historia de la linda Melosina*, published in 1489 and 1526, see Ivy A. Corfis, ed., *Historia de la linda Melosina* (Madison, 1986), and A. D. Deyermond, *"La historia de la linda Melosina:* Two Spanish Versions of a French romance," in *Medieval Hispanic Studies Presented to Rita Hamilton*, ed. A. D. Deyermond (London, 1976), pp. 57–65.

[17] On this chivalric convention and its currency, see Maurice Keen, *Chivalry* (New Haven, 1984), pp. 77–79. In Arthurian literature squires may for this reason prefer to be knighted by Lancelot rather than Arthur, as Gareth does. Larry Benson observes that a special bond ties the new knight to the man who gave him the order of knighthood: see Larry D. Benson, *Malory's Morte Darthur* (Cambridge, Mass. and London, 1976), pp. 102–03.

who stay in one place are less likely to appreciate the marvels of creation than those who experience the wonders of the world. The theme is reiterated by Thüring von Ringoltingen, the Swiss author who reworked La Couldrette's verse *Mélusine* into a German prose text in 1456, and who also ranks the snake-woman Melusina as a wonder of God's making.

The geography and the landscape of romance are only now receiving the detailed study that such complex subjects demand.[18] There are still too many geographical mysteries and marvels, coincidences and suggestions left unplumbed throughout this literature. For instance, there is the curious matter of the reference to the isle of Chile at the opening of *Perceforest*, represented as the most distant of the British Isles, beyond the Orkneys: "And after that is the isle of Chile, which is separated from all other islands by its great distance, and is placed towards the north wind in the midst of the sea, which island is barely known by few people."[19] "Chile" may be a scribal variant for Thule, as its source, Orosius, gives the word as "Thyle." All the authorities I have consulted to date trace the origin of the Latin American "Chile" back to an indigenous word. Ian Michael's discovery of a Castilian translation of *Perceforest*, not yet in print, does make one wonder. In the same way, the mysterious name "Miquelon," taken in conjunction with its neighboring island of St Pierre, does call to mind the enterprising Maguelonne of the romance and her foundation of the church of St Pierre on an island near Aigues Mortes, to commemorate her beloved Pierre de Provence lost at sea. The short romance of *Pierre de Provence et la Belle Maguelonne* was so widely distributed in Europe that it seems plausible that the Basque fishermen who named these Atlantic islands might well have known of it. I know better than to propose to unravel any such geographical riddles here, though they suggest that a number of additional place-names inspired by romance may indeed survive undetected. Instead, a few basic components of the chivalric journey merit closer scrutiny here.

Among the essential ingredients that ought to be reconsidered by students of journeys in later medieval chivalric fiction are real places as they are imagined by the authors of these romances – for instance, the three holy cities of Jerusalem, Rome, and Constantinople – or countries identified with particular chivalric legends – notably England, Spain, and Ireland. These actual locations were charged with centuries of accumulated meaning by history and religion. Different narratives often juxtapose these thematic centers with less famous places, to offer the illusion of a real journey. Romance geography intersperses

---

[18] Corinne Saunders, *The Forest of Medieval Romance* (Cambridge, 1993). Patricia Price's recent University of Minnesota dissertation investigates the geography of the English alliterative romances.

[19] "Et aprés est l'ille de Chile, qui est departie de toutes autres ysles par grant distance et est assise devers le vent de chirrion emmy la mer (chirrius est le vent collateral de bise par devers occident), laquelle ysle est a paine congneue de pou de gens." Jane H. M. Taylor, ed., *Le Roman de Perceforest*, première partie (Geneva, 1979), p. 62. Jane Taylor suggests that the island in question may be the largest of the Shetlands (*Perceforest*, p. 175).

such well-known sites with imaginative set pieces of a kind familiar to students of later medieval pageantry – the fountain in the forest, the magic rock (*perron fée*), or the enchanted island. By scrambling these geographical possibilities the creator of a romance could devise scenic effects ranging from the believable to the spectacularly weird.

Jerusalem continued to allure knights who still hoped to tread in the footsteps of the Third Christian Worthy, the crusader Godefroy de Bouillon. It remained the center of the world for the Christian knight through the fifteenth and sixteenth centuries, the ultimate prize in the contest between Christianity and Islam. When crusades were not available, a pilgrimage to Jerusalem conveyed some spiritual status to the real or the fictional knight, whether Paris of *Paris and Vienne* or Henry Bolingbroke, the future king of England. Both the *Siege of Jerusalem*, with its vision of the "vengeance of Jesus Christ" as a chivalric exploit of the Roman emperors Titus and Vespasian, and narratives of the First Crusade drawn from William of Tyre enthralled substantial numbers of readers well after 1500.[20] Both of these narratives depicted the capture of Jerusalem in historical time. The fictional recapture of Jerusalem for Christianity attracted a number of enterprising authors. Godfrey of Bouillon's kingship of Jerusalem was celebrated in both fictional and historical narratives, represented in English by Caxton's *Godefroy of Boloyne* of 1481 and *Helyas, the Knight of the Swan*, Robert Copland's translation of *La genealogie avecques les gestes et nobles faictz d'armes du trespreux et renommé prince Goddeffroy de Boulion*, printed by Wynkyn de Worde in 1512. The *Chronicque et histoire singuliere du chevalier Mabrian, lequel par ses prouesses fut roi de Hierusalem* was republished nine times in France between 1525 and 1600.[21] Renaut de Montauban of the *Quatre*

---

[20] Patricia Price's dissertation discusses the geography of the Middle English alliterative *Siege of Jerusalem*. For the three English texts on this subject, and the twenty surviving manuscripts in which they appear, along with much useful background material, see L. H. Hornstein, in *A Manual of the Writings in Middle English*, pp. 160–63; 319–21. For twenty-one French editions of this ferociously anti-Semitic romance, which appeared in print as *La destruction de Jhierusalem* in Geneva c.1478, see Cooper, "Nostre histoire," pp. 223–24. Among the sources of these works should be reckoned the Gospels, Josephus, and the twelfth-century *chanson de geste*, *La venjance Nostre Seigneur* or its Latin precursor. Medievalists have only recently begun to grapple with the vast popularity of this influential text across Europe. In 1481 Caxton printed *Godefroy of Boloyne*, his own translation from a French abridgement of William of Tyre's great Latin history of the First Crusade and the Latin Kingdom of Jerusalem, his *Historia rerum in partibus transmarinis gestarum*. Cooper, "Nostre histoire," pp. 207–08, lists eight French editions of *La genealogie avecques les gestes et nobles faictz d'armes du trespreux et renommé prince Goddeffroy de Boulion et des ses chevalereux freres* of Pierre Desrey, between 1499 and 1580. For *Helyas, the Knight of the Swan* and its connection with the French editions, see R. Lumiansky, in *A Manual of the Writings in Middle English*, p. 103. See Louis Cooper, ed., *La Gran Conquista de Ultramar* (Bogota, 1979), for the text based on the 1503 Salamanca edition, and Louis Cooper, ed., *La Gran Conquista de Ultramar: Biblioteca Nacional MS 1187* (Madison, 1989).

[21] Cooper, "Nostre histoire," pp. 208–09.

fils Aymon is represented as seizing Jerusalem from the Saracens after going there on pilgrimage. The same possibility interested that pseudonymous author, Sir John Mandeville. Like many other theorists he concluded that the sins of Christian rulers prevent them from mounting a successful new crusade. The idea of recapturing Jerusalem would also haunt Columbus and, most poignantly, in the end, Cortes.

All of its classical and ecclesiastical associations would seem to insulate Rome against any appropriation by the romance. Yet Rome's imperial and papal associations are commemorated in romances like *La Corónica de Adramón*, where repeated visits to Rome mark stages in the hero's progress toward kingship.[22] At the outset of *Meliadus de Leonnoys*, one of two French prose romances drawn from the *Compilation of Rusticiano da Pisa*, Sir Palamedes' ancestor is brought to Rome as a slave, and proceeds to save the emperor's life. In this narrative a declining Rome teeming with devious assassins must concede its military primacy to the court of the young King Arthur. Nevertheless, becoming emperor of Rome remained the ultimate accolade for a certain number of the knights of romance. Sir Torrent of Portyngale, whose romance was printed by Wynkyn de Worde around 1509, and by Richard Pynson around 1500, ended his adventures by being elected emperor. Important scenes of *Guillaume de Palerne* take place in and around Rome, where the foundling hero falls in love and elopes with the emperor's daughter Melior – both disguised as white bears. He, too, will later become emperor. In the continuation of *Huon of Bordeaux*, the hero's granddaughter Ide travels to Rome disguised as a man and becomes constable of the city; a miraculous change of gender permits her to consummate her marriage to the emperor's daughter. Among romances of antiquity, works like the *Sept sages de Rome* and *Les faitz merveilleux de Virgile* continued to exploit ancient Rome as a backdrop to romance in different ways.[23]

---

22   Anderson, preface to *La Corónica de Adramón*, vol. 1.

23   For *Guillaume de Palerne*, written in around 1194–97 under the patronage of the countess of St Pol, Yolande de Hainault, and this romance's English, Dutch, and Irish editions and translations, see C. Dunn, "Romances derived from English legends," in *A Manual of the Writings in Middle English*, pp. 34–37. *L'hystoire du chevalier Guillaume de Palerne* appeared in three French editions, the first in 1552 and the last around 1575; see Cooper, "Nostre histoire," pp. 216–17. For *Meliadus de Leonnoys*, a massive romance twice printed in the sixteenth century in France, in 1528 and 1532, see below, ch. 5. For bibliographical details, see Cooper, "Nostre histoire," p. 213; he is incorrect in referring to Rusticiano's text as a Latin work – the French is admittedly Italianate, but it is still French. For Sir Torrent of Portyngale, see *A Manual of the Writings in Middle English*, pp. 125–26. For the fortune of the *Sept sages de Rome* (two editions listed, 1492 and 1577) and the life of Virgil the Necromancer (five printings, 1520 through about 1535) among the printers of France, see Cooper, "Nostre histoire," pp. 224–25. Both of these books had a following elsewhere in Europe: the Crombergers printed the *Libro de los siete sabios de Roma* three times, in about 1510, 1534, and 1538. See Griffin, *The Crombergers of Seville*, pp. 153, 253. Griffin classes the *Siete sabios*, a *roman d'antiquité* that is also a frame-story, with

As mentioned above, Constantinople became a particular obsession of romances written after that city's fall to the Ottoman Turks in 1453. Esplandián is only one of many fictional knights to fight their way to the throne of Constantinople. Tirant lo Blanch recovers the Greek Empire for Christianity, but dies prematurely. In the romance that was one of Martorell's primary models, Guy of Warwick had fought before the emperor of Constantinople and then refused the hand of the emperor's daughter. French readers from 1510 to 1586 could purchase printed copies of the affecting tale of *La belle Helayne de Constantinople, mère de Saint Martin de Tours*, in seven different editions.[24] Luciana Stegagno Picchio has made a detailed study of the representation of Constantinople in romance tradition, from Chrétien de Troyes' *Cligés* in the late twelfth century up to *Palmerin*.[25]

Other cities and countries retained their magic for authors of different romances. Medieval versions of the legends of Troy remained in demand, and in print, through the sixteenth century, all across Europe. Babylon, Alexandria, Acre, Jaffa, and points east recur in any number of tales. Alexander's adventures carried his medieval admirers into lavish descriptions of the wonders of India. Kings of Hungary and Poland crop up in later medieval romances, testifying to a heightened level of awareness of the elegance of these eastern European courts, and to chivalric opportunities on the embattled frontiers of Christendom. The interest in Cyprus and Rhodes evinced by authors of later romances may also have been topical, following the dramatic events in those island strongholds. England and Spain become increasingly important as chivalric locales, frequently in combination, as the sixteenth century approaches: *Tirant lo Blanch, Olivier de Castille, Ponthus et Sidoine*, and *Amadís de Gaula* itself all manifest different Iberian and English associations. Writers of chivalric romance invariably display an acute sense of where the action was; they did their best to thrust their characters into the hottest spots available.

Among these romances' imaginary settings, one of the most popular remained the magic (or forbidden) mountain. Often this pinnacle conceals a treasure guarded by a lady, as in the *Mélusines* of Jean d'Arras and La Couldrette,

---

"traditional exemplum literature . . . which may have been read mainly by children." For some evidence of the export of this work to the Spanish Indies, from its appearance in a booklist of 1530, see Leonard, *Books of the Brave*, p. 101 (see also p. 98). For much more on Jerusalem, Rome, and Constantinople than can be included here, see *Jerusalem, Rome, Constantinople: l'image et le mythe de la ville au Moyen Age: colloque du Departement d'Etudes Medievale de l'Université de Paris-Sorbonne (Paris IV)* (Paris, 1986).

24 Cooper, "Nostre histoire," p. 215.

25 See Luciana Stegagno Picchio, "Fortuna iberica di un topos letterario: la corte di Costantinopoli dal *Cligès* al *Palmerín de Olivia*," *Studi sul Palmerin de Olivia: saggi e ricerche* (Pisa, 1966), III.102–03. Cooper records two sixteenth-century French editions of a fifteenth-century prose version of the romance of Guy of Warwick, p. 217. See also Dunn, in *A Manual of the Writings in Middle English*, pp. 29–31, where he documents the English, Irish, Latin, German, and French versions of this romance as late as the nineteenth century.

where the heroine's two sisters are assigned roles as security guards. Both romances indicate that the mountains, ladies, and treasures are still to be won, though only by knights descended from Mélusine. One of these mountains, in Armenia, is surmounted by the Castle of the Sparrowhawk, described in *Mandeville's Travels*: there the knight who keeps a successful vigil for a specified period will be rewarded by the lady in charge with his heart's desire, though only up to a point. In *Las Sergas de Esplandián*, the murdered enchantress (or distressed) damsel has left as her legacy a test of knightly prowess suitable for Indiana Jones. The winner is to be rewarded with a treasure left on her mountainous Atlantic island. This exploit involves the extraction of a sword from the stone doors of the chamber.[26] This last example combines the mountain treasure cavern with another pervasive feature of romance landscape, which might be appropriately labeled in modern American English the Fantasy Island. Garci Rodriguez de Montalvo's California certainly qualifies as such a place – an island stronghold close by the Terrestrial Paradise, inhabited by black Amazons in golden armor, supported by an air force of man-eating griffins. Apolidon's Firm Island, designed to evaluate true lovers, in book two of *Amadís de Gaula* ranks as another.[27] Both magic mountains and fantasy islands bear some family resemblance to the *perron fée*, the set piece of the "enchanted rock" or pillar familiar to students of the fifteenth-century tournament. Such stones, large or small, could be easily represented as theatrical set pieces, convenient as stage scenery for all sorts of pageants. In the *pas du perron fée* (the passage of the magic rock) of the Burgundian knight Philippe de Lalaing, held at Bruges on 28 April 1463, the knight who proposed the passage of arms rode out of a large "magic rock" set up in the marketplace. "At the far end of the space there was a rock fourteen to fifteen feet high, made with skill, well and agreeably worked, and painted in several colors: gold, silver, blue, black, red, and more."[28] It is notable that *Las Sergas de Esplandián* begins by whisking the new knight

---

[26] P. Hamelius, ed., *Mandeville's Travels*, EETS o.s. 153 (London, 1919 for 1916), pp. 97–98. *Amadís*, IV, ch. 130; continued in *Esplandián*, chs. 1–4; cf. Garci Rodríguez de Montalvo, *The Labors of the Very Brave Knight Esplandián*, trans. William Thomas Little (Binghamton, 1992), pp. 68–77.

[27] See Little's note in his translation of *Esplandián*, pp. 75–76, n. 16.

[28] Félix Brassart, ed., *Le Pas du Perron Fée* (Douai, 1874), p. 50. "Et au bout d'icelles cloustures, avoit ung perron de xiiij à xv pies de hault, fait par artiffice, bien et gentement ouvré et painst de diverses couleurs tant d'or d'argent, d'azur, de noir, de rouge comme d'aultres." Lancelot and Tristram duel at a "perron" in Malory, *Works*, ed. Eugène Vinaver (2nd edn, 1967; rpt. with additions and corrections, Oxford, 1973), II.568–69. See my article, "Display, Self-Definition, and the Frontiers of Romance in the 1463 Bruges *Pas du Perron Fée*," in *Persons in Groups: Social Behavior as Identity Formation in Medieval and Renaissance Europe*, ed. Richard C. Trexler (Binghamton, 1985), pp. 47–54. Keen suggests that the *perron* could be either a pillar or an "artificial mound," (Keen, *Chivalry*, p. 205). Sydney Anglo's important article on the *perron* in medieval and Renaissance tournaments should be consulted for more details on this matter. Cf. Sydney Anglo, "L'Arbre de Chevalerie et le perron dans les tournois," in Jean Jacquot and Elie Konigson, eds., *Les Fetes de la Renaissance* III (Paris, 1975), pp. 283–98.

straight from one of these traditional settings to the next. He awakens in the first chapter alongside the enchantress damsel's island; after he succeeds in pulling the sword from the stone doors, he is promptly carried off by ship to the forbidden mountain.

Pagan temples, ancestral tombs, and ruined or abandoned palaces also figure prominently in the scenery of the later medieval romance. One of the most notable scenes of Bagnyon's *Fierabras* has the Saracen Princess Floripas revealing her father's shrine full of golden idols to the captive Peers of France. A quite different effect is obtained in *Perceforest*, where the pre-Christian temple discovered in Britain presents a newly invented form of non-Jewish monotheism. In *Gyron le Courtoys* it is the antichivalric Brunes sans Pitié who discovers the cavern tomb of his great predecessor, Fébus, and hears the interpolated story of his exploits against the pagans and giants of ancient Britain. In *Mélusine* the heroine's rebellious and irascible son Geoffrey of the Great Tooth makes a similar discovery of his grandfather's tomb in the mountains of Albion. The thought in both places seems to be that this confrontation with mortality, chivalric decline, and past grandeur can reform the most dubious hero. The ruined palace as represented in the Amadís cycle, like the one on the Enchantress Damsel's crag, in books four and five, may be a related scene. The archaeological or antiquarian effect of these two settings may not be an accident. Like the Anglo-Saxon poet impressed by the ruins of Roman Bath, who imagined them to be *eald enta geweorc,* "the ancient handiwork of giants," medieval writers of romance admired the chivalry of the past and its relics. Physical evidence is here used to support the idea of knightly prowess as an ancestral legacy.

One "fantasy island" in particular deserves more extended treatment – in part as a fine example of a fantastic element in the landscape of romance, in part because, to us, it reads so much like a scene from science fiction. In this reader's view, the "science-fiction" tendencies of certain romances and romance epics should be better recognized. A strong interest in science and technology as well as in their notorious cousin, magic, colors the atmosphere of such works as the *Alexander* romances, the later sections of *Bevis of Hampton*, *Huon de Bordeaux*, and *Ogier le Danois*. In many respects these may be the direct precursors of modern science fiction. A direct line could well be traced through such authors as Cyrano de Bergerac and Jonathan Swift to Jules Verne. The matter deserves further exploration, but, regrettably, it cannot be pursued here.

The Castle of the Adamant, which draws ships to it by their iron nails, rested upon a clear scientific basis as far as its medieval and Renaissance witnesses were concerned. William Gilbert, the "father of magnetic philosophy," indeed cited the superstition that particular northern mountains attracted ships to their doom by their iron nails in his ground-breaking treatise of 1600. *Mandeville's Travels* locates the peril in a different quarter of the globe, but clearly imagines the same predicament. "For in many places of the see ben grete roches of stones of the ADAMANT, þat of his propre nature draweth IREN to him, And þerfore þere passen no schippes þat han ouþer bondes or nayles of IREN within hem, and ȝef þer do anon the roches of the ADAMANTES drawen hem tohem, þat neuer þei may go þens."[29] Both *Ogier* and *Huon of Bordeaux* involve their heroes in the same predicament, not surprisingly, since they are both navigating in the same waters, and depend on each other.[30] The second part of *Huon of Bordeaux* (dating from c.1216–29, translated by John Bourchier, Lord Berners around 1530 from a French prose text of 1455) brings Huon, blown off course at sea in a storm, and his ship, to the rock of the Adamant.[31] Here the ocean in which Huon is lost seems to be the Atlantic. To return to his goal he must pass by "the perilous Gulf," reputed to be one of the mouths of Hell, where indeed Huon converses with the damned soul of Judas and hears the outcries of Cain. In this telling, Huon's realistic and fantastic perils at sea rival his encounter with the magnetic castle. The captain climbs the mast to look for land, "at last he sawe afarre of an hye rocke / and on the heyght therof they sawe a thicke wode, and at the enter of the wode he sawe a lytell howse / wherof he thankyd god and descendyd downe."[32] Appearances, however, prove deceptive, as the author takes care to tell us in a scientific interpolation:

> for the plase that they sawe a farre of was a castell, and therin closed the rock of the Adamant: the which castell was daungerous to aproche / for yf enye shyppe come nere it and haue any Iron nayles within it, and a shyppe come within the syght therof, the Adamant wyll drawe the shyppe to hym. And therfore in those partes the shyppes that sayleth by that see ar made and pynned with wodden nayles, and without any maner of Iron, otherwyse they be loste and perysshyd. For the propertye of the Adamant is to drawe Iron to hym.[33]

This scientific description should be set against the first-person account of that spurious eyewitness, Mandeville:

> I myself haue seen o ferrom in þat see as þough it hadde ben a gret yle full of trees & buscaylle full of thornes & breres grete plentee, And the schipmen

---

29 Hamelius, ed., *Mandeville's Travels*, p. 180 (see also p. 109 and note. As the editor notes, Vincent de Beauvais' *Speculum naturale* (VIII.21) reported lodestones on the shores of the Indian Ocean. The note also adds *Herzog Ernst* to the list of romances that include this particular peril. Jean d'Outremeuse claimed in his *Miroir des histoires* to have written a "nouvelle gieste" on Ogier the Dane; if he was indeed also the real author of *Mandeville's Travels*, this might explain the curious overlap in subject matter. (See Hamelius, ed., *Mandeville's Travels*, II.11.) For William Gilbert's treatise, see *Encyclopedia Britannica* (11th edn, New York, 1910–11).

30 The continuation of *Ogier* draws on the second part of *Huon*, which drew to some degree on the first part of *Ogier*; the ultimate source seems an oriental legend, as in the *Thousand and One Nights*. See Togeby, ed., *Ogier le Danois*, p. 141.

31 Ibid., #39, p. 73.

32 Berners, trans., *Huon*, p. 368.

33 Ibid., p. 369

tolde vs þat all þat was of schippes þat weren drawen thider be the ADAMAUN-
TES for the IREN þat was in hem. And of the roteness & oþer thing þat was
within the schippes grewen such buscaylle & thornes & breres & grene grass
& such maner of thing, And of the mastes & the seyll 3erdes it semed a grete
wode of a groue. And suche roches ben in many places þer abouten.[34]

This attractive example illustrates at once the slipperiness of Mandeville and
the plausibility that made this book of imaginary travels more believable than
the narratives of Marco Polo. The author asserts that he has seen faraway islands
with his own eyes; all the rest is a shipman's tale. This strategy allows Mandeville
to incorporate much of the landscape of romance while preserving his credibility as a reporter. The most he can be accused of in this case is gullibility in
swallowing the story of the magnetic island and in repeating it to gull his readers
in their turn. Yet he does not say he believes the story himself.

The little house or hermitage that the captain saw in *Huon of Burdeux* turns
out to be a fabulous castle:

the fayrest and most rycheste howse in ye worlde, within the whiche was so
moch gold and rychesse that no man leuinge coude esteme the walue therof
/ for the pyllers within that howse were of Cassedony / and the walles and
towres of whyghte Alablaster. There was neuer dyscryued in [s]crypture nor
hystory the beauty of such a castell as this was, for whenne the sonne cast his
rayes on it it semyd a far of to be of fyne christal, it was so clere shynynge. In
this castell was nother man nor woman: but dede mennes bones lyenge at the
gate of this castell / at the porte there lay many shyppes, so that theyr mastes
semyd a far of to be a great foreste.[35]

This description of Castle Adamant encompasses fabulous beauty, the imagined wealth of distant lands, the struggle to establish a scientific rationale to
explain the marvellous, and the ultimate terror of the unknown. It would not
be difficult to read it as a kind of explorer's nightmare.

The episode where the hero is drawn to Castle Adamant is followed in both
Huon and *Ogier* by an escape by way of the fountain of youth. (Bevis of
Hampton also obtains the apples of youth. He employs them to secure the
conversion of his Saracen adversary.) The recovery of Eden and its association
with classical traditions of eternal youth haunted the authors of the Renaissance
romance epic no less than these authors of romances. Astolfo visits the Earthly
Paradise in Ariosto's *Orlando Furioso* (34:48ff) on his way to the moon and
back. There as in many earlier tales, and in Mandeville, Paradise Lost remains
bound up with the legend of an Eastern Christian empire ruled by Prester John,
still a well-established preoccupation of geographers and explorers of the
period.

Sir John Mandeville should be given some credit for encouraging interest in

---

[34] Hamelius, ed., *Mandeville's Travels*, p. 180.
[35] Ibid., pp. 369–70.

the recovery of the Earthly Paradise and a well or fountain of youth. He says he drank from it himself, though he never reached the Terrestrial Paradise itself.[36] The excerpt from the *Libro del conoscimiento de todos los reynos* cited in *Le Canarien*, an early fifteenth-century exploration narrative to be (discussed below, chapter six), evokes both the home of Prester John and the Terrestrial Paradise as plausible destinations.[37] The isle of California, the abode of black Amazons who terrify the besieged and besieging armies at Constantinople with their air force of man-eating griffins, is located "on the right-hand side of the Indies . . . very close to the region of the Earthly Paradise."[38] The Earthly Paradise itself proves more difficult to work into the plot.

Danain le Roux, the hero's friend and rival in *Gyron le Courtois*, believes that he has reached the Earthly Paradise when he has only entered the Val de Faux Soulas, the Valley of False Pleasure. "Celluy lieu a son ymaginacion est vng droit paradis terrestre / car yuer est par tout le monde et il fait illec aussi doulx et aussi plaisant comme sil fust le moys dauril ou le moys de may." "This place was to his fancy a real earthly paradise / for winter was throughout the world and it was as temperate and as delightful there as the month of April or May." (*Gyron le Courtois*, f. 326v.) An unprecedented moderation in climate convinces the knight that he has arrived in an Eden. This reaction is still common among northern invaders of "tropical paradises." The episode recalls Lerner and Loewe's characterization of Camelot as a place where "the rain may never fall till after sundown."

The narratives themselves help the student retrace the processes by which the authors of late medieval chivalric fiction planned the imaginary travels of their characters. Alongside their sources in ancient and medieval stories of wandering heroes, writers hoping to devise new routes to heroic achievement drew on the latest travellers' tales, among them the books of Sir John Mandeville and Marco Polo. History, recent or distant, offered further possibilities. Writers also might transmute their own travels and those of their friends and patrons into fiction.

Detailed studies of the sources of the Catalan *Tirant lo Blanch* allow Martí de Riquer to reconstruct the working methods of one fifteenth-century knight as he set about writing a romance. Joanot Martorell (c.1413–68) mingled his own experiences in England with the much earlier romance of *Guy of Warwick*, and written and oral accounts of fifteenth-century combat in Rhodes and Constantinople. Martí Joan de Galba, who finished the story after Martorell's

---

[36] Cf. Stephen Greenblatt, *Marvellous Possessions: The Wonders of the New World* (Chicago, 1992), p. 31.

[37] *Libro de la conoscimiento de todos los reynos*, trans. C. Markham, *The Book of Knowledge of All the Kingdoms, Lands and Lordships that there are in the World* (London, 1912). Elias Serra Rafols and Alejandro Cioranescu, eds., *Le Canarien*, in *Fontes rerum Canariaurm* (3 vols., La Laguna de Teneriffe, 1959), III.105. (For *Le Canarien*, see below, ch. 6.)

[38] Montalvo, *Esplandián*, trans. Little, pp. 456–57.

death, also pillaged Mandeville for placenames.[39] This grand narrative of a Christian recuperation of the Mediterranean world starts in the England of the Order of the Garter, and then voyages to Byzantium by way of Sicily and Rhodes. The hero proceeds to North Africa, and finishes his career by dying in his comrades' arms on the road to Constantinople. Along the way, the authors pepper their tale with references to landmarks of European geographic expansion. The king of Canary invades England in chapter five, though it had been European adventurers who invaded the Canary Islands, in a series of expeditions beginning as early as the 1340s, with its final phases not to take place until 1478 and 1496.[40] In 1460, representing the Canarians as enraged Saracen invaders of a Christian England, Martorell in a way justifies continuing Portuguese and Spanish interest in the conquest of the remaining islands, Fernández-Armesto suggests "with presumably conscious irony on the author's part."[41] Any "conscious irony" would have to lie in the author's awareness of the primitive nature of the natives of the Canaries, victims rather than instigators of invasion. Martorell's romance remakes them as classic non-Christian invaders, much like the Saracens of *King Ponthus*, who in turn reflect the Viking raiders of the early Middle Ages. It is notable that Martorell's king of Canary seeks revenge on England for the attacks of English pirates on his towns. *Tirant lo Blanc* might be interpreted as an expression of guilt and fear of reprisals for earlier acts of European aggression against the Canarians. To this reader, the event is less ironic than it is ominous. The Saracen King Abraham of Canary himself is described in terms that might be applied to Martorell's protagonist Tirant, "a hardy youth whose virile and restless soul was stirred by dreams of conquest."[42] The fictional Canarian invaders demolish England "pillaging the island, killing or enslaving Christians, and dishonoring their wives and daughters," much as certain European adventurers proposed to do to the Canarians.[43] Nevertheless, King Abraham knows all the rules of chivalry. He issues a cartel of defiance challenging the king of England to single combat, and is defeated in that battle by the Hermit William of Warwick, who has accepted temporary kingship in place of the young and frail English king, "lest the Saracen king be deceived."[44] The point of this fictional invention is to remake the Canarians as proper opponents for the Christian knights who oppose them; Fernández-Armesto observes how unequal the actual fight had been: "In reality, the wars

---

[39] Joanot Martorell and Martí Joan de Galba, *Tirant lo Blanc*, with an introduction by Martí de Riquer (Barcelona, 1979). For a concise English summary of Martí de Riquer's findings, see David H. Rosenthal's introduction to his translation of *Tirant lo Blanc* (London and New York, 1984), pp. xii–xviii.

[40] Felipe Fernández-Armesto, *Before Columbus* (Basingstoke and London, 1987), pp. 153–59, 171–85.

[41] Fernández-Armesto, *Before Columbus*, p. 221.

[42] *Tirant*, trans. Rosenthal, p. 7.

[43] Fernández-Armesto, *Before Columbus*, p. 181.

[44] *Tirant*, trans. Rosenthal, p. 19.

of the Peraza were squalid affairs, waged against neolithic savages who were scarcely fit opponents for a knight."[45] This episode makes it clear how permeable the boundary between exploration narrative and chivalric romance can be. It is a revealing moment, to be discussed further below (chapter six).

Later in his adventures, Tirant allies himself with his former opponent, King Escariano of Ethiopia, "a powerful black much taller than other men."[46] This character has been recognized by a number of critics as a figure based on the legend of Prester John. He, too, embodies the hope of encountering a long-lost Christian ally in the East.

> King Escariano, a tall, handsome black and a most valiant warrior, ruled the inhabitants of Ethiopia, who called him King Jamjam. He was rich, powerful, and adored by his vassals. His cavalry was mighty, and his kingdom was so big that it bordered not only on Tlemcen but on Prester John of the Indies' lands, through which the river Tigris runs."[47]

King Escariano tells Tirant that the preaching of three Franciscan friars had convinced him of the superior merit of Christianity in his youth.[48] Tirant instructs him in "everything a Christian knight should know about his faith," and the king is baptized in a solemn public ceremony.[49] An additional spur to his conversion is the earlier baptism of his queen Esmeraldina. In chapter CDIX King Escariano and his queen proceed to arrange for the baptism of his Ethiopian subjects. This chapter mentions a number of topographical features and curious customs of the country to lend verisimilitude to the narrative.[50]

The unknown author of the *La Corónica de Adramón*, writing about 1492, seems to exploit his own travels through Italy. Some of the romance's information about specific buildings, customs, and landmarks parallels guidebooks for pilgrims of the period.[51] Other idiosyncratic items can best be explained as the fruit of personal observation. At the same time, Gunnar Anderson stresses that this story is built upon a clear sense of symbolic geography. The hero's journey coils round the city of Rome, spiralling outward and back in, with three visits to the pope marking Adramón's ascent of the chivalric ladder, from the humble role of pilgrim, to the status of pre-eminent knight, and on to the throne of Poland.[52] The less specific portrayal of the Polish and Bohemian scenes suggests to the editor that the author drew on a written account of the Hussite heresy of the earlier fourteenth century rather than on personal experience.

Barbara Reynolds suggests that the "geographical precision" of *Orlando*

---

45 Fernández-Armesto, *Before Columbus*, p. 184.
46 *Tirant*, trans. Rosenthal, p. 525.
47 Ibid., p. 635; cf. p. 525ff.
48 Ibid., p. 534.
49 Ibid., pp. 560–63.
50 Ibid., pp. 639–41.
51 Anderson, ed., *La Corónica*, I.xxi–xxxiii.
52 Ibid., I:xxxiii.

Furioso makes it probable that Ludovico Ariosto had plotted the travels of his knights on a map.

> Every important event can be pinpointed: Orlando's attack on Angelica on the shore of Spain, just north of Barcelona; . . . Rinaldo's journey by boat along the Po to Ravenna, every ramification of the river (as its course was then) charted and described; Astolfo's flight on the hippogriff over Spain and along the north coast of Africa, south over Cyrenaica and into Ethiopia to the kingdom of Prester John. Even Alcina's island, unnamed, may be Japan, as shown on Contarini's map.[53]

New maps and travellers' accounts gave new tools to the creators of the later medieval and Renaissance romances and romance epics. Now the hero's journey, or the heroine's, could be traced on a printed map of a world that became more elaborate in its detail and more fantastic by the year. The landscape retained most of its old wonder, with certain problematic features reimagined or rationalized, but a surprising number of marvels resisting alteration in the face of discouraging eyewitness reports. This might perhaps suggest that sixteenth-century readers, like readers today, refused to surrender their belief in their favorite wonders of romance and ancient science.

The marvels that adorn the romances reflect in many cases a well-established belief that such prodigies existed in real life. The heritage of classical geography led the medieval and Renaissance traveler to expect to encounter "monstrous races," the exotic peoples that continued to be depicted in the romances of Alexander the Great. Human beings with no heads, with dogs' heads, or with one enormous foot, were all imagined to exist somewhere in the uncharted reaches of the earth. Sir Walter Ralegh noted down credible reports of a headless tribe just over the horizon in Guiana.[54] Other legendary beings had deep roots in the human imagination: Amazons, the snake-woman or mermaid, giants, dwarves, cannibals, fairies, the wild man. Such figures enlivened the landscape of romance as well as the maps of the more imaginative geographers. Their actual existence was still a possibility: they were regarded in many cases as emblems of the wonders of God's creation.[55]

The Alexander romances preserved and publicized the ancient image of India as the home of strange peoples all through the Middle Ages. In one celebrated Oxford manuscript the *Roman d'Alexandre* is found alongside *The*

---

[53] Barbara Reynolds' introduction to Ariosto, *Orlando Furioso* (Harmondsworth, 1977), II.20–21. The map Reynolds mentions was printed in Florence in 1506. Ariosto began work on his continuation of Boiardo's *Orlando Innamorato* in 1505, and published his poem in 1516.

[54] For a detailed account of this tradition, see John Block Friedman, *The Monstrous Races in Medieval Art and Thought* (Cambridge, Mass., 1981). Cf. Stephen Greenblatt, *Marvellous Possessions*, pp. 30–31, and notes, pp. 158–59, for additional bibliography.

[55] See Kurt Ruh, "Die 'Melusine' des Thüring von Ringoltingen," *Bayerische Akademie der Wissenschaften* (Munich, 1985), pp. 1–23.

Book of Marco Polo. Its status as an ancient work of high authority, together with its strong chivalric interest, made the story of Alexander much more successful than Polo among medieval audiences. The medieval artists' efforts to represent the curious alien beings of this text have, not surprisingly, attracted recent scholars. The early printers were as ravished by the visual possibilities of the narrative as the illuminators of many manuscripts had been. Johannes Bämler's 1472 Augsburg edition of the *Histori von dem grossen Alexander* had twenty-eight woodcuts, but this was a mere bagatelle compared to the 1514 Strassburg production of Mathias Hupfuss, which had ninety-three. The "many beautiful images" the printer advertised clearly entrapped purchasers.[56]

The Amazons of romance are most flamboyantly represented by Queen Calafia and her Amazons of the isle of California in Garci Rodriguez de Montalvo's *Las Sergas de Esplandián*, already discussed in brief, and to be discussed again later in connection with Sir Walter Ralegh's Latin American voyage. Thanks to their prominence in the imaginations of European travellers, the substantial literature devoted to their legend has grown still more formidable over the past few years. The classical origins of the legend are well known. Alexander had his encounter with the Amazons on the way to India. The continuators of Homer paid notable attention to the possibilities of Amazons at the siege of Troy. By the time Raoul Le Fèvre wrote his *Recueil des histoires de Troye* for Philip the Good of Burgundy in the 1460s, Hercules and Theseus could be depicted jousting against a pair of chivalrous Amazons, and Queen Panthasile with her thousand well-armed maidens could be brought onto the battlefield to good effect. Virgil's warrior and huntress, Camilla of *Aeneid* XI, also finds parallels in a fair number of romances. These medieval instances of fighting women have received rather less attention than their classical or Renaissance counterparts. All through the Middle Ages, in a variety of romances, female warriors most often appear on the scene as solitary figures, behaving much like the male knights errant they encounter. Huon's granddaughter Ide, who disguises herself as a knight to escape her father's passion and is later constable of Rome, may be a less familiar character. The thirteenth-century *Roman de Silence* centers on the knightly adventures of a girl raised as a boy, Silence. One of the models suggested for Silence is Avenable of *L'Estoire de Merlin* (also known as the *Vulgate Merlin Continuation*), who takes the name Grisandoles while she serves Emperor Julius Caesar as knight and seneschal.[57]

---

[56] For the German folk-books of Alexander, see Paul Heitz, *Versuch einer zusammenstellung der deutschen volksbucher 15. und 16. jahrhunderts nebst deren spateren ausgaben und literatur* (Strassburg, 1924), pp. 1–4.

[57] Little gives much useful bibliography on Amazons in his notes on Calafia and her origins: see his translation of *Esplandián*, pp. 457–58. Cf. Juan Gil, *Mitos y utopías del descubrimiento*, vol. 1 (Madrid, 1988). Medieval compendia of Trojan legends like Raoul Le Fèvre's *Recueil*, translated by William Caxton as *The Recuyell of the Histories of Troye*, are notable for their energetic and chivalric Amazons. See Raoul Le Fèvre, *The Recuyell of the Historyes of Troye*, trans. William Caxton, ed. H. Oskar Sommer (London, 1894),

Boiardo's Bradamante and Spenser's Britomart may be the most celebrated descendants of these heroines today. All of these ladies errant are Amazons of sorts, but, for the traveler, the possibility of encountering a bellicose society of such female warriors was the real menace.

Mélusine, half-woman and half-snake, legendary ancestress of the Lusignan family in Jean d'Arras' prose romance of 1393, also has classical precursors. She is the offspring of a Scottish king and a fairy, cursed for using her magic powers to punish her father for his betrayal of her mother. Each of Mélusine's sons is born with some physical oddity, like Geoffroi's "great tooth," as a sign of their supernatural origin.[58] One reflection of the widespread interest in this legend may be that Mélusine's castle Lusignan, complete with Mélusine, tail and all, appeared as a centerpiece on one of the tables at the duke of Burgundy's Feast of the Pheasant of 1454.[59] According to the romance, Mélusine and her sisters still haunt certain mystic places associated with their legend. Jean d'Arras makes a point of recording "sightings" of these hazardous females, in case his readers should be sceptical. Like the Amazons, they lend mystery and danger to the landscape.

A less flamboyant but equally self-reliant and mysterious heroine is Melior, the fairy mistress of Partonopeus de Blois (the English title of his romance is *Partonope of Blois*, and the Spanish, *El libro del conde Partinuplés*).[60] This story recycles the Cupid and Psyche theme with a gender reversal, so that it is the young knight who finds himself in bed with an invisible lady. The fact that she is empress of Byzantium as well as a powerful sorceress brings together two great fantasies of the late medieval knight, that of acquiring a fairy mistress and of winning Constantinople. Partonopeus' initial journey transforms a standard boar-hunt into a journey by magic ship into another world. There the knight passes through a great, uninhabited city to a castle staffed by invisible servants

---

II.366–70, 644–700; W. T. Culley and F. J. Furnivall, eds., *Caxton's Eneydos*, EETS e.s. LVII (London, 1890), pp. 150–53; Sarah Roche-Mahdi, ed. and trans., *Silence: A Thirteenth-century French Romance* (East Lansing, 1992); H. Oskar Sommer, *The Vulgate Version of the Arthurian Romances, Edited from Manuscripts in the British Museum*, II: *L'Estoire de Merlin* (Washington, 1908), pp. 282–92.

58 This feature needs to be compared to the birthmarks that identify lost princes like Esplandián, who has red and white letters on his chest at birth, giving his name and the name of his predestined lady in "latín muy escuro" ("a very obscure Latin") and "en lenguaje griego muy cerrado" ("very incomprehensible Greek") (Little's introduction to *Esplandián*, p. 43). For those critics to whom everything is text, Amadís' son might be almost the ideal hero.

59 Otto Cartellieri, *The Court of Burgundy* (New York, 1970), p. 143.

60 A. T. Bödtker, ed., *The Middle English Versions of Partonope of Blois*, EETS e.s. 109, no early printed texts of which have been identified; Adolfo Bonilla de San Martín, ed., *Libros de caballerías* (Madrid, 1907–18), II.477–615; Ignacio B. Anzoátegui, ed., *El Conde Partinuples* (Buenos Aires, 1944); Griffin, *The Crombergers of Seville*, p. 249 and item 192 of appendix I for the 1519 edition printed by Jacobo Cromberger; Leonard, *Books of the Brave*, p. 109; the earliest Spanish edition Leonard notes is that of Alcala de Henares, 1513.

where he encounters his unseen lady for the first time. This is exploration without bloodshed or any disagreeable interaction with the natives. Melior, for her part, travels on the clouds. In the Spanish text she informs her chosen mate that, although she has given herself to him, she retains her sovereignty, for she fears no man on earth, but only God.[61] This bold statement may contribute in its own way to make Melior a still less believable character in her own time. Alternatively, it may increase her appeal to the romance's trammeled female audience. Melior offers a different fantasy of travel and female authority.

The wild man appears most attractively in *Valentine and Orson*. The lost twin who is raised by a she-bear in the forest must inevitably meet his brother Valentine in combat, and must then be introduced into human society. Here the reader is allowed to become acquainted with a wild man: the widespread medieval dramatic and decorative motif assumes a disarming individuality. In his origins, the wild man has been identified with "the wood-spirit of popular belief. This creature, as modern folklore knows him, lives in the forest depths; has a hairy body, or green clothing; is frequently of great physical strength; sometimes carries an uprooted tree as a club . . ." Wild men and wild women were much on the mind of the late medieval knight, as events like the *Pas de la Dame Sauvage* held by the Burgundian knight Claude de Vauldray at Ghent in 1470 suggest.[62] The letter summoning knights to the joust describes a blonde wild woman, naked except for her long hair and a flowery garland, who inspires the knight's display of military skill. The knight claimed to have encountered her in the course of an allegorized journey: "Going forth on his first adventure, he left the wealthy kingdom of *Enfance* (Childhood), and came to a wild poor and sterile land called *Jeunesse* (Youth). Long time he wandered there, living only on his thoughts and feelings and on hope, which was his

---

61 "Agora, doncel, vos no pensedes que porque habedes hecho conmigo a vuestra voluntad que me tenedes a todo vuestro mandar; por todo ello no me doy nada yo, que el señorío es en mi poder, después de Dios. Ca piensan los hombres que después que aquesto ha hecho, que tienen las mujeres a todo su mandar. E si no guardades aquesto que yo vos mandaré matar de mala guisa así como dicho tengo. Ca yo no he miedo ni temor a ningún hombre del mundo, sino es a Dios mi señor, que está en cielo." Ignacio B. Anzoátegui, ed., *El Conde Partinuples*, p. 27. This may be another reason why Menéndez y Pelayo considered this romance indelicate.

62 Arthur Dickson, *Valentine and Orson: A Study in Late Medieval Romance* (New York, 1929), p. 114. For Claude de Vauldray's *Pas de la Dame Sauvage*, see Richard Barber and Juliet Barker, *Tournaments: Jousts, Chivalry, and Pageants in the Middle Ages* (Woodbridge, 1989), p. 124; Cartellieri, *The Court of Burgundy*, pp. 123–24; for the wild man tradition, see Richard Bernheimer, *Wild Men in the Middle Ages: A Study in Art, Sentiment, and Demonology* (Cambridge, Mass., 1952); Timothy Husband, *The Wild Man: Medieval Myth and Symbolism* (New York, 1980); Edward Savage, "The Transformation of the Wild Man from Pagan to Christian Mythology," in *Inroads* 2 (1989–90), pp. 13–19. For some discussion and illustrations of the wild man in theatrical tradition, see Bamber Gascoigne, *World Theatre* (Boston, 1968), pp. 16–18. Gascoigne suggests that the wild man in drama may go back to early Greek representations of Hercules.

favorite food. . . ."[63] This document might well be described as a custom-made romance. The image of life as a journey is here envisioned as the knight's ride through wilderness to meet a wild woman who becomes his lady. At the tournament itself, a whole cavalcade of savage men and women covered with golden hair led de Vauldray into the lists. Such events were much better enacted by day than by torchlight. The pageant of wild men at the French court in 1393, described in Froissart's *Chronicle*, nearly killed Charles VI and did kill four of his companions when the dancers' costumes caught fire.[64]

Giants recur especially in tales of heroic ancestors. *Gyron le Courtois* stresses combats against giants as a test of the modern knight's prowess. This romance also depicts the gigantic ancestors of the shrunken contemporary knight.[65] The grotesque Ardán Canileo of the Amadís cycle claims giant ancestors. In the same series of romances, Balán the giant becomes a key character who knights Esplandián. The name suggests that he might perhaps have been inspired by the Balán of the Charlemagne cycle. There, however, the character remains an undaunted Islamic opponent of the French, while in *Amadís* he is defeated by the Christian hero and later joins the defenders of Constantinople. The giant opponent appears early in heroic literature. David's defeat of Goliath, Odysseus' test of wits against Polyphemus, Beowulf's struggle with Grendel, King Arthur's prolonged contest with Ysbadadden Chief Giant in the Welsh *Culhwch and Olwen* and his duel against the Giant of St Michael's Mount all present variants on the theme. The idea that the primordial inhabitants of the land were giants recurs from the Bible to the Anglo-Saxon poem *The Ruin*, where the giants receive credit for building the Roman city of Bath. Saracen giants populate the world of Charlemagne. Some become allies, like Fierabras, who converts to Christianity after his duel with the peer Oliver, and dies a saint. Others, like Fierabras' father the Admiral Balan, remain intransigent and are exterminated by the Christians. In *Bevis of Hampton* a Saracen giant, Ascopart, at first helps Bevis and his lady, but later betrays them. It seems to be no coincidence that Ascopart declines to be baptized, afraid of drowning in the huge font prepared for him. Giants appeared with some frequency in the chivalric spectacles of the late Middle Ages, notably in the *Feast of the Pheasant* held by Duke Philip the Good of Burgundy in 1454 to drum up support for his crusade against the Turks

---

[63] Cartellieri, *The Court of Burgundy*, p. 123.

[64] Jean Froissart, *Chronicle*, trans. John Bourchier, Lord Berners (6 vols., London, 1901–03), VI.96–99.

[65] See Walter Stephens, *Giants In Those Days: Folklore, Ancient History, and Nationalism* (Lincoln, 1989). Fébus, the great-grandfather of Gyron le Courtoys, is represented as a gigantic knight. For giants in pageantry, see Montalvo, *Esplandián*, trans. Little, figure 10 (between pp. 326 and 327), the head of a Moorish giant from Cuéllar, Spain, for the feast day of San Miguel. Little reports that the entire figure, as it appears in the pageant, is ten feet tall. For colored pictures of giants and dwarves from a Catalonian pageant, see Mn. Antoni Bach, *Cardona, Vila Ducal* (Cardona, 1986), p. 88. Italian folk pageants also have their giants: see *Il Folklore* (Milan, 1967), p. 41 for the giant and giantess of Messina.

who had taken Constantinople. There a Saracen giant led an elephant into the great hall of the Hotel de la Salle at Lille, with Holy Church, really the chronicler Olivier de la Marche dressed as a Béguine, in a tower on its back. The giant symbolized the Islamic powers the duke intended to challenge.[66] Such giants, often representing Moors, still figure in folk pageants dating back to the Middle Ages, in Spain, Italy, and elsewhere, as do dwarves. At the *pas de l'arbre d'or* in 1468, the dwarf Master Peter and a giant helped to conduct the tournament.[67]

Dwarves were familiar figures at court in the later Middle Ages, as they continued to be in the Renaissance, up through the time when Velázquez painted them. The influential fifteenth-century court of Burgundy had its share: one account of Philippe de Lalaing's *Pas du perron fée* of 1463 includes a scene where a dwarf in the service of a mysterious *Dame fée* berates the knights of the ducal court.[68] In 1468 at the wedding feast of Duke Charles the Bold, his daughter's dwarf, Mme. de Beaugrant, rode in on a singing lion the size of a warhorse, and was lifted onto the table before the bride as a present.[69] Dwarves turn up throughout the history of romance as attendants of knights and ladies, facilitators of adventure, or, sometimes, scheming villains, like the evil dwarf who often betrays Tristram and Isolde. The insulting dwarf who drives Lancelot in the infamous cart in Chrétien de Troyes' *Chevalier de la Charrette* seems to be one of the earliest in a long line. Arthurian tradition does have its dwarf knight, Evadeam, shrunken by the spell of a rejected damsel, but he regains his true size in time.[70] Amadís' dwarf chamberlain Ardían began by serving his enemy: Amadís is called "the knight of the dwarf" during one phase of his chivalric career. Most of these dwarves do not seem to be supernatural beings. However, one especially potent figure belonging to this class is the dwarf king of the fairies, Oberon, who becomes Huon of Bordeaux' protector. The principal comic character of *Ysaïe le Triste* (c.1400) is the repulsive dwarf Tronc, son of Julius Caesar and Morgan la Fée, who becomes the resplendent fairy creature Auberon at the end of the story. In this respect the sequel to the prose *Tristan* also functions as a prologue to *Huon of Bordeaux*. Another memorable personage who combines diminutive size with magic is the dwarf magician Pacolet who befriends Valentine in *Valentine and Orson*. Pacolet's magic horse gives characters in this wide-ranging romance the power of flight.[71]

Turning from the human population of the world of romance to the animal

---

66 Cartellieri, *The Court of Burgundy*, p. 147.
67 Ibid., p. 125.
68 MS BL Harley 48.
69 Cartellieri, *The Court of Burgundy*, p. 162; the giants come later in the festivities.
70 Oskar Sommer, ed., *L'Estoire de Merlin*, pp. 457, 464; West, *French Arthurian Prose Romances*, p. 111.
71 See Katharine M. Briggs, *Pale Hecate's Team* (London, 1962) on the miniaturization of fairies in the sixteenth century. *Ysaïe le Triste: roman arthurien du moyen âge tardif*, ed. André Giacchetti (Rouen, 1989). For a modern vision of Pacolet, see Nancy Eckholm Burkert, *Valentine and Orson* (New York, 1989).

inhabitants opens up a new collection of marvels. There may be a dearth of mundane domestic animals in a number of works, but there is no shortage of heraldic monsters. Red and white dragons appear in Arthurian lore as national emblems, as in the legend of Merlin and Vortigern's tower, where the child prophet detects their presence underground as the cause of the tower's instability. Amadís' son Esplandián defeats a great serpent to win the Enchantress Damsel's treasure in his first adventure after becoming a knight. The dragon or serpent as guardian of a treasure is, of course, an ancient motif, represented in literature as early as *Beowulf.* Little notes that serpents recur throughout *Amadís.*[72] Esplandián's defeat of the serpent gives him a sobriquet: "the knight of the Great Serpent." His magic caravel, the work of the enchantress Urganda, has the shape of a winged snake with a mouth that spews fire. Urganda endows it with the power to carry Esplandián to any destination he wishes – unless fate or Urganda decide differently.[73] Dragons could also enliven chivalric pageantry; the banquet that had everything, the *Vows of the Pheasant,* included a fire-breathing dragon that swooped over the heads of the feasters. A second such dragon appeared in the play of Jason at the same feast, belching smoke, to be killed in hand-to-hand combat with the hero.[74] Lions lend a touch of exotic danger to the forests and enchantments of romance. They may prove friendly to the hero, as Yvain's lion did in Chrétien de Troyes's *Chevalier au lion.* A lioness suckles Amadís' son Esplandián, no doubt contributing to his prowess. Most often they serve as stock perils, guarding treasures or mysteries, as when Sir Lancelot must pass them to approach the Holy Grail in Malory, or Esplandián take his magic scabbard from the metal lion on the tomb at the Enchantress Damsel's crag. The knight Ardán Canileo of the Amadís cycle, the descendant of giants, bears some facial resemblance to a lion.[75]

The Californian variety of griffins, fed on male flesh by their Amazon keepers, terrify the besiegers and besieged alike at Constantinople in *Las Sergas de Esplandián.* Trained to attack males, they prove unable to distinguish between Queen Calafia's Christian opponents and her Turkish allies. Nevertheless, the griffins' strict obedience to their handlers gives Montalvo the chance to scold his readers for their own unruliness.[76] Otherwise, these heraldic beasts are not often permitted much in the way of character development. They serve for the most part as spectacular means of transportation and frightening special effects. These convenient creatures need to be seen amid a variety of fantasies of flight that preoccupy romances from an early period on, taking up the theme of the myth of Dedalus (and Icarus). In Ariosto's *Orlando Furioso,* Astolfo flies

---

[72] Montalvo, *Esplandián,* trans. Little, p. 75, n. 16.
[73] Ibid., p. 538.
[74] Cartellieri, *The Court of Burgundy,* p. 146.
[75] Montalvo, *Esplandián,* trans. Little, p. 75. For Ardán, see Edwin B. Place and Herbert C. Behm, trans., *Amadís* (Lexington, 1974–75), II, ch. 61, p. 613; Montalvo, *Esplandián,* trans. Little, p. 102, n. 4.
[76] Montalvo, *Esplandián,* trans. Little, pp. 461–65.

on a hippogriff to the land of Prester John. Alternatively, the fantasy of flight can be fulfilled by magical or mechanical means. The magic horse of Chaucer's *Squire's Tale* is presented as a misunderstood wonder of technology. A similar magic horse reappears in *Cleomadés*, and in *Valentine and Orson*. The sheer geographic scope of many romances propels authors to invent such devices, in order to move the characters around with the necessary speed to sustain the action.

Other monsters of romance defy classification. Malory's Questing Beast, the *Beste glatissant, Beste diverse,* or *Beste merveilleuse* of the French books, is more often heard than described. Pursued by Pellinor and later by Palamedes, in Malory it strikes King Arthur as "the strongeste beste that ever he saw or herde of." A characteristic sound announces its appearance: "the noyse was in the bestes bealy lyke unto the questyng of thirty coupyl houndes."[77] While Malory may be sparing of descriptive details, the *Tristan en prose* explains the *Beste glatissant* as a creature with "the feet of a stag, the thighs and tail of a lion, the body of a leopard, and the head of a serpent." The barking or howling sound from its belly is made by its whelps. This composite monster is explained as the offspring of a wicked damsel and the devil. It seems rather reminiscent of the grotesque creatures that prance on the margins of the livelier late medieval manuscripts, and have been recently elucidated by Michael Camille.[78] The undescribed but noisy monster of the Irish forest in *Olivier de Castille* may be a relative; here, too, the author leaves almost everything up to the reader's imagination.

Noticeable affinities connect the principal beasts that lurk in the forests of the late romances with the fearsome, whimsical and astonishing creatures popular among later medieval heralds. Rodney Dennys observes that the griffin became widely used in heraldry only in the fifteenth century, though the heralds of those days liked to place it on the coat of arms they attributed to Alexander the Great. Composite, chimerical animals, sometimes unique to a single coat of arms or heraldic treatise, also seem characteristic of the later medieval heraldic imagination. Dragons and lions have a much longer history as military emblems, though, going back to antiquity. Curiously enough, a two-tailed mermaid with a coronet is called a "Melusine" in German heraldry.[79] There are undoubtedly cross-influences running between heraldry and romance, much like those that link the romance and the saint's life.

This chapter surveys a few of the principal features of the romance landscape. Much more detailed analysis is needed before the materials presented

---

[77] Malory, *Works,* ed. Vinaver, I:42.

[78] West, *French Arthurian Prose Romances,* pp. 38–39. Cf. Fanni Bogdanow, *The Romance of the Grail: A Study of the Structure and Genesis of a Thirteenth-century Arthurian Prose Romance* (Manchester, 1966), pp. 124–26; L. R. Muir, "The Questing Beast: Its Origin and Development," *Orpheus* 4 (1957), pp. 24–32; Michael Camille, *Image on the Edge: the Margins of Medieval Art* (Cambridge, 1992).

[79] Rodney Dennys, *The Heraldic Imagination* (New York, 1975), pp. 124–25, 133–95.

here can be understood in depth. For this, the reader needs to resort to the many excellent individual studies of particular topics, at least some of which are indicated in the notes to this chapter. Still, a quick overview like this one can begin to suggest the imaginative wealth of the materials that the romancers of the later Middle Ages drew upon, and the seductive variety of the worlds they created for their audiences. Barbara Reynolds remarks of Ariosto that "One of the most remarkable features of the art of Ariosto is the precision with which he represents the real world in which he sets his other world of legend and fantasy . . . it seems to be Ariosto's desire to take the entire earth as a stage for his events, with the moon as an extension."[80] This thirst to encompass the known world was shared by Aristo's medieval predecessors: the element of geographic variety lends excitement to numerous romances.

In Strauss' opera *Arabella* (first performed in 1933, with a libretto of 1929 by Hugo von Hoffmannsthal) the heroic Croatian landowner Mandryka captures the imagination of the audience as he describes a forest "full of gypsies and hermits" – the forest of romance, which he has just sold to a Jew for a fat price.[81] It is tempting to read this line as a throwaway sketch of the destruction of the world of romance by the sordid forces of capitalism; it seems to be assumed that the Jew will cut down the trees. The loss here is not viewed as biological but as spiritual. In the fifteenth and sixteenth centuries it was the opposite case. Readers of this period experienced a dizzying expansion of the romance landscape. This in a way counterbalanced the earlier medieval trend toward the domestication of the European environment through deforestation and agrarian settlement. The Anglo-Norman poet Wace had complained in the mid-twelfth century that he had visited the suppposedly enchanted forest of Brocéliande without finding any of the wonders of romance. "A fool I went, a fool I came back." Familiarity began to breed contempt. The writers of the later Middle Ages had to look to the margins of the known world, or to the distant past, or both, for marvels to test their knights and ladies. The reports of Columbus, Cortes, and their contemporaries offered satisfying proof that the landscape of romance was in no immediate danger of extinction.

[80] Reynolds' introduction to her translation of *Orlando Furioso*, II.20.
[81] Cf. Peter Branscombe, "Arabella, Vienna and the 1860s," in the program for the 1990 Royal Opera House production of *Arabella* (London, 1990), n. p. "Hoffmannsthal flattered himself that with the figure of Mandryka he had brought something quite new to the Viennese stage: a glamorous and mysterious stranger from the farthest corner of the empire." I am indebted to Sir Jeremy Isaacs, who was then General Director of the Royal Opera House, Covent Garden, for directing my attention to *Arabella*.

PART TWO

Exploration and Chivalry:
Case Studies

"This was the sort of place the Conquistadores landed in," Hilary said. *"Cortés landed in just such another, and burned his ships on the beach behind him. When we go down the coast, we will draw the very beach where he landed. Imagine landing like that, a thousand miles from any store, or any friend, in an unknown world. It was a lonely night for those fellows, when their ships were burned and they turned inland to what was waiting for them."*

"I would not pity them too much," Margaret answered. *"They were there from choice, mainly from greed; nor were they novices at the work. They had also three great advantages, guns, horses and Cortés. The prizes to be won were enormous, and the dangers to be faced only thirst, which was probably chronic with them; hunger, which they must have known in Spain; and death, which they would have had on the gallows if they had not emigrated."*

"I see all that," he said; *"yet there it is. Cortés came to the difficult new thing and did it. Then four hundred years afterwards, fellows like me appear, who write how Cortés did it and how he ought to have done it. Do you think that we last fulfil a function?"*

They had now turned off on their way to the house through the forest.

"Yes, Hilary," she said. *"It is even called a kind of wisdom."*

Something in her tone made him pause to look at her.

"I don't quite see your point," he said.

"It is a kind of wisdom," she said, *"to be wise after the event."*[1]

THE SECOND PART OF this study moves from the literature of late medieval and Renaissance chivalry to its applications in the annals of exploration. Links between chivalry and exploration have been noted by ancient and modern students of the subject. The level, nature, and importance of the connections have yet to be discussed in any depth. This happens largely because many pertinent specialist studies of chivalry mention this aspect of their subject only as a parting shot. Exploration supplies a provocative conclusion, but following up on the question remains beyond the scope of the author's work.

Tracing the continuing influence of any aspect of the Middle Ages can be a delicate matter. The well-trained medievalist recoils from the notion of study-ing his or her period solely as a prefiguration of later eras. This is a sure way to distort one's findings. But this delicacy of principle also isolates and protects the Middle Ages from their natural historical consequences. It frustrates longterm projects that cross the artificial boundaries erected by scholarship itself. The student who approaches these barriers finds herself in the position

---

[1] John Masefield, *Sard Harker* (1924; rpt. Harmondsworth, 1963), pp. 81–82.

of the Good Knight without Fear in *Gyron le Courtoys*, as he rides into the *Val de Servage* and hears the portcullis crash down behind him and the men in the tower shout that there's no going back.[2] The pillar that marks the path reads: "This is the way whence there is no returning. None who enter can ever leave again until the coming of the good knight who must die for love."[3] Let us nevertheless adventure.

In this half of the book I reread a variety of exploration narratives from the viewpoint of the chivalric romances that haunt them. This collection of case studies begins with that influential pair of literary collaborators, Marco Polo and Rustichello (or Rusticiano) da Pisa, in 1298–99, as the author of Arthurian romance notes down the Venetian traveler's reminiscences of Mongol Cathay, or so he claims, at least. It ends in the early seventeenth century with the wonders of Captain John Smith's global career in chivalry and exploration, as reported by himself. In between, Gadifer de la Salle, Henry the Navigator, Hernan Cortes, Cabeza de Vaca, Sir Walter Ralegh, Hakluyt, and Garcilaso de la Vega all offer useful variations on the theme. This is not a comprehensive study. New research now underway will open up other dimensions of the material. Instead, my goal here is like that of the unfortunate Gadifer de la Salle, to open a path between disciplines and periods.

---

2 *Gyron le Courtoys*, f. 289v: "jamais ne retournerez ne par ceste voye ne par autre. Allez avant, si verrez adonc tout clerement quelle avanture c'est que vous devez trouver." All references to *Gyron le Courtoys* cite *Gyron le Courtoys*, c.1501, facsimile reproduction (1977; rpt. London, 1979). The translations, unless otherwise noted, are mine. The themes of the deadly choice of pathways by the traveler, the warning of Abandon Hope, and the preoccupation with fathers and genealogy are distinctly Dantesque. Did Dante know Rustichello's work?

3 *Gyron*, f. 289r: "Cy est le pas sans retour. Nul ne si mettra qui iamais puisse retourner iusques a tant que le bon chevalier, celluy qui doit mourir pour amour y viendra."

CHAPTER THREE

Marco Polo and Rustichello da Pisa:
the traveler's romance

IN THE ANNALS OF medieval romance it is uncommon for readers to know anything about the author. Even in the case of the greatest artists, Chrétien de Troyes, for instance, little beyond a local habitation and a name is left to us. Other masterworks like the Lancelot-Grail cycle or *Sir Gawain and the Green Knight* remain obstinately anonymous, although some of the participants do name themselves, and optimistic scholars have always had their theories. It is then somewhat remarkable that we know what we know of Rustichello (or Rusticiano) da Pisa, Marco Polo's secretary and "ghostwriter." We know that these two somewhat unlikely collaborators encountered one another while they were both prisoners of the Genoese. After his return from his now celebrated travels to China, Marco Polo had become involved in the wars of Venice. In Ramusio's biography he was one of the prisoners of war taken at the battle of Curzola on 6 September 1298, after service as "gentleman commander" of a galley. The specifics of the story are somewhat in doubt; the conflict between Venice and Genoa provided other opportunities for Polo to get himself captured.[1]

How Rustichello got into prison himself still seems a murky business. The Pisans had also had their differences with the Genoese. L. F. Benedetto observes that so many Pisans had been incarcerated in Genoa that during one phase of the struggle they had a prison all to themselves. Rustichello's most memorable deed up to that point had been his production of the massive Arthurian prose romance known today as the "Compilation of Rusticiano da Pisa," which he says is based on a manuscript left in Italy by the future Edward I of England on his way to his crusade in 1271–72. Some scholars conjecture further that Rustichello may have traveled to Palestine in Edward's train.[2] If he did, he could have witnessed that prince's narrow escape from assassination by descendants of the devotees of the Old Man of the Mountain, a personage described in a notable episode of *The Book of Marco Polo*. He might also have heard an account

---

[1] Ronald E. Latham, ed. and trans., *The Travels of Marco Polo* (Harmondsworth, 1958), p. 16. For qualifications, see L. F. Benedetto's editorial introduction to Marco Polo, *Il Milione*, Comitato Geografico Nazionale Italiano Pubbl. 3 (Florence, 1928).

[2] Latham, ed. and trans., *Travels of Marco Polo*, p. 16.

of this adventure on Edward's return to Italy later in 1272. No two manuscripts present Rustichello's collection of Arthurian and pre-Arthurian narrative material in quite the same form. The printers of the sixteenth century complicated matters by issuing the bulk of the text in two volumes, *Gyron le Courtoys* and *Meliadus de Leonnoys*, with the second half of the manuscript appearing in print first.[3]

The linguistic evolution of both works should command attention, since it reflects the diverging readership and reputation of each text. The history of their translations promoted the two books' divergence. By the fourteenth century, the *Book of Marco Polo* had become available as a Latin and an Italian text. It was so widely distributed in these translations that later scholars express surprise at its French origin. Polo's sixteenth-century biographer Ramusio himself believed that the original work must have been written in Latin.[4] Rustichello's contemporary, Ramon Lull, evokes the same surprise by writing certain texts in his own vernacular, Catalan, rather than in Latin – the *Libre del orde de cavayleria* (*The Book of the Ordre of Chyualry*), to name one. The translators and disseminators of Marco Polo's book may choose on occasion to recall the original identity of the volume as a French courtly work. They also supply it with new identities, as a work of authority to be consulted by the learned in Latin, and as a text to be read in most European languages.[5]

By contrast, the *Compilation of Rusticiano da Pisa* remained in the vernacular. Its French loses its Italian features over time as the language is corrected and modernized in later editions. The romance continued to be read as an aristocratic French text. It maintains its character as an impressive, high-prestige volume through to its latest appearances in printed form, the reprints of 1979–80. Its sixteenth-century Parisian printers issued it in the company of other massive Arthurian works: Vérard, the publisher of *Gyron le Courtoys*, also printed *Lancelot du Lac*, and *Merlin*. Galliot du Pré, who printed the first edition of *Meliadus*, was also responsible for the earliest printed texts of *Perceforest*, Chrétien de Troyes' *Perceval* (1530) and the *Histoire du Sainct Greaal. Meliadus* was to be reissued in 1533 by Denis Janot, perhaps better known as the publisher of Rabelais, Villon, *Tristan* (1533) and *Amadís de Gaule*.[6] Rustichello's work continued to appear in distinguished company.

While Rustichello's *Compilation* does not seem ever to have been available in English, it was much read in France, Italy, and Spain for three centuries.[7] Its

---

3 *Gyron le Courtoys* (Paris: Antoine Vérard, c.1501; rpt. 1506 and 1519). *Meliadus de Leonnoys* (Paris: Galliot du Pré, 1528; rpt. 1532). (Hereafter referred to as *Gyron* and *Meliadus.*)

4 Marco Polo, *Marco Polo: The Description of the World*, ed. and trans. A. C. Moule and Paul Pelliot (London, 1938), p. 44.

5 Moule and Pelliot give a sizeable list of MSS and printed editions, pp. 509–516.

6 C. E. Pickford's introduction to *Meliadus de Leonnoys 1532*, facsimile reproduction (London, 1980), pp. iii–iv.

7 Why Ben Jonson identified Prince Henry with Meliadus in his verses for *Prince Henries*

two French editions found sixteenth-century Italian translators: *Girone il Cortese* uses the 1501 text of *Gyron le Courtoys*, and, in Donald Hoffman's opinion, improves upon it. *Il gran re Meliadus* (1558–59) translates *Meliadus de Leonnoys*.[8] Rustichello's *Compilation*, or else "King Edward's Book" that he claimed as his source, found its way into the Hispanic peninsula earlier still. Harvey Sharrer refers to "numerous Catalan and Aragonese documents and letters" that refer to *Meliadus, Palamedes*, and *Gyron le Courtoys*.[9] French manuscripts of *Meliadus, Gyron* and *Tristan* appear in the royal libraries of Aragon in the fourteenth century.[10] William J. Entwistle argues that the Spanish author of the *Libro del esforzado caballero Don Tristan de Leonis* might have followed Rustichello's source for the chapters that correspond to *Gyron le Courtoys*, rather than Rustichello himself.[11] A late-fourteenth-century manuscript fragment tells part of the story of Branor le Brun in language close to that of *Don Tristan*, suggesting that the printer had a translation of this date as one of his primary sources.[12] Rustichello's *Compilation* may also have influenced at least one Greek poet around 1300, the author of "Ho Presbys Hippotes" ("the Old Knight"), who treats an episode similar to the opening of *Gyron le Courtoys*.[13]

Rustichello's extensive romance remains the first known Arthurian narrative to be written by an Italian, although the Italian wrote it in French, the same language he would use in Marco Polo's book. William Calin has pointed out that the use of French in this and other exploration narratives of the thirteenth century must reflect the desire to reach a secular, international, courtly audience.[14] Rustichello's special attraction for Polo might have been his expertise as

---

Barriers (performed 6 January 1610), and which of several Arthurian Meliaduses he meant to evoke, is difficult to say. G. D. West identifies six in his *An Index of Proper Names in French Arthurian Prose Romances* (University of Toronto Romance Series 35, Toronto, 1978), but Tristan's father is the principal figure to bear the name.

8 Donald Hoffman, in *The New Arthurian Encyclopedia*, ed. Norris J. Lacy *et al.* (Chicago and London, 1991), pp. 197, 213–14. For further details on these versions, he cites Francesco Tassi, ed., *Girone il Cortese: romanzo cavalleresco di Rustico o Rusticiano da Pisa* (Florence, 1855); see also Edmund G. Gardner, *The Arthurian Legend in Italian Literature* (London, 1930), pp. 47–63.

9 *The New Arthurian Encyclopedia*, p. 425.

10 William J. Entwistle, *The Arthurian Legend in the Literatures of the Spanish Peninsula* (1925; rpt. New York, 1975), p. 90.

11 *Libro del esforzado caballero Don Tristan de Leonis* (Valladolid: Juan de Burgos, 1501); Entwistle, *The Arthurian Legend*, pp. 113–14; 118–121.

12 The fragment, MS Madrid, Biblioteca Nacional, 20262 (no. 19), is discussed in Harvey Sharrer, *A Critical Bibliography of Hispanic Arthurian Material, I: Texts: The Prose Romance Cycles* (London, 1977), pp. 27, 30.

13 Norris J. Lacy, in *The New Arthurian Encyclopedia*, p. 368, citing Pierre Breillat, "La Table Ronde en orient: le poème grec du *Vieux Chevalier*," *Mélanges d'Archéologie et d'Histoire Publiés par l'Ecole Française de Rome* 55 (1938), pp. 308–40.

14 Strangers Conference discussion, University of Minnesota, 25 February 1994.

a writer in French. Unless Rustichello and Polo conversed in French, the project demanded translation skills as well as notetaking ability.

Primary studies comparing Rustichello's romances with the *Book of Marco Polo* demonstrate an extensive amount of overlap between the two, both in language and content. Ronald Latham asserts that "Rustichello's share in the joint venture has probably been underrated."[15] The work of detailed comparison undertaken by L. F. Benedetto as part of the earliest critical edition of the Polo manuscripts only begins to point out the nature of Rustichello's contribution. The casual storytelling style of the first of the French manuscripts remains unmistakeably Rustichello's. In many passages Rustichello repeats expressions or speeches he had used before in the annals of the knights of Uther Pendragon and King Arthur. Latham tries to differentiate in his translation between "the bald and businesslike quality of Polo's topographical notes and the self-conscious artistry of those romantic interludes that betray most clearly the hand of Rustichello."[16]

Authorities on medieval travel literature still express genuine discomfort when they must confront the element of romance in the *Book of Marco Polo*, and the fictional nature of *Mandeville's Travels*. Mary Campbell's comments illustrate this viewpoint most effectively:

> But Rusticello's immediate impact on the work appears to have been relatively superficial. He is responsible for the language of romance that suffuses the narratives of the Tartar wars at the end of the work and perhaps for the more thoroughly fictional of the stories that replace data in chapters on cities Marco did not visit. The structure of the work, the selection of its material, and most of all the conception of the act of telling it displays are all Marco's – or, as that name renders a rather problematic voice, are at any rate not the contributions of Rustichello's genre. Would a professional romancer have said this: "And after we had begun about the Greater Sea then we repented of it . . ., because many people know it clearly. And therefore we will leave it then, and will begin about other things."[17]

This objection is surprising, since Rustichello's own romances, like those of many of his contemporaries, abound in similar remarks: "When they set forth they rode so much that they came to Camelot, but before they arrived several great and marvellous adventures happened to them, which I will not describe to you at all in this book, since in my book of the Brut they are reproduced at length."[18] The English-speaking reader runs across many similar items in Malory. A specialist in romance might be inclined to argue that such blunt acts

---

15 Latham, ed. and trans., *Travels of Marco Polo*, p. 17.
16 Ibid., p, 28.
17 Mary B. Campbell, *The Witness and the OtherWorld: Exotic European Travel Writing 400–1600* (Ithaca, 1988), p. 93.
18 *Meliadus*, f. ix(v): "Quant ilz se furent mis en la voie ilz cheuaucherent tant par leurs iournees que ilz vindrent en la cite de Kamalot mais auant que ilz y fussent arriuez il leur

of omission are all too characteristic of the longer prose romances, particularly those of King Arthur. Their effect is to create the sense of a dense network of interlocking adventures, some visible and some left to the imagination.

Campbell's next paragraph continues "What is significant about the collaboration is not so much the degree to which the fiction writer adulterated the words of the documentarist, but the fact of the collaboration itself."[19] "Adulterated" does still convey a strong pejorative effect. Campbell proceeds to analyze the autobiographical viewpoint of Marco. ("Marco is a merchant, and therfore he witnesses with the eye of a merchant, as Egeria had with the eye of a nun.") Latham is a bit less restrictive: "Primarily they were the eyes of a practical traveller and a merchant, quick to notice the available sources of food and water along the route, the means of transport, and the obstacles interposed by nature or by man . . ."[20] The problematic figure here is not the economically defined eyewitness, "Marco the Merchant," like "Caxton the Merchant," a being limited to his professional identity. Presumably all merchants, and all nuns, see with the same eye. None can see beyond the confines of the collective in which they are grouped, and which too often is viewed as a stereotype. This, in a way, recalls Chaucer's portraits in the General Prologue to the *Canterbury Tales*: these writers become the Knight, the Merchant, the Prioress. What we have is the modern critic's version of the medieval Estates Satire tradition so expertly analyzed by Jill Mann.[21] The difference lies in the fact that Chaucer creates for many of his characters personal idiosyncrasies that transcend or illuminate their social status. This potential for personal growth, mixed motives, or quirkiness is too often denied by the modern scholar to his or her representative Knight, Squire, Merchant or Nun.

In some cases a work of literature can be identified without question as the product or the exclusive property of a single class. This is not the case here. The *Book of Marco Polo* confronts us with the collaboration of a merchant and a courtly writer of romance. As in the cases of many later medieval literary artifacts, including the writings of Chaucer and Caxton – both authors of mercantile origin or antecedents with extensive courtly experience and courtly

---

aduint plusieurs grandes et merueilleuses aduentures / lesquelles ie ne vous deuiseray mie en cestuy liure: car en mon liure du Brut sont toutes au long contenues."

[19] Campbell, *The Witness*, p. 93.

[20] Latham, ed. and trans., *Travels of Marco Polo*, p. 19.

[21] *Chaucer and Medieval Estates Satire: The Literature of Social Classes and the General Prologue to The Canterbury Tales* (Cambridge, 1973). A number of romances show fictional merchants and knights collaborating or even assuming one another's roles. As early as *Fleur et Blanchefleur*, the prince disguises himself as a merchant in order to penetrate the Saracen stronghold where his beloved is hidden; the theme recurs elsewhere as well. In *Valentine and Orson*, a courageous merchant steps forward to defend the falsely accused empress of Byzantium, fights a judicial duel against her archenemy the bishop, and is ennobled as a reward for his valor.

audiences – we need to recognize the interplay between merchant and court to understand these compositions.

Experimental alliances between knights and merchants proliferate throughout the period under discussion in this study. The earlier version of *Le Canarien*, to be discussed in the next chapter, identifies the merchant as an agent of the crusader. In Gadifer de la Salle's proposal for a new African expedition, following the frustration of his enterprises in the Canary islands between 1402 and 1404, he suggests that a trader should be delegated to spy out conditions before any flotilla sets sail. Henry the Navigator's African tentatives combined mercantile and crusading elements to similar effect. Factual and fictional works alike picture the merchant as a gatherer of intelligence, a privileged traveler who finds a welcome in strange ports, a bearer of tidings from distant lands. In Chaucer's *Man of Law's Tale*, the Sultan of Syria makes a habit of questioning his merchants "whan they cam from any strange place" to find out "tidynges of sondry regnes, for to leere / The wondres that they myghte seen or heere."[22]

The alliance of the knight and the merchant are reflected in a different way in the printing industry of the later fifteenth and sixteenth centuries. Grant Uden's book about William Caxton and his patron Anthony Woodville, Lord Rivers, in fact bears the title *The Knight and the Merchant*. Successful merchants like Caxton might function as diplomats in trade negotiations, or as financial agents of their own and other countries. They moved in court circles as powerful, familiar figures. Many merchant families aspired to noble status, and achieved it for their offspring; the Chaucers and the de la Poles in England are good examples of this form of advancement.[23]

The early printers quickly became adept at retailing chivalric literature to knightly audiences, sometimes with the patronage of knights or princes. Tales of knights and ladies are supplied with the clear recognition of a substantial demand from within and beyond their traditional audience. The symbiotic relationship of the merchant and his customer played a key role in the ongoing development of this literature as a salable commodity. The appearance of chivalric terms like "merchant adventurer" and "enterprise" in the mercantile vocabulary during the sixteenth century suggests that merchants of this period may have based their images of themselves more on knightly values than on a tradition of "bourgeois prudence."[24]

---

22 Geoffrey Chaucer, *Man of Law's Tale*, lines 178, 181–82.
23 Grant Uden, *The Knight and the Merchant* (London, 1965). For Caxton's mercantile career, see George Painter, *William Caxton* (London, 1977). Geoffrey Chaucer's father was a successful London vintner in the mid-fourteenth century; his great-great-grandson, John de la Pole, earl of Lincoln (c.1464–87), was presumptive heir to the English throne at the time of the Battle of Bosworth Field in 1485. The Pole family, into which Chaucer's granddaughter Alice married, began as merchants of Kingston-upon-Hull. The Berkeleys of Gloucester built their dynastic fortunes on trade even earlier.
24 For more about the interplay between the merchant and the court, see Sylvia Thrupp, *The Merchant Classes of Medieval London*. Henry Lovelich, a London merchant, produced

For all of these reasons, the notion of the merchant as a straightforward, economic being, focused on his own profit to the exclusion of all other concerns, rings false. The image belongs to medieval estates satire or Marxist political theory, not to the analysis of actual human beings or their written artifacts. Such an objection of course complicates the effort to separate the strands of the *Book of Marco Polo* into sharply differentiated mercantile and chivalric voices. Twentieth-century readers need to recognize that there are times when the merchant and the romancer may sing in unison.

The difficulty, for many modern readers, does not seem to stem from the merchant but from the writer of romances. The merchant knows his place, or rather we know it. As the eyewitness, by rights he ought to be the principal author of the text, the "true and only author."[25] The romancer remains a mystery, an intrusion. Much editorial effort and much of the translator's skill goes into differentiating "Marco's" from "Rustichello's" voice. In manuscript studies the hope is always to find a text that includes "Marco's later revisions and corrections."[26] Too many editors work overtime to efface the romancer and expurgate his text.

In fact, the two voices are not separable. Scholars point to bits of the book — words, phrases, scenes, stories — that must be Rustichello's, because they are lifted straight out of his earlier manuscripts. But a dissection of this kind strips the work of its distinctive character. The interaction of the merchant and the writer of chivalric romances creates the effect of a duet that runs throughout their book. The two voices cannot be disentangled. As the two prisoners talk, the merchant narrates his observations to the romancer, who writes it down in his own language. Rustichello becomes Marco Polo's first auditor, editor, and critic. He is the essential intermediary — another kind of merchant, perhaps?[27] The Italianate French words on the page have to be read as those of the romancer. Whether Rustichello is translating, transcribing, evaluating, censoring, or embellishing Marco Polo's speech, his is the hand that wrote the text we have. It has been suggested that he is also responsible for many of the interpolated stories that punctuate the list of cities visited by Marco. Orlandini suggested that the book's structure and all of the interpolated tales are Rustichello's; Frances Wood goes farther still by questioning Marco Polo's status as an eyewitness and giving Rustichello principal credit for the book.[28] The thought annoys too many readers who resent Rustichello crowding between them and

his translations, *The History of the Holy Grail* and *Merlin,* around 1450. In 1281–82 "an old merchant from Goslar" is reported to have won a tournament at Magdeburg and received a local beauty as his prize. (See Barber and Barker, *Tournaments,* p. 56.)

25 Benedetto, trans. in Moule and Pelliot, ed. and trans., *Marco Polo,* p. 43 n.

26 Campbell, *The Witness,* p. 96 n. 8.

27 In Baudelaire's *Poésies en prose,* the poet's mistress castigates him as a "marchand de nuages." Baudelaire's "merchant of clouds" well describes Rustichello.

28 Moule and Pelliot, ed. and trans., *Marco Polo,* 43 n.; Frances Wood, *Did Marco Polo Get to China?* (London, 1995).

the heroic figure of the authentic traveler – a figure created in whole or part by Rustichello himself. It is perhaps surprising that Marco Polo continues to be considered the author, and Rustichello only his scribe, the transcriber, even though Rustichello does the writing and uses his own language, which is disturbing because it is the language of Arthurian romance. But Rustichello can himself claim the status of an eyewitness in a different sense. If he has not been to Cathay, he has at least been alongside Marco Polo in Genoa. The tendency to denigrate his voice and his work reflects a widespread disrespect for the scribes who supply us with all the written evidence we have of the Middle Ages. It also reflects the devaluation of romance that runs through many recent critical studies.

Alternatives that recommend themselves to modern students of exploration literature confronted by romance are to ignore the romance almost totally, as Stephen Greenblatt does, or to fight it off in the manner of Mary Campbell. One can push the romance into the background ("The romances of Arthur and Alexander provide a background of fictional experience against which to measure the actual").[29] Contemporary criticism would much rather celebrate the rise of the realistic novel, with "its freedom from the cruder qualities of the supernatural emphasized by *Wonders* and the Alexander romances."[30]

Too often in studies of this material works like *Mandeville's Travels* and the romance play a curious subsidiary role in a history of literature focused on the rise of the novel, with the novel starring as the heroic protagonist. Travel literature becomes an intermediate stage, wedged between "the novel's prehistory in medieval narrative and prose" and *Robinson Crusoe*, and characterized by "precocious realism."[31] Campbell's discussion clearly defines the hierarchy of genres endorsed by most critics today.

For Campbell, the romance becomes a backward and even pernicious form of reading. Campbell embraces Auerbach's characterization of the courtly romance as an "artless" form of literature. The romance, for Campbell, is always ugly and greedy, a sinister genre responsible for much evil in world history. Mary Campbell's effort here resembles the enterprise of Juan Luis Vives, who also struggled to reduce the romance to the status of a children's literature – but for Campbell, the chivalric romance is a purely masculine children's literature, while Vives knew it as a threat to the morals of female readers. In Campbell's assessment, the infantile male ego craves such stories of self-aggrandizement and then enacts them in deeds of inhumanity all across the globe.

In fact, as the first part of this study attempted to indicate, the Middle Ages produced many sorts of romances, in prose and in verse, long and short, chivalric and antichivalric. Rather than picturing Rustichello as a generalized writer of "romance," it is important to see what kind of romance he wrote. One

29 Campbell, *The Witness*, p. 121.
30 Ibid., p. 106.
31 Ibid., p. 123.

can then better estimate its interplay with the reminscences of Marco Polo, as well as its influence on the world at large.

In the world of romance, Rustichello's identity is again a problem. As discussed above, he is by his own account a transcriber of another manuscript, one supplied by King Edward. There is some evidence that some of his material may have circulated independently, which would support this statement. To the modern Arthurian scholar he figures as a "compiler," and his text is "the compilation of Rusticiano da Pisa." In manuscript, it is a body of work subject to much *mouvance*, variation from one copy to the next. C. E. Pickford notes that ten different versions have been identified, surviving in more than thirty manuscripts, none of which contains the complete text. As with the *Book of Marco Polo*, some of this variation may be due to scribal efforts to regularize or comprehend the Italianate French of Rustichello's original. In this study attention will be centered on Rustichello's work as it was made accessible to the reading public of the sixteenth century in the editions of the Parisian printers Antoine Vérard and Denis Janot. These also happen to be the texts most readily available to the present-day reader, since facsimile reproductions have been issued by Scolar Press. As Benedetto noted, these sixteenth-century publications offer versions of Rustichello's work that have been edited to bring his archaic, Italianate French up to date, so they are not a good guide to correspondences of vocabulary or phrase with the text of the *Book of Marco Polo*. They are also unsatisfactory as representations of the shape of Rustichello's original work. Here the text is chopped into two substantial volumes, which still omit sections of the *Compilation* that overlap with the prose *Tristan*, itself published separately. For these reasons I will have occasion to refer to the *Compilation* as it appears in manuscript. Still, the advantages of accessibility and the pertinence of the printers' version of Rustichello to this particular study make it appropriate to focus some attention on the printed editions.

Rereading *Gyron le Courtoys* and *Meliadus* from the perspective of the explorer reveals first of all the parallels of language and event that earlier scholars like L. F. Benedetto and Ronald Latham have noted. These parallels begin with the first words of the preface. *Gyron le Courtoys* addresses itself to "Lords, emperors, kings, princes, dukes, counts, barons, knights, viscounts, burghers and all worthy men of this world who have the will and desire to entertain yourselves in romances, take this one and cause it to be read from top to bottom."[32] Marco Polo's book opens with the same catalogue of auditors: "Emperors and kings, dukes and marquises, counts, knights, and townsfolk,

---

[32] Gyron, f. 1v: "Seigneurs / Empereurs / Roys / princes / ducz / contes / Barons / Chevaliers / Vicontes, Bourgeois et tous les prudhommes de cestuy monde qui talent auez et desir de vous delecter en rommans prenez cestuy cy et le faictes lire de chief en chief." Compare "Seignors enperaor et rois, dux et marquois, cuens, chevaliers et borgiois, et toutes gens qui volés savoir les deverses jenerasions des homes . . . si prennés cestui livre et le feites lire" (Marco Polo, *Il Milione*, ed. Benedetto, p. 3).

and all people who wish to know the various races of men . . . take this book and have it read to you."[33] Young Marco Polo first appears at the court of the Great Khan in much the same way that young Tristan appears at Camelot.[34] Other parallels of language and content surface in an attentive reading of the two works. Rustichello's description of Camelot in *Meliadus de Leonnoys* finds echoes in Marco Polo's description of the Great Khan's residence at Chagannor:

> They came to the court of the noble and mighty King Arthur. And they found him in his city of Camelot, which was at that time the noblest city, the most dreaded and the richest that King Arthur held, with the exception of the city of London. These two cities were at that time the noblest cities of the kingdom of Logres, but the king enjoyed staying at Camelot more, because the place was more comfortable and located in a place suitable for recreation, with woods and streams and many fountains and plains.[35]

> He enjoys staying in this palace because there are lakes and rivers here in plenty, well stocked with swans. There are also fine plains, teeming with cranes . . .[36]

The final section on the Tartar wars is confidently ascribed to Rustichello, in most cases because it does not interest the modern critic: "we can safely see the hand of Rustichello in the conventional battle-pieces that largely fill the last chapter of the present work, with their monotonous harangues and their insistence on all the punctilio of 'Frankish' chivalry."[37] The thought, then, is to ascribe to Rustichello as many as possible of the parts of Marco Polo's book that the contemporary reader dislikes. These comments reflect the explicit distaste for chivalric literature in general and chivalric fiction in particular that pervades too many studies of *The Book of Marco Polo*.

The example of *praeteritio* cited earlier by Campbell seems to this reader altogether typical of romance. This is a form of torment often visited on readers by authors of romances. All too often the narrator informs us that many more adventures could have been described if time had permitted: "[But for tho

---

33 Latham, ed. and trans., *Travels of Marco Polo*, p. 33.

34 Ibid., p. 17.

35 *Meliadus*, f. ix(v): A la court du noble et puissant roy Artus vindrent. Et le trouerent en sa cite de Kamalot qui estoit en celluy temps la plus noble cite / la plus crainte & la plus riche que le roy Artus eust / fors la cite de Londres. Ces deux citez estoient en celluy temps les plus nobles citez du royaulme de Logres / mais *a la cite de Kamalot demouroit plus voulentiers* le roy: que en lieu que il eust / pource quelle estoit plus aisee et en lieu de soulas et deduit / en foresz et riuieres/ et a grant plante de fountaines et prayries."

36 Latham, ed. and trans., *Travels of Marco Polo*, p. 107. "Car sachiés que le grant kan demore a ceste cité en cest palais voluntieres, por ce que il hi a lac et rivier assez, la ou il demorent cesnes assez. Et encore il hi a biaus plain es quelz ont grues assez . . ." Marco Polo, *Il Milione*, ed. Benedetto, p. 61.

37 Latham, ed. and trans., *Travels of Marco Polo*, p. 18.

adventures were with wylde beestes] and nat in the q[uest of the Sancgreal, therfor the tale ma]kith here [no] menci[on therof; for it wolde be to longe to telle of alle tho adventures that befelle] them."[38] Such omissions are especially common in *Meliadus*, where the author prefers to refer readers to the prose *Tristan* rather than duplicate episodes, even when they are as essential as Tristan's climactic duel with the archvillain Nabon le Noir. The authenticating effect of these omissions is equivalent to Chaucer saying he does not know the name of one of his Canterbury pilgrims. This persistent habit of abridgement or cross-reference gives the reader a sense of the depth of the romance's fictional world, teeming with more adventures than the most energetic teller can relate.

The romance is not only open-ended, designed to accommodate as many sequels as its continuators care to attach. As this technique suggests, it is also open to addenda in the beginning or middle of the story. For the classically-minded reader this is a significant literary defect. It suggests that the romance is flawed by Aristotelian standards. Its beginning, middle, and end are all subject to revision. "There is no stability", as Malory once complained. This feature lays the romance open to critics like Campbell, who detect, in its insatiable appetite for new stories, sad evidence of human, especially masculine, greed. For the reader who enjoys romances, though, this open-ended quality becomes an attraction rather than a defect. It allows the romance to accommodate a variety of disparate material. As Giovambattista Giraldi Cinthio pointed out in 1549, this ability to welcome diverse ingredients from all points of the compass is one of the greatest charms of the genre.[39] This effect also makes the romance more "realistic" than genres built around artificial stopping points. Life on earth, after all, is a kind of "never-ending story"; all of human history is interconnected. The romances recognize this in a way that is impossible in other narrative genres.

Rustichello's book is in large part what Hollywood now calls a "prequel" that attaches itself to the prose *Tristan*. Written after both the prose *Lancelot* and *Tristan*, it devotes itself to the adventures of the fathers of Tristan, Arthur, Palamedes, Lancelot, and Erec. (With *Perceforest* an enterprising fourteenth-century author would move the history of Arthurian chivalry several genera-tions further backward, to the days of Alexander.) This approach accords with one of the romance's chief preoccupations, the question of the decline of chivalry, and of the rivalry between generations of knights. The initial episode, when the 120-year-old knight Branor le Brun challenges King Arthur's knights of the Round Table to joust and trounces them all soundly, announces this theme. Incidentally, the history of the dissemination of Rustichello's

---

38 Sir Thomas Malory, *Morte Darthur*, II.1013.

39 "I say this because diversity of actions carries with it the variety that is the spice of delight and so allows the writer a large field to use episodes, that is, pleasing digressions, and to bring in events that can never, without risk of censure, be brought into poems of a single action." Giraldi Cinthio, *On Romances*, trans. Henry L. Snuggs (Lexington, 1968), p. 23.

Compilation suggests that this was the episode that most interested its readers – as it most interested Rustichello himself, who seems to have inserted it at the beginning of *Gyron le Courtoys*. This motif is reinforced later when the degenerate Brunes sanz Pitié, the most anti-chivalric knight of the prose *Tristan*, descends into a cave where Fébus, Gyron's great ancestor, is entombed. Knights were really knights in Fébus' day: a hermit recounts Fébus' invasion and conquest of three pagan kings of western Britain and their attendant giants before his death from unrequited love. There is more than a suggestion here that the conquest of foreign lands, especially when they are non-Christian, is the knight's highest calling. In *Meliadus* the author remarks several times that if King Arthur had not been so fun-loving he could have conquered most of the world: "he would nevertheless have easily been able to conquer the whole world and subjected it to himself by force of knighthood if he had wanted to."[40]

As the work was reconfigured by its sixteenth-century Parisian publishers, both halves of Rustichello's *Compilation* were made to begin in traditional fashion, with the arrival of a strange knight to challenge King Arthur's court. This is the opening motif familiar to English-speaking readers from a variety of episodes in Malory's *Morte Darthur* and the first section of *Sir Gawain and the Green Knight*. Vérard's edition of *Gyron le Courtoys* begins with the ancient Branor le Brun returning to discomfit the knights of Camelot. *Meliadus de Leonnoys*, remarkably for the purposes of this study, introduces Camelot through the eyes of a Babylonian knight, one Esclabor. Esclabor enters Arthurian history as the father of Tristan's great rival, the Saracen knight Palamedes. Sent to Rome along with his family in tribute to the emperor, Esclabor displays a knack for rescuing rulers in distress. After interposing himself between the elderly emperor and a lion escaped from the imperial zoo, Esclabor is able to demand his freedom as a reward. This and the episode of the Good Knight Without Fear (*le bon chevalier sans peur*) in the Val de Servage help to establish the struggle for freedom as one of the most powerful themes of the *Compilation*. His experience of court intrigue leads Esclabor to forsake Rome for England; he hears that a young king, Arthur, has established a court that values knighthood above all else. In *Meliadus de Leonnoys* we approach Camelot for the first time from the viewpoint of a Babylonian traveler. The angle of entry is distinctive; while the author does not exploit the possibilities of the situation as melodramatically or satirically as a twentieth-century reader might expect, the importance of the idea deserves recognition.

The arrival of Esclabor and his brother at King Arthur's court is the mirror image of the Polo family's arrival at the court of the Great Khan. It is also notable that just as Marco Polo ingratiates himself with the Great Khan by learning the local languages, so Esclabor assimilates perfectly into the culture of Camelot: "both of them conversed and conducted themselves in the same manner as

---

[40] *Meliadus*, f. ii(r): "qui toutesfois eust bien peu tout le monde par force de cheualerie auoir conquis & mis en sa subiection sil eust voullu."

those of the household, speaking and chatting so politely that King Arthur valued them highly and believed in truth that they were Christians. "[41]

Latham follows Orlandini partway when he suggests that several of the interpolated stories in the *Book of Marco Polo* might also be Rustichello's own work. The tale of the sheikh of the Mountain and the assassins (also in Mandeville), the Magi, the *Roi Dor*, the legend of St Thomas of India, and other enlivening tales punctuate Marco Polo's travels.[42] In this connection it should be noted that Rustichello displays great fondness for the interpolated story in his *Compilation*. In *Gyron le Courtoys* I counted as many as twenty-seven interpolated stories. *Meliadus* often resorts to the same device. This predilection makes the term "compilation" even more accurate as a description of Rustichello's romance – a term that would also be applicable to *The Book of Marco Polo* if Rustichello could be identified as the supplier of the stories interpolated there. Both works take on some of the qualities of the frame-story, the *roman à tiroirs*. Like *The Seven Sages of Rome*, Chaucer's *Canterbury Tales* or *The Arabian Nights*, they imbed short stories in a large-scale narrative. This technique allows Rustichello to move back in time several generations. His work is a family romance in which the interpolated stories animate the hero's long-dead ancestors in competition with the knights of King Arthur's day. Gyron in his prime is set against Gyron the apprentice knight, who is told by his mentor Galeholt le Brun that he cannot expect to be any good before he attains the age of thirty-five. The layering of past on present action, the youth against the maturity of the same character, gives the *Compilation* the effect of a sophisticated frieze of interconnected stories. The stories also provide effective shifts from third-person to first-person narration.

The stories in *The Book of Marco Polo* offer a similar change of direction, supplying a variety of action, historical depth, and background to the contemporary personages Marco Polo encounters. The tale of the Old Man of the Mountain, also to be found in Mandeville, chimes with Polo's later description of the Great Khan's city of Quinsai "which means to say in French the city of heaven . . . *where so many pleasures may be found that one fancies himself in Paradise.*"[43] Both of these are accounts of earthly paradises of different kinds, one masterminded by an evil Saracen for the delusion of his henchmen, and one set forth as an enticement to the enterprising traveler to Cathay. There are miracle stories in which the Three Magi appear, excerpts from the life of St Thomas of India, and selections from the military history of the Tartars. The tendency to characterize the chivalric narratives as "monotonous" downplays

---

[41] *Meliadus*, f. x(r): "en telle maniere sentretiennent & demeinent comme font ceulx de la maison en parlant & deuisant si courtoisement tous deux que le roy Arthur les prisoit moult et cuidoit vraiement que ilz feussent crestiens."

[42] Latham, ed. and trans., *Travels of Marco Polo*, p. 18.

[43] Moule and Pelliot, ed. and trans., *Marco Polo*, p. 326; italicized addition from Ramusio and an earlier Latin version, Z.

their variety. The failed Tartar invasion of the fantastically rich island of Çipingu (Japan), the Great Khan's conflict with his uncle Naian, the exploits of King Caidu's militant and unvanquished daughter Aigiaruc detail altogether different sorts of adventures. They vary the account of Polo's travels and mercantile observations, which threatens to become equally "monotonous" and formulaic in its own way, with a contrasting layer of chivalric or evangelical experience. Rustichello deploys armies and saints across this quadrant of the globe in artful fashion to supplement the wanderings of the merchant hero.

The story of the Tartar princess might appeal in particular to the audience of the romances. Like Turandot, in some ways her descendant, Aigiaruc, "which means to say in French Shining Moon," refuses to marry any man who cannot defeat her in a contest.[44] Here the contest is not the traditional, decorous exchange of riddles, or a footrace like that of her Greek predecessor Atalanta, but a wrestling match. Aigiaruc does recall the Saracen princess of romance in her warlike abilities; she is little short of a giantess, as well as a great beauty. Her attributes recall the tradition of female physical prowess exemplified by Floripas of Bagnyon's *Histoire de Charlemagne*. They also look ahead to the woman warriors of the Italian romance epic. The story is most unconventional in that it does not end with the defeat and marriage of the princess. It does flirt with the standard conclusion. A handsome prince, son of the king of Pumar, accepts her challenge. He is so elegant, rich, and strong that her father suggests to Aigiaruc in private that she should allow herself to lose. She rejects this parental hint: "And I tell you that king Caidu caused his daughter to be told in secret that she should let herself be conquered. But his daughter said she wouldn't do that for anything in the world."[45] In fact "Shining Moon" does defeat the prince, much to the annoyance of her parents. We last hear of her serving her father in battle, dragging enemy warriors from their horses, "nor in all the press of combat did he have any knight more worthy than she." "Shining Moon" remains undefeated, whether in martial arts or in knightly warfare on horseback.[46]

This unconventional approach to the story of the pagan princess leaves the tale open-ended, defying all the reader's expectations. Just as Kublai Khan's army failed to conquer the gold of Japan, so the princes of Asia have failed to subdue the warrior princess. Rustichello writes of her in the present tense, leaving open the possibility that she might still be awaiting her destined bridegroom somewhere in the depths of Tartary. Both of these objects of attraction remain open to conquest. When Christopher Columbus set his sights on the fabled isle of Çipangu, he might not have been the first of Marco Polo's readers who hoped to step into this alluring, factual romance. These narratives invite

---

[44] Marco Polo, *Il Milione*, ed. Benedetto, p. 220: "que vaut a dire en françois lucent lune."

[45] Ibid., p. 221. "E si vos di que le roi Caidu fist dire a sa fille priveement qu'elle se devisse laisser vincere. Mes sa fille dist qu'ele ne le firoit por rien dou monde."

[46] Ibid., p. 222. "Ne en toute la meslee ne avoit chevaliers que plus hi vaillist d'ele."

chivalric as well as mercantile audience participation. Where the *Compilation of Rustichello da Pisa* remains a collection of past exploits loosely associated with Arthur's Britain, *The Book of Marco Polo* can be read as a guide to future adventures for the emperor, prince, and knight, as well as the merchant and the missionary. There are evil customs yet to eradicate, populations to subdue and convert, treasures and princesses yet to be won in the wilds of the East.

Rustichello's romances also explore darker aspects of the knight errant's experience. The stories they tell are as much a deterrent to travel as encouragement. *Gyron le Courtoys* ends in frustration and failure for all of its principal heroes, as the teller recognizes. By the end of this section of the narrative, the three best knights left alive in the world are prisoners, and one of them is also insane. Gyron is not only imprisoned but forced to witness the death of his mistress in childbirth, helpless to assist her. He loses custody of his infant son to his evil captor; the child is nourished in malice and cruelty. The printer of *Meliadus de Leonnoys* insists on ending his volume by relating the death of the hero. All of this runs quite contrary to any characterization of the romance in general as a genre given over to childish self-gratification. How it might have related to Rustichello's own, presumably later, experience of imprisonment remains a mystery.[47]

The struggle for freedom from servitude recurs throughout the *Compilation of Rustichello da Pisa*. The threat or the experience of enslavement provoke powerful reactions among the romance's main characters. In *Meliadus de Leonnoys*', the first main character, the Babylonian knight Esclabor, declares to the Roman emperor that freedom is the only reward he would value. "I am your serf (or perhaps slave?) in servitude. I do not wish to be one any longer. Set me free! All I ask of you is freedom."[48] The Val de Servage episode in *Gyron le Courtoys* preoccupies itself with the issue of enslavement. Every foreigner who enters the valley becomes the prisoner and servant of the giant Nabon le Noir. The Good Knight without Fear refuses to accept this fate with resignation. He claims that he would rather live in the forest as a Wild Man than subside into servitude. His entrapment through a maiden's deceit, starvation, and loss of freedom will eventually drive him insane. In a paradoxical twist, his insanity lends him a measure of freedom as it negates his prior identity as a Good Knight. He is released from his cell, since he is now regarded as a fool rather than a dangerous potential assassin. The madman's liberation from the constraints of chivalric morality allows him to take vengeance upon the maiden who betrayed him. His reversion to a life of savagery is more complete than he

---

[47] There is no indication that Rustichello worked on his romance in prison. He was presumably at liberty when he obtained access to Edward I's manuscript. We do owe a later romance, Sir Thomas Malory's *Morte Darthur*, to its author's imprisonment.

[48] *Meliadus*, f. iiii(r): "Vostre serf suis en seruage / ie ne le veux plus estre faictes moy franc / ie ne vous demande que franchise."

envisioned on his arrival in the valley – he also kills a boy who mocks him, and becomes very good at throwing stones, rendering the castle uninhabitable.[49]

Readers of the printed version of Rustichello's *Compilation* would return to the Val de Servage at the end of *Meliadus*, when Tristan finally kills the giant and frees his captives. The actual duel is omitted, as it is to be found in "the book that has been made of the deeds of Tristan of Leonnoys."[50] Instead, *Meliadus* offers the combat of Lancelot and Palamedes against Nabon's messengers. This is followed by a kind of chivalric detective story: Gyron, Danain, Lac, and the Good Knight without Fear are held in a secret prison, known only to the dead giant and his near relations, so that a quest must be undertaken for their rediscovery. The conclusion seems to be the work of the printer, who fails to make much of the release of the heroes of *Gyron le Courtois*. Rustichello's text did mention that the captive knights would be released in a decade or so, but it left them imprisoned. The best knights of this chivalric world wind up as frustrated beings in a state of suspended animation.

Of the many tales that make up *Gyron le Courtoys*, the "valley of servitude" (val de servage) cries out most loudly to be connected to the history of exploration. The romance's climactic adventures in the "valley of false pleasure" (faulx soulas) and the "valley of anger" (courroux) might be read with equal plausibility as allegories of the explorer's experience. Gyron's best friend and nemesis Danain le Roux, newly reconciled with him, chooses the pathway to false pleasure at an ominous crossroads. Both roads lead to certain death, the inscription on the mandatory (and minatory) stone ("perron") at the entrance warns them. "For if you wish to turn aside here, you will never lose your way, but in one or the other [path] you'll die."[51] Initially apprehensive, as the climate changes from winter to spring, Danain believes he has found paradise.[52] Indeed, the paradise he finds bears some resemblance to the domain of the Old Man of the Mountain as described in *The Book of Marco Polo*.

> He had had made in a valley between two mountains the biggest and most beautiful garden that was ever seen, planted with all the finest fruits in the world and containing the most splendid mansions and palaces that were ever seen, ornamented with gold and with likenesses of all that is beautiful on earth, and also four conduits, one flowing with wine, one with milk, one with honey, and one with water. There were fair ladies and damsels, the loveliest in the world, unrivalled at playing every sort of instrument and at singing and dancing. And he gave his men to understand that this garden was Paradise . . . When they awoke and found themselves in there and saw all the things I have told you of, they believed they were really in Paradise. And the

---

49 *Gyron*, cccxi(r).
50 *Meliadus*, f. ccxxviii(v).
51 *Gyron*, f. ccxxv(r): "Car se tu ty veux desvoyer / Jamais jour ne te desuoyeras / ains en lung ou lautre mourras."
52 *Gyron*, f. cccxxvi(v): "celluy lieu a son ymaginacion est ung droit paradis terrestre."

ladies and damsels stayed with them all the time, singing and making music for their delight and ministering to all their desires.[53]

On first entering the valley of *faulx soulas*, Danain first experiences the change in climate, from winter to May, with grass, trees and singing birds: "les oyseletz y alloient chantans darbre en arbre." Then he comes to the first of the two towers, the fairest he has ever seen in his life: "car elle estoit dehors ouuree dor et painte a dames et a damoyselles." Prefiguring Christine de Pizan's City of Ladies, this "marvellous" tower is painted with images of women, not a male figure among them. Danain hears the sound of a harp, and the voice of a maiden singing from a pavilion alongside the tower. He gives his horse to his squire, who warns him to be careful – he's a long way from home. Danain pays no attention. He enters the tent and confronts a stunning maiden in bed, chaperoned by four others, all dressed like queens. Danain takes off his helmet to speak to them. The progressive loss of identity of the knight is completed as he becomes so enraptured with the beautiful maiden in the bed, Aube (Dawn), that he forgets everything in the world except her.[54] The maidens instruct him that if he wants the pleasure of their company, "partir a nostre soulas," he must first defeat one of their enemies. Every day's act of prowess is rewarded by a return to the ladies' society.[55]

In both tales the deluded young warrior finds himself in a valley full of fair maidens adept in music, whose charms seduce him into undertaking any perilous mission in order to return to their company. Instead of the Old Man, "le Viel," the fiendish Saracen mastermind of the assassins, *Gyron le Courtoys* depicts an ongoing war of the sexes between sons and daughters of neighboring knights. Thanks to their fathers' rash vows, none of them can marry until the other side has been vanquished. The valley's "forte advanture" – the "strong adventure" – involves the daily fording of a hazardous river, a different kind of "passage perilleux" than the one Gyron encountered earlier in the romance. Gyron's is a "passage of arms" that involves jousting against twenty-one knights. Danain's literal "passage" of the river looks forward to the "passage

---

53 Latham, ed. and trans., *Travels of Marco Polo*, pp. 70–71; Marco Polo, *Il Milione*, ed. Benedetto, p. 33. "Il avoit fait fer entres deus monagnes, en une valé, le plus grant jardin et les plus biaus que jamés fust veu. Il hi a de tous buen fruit dou monde. Et qui avoit fait fer les plus belles maison et les plus belles maison et les plus biaus palais que unques fuissent veu: car il estoient dorés et portrait de toutes les belles coses dou monde. Et encore hi avoit fait faire conduit, que por tel coroit vin, et por tel lait, et por tel mel, et por tel eive. Il hi avoit dame et dameseles, les plus bielles dou monde, les quelz sevent soner de tuit enstrumenti et chantent et calorent miaus que autres femes. Et faisoit le Vielz entendre a ses homes que cel jardin estoit parais. . . . Et quant les jeunes estoient desvoilés, et il se trovent laiens et il voient toutes cestes couses que je vos ai dit, il croient estre en parais voiramant. Et les dames et les dameseles demouroient tout jor con elz sonant et cantant et faisant grant soulas . . ."

54 *Gyron*, f. cccxxxv(r).

55 *Gyron*, f. ccccxxxiii(v).

perilleux" by sea that figures among Gadifer de la Salle's adventures in the Canary Islands, to be discussed in the next chapter.[56] Once Danain has crossed the river, he must fight as the ladies' champion against a defender of a tower populated by knights. His ultimate defeat only forces Danain to change sides and fight against the next arrival.

Another critical difference between these two deadly paradises is that in *Gyron le Courtoys* the maidens are given a chance to lament their own imprisonment. In both tales they are entrapped as much or more than the warriors they seduce, but only in Rustichello's romance are they given voices with which to object. "Ah, sir knight, have pity upon us; we are all captives."[57] The readers of Marco Polo will never know whether the women employed by the Old Man of the Mountain were happy temptresses or desperate slaves. Their view of the situation is never taken into account.

Gyron's descent into the "valley of anger" (*val de courroux*) begins with a torrent of unprovoked verbal abuse directed at the most courteous knight of his day from the safety of a tower. This treatment arouses Gyron's own anger, as the lord of the castle notes with some amusement: "do these little words rile you?"[58] Here, courtesy is a handicap. Gyron spares the lord of the tower, not because he likes his attitude, but on chivalric principles: "I should not consider your evil nature, but the courtesy that knights should do and have."[59] When the defeated lord invites him to stay overnight, swearing by "the faith he owes to all the knights errant in the world" that Gyron will come to no harm, Gyron accepts his invitation. This is, of course, a trap. His hosts only affect marvellous courtesy until they can separate Gyron from his armor and capture him in his sleep. Here and elsewhere in the romance, chivalric morality turns against its practitioner.

All of these stories explore the limits of the chivalric code. They question the usefulness of chivalric principles to their practitioners in a world where many others seem to have no principles at all. Chivalric morality, represented by maxims throughout the *Compilation*, leads these knights to tackle impossible problems, risking their lives for total strangers of dubious moral character. The

---

56 Compare the *Pas Perilleux* in René of Anjou's *Le Livre du Cueur d'Amours Espris* of 1457, which is both a "dangerous crossing" and a passage of arms where the Knight Heart encounters the Black Knight *Soussy*, Care or Trouble, on a rickety bridge over the Stream of Tears. This scene is represented in two of the elegant miniatures of MS Vienna Cod. Vind. 2597, folios 18v and 21v, reproduced in *King René's Book of Love*, introduction and commentaries by F. Unterkircher (1975; New York, 1980). The perilous river crossing had been a staple of romance at least since Chrétien's *Chevalier de la Charrette*, where Lancelot and Gawain experienced variations on this theme, with Lancelot's crossing of the infamous sword bridge and Gawain finding himself trapped at a ford.

57 *Gyron*, f. cccxxxv(r): "Haa sire cheualier ayez mercy de nous / nous sommes toutes emprisonnees."

58 *Gyron*, f. cccxxxix(r): "vous courroussez vous de ces petites parolles?"

59 *Gyron*, f. cccxxxix(r): "Je ne doys mye regarder a la vilenie de vous / mais a la courtoysie que chevaliers doyuent faire et avoir."

Good Knight without Fear claims that he would never have trusted the maiden who fooled him if he had ever done wrong to any woman. The knights of Rustichello's *Compilation* confront men and women who play the system for their own advantage. When a knight faces a moral quandary the consequences of his decision to intervene remain uncertain. For every good deed that brings the hero glory, another results in peril and embarrassment. Should Gyron fight to free the knight and lady he finds bound to a tree in their underclothes in the depth of winter? Should he persist after being told of the knight's criminal record as parricide and seducer of his brother's wife? Being Gyron, he does release the captives. Since this is the world of Rustichello's *Compilation*, it is not long before the rescuer finds himself and his lady friend tied to a tree in their turn, of course by the very knight he rescued.

In spite of such experiences, the knights of Rustichello still regard themselves as bound to take up arms against evil customs. A reader bearing this in mind might note with interest the number of peculiar and most unchristian customs that Marco Polo describes in his book. The volume might even be read as a compendium of evil customs to be eradicated by future conquerors. To its regal and courtly readers, this element of the text offers a variety of chivalrous excuses for invasion.

Throughout the *Compilation* the forest maintains its role as the primary backdrop for the action. Events of importance do not often take place at court. For the most part the knights of this romance are to be found prowling through the shrubbery in search of adventures, tournaments, ladies to kidnap, kidnapped ladies, or marauding giants. While the romancer revels in descriptions of the glories of courtly life, some effort is spent on undercutting the prestige of the court. Both printed texts begin at courts that are about to lose their prestige. In *Meliadus*, the Roman court is in decline, and the emperor is old. Intrigue and assassination plots seethe beneath its ceremonious surface. When we first see King Arthur's court in *Gyron le Courtoys*, the ancient knight Branor le Brun has just arrived to humiliate the knights of the Round Table. At the end of the volume, it is Gyron's wicked son who demolishes the best King Arthur has to offer. Only the Saracen Palamedes saves Camelot from total defeat. The vast bulk of the volume follows Gyron and his friends through the woods in pursuit of their adventures; it is one long journey. The knight errant is by profession a wanderer, a long way from home. Danain le Roux's squire tells him so in the Valley of False Pleasure: "for you are here all alone and in a strange land. Remember that you are now too far from Maloanc."[60]

The Book of Marco Polo would seem, initially, to take the opposite approach. Marco Polo describes the court of Kublai Khan at the height of its glory. We do still notice the ruined palaces of past civilizations as we approach the Khan, and

---

[60] *Gyron*, f. cccxxvii(r): "car vous estes ycy tout seul et en estrange contree / Souviengne vous que vous estes a cestuy point trop loing de Maloanc."

within Cathay itself.[61] There is a sense that however marvellous the present state of things, the greatest splendors of Asia may be things of the past. Ramusio's revised Latin text intensifies this effect by noting that the Great Khan's death prevents the Polos themselves from returning to Cathay: "And while Masters Nicolau, Mafeu, and Marc were making this journey they learnt how the great Khan was cut off from this life, and this took away from them all hope of being able to return any more to those parts."[62]

In both works the distancing of the principal court in time or space enhances the wonders of the past at the expense of the present. The technique is designed to reverse our perspective. If we think of King Arthur's knights as far, far better than our humdrum contemporaries, it might seem logical that Arthur's father's generation should have been greater still. The underlying model of history is one of continual decline from a state of near-perfection. This chivalric account of human affairs reflects entropy rather than progress. On a practical level, this approach glorifies Rustichello's characters and his book. An upstart competitor, it challenges the prose *Tristan*, the Lancelot-Grail cycle, and the other grand romances of its own century by presenting itself as a chronicle of a still more ancient and superior brand of chivalry. In the same way the late Great Khan's faraway court makes any mere European court look small. One wonders if that could have been the effect of the text on the "emperors" Rustichello addressed.

Literal giants are prominent in these texts, as knights' opponents in Rustichello's romance and also as wonders for the Polos. The prehistory of Britain as it had been developed by Geoffrey of Monmouth and his more inventive successors postulated an early race of British giants. They were not alone. The tantalizing biblical line "There were giants in the earth in those days" can be read as a compliment to the achievements of past civilizations, as the verse concludes, "mighty men which were of old, men of renown."[63] It can also be read as a statement of fact. As mentioned before, the tendency of the Old English poets to describe past architectural triumphs as *eald enta geweorc*, "the ancient handiwork of giants," most explicit in *The Ruin*, shows the Anglo-Saxons marvelling at the monumental structures left by the Romans as projects only giants could have completed. In Rustichello's romance, the pagan kings of early Britain are alternately served by local giants, and persecuted by them. Scattered giants survive as tyrants up to the days of King Arthur. We are also given to understand that the knights of olden days, like Gyron's great ancestor Fébus, were themselves gigantic in stature. Logically, as his opponents grow to superhuman proportions, the hero who confronts them must grow in prestige if not in physical size. Combat between warriors of unequal size has an interminable history in heroic literature: David and Goliath, Beowulf and Grendel find many counterparts all across the globe. This element recurs among Marco

---

[61] As at Balc, in Moule and Pelliot, ed. and trans., *Marco Polo*, p. 44.
[62] Ibid., p. 19.
[63] Genesis VI.4.

Polo's reminiscences, as in the Tartar princess who is little short of gigantic, or the natives of Zanzibar who, in the French text "are so stout and so large-limbed that they seem giants."[64]

We still lack a large-scale English-language study of the *Compilation of Rustichello da Pisa*, in manuscript or its printed editions, though Løseth and Lathuillière offer important overviews in French.[65] An amplified discussion of what a detailed study of Rustichello's fictional world can do for the *Book of Marco Polo* is also much to be desired. This preliminary study may begin to suggest some basic lines of inquiry. The dual purpose of the chapter is, first, to attempt a chivalric reading of *The Book of Marco Polo*, since the chivalric readership of his volume has been rather left out of the discussion. Secondly, it tries to demonstrate how such a chivalric romance of Rustichello da Pisa can serve as a guide to the concerns and preoccupations of this key group of readers – the "Lords Emperors and Kings, Dukes and Marquesses, Counts, [and] Knights" evoked by Rustichello as the primary audience of his writings.[66]

---

[64] Moule and Pelliot, ed. and trans., *Marco Polo*, p. 192; italics from P omitted.
[65] Eilert Løseth, *Le roman en prose de Tristan, le roman de Palamède, et la compilation de Rusticien de Pise: analyse critique d'après les manuscrits de Paris* (Paris, 1891); Roger Lathuillière, *Guiron le Courtois, Etude de la tradition manuscrite et analyse critique*, Publications Romanes et Françaises, LXXXVI (Geneva, 1966).
[66] Moule and Pelliot, ed. and trans., *Marco Polo*, p. 73.

CHAPTER FOUR

Gadifer de la Salle: native kings and traitor knights

L'entencion de Gadifer est d'essaier d'ouvrir le chemin.
(Gadifer's intent is to try to open the path.)[1]

FELIPE FERNÁNDEZ-ARMESTO HAS stressed the importance of the conquest of the Canary Islands for understanding European attitudes to exploration. "Apart from Genoese surrogacy, it is the Canary Islands that are the key to everything that is most spectacular in the rise of Castile. Allegretto Allegretti thought that America *was* 'another Canary Island'."[2] That archipelago remained a primary goal for Henry the Navigator, who never attained it, and, later, for Ferdinand and Isabella, whose agents did not complete their conquest until 1496. As Fernández-Armesto suggests, the history of this struggle may be even more useful for testing the links between chivalry and exploration, romance and exploration narrative, the crusader knight and the conquistador. The metamorphosis they convey resembles the "morphing" effect of computer-aided animation. One picture melts into another. The reader watches as the knight turns explorer and then becomes a curious hybrid of slave trader and missionary. *Le Canarien*, the chronicle of the French expedition of 1402, anticipates most of the motives, reactions, and expedients that would challenge Christopher Columbus ninety years later. An attentive rereading of *Le Canarien* shows the chivalric imagination defining exploration as a knightly adventure. It merits closer study.

The expedition of 1402 had as its French protagonists three notable figures: the partners Gadifer de la Salle (c.1350–c.1422) and Jean de Béthencourt (1362–1422) and their rebellious subordinate, Bertin de Berneval. Each represents one aspect of the problem.

Gadifer de la Salle is notable as an eminent fourteenth-century knight whose biography reveals literary interests and chivalric preoccupations. The La Salles must have been a literary family. Gadifer and several of his relatives bear names

---

1 *Le Canarien*, III.107. All references to *Le Canarien*, unless otherwise noted, are taken from Alejandro Cioranescu and Elias Serra Rafols, eds., *Le Canarien*, in *Fontes rerum Canariarum* (3 vols., La Laguna de Teneriffe, 1959). (Hereafter referred to as *Le Canarien*.)
2 Felipe Fernández-Armesto, *Before Columbus: Exploration and Colonisation from the Mediterranean to the Atlantic, 1229–1492* (Basingstoke and London, 1987), p. 221; cf. pp. 7, 169–222.

taken from a variety of works of chivalric fiction, some *romans d'antiquité*, and some Arthurian. Gadifer was himself a reader who brought books with him on his voyage to the Canary Islands. His name crops up among the members of the Court of Love cultivated by Charles VI and his uncles and regents the dukes of Bourbon and Burgundy.[3] Gadifer had by the age of fifty-two or so established a solid knightly reputation, though not one altogether without blemish. He had seen extensive military service as a partisan of France, specifically of the duke of Berry, later of Louis, duke of Anjou, whom he served in Italy, and later still of Louis, duke of Orleans (1372–1407). One of his prized chivalric possessions, the collar of Louis' chivalric order of the Porc-épic or Camail, granted to him in 1400, was stolen in the course of his Canarian expedition.[4] Gadifer is reported to have engaged in crusading ventures with the Teutonic Knights in Prussia on at least two, perhaps three occasions, once around 1378, and again in 1390–91, with Boucicaut (possibly alongside the future Henry IV of England). Between these ventures he served under the duke of Bourbon at the siege of Al-Mahdiya in North Africa in the summer of 1390, and with the Hospitallers at Rhodes. Gadifer's high reputation among his contemporaries partly stemmed from this international crusading activity. Antoine de la Sale, who may or may not have been a relative, makes Gadifer the bearer of the banner of the Virgin Mary in the Prussian crusading episode of his romance *Petit Jehan de Saintré* of about 1455.[5] A banner of the Virgin accompanies Gadifer on his

---

3   Maurice Keen, "Gadifer de la Salle: A Late Medieval Knight Errant," in *The Ideals and Practice of Medieval Knighthood: Papers from the First and Second Strawberry Hill Conferences*, ed. Christopher Harper-Bill and Ruth Harvey (Woodbridge, 1986), p. 79.

4   For Louis of Orléans' "pseudo-order" of the Porc-épic or Camail, see D'A. J. D. Boulton, *The Knights of the Crown: The Monarchical Orders of Knighthood in Later Medieval Europe, 1325–1520* (Woodbridge, 1987), pp. 274, 329, and Hélie de Brémond d'Ars-Migré, *Les Chevaliers du Porc-Epic ou du Camail, 1394–1498* (Mâcon, 1938). One of the great moments of the *porc-épic* in pageantry came at the coronation of Louis XII in 1499. See Theodore Godefroy, *Le Cérémonial Français* (Paris, 1649), I.241–45. Porcupines run rampant all over the décor throughout the event. The banquet ends with a float bearing a fair maiden and a gigantic mechanical porcupine that raised its bristles at the spectators, "vn grand Porc espic, monté sur vne terrasse, qui par engin se remuoit & herissoit ses plumes." For Gadifer de la Salle's Teutonic expeditions, see Keen, "Gadifer de la Salle." Paravicini gives Gadifer a third visit to Prussia, with the questionable date of 1357.

5   Antoine de la Sale, *Little John of Saintré*, trans. Irvine Gray (London, 1931), p. 233. For René II, duke of Lorraine's use of a banner of the Virgin in his campaign against Charles the Bold of Burgundy in 1476–77, see Philippe Contamine, *War in the Middle Ages*, trans. Michael Jones (Oxford, 1984), pp. 300–01. On the increasing reliance on standards to replace heraldic banners and pennons in the later fifteenth century, see Malcolm Vale, *War and Chivalry: Warfare and Aristocratic Culture in England, France and Burgundy at the End of the Middle Ages* (London, 1981), pp. 97–98, citing Contamine's *Guerre, état, et société*, pp. 675–6. Keen observes that Antoine de la Sale was "a knight, a great traveller, an expert in heraldry and the lore of the tourney, and the bastard son of one of the most famous (or perhaps rather infamous) *routier* captains of his age, Hawkwood's great rival, Bernardino de la Sale" (Keen, *Chivalry* (New Haven, 1984), p. 208). As a knightly author

voyage to the Canary Islands in the frontispiece of MS BL Egerton 2709. Such a banner is also borne before the Christian army at Al-Mahdiya in Froissart's account of the duke of Bourbon's expedition.[6]

Jean de Béthencourt, Gadifer's partner in the Canarian expedition, was a Norman noble, ten years his junior. He knew Gadifer as a fellow member of the duke of Orléans' household. Both of them seem to have taken part in the duke of Anjou's foray into Italy, and they were both in the duke of Bourbon's army before Al-Mahdiya. Béthencourt was the chief investor in the project. As Cioranescu remarks, he took upon himself the financial and political aspects of the enterprise. Gadifer's version of the chronicle suggests that Béthencourt was physically incapacitated in some manner that limited his martial capabilities.

In the earlier text of *Le Canarien* Béthencourt plays the role of the false friend. Sent to collect fresh supplies and reinforcements from Spain, he made use of his connections at the Castilian court to cut a deal for himself. In return for sovereignty over the Canary Islands, he did homage to the king, ignoring both his partner Gadifer and his own mentally erratic sovereign, the king of France. Béthencourt anticipated Columbus in the contractual approach he took to his future conquests. Like Columbus, he wanted to secure for himself a position as ruler of his new domain, a fixed share of the proceeds of trade with the islands, and the support of a powerful overlord. Furthermore, like Columbus, he took the precaution of ensnaring these rash royal promises in writing. The later history of Béthencourt's claim to the Canary Islands involves his nephew Mathieu's misgovernment and Mathieu's sleazy second career reselling his own and his uncle's claims of sovereignty in various courtly markets. The Béthencourt text transforms Gadifer's scouting report into a family romance chronicling the tribulations of the heirs of Jean as conqueror. The tale of the man who would be king becomes a romance of disinheritance

In *Le Canarien*, Bertin de Berneval, the "man of good diligence" so highly recommended to the principal partners of the expedition, turns into the chief villain of the tale. His descent from explorer's assistant to pirate and slave trader heightens the drama of *Le Canarien*. Disenchanted with the realities of life on

who wrote one of the key romances of his period, he should be set beside Joanot Martorell and Sir Thomas Malory.

6   Jean Froissart, *Chronicle*, trans. Sir John Bourchier, Lord Berners (6 vols., London, 1901–03), V.358–441. (Hereafter referred to as Froissart, *Chronicle*.) "And bycause that the great galees coulde nat aproche nere to the lande, the men yssued out in bottes, and toke lande and folowed the baner of Our Lady." "The duke of Burbone, who was as chefe of the Christen armye there, was lodged in the myddes of his company ryght honorably, his baner displayed, poudred, full of floure du lyces, with an ymage of Our Lady in the myddes, and a scochynne with the armes of Burbone under the fete of the ymage." V.401. Gadifer's banner is reproduced in *Le Canarien*, III.12–13. For background on the "gradual westward shift of the crusading trajectory," see Fernández-Armesto, *Before Columbus*, pp. 121–48. St Louis had turned his crusade of 1269 in this direction, rather to the disgust of Joinville.

I. Gadifer de la Salle sets sail for the Canary Islands under the banner of the Virgin, 1402 (British Library, MS Egerton 2709).
By permission of the British Library Board

the isle of Lanzarote, he attempts to recoup his losses by robbing and marooning his fellows, offering to trade some captured natives to the shipmen to pay for his passage back to civilization. For the narrators, Bertin is not merely a betrayer of all the chivalric values of honor among knights. He also becomes a Judas to the islanders. In *Le Canarien*, Bertin de Berneval plays the well-established role of the traitor knight to the hilt.

Jean de Béthencourt and Gadifer de la Salle seem to have ventured south to Africa for the first time as part of Louis II of Bourbon's expedition to Barbary in 1390.[7] This mission against the port of Al-Mahdiya was organized by the Genoese in an effort to eliminate a pirate stronghold. It is worth looking at Jean Froissart's account of the event to see how that pre-eminent chronicler of fourteenth-century chivalry evaluates the enterprise. For two broiling months a Christian crusading army of French and English troops camped before the city Froissart considered an African Calais. (In fact, Froissart has difficulty with the name of the place, and it comes out in Lord Berners' Tudor English translation as "Aufryke in Barbary.")

> For on that coste it is the chiefe key of Barbary and of the realmes that foloweth: first, the realme of Aufrike, of Mallorques, and of Bougy. And if God of his grace wyll consent that we maye wyn this cytie of Aufrike, all the Sarazyns wyll trymble, to the realme of Liby and Sury, so that all the worlde shall speke therof; and by the ayde of other christen realmes and ysles marchyng nere to Aufrike, we shall always be refreshed with vitayls and newe men: for this is a common voiage. For every man wyll desyre dayly to do dedes of armes, and specially on Goddes enemyes.[8]

Both Béthencourt and Gadifer de la Salle received financial aid from the duke of Orléans to enable them to participate in this enterprise. Béthencourt achieved a mention as one of the ranking officers whose banners were displayed before the Christian encampment.[9] In the end, the crusaders were defeated by the climate, first the heat, and then their fear of the approaching winter with its storms. "The great heate and brinnynge of the sonne dyd put the Crysten men to great payne and traveyle, for whan they were in harnesse, by reason of the heate, it brente them within their armure."[10] Like Danain le Roux in *Gyron le Courtoys*, they were emphatically not in their own country. The inhabitants of the port for the most part sensibly refused to come out and face the crusading army in a pitched battle, preferring to harass them with hit-and-run attacks or by hurling projectiles from a safe distance. *Le Canarien* seems to refer to this experience, common to both Gadifer and Jean de Béthencourt, when it

---

7 Fernandez-Armesto, *Before Columbus*, pp. 148, 174–75. Duke Louis II of Bourbon (1337–1410) was Charles VI's maternal uncle.

8 Froissart, *Chronicle*, trans. Berners, V.397.

9 Ibid., V.402: "the lorde of Bertencourt with penon."

10 Ibid., V.410; cf. pp. 428–29. On the role of the seasons in medieval warfare, see P. Contamine, *War in the Middle Ages*, trans. Michael Jones (Oxford, 1984), pp. 227–28.

mentions how those who were "before Africa" ("devant Afrique") – using Froissart's term for Al-Mahdiya – "saw the best and fairest of all their forces, and it is something to be much feared in battle, folk armed with projectiles, especially in those parts, for one cannot be so heavily armored as here in our country, on account of the land, which is somewhat hotter."[11] The recollection sums up the French experience of the siege.

The one warrior present who made a name for himself by his individual prowess was a young Berber, called by Froissart "Agadingor Dolyferne." The element "Olyferne" recalls Nebuchadnezzar's general Holofernes, decapitated by Judith. Agadingor is attractively depicted as a lover and chivalrous gentleman. He would be a most suitable opponent for any Christian knight, but he is maddeningly elusive.

> he was always well mounted on a redy and a lyght horse: it semed whan the horse ranne, that he dyd flye in the ayre. The knyght semed to be a good man of armes by his dedes: he bare alwayes of usage thre fedred dartes, and ryght well he coulde handle them, and acordynge to their custome he was clene armed with a longe whyte towell aboute his heed: his aparell was blacke, and his owne coloure browne, and a good horseman. The Crysten men sayde they thought he dyd suche dedes for the love of some yonge lady of his countrey . . .[12]

Elements of this description find echoes in Joanot Martorell's portrait of the king of the Canary islands, to be discussed in the final section of this chapter.

Agadingor's proposal for a duel of honor between ten Saracens and ten Christians is cheerfully accepted by a French squire, to the annoyance of the leaders of the expedition, who object that they were not consulted in advance. In fact, it comes to nothing – perhaps, Froissart suggests, because the presence of a Christian army in full battle array deters the Saracens from making their appearance. Instead, the Christians stand broiling in their armor for some time, before they give vent to their frustrations in an ill-advised attack on the city. The event brings out the thirst to achieve personal distinction that overpowers the crusading army. It also betrays the need and desire of those in charge to dampen chivalric initiative where it threatens to subvert their authority. International chivalry is a force harnessed here by the Genoese for political and economic ends. Its nature made it difficult to control.

In another notable episode, the citizens of Al-Mahdiya send their interpreter (in Tudor English, a "trucheman") to ask why they should be the objects of a crusade. They are accustomed to skirmishes over trade with their perennial

---

11 Froissart, *Chronicle*, trans. Berners, III.97–99. "Virent le meilleur et le plus bel de toute leur puissance, et c'est une chose qui moult doit estre doubtée en bataille, que gens de trait, espiciaument en ces marchez par dessa; car on ne puet mie estre si fort armé comme se c'estoit en nous marchez, pour le pais, qui est un po plus chaut."

12 Ibid., V.404–05.

rivals, the Genoese, but why should this concern the knights of France and England? After much consultation among the leadership, a comprehensive religious justification is proffered:

> bycause the sonne of God, called Jesu Chryst, and trewe profyte, by their lyne and generacyon was put to deth and crucyfyed: and bycause they had judged their God to deth without tytell or reason, therfore they wolde have amendes, and punysshe that trespace and false judgement that they of their lawe had made; and also bycause they beleved nat in the holy baptyme, and are ever contrary to their faythe and lawe; nor also bycause they beleved nat in the Virgyn Mary, mother to Jhesu Cryst: for thes causes and other, they sayd, they toke the Sarazyns and all their secte for their enemyes, and sayd howe they wolde revenge the dispytes that they had doone, and dayly do to their God and Crysten faythe.[13]

This reply is received with derision, as "nothynge reasonable, for it was the Jewes that put Chryst to dethe, and nat they." The crusaders' defence of their own actions ignores any economic motive. The Genoese and their difficulties with the Barbary pirates are brushed aside as a motive for action. The knights of France and England depict themselves as single-minded holy warriors. It seems equally clear that the crusading leadership are determined to conflate non-Christian groups into a single category, all deserving of the same divinely ordained punishment. While the political and economic aspects of the expedition are apparent to the historian and his readers, not to mention the besieged townsfolk of Al-Mahdiya, the duke of Bourbon and his army insist on presenting themselves as holy warriors pursuing the *"vengeance Jesu-Christ."* When they returned to Europe, they could report that the Virgin Mary miraculously shielded them from the ambushes of their cunning opponents on at least one occasion.

> As the Sarazyns aproched, they sawe sodenly before them a great company of ladyes and damosels, all in whyte colour, and one in especyall who in beauty without comparison exceded all the other, and there was borne before her a baner all of whyte and reed within. With this sight the Sarazyns were so abasshed, that they lacked spyrite and force to go any further . . .[14]

The banner of the Virgin reappears here as a powerful sign of divine protection. In this miraculous episode the Virgin herself follows a banner. Given this context, the identification of Gadifer as the Virgin's standard-bearer in Antoine de la Sale makes him a potent figure. It is an emphatic emblem of the author's approval.

Froissart's presentation of the duke of Bourbon's expedition to Barbary is itself full of interest. The historian does not offer a continuous narrative.

---

[13] Ibid., V.407.
[14] Ibid., V.407–08.

Instead, he punctuates his account of the two-month siege with two other chivalric events. The first is the tale of a parallel siege in France, leading to the capture of the robber knight "Aymerygott Marcell."[15] The second reports on the earl of Ostrevant's participation in a tournament held at London by Richard II. Froissart closes his narrative of the voyage to Barbary with the king of France's complex response to the crusaders' report. All of these events are linked by their associations with the long conflict between France and England that is Froissart's principal subject.

The first interruption, the tale of Aymerygott Marcell, starts out as a swash-buckling conflict between the renegade knight and the French authorities. It turns into an exercise in chivalric psychology and political influence. Aymerygott, a Limousin, exemplifies for a number of modern scholars the abuse inflicted on France by the Companies. At the outset of the episode, three captains noted for taking base advantage of the Hundred Years War to pillage the countryside must decide whether or not to abide by a truce with England. One complies, one pretends to comply, and the third, Aymerygott, conducts business as usual. Froissart, who is never shy about supplying dialogue, dramatizes his reasoning: "On a tyme he said to his olde companyons: 'Sirs, there is no sporte nor glory in this worlde amonge men of warre, but to use suche lyfe as we have done in tyme past; what a joy was it to us whan we rode forthe at adventure, and somtyme founde by the way a ryche priour or marchaunt . . .' "[16] In Froissart, even the robber knights envisage themselves as "living the life of kings" in a world of knightly performance – "and they called themselfes adventurers."[17] Later on, when he is besieged by the authorities, Aymerygott sends word to England, in an effort to get Richard II to object to the French action against him as an infringement of the truce. In the end, his uncle's disregard of his command not to venture out of the castle loses Aymerygott his stronghold, and his cousin's desire to curry favor with the French establishment loses him his head. For Froissart, Aymerygott serves as an example of a knight who might have been "a man of great valure," had he chosen the path of virtue. Aymerygott is admired for his abilities. The seductive power of the "lifestyle of the rich and famous" is acknowledged as a factor in his corruption. Still, the contrast in character and fate between the knights who go to Barbary and this one who stays home is pointed by the conscientious historian himself.[18] For Froissart, there are clear distinctions to be drawn between the "adventurer" and the crusader.

Froissart's second interpolated story depicts a London tournament attended

15 His name is Merigot Marchès in Keen, *Chivalry,* pp. 230–31; cf. H. Duplés-Agier, ed., *Registre Criminel du Chatelet de Paris, 1389–92* (Paris, 1861–64), II, p. 210; cf. G. W. Coopland's note to Philippe de Mézières, *Le Songe du Viel Pelerin* (Cambridge, 1969), II.98.

16 Froissart, *Chronicle,* ed. Berners, V.365

17 Ibid., V.365.

18 Ibid., V.396.

by the young earl of Ostrevaunt, William of Hainault. The attentive reader may have noted that the earl's banner waved over the Christian camp at Al-Mahdiya, borne by a delegation from Hainault. The earl himself was back home. The center of interest for Froissart here, besides the fascination of the elegant chivalric performance he describes, is the political fallout occasioned by the earl's decision to cross the channel. The young nobleman's decision to visit his "English cousins," and, worse yet, to accept the Order of the Garter from Richard II, makes him an object of suspicion in Paris. The French are under no illusions regarding the use of orders of knighthood to build alliances, though Froissart finds it prudent to suggest that there may be more paranoia than real grounds for suspicion in this case.

Froissart concludes with the Christian army's return to Europe. The crusaders proceed to suggest that the king of France follow up with an expedition of his own to North Africa. "Syr, ye have devocyon and great ymagynacion to go over the see, to fyght agaynst the infydels, and to conquere the holy lande." Charles VI, two years away from his first mental breakdown, gives them a receptive hearing: "That is trewe, quod the king; my thought nyght and day is on none other thyng."[19] But the king is deflected at once, first by a suggestion that he can only hope to succeed if he first unites Christendom under a single Pope. This would entail an invasion of Italy to depose the Roman pontiff Boniface IX in favor of Clement VII at Avignon. The projected invasion of Italy is deferred, in its turn, to take advantage of an offer from Richard II to negotiate an end to the Hundred Years War. This pattern of crusading fantasies displaced by more pressing local realities is full of reverberations for the future.

Possibly inspired by their experiences in Barbary twelve years earlier, or, as Fernández-Armesto suggests, guided by a map, the two veteran crusaders Gadifer de la Salle and Béthencourt set out from La Rochelle on 1 May 1402. They had obtained a crusading indulgence from the imprisoned Avignon Pope Benedict XIII, the pontiff preferred by their common patron Louis of Orléans.[20] The events of their voyage are well summarized by Cioranescu and, in English and more concisely, by Keen and Fernández-Armesto.[21] After some legal difficulties in Seville, the expedition arrived on the island of Lanzarote in July. Their first concern was to put up their fortress, which they called Rubicon, the name perhaps a reflection of Gadifer's interest in Roman history. The local population responded politely to offers of friendship, protection, and religious instruction. The neighboring island of Fuerteventura proved less welcoming, since the inhabitants had already been raided by slavers. Deterred by this setback, the partners decided their current resources were inadequate to the task of conquest. Béthencourt returned to Spain for supplies and reinforcements, and

---

19 Ibid., V.434–35.
20 Otto Cartellieri, *The Court of Burgundy: Studies in the History of Civilization*, trans. Malcolm Letts (1925; rpt. New York, 1970), p. 7.
21 Keen, "Gadifer," pp. 80–82.

stayed away for rather a long time while he negotiated with the Castilian court. This left Gadifer de la Salle and his party in difficult straits. The hard times helped provoke Bertin de Berneval to mutiny while Gadifer was off on the desert Isle des Louppes, hunting seals to provide shoeleather. Bertin helped himself to the personal property of his fellow explorers and fled on a convenient Spanish ship with the booty, including a group of captive islanders. The remaining crusaders were left to cope with a rightfully enraged local population and their own indigence. Perhaps not surprisingly, they descended at this point to all-out warfare and the sale of slaves themselves. Gadifer did succeed in subjugating and converting the resourceful king of Lanzarote and his people, and carried out a tour of the remainder of the archipelago. Béthencourt reappeared in April 1404 to announce that he was the new lord of the Canary Islands. On his return to Spain, Gadifer discovered he had no legal recourse in the case, perhaps, as Keen suggests, because he had nothing in writing to support his claim. His version of the chronicle presents his justification of his own deeds, together with his recommendations for future conquests. He spent most of his remaining years on active duty in the service of Orléans. The Canarian project did not profit Béthencourt or his heirs to any great extent. It seems to have added lustre to Gadifer's already high reputation as a knight; in *Le Jouvencel* Jean de Bueil ranked him with the great Bertrand du Guesclin.

The record of the invaders' experience survives in two versions. The earlier of the two texts of *Le Canarien* (British Library MS Egerton 2702) reflects Gadifer de la Salle's views. This is easily the more elegant of the two surviving manuscripts, registered in the library of the dukes of Burgundy from 1420–c.1650.[22] This text was pruned by the Béthencourts and supplemented with a variety of courtly and domestic additions around 1490 to produce a distinctive second account of the 1402 expedition. This version is preserved in the decidedly less formal MS Montruffet (Bibliothèque Municipale de Rouen).

Their approach links the two texts of *Le Canarien* with several established genres of chivalric literature. This text is first of all a chronicle of noble deeds, attempting on a smaller scale what Froissart does at length: "and because it was once the custom to put in writing the exploits that princes and conquerors performed, just as one finds in old stories" (or ancient histories?).[23] From the outset, the authors label *Le Canarien* as another narrative of "bonne chevalerie" in the grand old tradition. The narrative also presents aspects of the specialized chivalric biography, like the lives of Boucicaut or Jacques de Lalaing – or, at certain moments, autobiography. Gadifer may have drafted parts of his version. It certainly reflects his perspective, to such an extent that Béthencourt's

---

[22] *Le Canarien*, III. 151–53, 159; Georges Doutrepont, *La littérature française à la cour de Bourgogne* (Paris, 1909), pp. 243–44.

[23] *Le Canarien*, III.17: "et pour ce que iadis souloit on mectre en escript les bonnes chevaleries que les princes et les conquereurs souloient faire, ainsi que on treuve es ansiens hystoires . . ."

descendants needed to protect their family's good name by drastic editorial intervention. This is both the tale of an expedition and of the deeds of particular knights. Gadifer identifies his voyage as "the deed he had undertaken against unbelievers, which God grant him to complete to his honor and the salvation of many souls."[24] *Le Canarien* is a *livre des faits*, a "book of deeds," like the approximately contemporary *Livre des fais du bon messire Jehan le Maingre, dit Bouciquaut* of 1409.[25]

In the duke of Burgundy's library, the descriptive sections of Gadifer's *Livre de Canare* would complement the reports of Duke Philip the Good's own agents, sent out as scouts in preparation for the duke's own crusading project; Bertrand de la Broquiére's *Voyage d'outremer* is the best-known of these reports. Philip the Good is not often considered as a patron of exploration. This may be, perhaps, because the voyages he sponsored were aimed at preparing for a new crusade, one that never escaped the shores of France.[26]

The imaginative reader might also detect affinities between *Le Canarien*'s record of an act of knightly prowess and some of the later tournament records of the Burgundian court, chronicling the performance of *pas d'armes* (passages of arms) like Jacques de Lalaing's *Pas de la fontaine de pleurs*, held at Chalon-sur-Sâone in 1450, the *Pas du perron fée* of his brother Philippe de Lalaing (Bruges, 1462–3), or the *Pas de la dame sauvage* of Claude de Vauldray (Ghent, 1470).[27] *Le Canarien* describes Gadifer's escape from the Isle des Louppes as a *perilleux passaige*, a term the editors associate with the *passaige d'outremer*, a crusading expression. But the *passage perilleux* had long been a staple of the romances. In *Gyron le Courtoys* the *passage perilleux* is a test set up by Galehot le Brun, and there are numerous risky *passages* or *pas* elsewhere, which can be either paths or places of adventure, like the *passages sans retor* leading into the *val de servage*, also in *Gyron le Courtoys*, or the *pas perilleux* where Heart fights with Trouble on a rickety bridge over the Stream of Tears in King René of Anjou's *Livre du cuer d'amours espris*.

Most telling of all is the identification of the expedition to the Canary Islands as an "estrange emprise:" "And noone should wonder at it if they undertook to make such a conquest. And many other knight in the past has set about equally strange enterprises."[28] *Emprise* can carry the simple meaning of "enterprise"

---

24 Ibid., III.57: "le fait qu'il a entrepris sur mescreans, lequel Dieu lui doint acomplir à son honneur et au sauvement de maintes ames."

25 *Livre des fais du bon messire Jehan le Maingre, dit Bouciquaut, Mareschal de France et gouverneur de Jennes*, ed. Denis Lalande (Geneva, 1985).

26 See Doutrepont, *Littérature*, pp. 242–65 for Philip's projects, embassies, and extensive collection of books on the subject, including *Le Canarien*.

27 For descriptions of all of these events, and discussion of the Burgundian *pas d'armes*, see Cartellieri, *The Court of Burgundy*, trans. Malcolm Letts.

28 *Le Canarien*, III.95: "Et nul ne se doit esmerveiller s'il ont empris de faire une telle conqueste . . . Et maint autre chevalier ou temps passe ont fait dausy estrangez emprisez . . ."

or "project," but it also belongs to the world of chivalric vows to perform some notable action, usually a series of jousts. These intentions were sometimes marked by the adoption of an *emprise*, a badge identifying the knight dedicated to this purpose. The *emprise de bracelet* described in the *Livre des faits de Jacques de Lalaing* and *Petit Jehan de Saintré* may be the best known of these late medieval chivalric rituals.[29] *Le Canarien* does not record that the French expedition adopted any visual emblem, but the chronicle does label the project as a "strange enterprise" like those undertaken by great knights of the past. The term also carries our sense of "enterprise" as "energy or initiative." *Le Canarien* complains, "And one should not doubt that many things were left undone in the past out of a lack of enterprise."[30]

The target audience of Gadifer's version of *Le Canarien*, as the text and the character of the manuscript both indicate, must be the princes of France. While the pragmatic Béthencourt had turned to the nearby Castilians for support, on principle or out of necessity Gadifer de la Salle still addresses his proposals to a French audience. The appearance of the manuscript in the duke of Burgundy's library catalogue of 1420 confirms that he had found one auditor of this kind, a powerful Valois prince with crusading ambitions. To do this Gadifer had to reach out to the son of the assassin of his murdered patron, Duke Louis of Orleans, perhaps to the assassin himself. John the Fearless had gone with Boucicaut to fight the Turks, encountering disaster at Nicopolis in 1396.[31] Philip the Good's crusading ambitions may reflect a desire to emulate and compensate for his father's experience; as early as 1421 he sent out a scout, Gilbert de Lannoy, to investigate the possibilities.[32]

Reading *Le Canarien* as a chivalric document focuses attention on several key aspects of the text. Romance elements permeate the exploration narrative. The landscape of the islands themselves, in the case of Tenerife, Grand Canary, Palma, Gomera and Hierro, volcanic mountains rising from the ocean, might evoke the magic mountains or islands of romance. The names their European invaders imposed on these places unquestionably call up echoes from the world of the romance: *l'isle Lancelot*, the island Lanzarote, preserved the name of a previous explorer, the Genoese Lancellotto Malocello, but the word cannot help evoking the great Arthurian knight as well. This island reminded Gadifer of Rhodes – he could have been speculating about its possibilities as a similar crusader stronghold.[33] The island "Ercanie" is also "dite Forte aventure," (Fuerteventura) – a "strong adventure," exactly Malory's term. Then there are other islands, of iron (l'isle de Fer/ the Spanish Hierro), Hell (l'isle d'Enfer) and

29 Larry D. Benson, *Malory's Morte Darthur* (Cambridge, Mass., 1977), pp. 169–72; Keen, *Chivalry*, p. 212.

30 *Le Canarien*, III.107: "Et ne doubte l'en point que moult de choses sont demoureez ou temps passé par faulte d'emprise."

31 See Aziz Suryal Atiya, *The Crusade of Nicopolis* (London, 1934).

32 Doutrepont, *Littérature*, pp. 245–46.

33 *Le Canarien*, III.139.

Wolves (Louppes), though the wolves in this case are seals (*loups de mer*). Leagues to the south, the isle of Kings (*les Roys*) is rumored to be populated by red folk.[34] Each name voices its own challenge to the would-be conqueror. The names the Frenchmen give to their own fortresses, Rubicon and Riche Roche, conjure up the images of Caesar on his way to claim the rule of Rome, and of enrichment, taking us back to the magic rock or mountain with its treasure. The expedition encounters *sirenes*, which turn out to be a marvellously strange sort of fish, portending danger at sea. With the help of the excerpt from the *Libro del conoscimiento de todos los reynos* that the chroniclers insert "because Gadifer had a great desire to know the truth," the nearby mainland becomes a convenient shortcut to the legendary River of Gold, the land of Prester John, and the Earthly Paradise.[35] Perhaps the most seductive geographic fantasy of the later Middle Ages is cited straight out of an authoritative reference work, the eyewitness testimony of "a friar."

Gadifer's version of *Le Canarien* concerns itself much with matters of principle, chivalric and Christian. The chivalric morality of Gadifer's chroniclers centers on the ideal of loyalty, on keeping one's word. Naturally, Gadifer stands as a scrupulous model of these primary knightly virtues, traits his contemporaries lamented as the preliterate tradition of oral agreement lost its legal force in the bureacratic courts of Europe.[36] Gadifer is pictured as holding fast to the old ideal. He will make no treaty with the natives in the absence of his comrade Béthencourt.[37] This contrasts flatly against the conduct of Béthencourt in Spain, treating with the king of Castile for sovereignty over the islands "without mentioning his comrade who had remained there for them both."[38] Francisco Calvo, the good captain of the nef La Morelle, stands forth as another shining counter-example when he resists de Berneval's proposition to get rich quick by marooning Gadifer, declaring "never should it please God for them to do such a disloyal thing to such a knight."[39] In the world of the *Canarien*, keeping one's word and remaining true to a partner are uncommon virtues. The text expresses Gadifer's outrage at his own betrayal by Jean de Béthencourt, Bertin de Berneval, and others. The betrayal of a pledge, of fellowship, is portrayed as both a chivalric and a religious failure. Bertin de Berneval is a triple traitor, betraying Gadifer, the trusting islanders, and his own accomplices.

34 Ibid., III.125.
35 Ibid., III.97: "le chemin est brief, aise et po coustable au reguart des autres chemins." Cf. pp. 101 and 125.
36 Chaucer's *ballade* "Lak of Stedfastnes," a work roughly contemporary with Gadifer's expedition, mourns this change: "Somtyme the world was so stedfast and stable / That mannes word was obligacioun." Cf. *Riverside Chaucer*, ed. Larry D. Benson (Boston, 1987), p. 654.
37 *Le Canarien*, III.25.
38 Ibid., III.33: "sans faire mencion de son compaignon qui estoit par dessa demouré pour eux deux."
39 Ibid., III.37: "que ja Dieu ne pleust qu'ilz feissent une tele desleauté à un tel chevalier."

So you can see and know the great disloyalty of Bertin de Berneval, who committed three chief treasons: one was against Gadifer, their captain, whom he left on the desert island to die of hunger and also deprived him of men, food, and munitions; the second, that under the cloak of good faith he invited the king of the Island Lancelot, who had been reassured by him and by us all, and captured him and his people and sold them to the Spaniards to carry into slavery; the third, that when he was through with his own sworn companions, he left them behind, for which reason they died, and departed with his prey.[40]

The narrator notes in particular the way Bertin welcomes the native king to supper: "That was the kiss of the traitor Judas, when he delivered our Savior Jesus Christ into the hands of the Jews to crucify him and put him to death."[41]

Le Canarien can be read as a romance of friendship betrayed – a theme that also surfaces in such works as *Gyron le Courtoys* and the romance of Alexander. Where the classic "romances of friendship" like *Amis et Amiloun*, *Claris et Laris*, and later *Olivier de Castille et Artus d'Algarbe* celebrate male bonding as a glorious thing, other chivalric narratives lament the treachery of one knight to his companion. One of the most effective and longest-running dramas of *Gyron le Courtoys* involves Guiron and his best friend Danain le Roux, who begin as inseparable buddies, become entangled with one another's women, and nearly execute one another on several occasions before they are reconciled and part at the crossroads to undertake their final quests. *Le Canarien* has great fun portraying Bertin as an anti-chivalric villain. The narrator even throws in a few parodic flourishes, as in the scene where Bertin proposes something to his men that will tend to their advancement and honor, and swears them to secrecy.[42] Later on, Bertin plays the part of the traitor knight to the hilt. He hands over the Poitevin women of the party to be raped by the Spanish sailors, and taunts Gadifer with his age, from a safe distance: "I want Gadifer de la Salle to know that if he were as young as I am, I'd go kill him, but since he isn't, if I should take it into my head I'd arrange for him to be drowned at the Isle of Wolves; that way he can go fishing for seals."[43] In the end he abandons his own men on the seashore with a faintly Arthurian injunction: "Advise yourselves as best you

---

40 *Le Canarien*, III.55: "Or povez voir et cognoistre la grant deleauté Bertin de Berneval, qui fit III traisons principales: l'une si fut contre Gadifer, leur capitaine, qu'il lessa en l'isle deserte pour mourir de fain et anxi le desgarnir de gens, de vitaillez et d'artillerie; l'autre, que soubz ombre de bonne foy il manda le roy de l'isle Lancelot, qui estoit asseuré de lui et de nous touz, et le print lui et ses gens et les livra aus Espaigneaulx pour mener en servage; la tierce, que ses propres compaignons aliez de serment, quant il eut fait de eulz, il les lessa en terre, par quoy il sont depuis mors, et s'en ala avec sa praie . . ."

41 Ibid., III.43: "Ce fut le beser Judas le traistre, quant il livra nostre Sauveur Jhesucrist en la main des Juifs pour le crucifier et mettre à mort."

42 Ibid., III.37.

43 Ibid., III.47: "Je vueil bien que Gadifer de la Sale sache que se il feust ainsi jeune comme moy, que je l'alasse tuer; mais pour ce qu'il ne l'est mie, s'il me monte un pou en la teste, le l'iray faire noier en l'isle de Louppes: si peschera aux loups marins."

can, for you're not coming with me."[44] Bertin certainly ranks as an anti-Arthur. The deadly consequences of such betrayals of faith were felt by Gadifer and his party, first marooned on a desert island, and then left to fend for themselves amid the righteously outraged population of Lanzarote.

Gadifer's manuscript promotes two key aspects of his character. First and foremost, Gadifer wants to be seen as a crusader, opening the path to the next great foray of Christendom against Islam. Even after the failure of his *estrange emprise*, Gadifer proposes to sponsor new voyages further south in pursuit of his goal. This time he would send a trading vessel "en maniere de marchans" to investigate the terrain before launching another expedition of conquest.[45] For Gadifer, trade makes good cover for the advance scout of a future crusade. When Antoine de la Sale depicted Gadifer in *Petit Jehan de Saintré* as the bearer of the banner of the Virgin Mary in his hero's crusade, he reproduced a portrait endorsed by Gadifer's manuscript. The Egerton manuscript of *Le Canarien* shows on its frontispiece the boatload of French invaders, with Gadifer standing beneath the banner of the Virgin. Even after the failure of this particular enterprise, Gadifer pictures himself as a scout, and advertises the Canary Islands he has explored as the logical next step for the crusading monarchs of Europe. The path opened by Gadifer de la Salle leads, by his account, to the River of Gold of the *Libro de conoscimento de todos los reynos*, and to Prester John. This idea seems central to his sense of himself.

Gadifer's concept of the crusade would appear to be modeled on the formula of conquest followed by mission advocated by Innocent IV in the mid-thirteenth century, and described by Benjamin Z. Kedar.[46] *Le Canarien* begins by describing past expeditions of conquest undertaken in the hope of converting infidels, "en esperance de les tourner et convertir à la foy crestienne" ("in the hope to turn and convert them to the Christian faith"), but more often the verb employed is "mettre," as in "convertir et mettre à nostre foy." ("To convert and put them to our faith.")[47] In this formulation the natives are imagined as passive beings, to be put to Christianity as they might be put to work. Until the French establish dominion over the *isle Lancelot*, the clergy preach to the natives without much apparent effect, as they indicate earlier missions had done.[48] In the end, the natives of Lanzarote are subdued, led to baptism, and then instructed in the Christian faith: "and we had more than eighty prisoners in the castle of Rubicon, and a great plenty of them dead, and we had reduced our enemies to such a state that they did not know what to do any more, and came

[44] Ibid., III.55: "Donnez vous le meilleur conseil que vous pourrez, car avecques moy ne vous en vendrez vous point."

[45] Ibid., III.107.

[46] Benjamin Z. Kedar, *Crusade and Mission* (Princeton, 1984), pp. 159–61.

[47] *Le Canarien*, III.15, 17, 117.

[48] Ibid., III.73–75.

day by day to surrender, one after another, until there were few left alive who were not baptized, especially of the folk who could hurt us."[49]

Le Canarien includes a summary of basic Christian beliefs, perhaps as an example of the teaching that Gadifer offered to the Canarians, and also as evidence that Gadifer and his men were indeed concerned to convert as well as to conquer. "And for this reason Gadifer organized a teaching such as he knew how to present and organize, as simply as he could, to introduce those that we baptize there [to the Christian faith.]"[50] The capsule version of the Bible presented here is full of interest, preserving as it does the essence of Christianity as advocated by Gadifer and his clerical advisors. Beginning with the book of Genesis, the teacher surveys the Bible, with stress on such essential subjects as Adam and Eve, Noah, and the tower of Babel. The children of Israel, singled out by God as a holy people, are rejected for their lack of faith in Jesus. By contrast, all who join Jesus's disciples in their beliefs are to be saved, while those who fail to believe are "on the road to Hell."[51] This narrative section is followed by a listing of the articles of Christian faith, the ten commandments – reduced to two here, belief in God and the "Golden Rule," interestingly in Hillel's formulation rather than Jesus': "do not do to another what you would not want done to yourself."[52] Communion, confession, the importance of labor in one's appointed calling, and avoidance of sin are the final subjects touched upon briefly in Gadifer's summary of his faith.

The most startling feature of this section for the twentieth-century reader may be its casual pronouncement of a racial anti-Semitism associated with skin color. *Le Canarien* remarks concerning the Jews:

> But they did not choose to believe [Jesus] nor recognize his coming, so they crucified him and put him to death, in spite of the marvellous miracles he did in their presence; for which reason they were all ruined, as everyone knows. For in all the world no Jew exists who is not subjected to the control of others and who does not go day and night in terror of his life, and for this reason they are so palefaced.[53]

---

49 Ibid., III.79: "et avions plus de IIII^{xx} prisonniers au chastel de Rubicon et en y avoit eu grant foison de mors; et tenoions nous ennemis en tel point qu'ilz ne savoient plus que faire et se venoient de iour en iour rendre en nostre mercy, puis le uns puis les autres, tant qu'ilz sont pou demouré en vie qui ne soient baptisiez, especialment de gens qui nous puissent grever."

50 Ibid., III.85: "Et por ce a Gadifer ordenné une instruction ainsi qu'il a sceu faire et ordonner, le plus legierement qu'il a peu, pour introduyre ceuls que nous baptisons par dessa."

51 Ibid., III.91: "en voye de perdicion."

52 Ibid., III.93: "que l'en ne doit faire à autruy mais que l'en vouldroit que autruy ly faist." Hillel's version of this principle is preserved in the Talmud, Tractate Mo'adin, Masechet Shabat 31:A, and therefore widely available, but where *Le Canarien* might have found it is impossible to determine.

53 Ibid., III.91: "Mais ilz ne le vouloient croire ne cognoistre son advenement, ains le

Skin color – in this case, interestingly, pallor – and servitude are both represented here as divinely ordained punishments for an ancestral act of deicide. The implications of this belief for the Canarians, threatened themselves with exile and slavery, need to be underlined. This instruction does not simply prepare the Canarian proselyte to share his teachers' beliefs about the Jews, or to recognize a Jew by the color of his or her skin if he should indeed happen to see one. One of the key features of the lesson is the importance of recognition. The islanders do not "recognize their Creator." The Jews refused to know, or, by extension, to acknowledge Jesus as the Messiah. *Le Canarien* uses two related words, "recognoissent" and "cognoistre." "Recognizance" is a term used in feudal law to describe the return of a fief to its overlord. Definitions more familiar to modern users of the verb in French and English include "to identify," "to know again," and "to acknowledge." By accepting Christianity, the Canarians may be able to avoid the enslavement that Gadifer's mission tells them is the fate of the Jews. The experience of an overwhelming sense of terror, also to be escaped through the church, would not have been new to the natives of Lanzarote or Fuerteventura by this time.

The passage may also convey an undercurrent of warning to the sceptical reader. Those who do not believe marvels, "les merveilleusez miraclez," whether performed before their own eyes or narrated to them long afterwards, become subject to divine condemnation. Faced with a chronicle teeming with marvels, the reader who withholds his or her belief is re-enacting the role played by the Jew. By believing in the wonders set out in the text, the reader reaffirms his or her Christian identity, and his or her claim to salvation.

This section of the text is presented as Gadifer's own work. The writer remarks that he is not a cleric. "And so they might understand the better Gadifer made and planned this book after the simplest fashion he could, according to the small wit God gave him, for he's no clerk."[54] He trusts that God will send better scholars, "aucuns bons clers prodommes," to continue his teaching of the islanders. Here Gadifer becomes a secular missionary, a role that the knights of fiction also adopt with some frequency.[55] By recording his lesson in basic

crucifierent et le mistrent à mort, non obstant les merveilleusez miraclez qu'il faisoit en leur presence; par quoy ilz sont touz destruiz, ainsi que chascun scet. Car en tout le monde n'a Juyf qui ne soit en subjection d'autrui et qui ne soit jour et nuit en paour et en cremour de leur vie, / et pour cela sont ainsi descoulourez."

54 Ibid., III.95: "Et afin que mieulx le puissent entendre Gadifer a fait et ordenné ce livre au plus legierement qu'il a peu faire, selon se pou d'entendemet que Dieu li a donne, car il n'est mie clerc . . ."

55 In Boiardo's *Orlando Innamorato* it is the knight Orlando himself who baptizes his noble Saracen opponents, the Tartar khan Agricane as he lies dying after his great duel with Orlando (trans. Charles Stanley Ross (Berkeley, Los Angeles, and Oxford, 1989), I.xviii, lines 29–55; xix, lines 1–17, 25–28; see also Ross' note, p. 853) and the courteous Saracen knight Brandimarte in prison (II.xii.8–31; Brandimarte in turn arranges for the conversion of all the Saracens of Damogir, II.xiii.34–49). This is an ongoing theme of the poem: Orlando's rival, Ranaldo (Renaut de Montauban of the *Quatre fils Aymon*), converts

Christianity as part of the tale of his deeds, Gadifer de la Salle lays claim to a higher moral authority. Whatever rampages his comrades may have committed in the Canary Islands, he portrays himself fulfilling the highest ideals of Christian knighthood, as crusader and missionary. In this way the Gadifers differentiate themselves from the Aymerygott Marcells and the Bertin de Bernevals. The prestige of the role invites competition. Not surprisingly, the B manuscript ascribes this exposition of Christian doctrine to Béthencourt and his chaplains, not to Gadifer.

A second distinctive feature of Gadifer's personality as depicted in *Le Canarien* is his penchant for speaking out as a social critic. The section of the manuscript where he enlarges on his ideas for improving European society was omitted from the later version, and it seems to irk its editors.[56] Gadifer is here depicted meditating on the state of the world, and addressing his prescription for reform to the clergy and princes of his day. This apparent digression also reflects a lively chivalric tradition, though not one that is much stressed in postmedieval studies of chivalry. The obligation of the older or the retired knight to serve as critic of his society had been enacted in real life by Ramon Lull, and in Gadifer's lifetime by the chancellor of Cyprus, Philippe de Mézières (1327–1405), the contemporary figure perhaps closest to Gadifer in character. The hermits of Arthurian romance (especially the *Queste del Saint Graal*) may have been the original models for this role. Sir Dinadan of the prose *Tristan*, that outspoken critic of knighthood itself, furnishes an alternative approach. The sense that they were the natural advisors of princes may have encouraged experienced knights like Gadifer to voice their views of what was wrong with the world. The world is *desvoyé*, gone astray, and Gadifer presents himself as its pathfinder, pointing out the true direction to the leaders of his country.[57]

In his complaint, Gadifer stresses again the failure of loyalty evident in Western society: "and in many places one deceives the other and they fail to

---

Prasildo, Iroldo, and the Saracen Princess Fiordelisa (I.xvii.34–37); Fiordelisa goes on to effect the conversion of her father King Dolistone and all of Armenia (II.xxvii.34–35). The Saracen knight Rugiero, descendant of Hector of Troy and ancestor of the House of Este, will himself become Christian, according to prophecy, although the poem breaks off before this event can occur (I.xxi.54–55, 61; xxii.4). In these scenes the knight replaces the priest. For important conversion scenes in a variety of earlier chivalric narratives, see Sir Thomas Malory, *Works*, ed. Eugène Vinaver (2nd edn, 1967; rpt. with additions and corrections, Oxford, 1973), II.841–45; the conversion scene is given equal weight in the French and Spanish texts of the *Tristan en prose*. Jean Bagnyon, *L'histoire de Charlemagne (parfois dite Roman de Fierabras)*, ed. Hans-Erich Keller, Textes littéraires français (Geneva, 1992), bk 2; Henry Watson, trans., *Valentine and Orson*, ed. Arthur Dickson, EETS o.s. 204 (London, 1937; rpt. New York, 1971).

56 *Le Canarien*, III.114, n. 44.

57 Ibid., III.109, 107. (Gadifer also complains that Béthencourt "s'est malement desvoyé de la droite voye à laquelle Dieu le ramenoit" ("wandered afar from the straight path on which God was leading him"), ibid., III.95.)

recognize honor."[58] He objects in particular to the Great Schism: "For you see that we have two popes, one of whom we support and one the Romans support; and yet we can only have one, as God ordained, but we don't know which it is."[59] The prelates of his day have failed to regulate their own affairs; they do little better as advisors of princes, meddling in matters beyond their competence. Gadifer urges the secular rulers of his day to straighten out the church as well as the rest of society. The advisors of Charles VI who were urging him to suppress the Roman pope as a first step towards Western unity in the face of Islam took the same view. Much of what Gadifer says is widespread among his contemporaries; Philippe de Mézières addresses these same matters in much greater detail.[60] In many respects Gadifer's abbreviated and generalized discussion seconds Philippe's much more elaborate proposals. This is hardly astonishing, since Gadifer would have been exposed extensively to Philippe's program in the orbits of Bourbon, Boucicaut and Louis of Orléans.

This critical view of his surroundings is not accompanied by much in the way of direct self-criticism. This may be altogether natural in a document that was written in some senses as an apology. Gadifer is presented here as a man incapable of deceit, motivated as much by desire for the common good as by singular profit. *Le Canarien* admires traditional knightly virtues – loyalty, physical endurance, daring, generosity. Any degrading actions performed by Gadifer or his men, such as selling the people of the islands into slavery, are acts of desperation, the necessary strategies of a survivor. "And we devoted ourselves as much as possible to capturing people, for this was our only hope at the time, so if any ship came from Spain or elsewhere, we might exchange captives for food, since Béthencourt had abandoned us altogether."[61] Elsewhere, talking of their sin in eating meat on fast days, since they had nothing else, the writers remark that "need knows no law."[62] In the version of the chronicle supporting Béthencourt's viewpoint, Béthencourt applies much the same comfortable doctrine when he writes to Gadifer of his homage to Castille: "My very dear

---

58 Ibid., III.109: "et en mainte lieu decepvent l'un l'autre et mescognoissent honneur."
59 Ibid., III.111: "Car vous voyez que nous avons deuz papez, dont nous tenons à l'un et les Romains à l'autre; et si n'en povons entre nous et eulx avoir que un, ainsi que Dieu l'ordonna, mais nous ne savons lequel c'est."
60 Compare *Le Songe du Viel Pelerin*, I; bk 1, 99v1–102v2, Queen Truth's arraignment of the clergy in the city of Avignon, and bk 3, where Philippe urges Charles VI to take the lead in urging the church to resolve the schism before proceeding on a last grand crusade. The knights of Philippe's *Order of the Passion*, which Louis of Orléans had promised to support and the duke of Bourbon and Boucicaut had agreed to join, were to pause in Italy to promote a peaceable end to the schism. Atiya, *The Crusade of Nicopolis*, pp. 133, 136, item 7.
61 *Le Canarien*, III.63: "Et mettons toute la diligence que nous povons de prendre gens, car c'est tout nostre reconfort quant à present, a fin que s'il vient aucun navire d'Espaigne ou d'ailleurs, que nous puissions changer gens pour vivres, veu que Bettencourt nous a du tout habandonnez..."
62 Ibid., III.35: "neccessité n'a loy."

brother and friend, one must endure many things. What's past, one must forget, always doing the best one can."[63] Where Bertin is concerned, Béthencourt cannot resist saying "I told you so."

The behavior of the French invaders as recorded in *Le Canarien* recalls the late Harvey Leibenstein's economic concept of "selective rationality" as the psychological foundation of economic decisions, the compromise between "the way people would like to see themselves behave and the way they would wish to behave in the absence of any constraints."[64] Chivalric morality does not deter Gadifer and his men from capturing the natives of the Canary Islands and selling them into slavery. At the same time, Gadifer's chronicle deplores the treacherous and cruel actions of Bertin de Berneval, which cost the remaining Frenchmen the trust of the inhabitants of Lanzarote. On a strategic level *Le Canarien* remains pragmatic. Gadifer eagerly anticipates the easy conquest of peoples who do not know the use of projectile weapons, who have no arrows or guns, and indeed fear archers more than anything else."The people are without armor or sense of battle, for they do not know what war is, nor can they obtain aid from other peoples . . . and they are not folk to be much feared, unlike other nations, for they are people without projectile weapons."[65] Here Gadifer recalls his contrasting experience at Al-Mahdiya: those who were "devant Afrique," (Gadifer uses the same term as Froissart) saw the brightest and best of the Saracen forces, and the redoutable power of artillery in battle, especially in hot climates where heavy armor is impractical.[66] The natives of the Canaries offer a different proposition. Better still, in other yet undiscovered isles to the south, he has heard there are people who have never experienced any form of warfare: "et sont gens qui oncques ne virent guerrez."[67] The fictional thirteenth-century knights of *Gyron le Courtoys* express shame at the idea of fighting an unarmed man, and scorn to stain their swords with the blood of a mere giant. The actual fourteenth- or fifteenth-century knight does not apply these principles to combat against "unbelievers of different laws and languages."

The experience of exploration for the knight results in a loss of identity, another long-standing theme of epic and romance. He misses his accustomed

---

[63] Ibid., II.107: "Mon très cher frere et amy, il fault souffrir biaucoup de choses. Se qui est passé, il le fault oublier, en fesant tousjours le mieulx que on pourra."

[64] Harvey Leibenstein, *Beyond Economic Man* (Cambridge, Mass., 1976).

[65] *Le Canarien*, III.49, 97: "Les gens sont sans armeurez et sans sens de batailles, car ilz ne scevent que c'est de guerre et si ne povent avoir secour d'aultre gent . . . et ne sont mye gens qui facent trop a redoubter, anxi que seroient autrez nacions, car il sont gens sans trait."

[66] For a detailed report on the military equipment of fifteenth-century Islamic armies and their Christian contemporaries, see the work of Philip the Good of Burgundy's emissary Bertrandon de la Broquière, *Le Voyage d'Outremer de Bertrandon de la Broquière*, ed. C. Schefer (Paris, 1892), pp. 227; 269–271; the pertinent section on Turkish archery is cited, with English translation, in Malcolm Vale, *War and Chivalry*, pp. 105, 112.

[67] *Le Canarien*, III.107.

food, clothes, bedding, even his horse. (Here it is impossible to resist quoting Jean Giraudoux: "The horse as everyone knows is the most important part of a knight.")[68] From the moment he disembarks, the knight is not quite himself. *Le Canarien*, in a number of places, expresses Gadifer's uneasiness and frustration at the loss of control over his own movements that arises from the unaccustomed dependence on boats and their sailors. He is "in great pain at heart because he was in such subjection that he couldn't help himself by means of his own property."[69] Even though he paid for the ship, he cannot enforce his will on the recalcitrant mariners. He is pleased to note that on Fuerteventura the terrain would permit riding all across the island: "puet on chevaucher partout."[70]

The disappearance of standard articles of diet and clothing also demoralizes the members of the expedition in significant ways: "We who were accustomed to live on bread, were for a long time without bread and wine; and we lived on meat, for we were forced to. And we went two and a half years sleeping right on the ground, without sheet, linen or blanket, except the poor, torn garments that we had on, which distressed us greatly."[71]

Le Canarien dwells persistently on the deprivation of bread and wine.[72] These are basic staples of the European diet. They are also the elements of communion. At the same time, the writers fret over the fact that they have difficulty performing the fasts enjoined by the church. "If food did not arrive within the month, we would have to eat meat throughout Lent."[73] Gadifer's ultimate trial on the Isle des Louppes leaves him marooned eight days without food, drinking the dew he catches in a cloth. To escape, he must venture in a small boat across "the most horrible strait of sea that anyone knows."[74]

Clothing also proves vital, as essential equipment, and as a sign of identity, whether corporate or individual. After all, the natives are defined as naked,

---

68 Jean Giraudoux, *Ondine: Pièce en Trois Actes d'après le conte de De la Motte Fouqué* (Paris, 1974), I.2, also cited in Contamine, *War in the Middle Ages*, p. 126.

69 *Le Canarien*, III.27–29: "en grant dolour de cuer de ce qu'il estoit en celle subiection quil ne se pouoit aidier du sien propre."

70 Ibid., III.135.

71 Ibid., III.117: "Nous qui avoions acoustumé à vivres de pain qui avons esté longuement sans pain et sans vin; et avons vescu de char, car aire le convenoit. Et avons esté deux ans et demy couchans à terre plaine, sans drap, linge ne lange, fors qu'en la povre robe dessirée que nous avions vestue, dont nous fuymez mout grevez . . ."

72 Ibid., III.47, 67, 85, 117, and elsewhere.

73 Ibid., III.85: "Mais s'il ne nous vient vitailles dedens un mois, nous sommez du tout à la char contre sainte quarantaine"; see also III.35: "car d'environ Noel mil CCCC et deux jusques aprés la Saint Jehan Baptiste mil CCCC et trois nous n'avions mengié de pain ne beu de vin et avons vesqu de char et en karesme et en charnau, car necessité n'a loy" ("for from Christmas 1402 until after the feast of St John the Baptist 1403 we have not eaten bread nor drunk wine and have lived on meat both in Lent and on meat days, for need has no law").

74 Ibid., III.51: "le plus horrible passaige de mer que nul sache."

although on closer inspection they do seem to wear various key articles of clothing. Their kings differentiate themselves from other warriors by means of costume.[75] Among the losses Gadifer regrets is his golden collar of the Order of the Camail, his own badge of chivalric rank and affiliation.[76] Gadifer goes off to hunt seals to supply his men with shoes. As time goes by the Europeans are threatened with nakedness themselves; unlike the islanders, they are indeed "ashamed of their private parts."[77] If all else fails, Gadifer records his own "modest proposal": they must kill all the fighting men, as they had begun to do, baptize the women and children, and adopt the natives' way of life.[78]

Aspects of Gadifer's knightly culture do contribute to his ability to survive. Certainly the comforting thought that endurance is a proof of heroism helps to raise his morale. Gadifer in particular is depicted as the hero turned victim, as well as conqueror, missionary and pathfinder. He and his loyal followers are distinguished from their companions by the suffering they undergo in pursuit of their goal, as well as by their military enterprises. Part of the business of *Le Canarien* is precisely to record the many hardships that Gadifer endured, to the enhancement of his fame as a knight.

On a practical level, the fact that knights were encouraged to hunt as part of their basic training stood Gadifer in good stead. When Gadifer descends on the inhabitants of the islands, it is as a hunter, chasing down his prey and counting the captives, as he hunted the seals (*loups de mer*) of the Isle des Louppes. Each foray ends with an accounting of the "bag." The most brutal "hunt" is assigned to one of the party's native translators rather than Gadifer himself: "Peter the Canarian chased three and took a woman from them and took two others in a cavern, one of whom had a suckling infant that she smothered for fear it might cry."[79] Of the natives of Fuerteventura, Gadifer reports: "They can only be captured alive with great difficulty."[80]

The depiction of the Guanches, the natives of the islands, stresses their nakedness, unbelief, and diversity of faith and speech. These people are "unbelievers of various laws and varied languages," "and do not recognize their Creator and live to some extent like animals and their souls are on the path to

---

[75] Ibid., III.61: "Ainsi se parti Afche et se vesti comme roy." "Then Afche went off and dressed himself as a king."

[76] Ibid., III.35: "un collier d'or de la devise Monseigneur d'Orliens . . . et pesoit le dit coller qui estoit à Gadifer deux marcs d'or ou environ" ("a golden collar of the emblem of Monseigneur d'Orléans . . . and the said collar, which was Gadifer's, weighed about two marks of gold").

[77] Ibid., III.141: "honteus de leurs menbres." For the seals, cf. III.39.

[78] Ibid., III.63.

[79] Ibid., III.71: "Pietre le Canare en chassa trois et leur toli une femme et en print deux autres en une cave, dont l'une avoit un petit enfant alectant, qu'elle entrangla, pour la doubte qu'il ne criast."

[80] Ibid., III.137: "et a poine les peut on prendre vis."

perdition."[81] Amongst them, *Le Canarien* distinguishes different groups by their physical appearance, speech, or curious customs. The chronicler also attempts to differentiate between social classes among the natives. L'isle des Palmes is populated by simple, respectable folk, while Grand Canary supports a large class of noblemen.[82] Some are actively hostile to foreigners, while others have not yet experienced the raids of slaving ships. A martyred community of friars leave word that the island of Grand Canary is populated by traitors: their "testament said this: that no one should trust them, whatever appearance they present, for they are traitors and are six thousand gentlemen according to their estate."[83] The inhabitants of La Gomere speak so strangely because they are marked by a prince's curse.[84] *Le Canarien* envisions these people as promising opponents for the future. Indeed, Gadifer busies himself investigating the lie of the land, with a view to new conquests.

The interpreters who make it possible for the French to speak to the natives of the islands emerge as essential figures. The frightening intimacy of the relationship between translator and translated is exemplified by the interpreter Béthencourt hired, Alfonso the Canarian. He has lived among the invaders, knows all the secrets of their household, and supplies dangerous information to his relatives: Alfonso "lived continually with us and knew our ways and our poverty and purposed nothing but our ruin."[85] The female interpreter, Isabel, seems to be recognized as more trustworthy. She is vital to Gadifer's party, who plead with Bertin de Berneval for her return as he is about to carry her off into slavery. "Leave us Isabel the Canarian, for we do not know how to talk to the natives who live in this island." Bertin's folk instead fling the unfortunate Isabel into the sea, where she would have drowned if Gadifer's men had not been there.[86]

This Isabel needs to be recognized as the first of a series of female mediators between cultures who demand attention in this study. On one level, they play a role analogous to the helpful but often nameless "damsel" of chivalric tradition, leading knights to adventures and, on occasion, rescuing them or being rescued themselves. Elsewhere, they seem to be viewed as variants of the Saracen princess who saves and sometimes marries the hero or one of his friends. Cortes' Doña Marina, Pocahontas, even Sacajawea, can be seen as continuing the series. In the Canary Islands, Isabel would be succeeded by the end of the

---

81 Ibid., III.85: "mescreans de diverses loys et divers langages" "et ne recognoyssent leur createur et vivent en partie comme bestez et sont leur ames en voye de perdicion."

82 Ibid., III.77: "simples gens et de bon condicion." Cf. III.131.

83 Ibid., III.75: "lequel testament dit ainsi: que nul ne se fie en euls, pour semblant qu'il facent, car ilz sont traistrez et sont VIm gentils hommes selon leur estat."

84 Ibid., III.127–29.

85 Ibid., III.59: "lequel demouroit continuelment avecques nous et savoit nostre comune et nostre povreté et tiroit du tout à nostre destruction."

86 Ibid., III.53: "Laissez nous Isabel la Canare, car nous ne saurions parler aux habitans qui demourent en ceste isle."

century by Francisca de Gazmira, the Canarian laywoman whose mission to her own people proved more effective than the many earlier attempts at Christianization from the outside.[87]

The king of Lanzarote also turns out to be a most attractive character, perhaps in spite of his chroniclers. He is never given a name, while the male members of the French expedition are carefully listed, as is customary in a record of chivalric enterprise.[88] Even after baptism, we are never told what to call him. Yet this island king's exploits make him a more than worthy opponent of the knights who surround him. He first appears by appointment to establish friendly relations with Gadifer and Jean de Béthencourt, "and they confided themselves in the friendship of the aforementioned knights, as friends and not as subjects, which knights promised to protect them against all who wished to harm them, as much as they could."[89] Béthencourt's later agreement with the king of Castile ignores the sovereignty of the king of Lanzarote as well as Gadifer's rights as partner. The king next appears as a betrayed guest, captured by Bertin de Berneval as he sleeps off the effects of Bertin's dinner party. In identifying Bertin's treacherous overtures to the king as "the kiss of Judas," *Le Canarien* suggests a further identification of the captive monarch with Jesus. As hero and as victim, the king of Lanzarote claims the most powerful role.

This treatment of the king may reflect, in part, the problem Europeans experienced in interpreting the conflicting visual signals sent out by the image of the crowned naked man.[90] This problem also perplexes students of the Alexander romances, with their images of naked Brahmins and their crowned king, as recently discussed by Thomas Hahn. The only representation of a crowned, naked man in the Christian tradition is that of the crucified Christ, as Jill Keen has astutely observed.[91] The king's struggle to maintain the respect of the knights and their royal patrons certainly accords with later problems native kings experienced as they fought to establish their royal status before European audiences. Recognition of a native king as a sovereign in the same sense as the king of France or Castile remains sporadic.[92]

Still, the king of Lanzarote refuses to play the part of Jesus to the bitter end.

---

[87] Fernández-Armesto, *Before Columbus*, pp. 210–11.

[88] Cf. *Le Canarien*, III.81–83.

[89] Ibid., III.25: "et se misterent en l'amistance des chevaliers dessus dis, comme amis non mie comme subgiez, qui les promidrent à garder de tous ceuls qui leur voudroient mal faire, à leur povoir."

[90] In the later MS B of *Le Canarien* the islanders are most often shown wearing loincloths, but the pictures of the chained king in the act of escaping do represent him as a naked man, as in *Le Canarien*, II.63, 125. His crown is more clearly visible in the illustration reproduced in II.121.

[91] Jill Keen, private communication, University of Minnesota, February 1994; T. Hahn, "Imagining the Exotic: Visual Representations of 'Indians' in Late Medieval Vernacular Manuscripts," presented at 'Strangers in Medieval Society', 26 February 1994, University of Minnesota.

[92] See P. E. Russell, "White Kings on Black Kings: Rui de Piña and the Problem of Black

Instead he displays a level of prowess that compels the admiration of the chronicler.

> When the king saw himself in such a pickle and knew the treason of Bertin and his comrades and the offence they were committing against them, like a bold, strong, and powerful man he broke his bonds and freed himself from the three men who were guarding him, of whom one was a Gascon who ran after him; but the king turned on him and struck him in great fury such a blow that the others let him pass; and this was the sixth time he had freed himself from the hands of the Christians by means of his skill.[93]

Later on Gadifer captures the same king, attempting to gain revenge for the killing of some members of his party. In an episode to be often repeated in the annals of European exploration, the king's rival Afche tries to use the French knights to help him gain the throne. Most conveniently, Afche is the uncle of Alfonso the translator. Through Alfonso, Afche characterizes the king as an implacable enemy: "and he made him say that the king hated him greatly and as long as he lived we would never get anything out of them without much effort, and that he was altogether guilty of the death of his men . . ."[94] In retrospect *Le Canarien*, addicted to the mathematics of treason, recognizes that Afche is a double traitor, betraying his liege lord and plotting to betray Gadifer himself once he becomes king. At the time, though, Gadifer is enchanted by the prospect that Afche and his men will accept baptism. He would not be the first European attracted by the prospect of replacing an intransigent non-Christian monarch by a helpful convert, nor would Afche be the last native prince to offer to accept baptism in return for military aid in a *coup d'état*.[95] This solution was far more common in romance than in real life: variations on the theme conclude *Fierabras* and *Les Trois Fils du Roi*.

The king of Lanzarote, chained in the fort Rubicon with a pair of irons that wound him, is not finished yet, and he escapes again: "by night the first king escaped from the prison of Rubicon and carried off the irons and the chain that bound him. And as soon as he got back to his dwelling, he had the aforementioned Afche seized, who had made himself king and had also betrayed him,

---

African Sovereignty," in *Medieval and Renaissance Studies in Honour of Robert Brian Tate*, ed. Ian Michael and Richard A. Cardwell (Oxford, 1986), pp. 151–64.

[93] *Le Canarien*, III.43: "Quant le roy se vi en tel point et cognut la traison du dit Bertin et de ses compaignons et l'oultrage qu'il leur faisoient, comme homme hardi, fort et puissant, rompi ses liens et se delivra de trois hommes qui en garde l'avoient, desquelz estoit un Gascon qui le poursuy; mais le roy retourna sur lui et le frappa par grant hayr un tel cop que les autres lui firent voye; et c'est la VIe fois qu'il s'est delivré des mains de crestiens per son appertise."

[94] Ibid., III.59: "et lui manda que le roy le haioit moult et que tant qu'il vesquist nous n'aurions rien d'euls si non à grant payne, et qu'il estoit du tout coulpable de la mort de ses gens . . ."

[95] Cf. Russell, "White Kings."

and had him stoned and burned."[96] Again, the king of Lanzarote refuses to subside into the role of victim.

The ultimate accolade comes when the king is taken once more; the chroniclers describe him as one "who gave us enough difficulty on several occasions."[97] He and his household agree to accept baptism. The king's words and attitude convince the chronicler that he will be "a good Christian." Around 1500, the Castilian translator of Bagnyon's *Fierabras* would justify the execution of a Saracen prince on the grounds that "even if . . . he agreed to be baptized, he would never be a good Christian." From this point the native ruler is to be held to a new standard, that of an orthodox Christian believer. This is the point where Gadifer inserts his instruction in basic Christianity. When the king becomes, essentially, Gadifer's Sunday-school pupil, he loses much of his stature as a royal Houdini.

These conflicting pictures of the islanders and their king bring into focus a major problem for the chivalric chroniclers of exploration. Chivalrous exploits require the challenge of a worthy opponent. As later historians testify, hunting down stone-age tribesmen does not qualify as an act of prowess.[98] In fact, such an act subverts the chivalric principles of many fictional icons of knighthood. The knights of *Gyron le Courtoys* would not dream of applying their swords to an unarmed or unequally armed enemy, however gigantic. The portrayal of the king of Lanzarote as a formidable enemy and a man of honor and prowess in his own right sullies the honor of his French opponents. It also runs the risk of diminishing their achievements. Even without any knowledge of metalworking, the king of Lanzarote manages to give the armed men of late medieval France a good deal of trouble.

Le Canarien works hard to identify knightly deeds for proper recognition. In the process it alternates uneasily between characterizing the Guanches as fearsome adversaries and proclaiming them easy prey. In the list of those who did their duty in the service of Gadifer and his cause, the authors select for special notice Johan Le Masson and Girard de Seurberay "who always risked themselves the most and confronted their foes several times and always won."[99] On one occasion *Le Canarien* is able to depict a single combat between Girard and a native warrior, though it is more like a wrestling match than a duel in form. Gadifer's bastard son Hannibal is recognized twice later for rescuing the explorers' boat by the vigorous use of an oar, wounded as he was, while all but one of

[96] *Le Canarien*, III.63–64: "par nuit, le premier roy s'eschappa de la prison de Rubicom et emporta les fers et la chayne dont il estoit lié. Et / tantost qu'il fu à son hostel, il fit prendre le dessus dit Afche qui s'estoit fait roy et aussi l'avoit tray, et le fist lappider de pierres et ardoir."

[97] Ibid., III.85: "qui nous avoit assez donné de payne par plusieurs foys."

[98] Fernández-Armesto, *Before Columbus*, p. 184.

[99] *Le Canarien*, III.83: "qui sont toujours les plus aventurez et se sont plusieurs foys encontré ou leurs ennemis et tous jours les ont vaincuz."

the rest cower on the bottom to avoid "a great pelting of stones."[100] The risk of death is still real, but in trying to make Gadifer's experience against the Guanches conform to chivalric tradition, the chroniclers are struggling to make bricks without straw.

In practice, the knight experienced the ambivalence of his role as both protector of the people and their oppressor. In Ramon Lull's *Libre del orde de cavayleria*, the knight is ordained to guard the laborers and also to intimidate them into working. The French invaders of *Le Canarien* begin by identifying themselves as friendly protectors of islanders already harassed by slaving raids. The treachery of Bertin de Berneval exposes these promises as hollow. To the natives of Lanzarote, the French must either be wolves in sheep's clothing, or impotent to save themselves, let alone anyone else.

As in a number of romances, so here the unbeliever questions the Christian's credibility: "How will you protect us when you betray one another? Therefore it seems to us that you do not possess such a strong and good faith as you would have us believe."[101] The theme of the non-Christian pointing out the shortcomings of Christian moral practice recurs especially in the Charlemagne tradition: it goes back to the *Pseudo-Turpin*, and forward to Boiardo's *Orlando Innamorato*. There, the Saracen king asks whether the Christians value money or valor more greatly. In the earlier text, the Saracen king Agiolandus refuses baptism after witnessing the dire contrast between wealthy bishops and beggars in Charlemagne's camp. Those cases stress the contrast between Christian materialism and the self-denying charity advocated by Jesus.

Le Canarien shifts the focus to the prime chivalric virtue, loyalty. Christians who betray one another also betray their faith. *Le Canarien* protests in its turn that Bertin's treason as unbelievable in a Christian: "This treason was damnable and against the catholic faith, since we were engaged in serving God, innocent, and without fault for which one should so betray us to death. And truly we never imagined that such great inhumanity might be found in the heart of a Christian man."[102] Such episodes lay the missionary open to attack as a hypocrite, an imperfect practitioner of the faith he represents as divine perfection. Their true audience, of course, is the Christian reader, whom the authors hope to induce to see themselves as they might appear to a critical observer from outside the community of their own faith.

---

[100] Ibid., III.121, 133: "moult grant get de pierres."

[101] Ibid., III.57: "Coument nous garderiez vous quant vous mesme traissez l'en l'autre? pour quoy il nous samble que vous ne tenez mie si ferme ne si bonne foy comme vous nous donnez à entendre." For a discussion of the theme, see Charles S. Ross' introduction to Boiardo, *Orlando Innamorato*, pp. 21–24.

[102] *Le Canarien*, III.39: "Or estoit ceste traison dampnable et contre la foy catholique, regardé que nous estions en service de dieu, innocens et sans coulpe parquoy on nous deust / ainsi trair à mort. Et vraiement nous ne pensesons jamais que si grant inhumanitee se peust mectre en courage de homme crestien . . ."

*

Around 1460, when Joanot Martorell was adapting his earlier romance of *William of Warwick* into the opening section of *Tirant lo Blanch*, he changed an invasion of England by the Moorish kings of Tangier and Gibraltar into an act of vengeance by the king of the Canary Islands. The more populous islands of the chain were at that time still resisting their Castilian invaders. Their ultimate conquest would preoccupy Castilian monarchs between 1478 and 1496.[103]

It is not necessary to assume that Martorell drew on any version of *Le Canarien* as a source for his king of the Canary Islands. The idea of the archipelago as a stepping stone to the River of Gold, Prester John, and the reconquest of the Holy Land was well disseminated by 1460, as numerous sources beyond *Le Canarien* attest.

The image of the king that Martorell devises in *Tirant* contradicts the evidence of *Le Canarien* – Fernández-Armesto suggests, out of "presumably conscious irony."[104] It certainly makes a valiant attempt to resolve the chivalric problem posed by the king of Gadifer's chronicle. Early in *Tirant lo Blanc* a Canarian fleet swoops down on England to take revenge for English raids on the Canary Islands. The islanders proceed to rape and pillage the English countryside right and left. After Martorell's hero, the hermit-knight William of Warwick, ignites a form of Greek fire in the besieging Canarians' camp, the king, whom Martorell names Abraham, issues a cartel of defiance to the king of England, offering to meet him in single combat. If he loses, his troops will depart at once. The English king is a delicate young man (modeled perhaps on Richard II or Henry VI). He accepts the challenge, but abdicates in William's favor, so as not to deceive the Saracen. King Abraham makes his appearance on the field wearing a round helmet under his turban, and armed with a bow and arrows. Throughout the passage, he recalls Froissart's portrait of Agadingor Doliferne, the elusive young knight of Barbary who evades capture by the duke of Bourbon's men at the siege of Al-Mahdiya. In fiction a similar personage proves much easier to deal with. William of Warwick dispatches him as a matter of course. After the king's inevitable defeat, the surviving Canarians refuse to honor his agreement, so a final confrontation in battle must take place. Again, there are no surprises: the Saracen invaders are slaughtered without mercy.[105]

Looking at Martorell's work from the vantage point of *Le Canarien*, we can judge how the king of the Canary islands has been reinvented to comply with contemporary experience against "the brightest and best" of the Saracen forces, not to mention the conventions of romance. He now possesses the projectile

---

[103] See Fernández-Armesto, *Before Columbus*, pp. 184–85, 212.

[104] Ibid., p. 221.

[105] Joanot Martorell and Martí Joan de Galba, *Tirant lo Blanc*, ed. Martí de Riquer (Barcelona, 1979). The English translation I use is that of David H. Rosenthal (London and New York, 1984), p. 34.

weapons that Gadifer encountered "before Africa," but which the king of Lanzarote lacked. Where the original Canarians were invaded, King Abraham invades. Unlike his Canarian predecessor, he is literate. More than this, he is adept in chivalric language, capable of initiating a formal chivalric duel to decide who should rule England.

The reinvention underlines how far the original king of Lanzarote and his people fell short as opponents. This is a sensitive matter for the fifteenth-century chivalric audience of stories of exploration. Romance rushes in to adjust the most inconvenient facts. The effect for this twentieth-century reader is less one of conscious irony than of self-justification. In the arena of fiction, at least, the Christian knight can triumph in a just cause, defending his home-land against the treacherous forces of disbelief. *Tirant lo Blanch* offers a telling example of the interplay between chivalry and exploration. Here, the experience of exploration is reimagined to conform with chivalric convention. In particu-lar, the inconvenient native opponent must be reshaped into a plausible Sara-cen. An undercurrent of guilt runs beneath the story: what if the natives of the Canary Islands did arrive one night to do unto the Europeans as the Europeans had done unto them? Martorell's approach to the subject brings reality back into line with the established norms of imaginative fiction. More than that, it supports contemporary efforts to complete the subjugation of the islands by erasing most of the attendant moral difficulties.

There are places where Martorell's perspective repels the modern reader. The technicality that substitutes one king of England for another for purposes of combat may come across to us less as an admirable stratagem than as a dubious act of chicanery. It may also betray a widespread late-medieval cynicism as to God's decisive role in contests of this kind. God is more likely to assist the Christian champion if he happens to be an invincible veteran than if he is only a sickly adolescent. Martorell enjoys the drama of the single combat, but he has few illusions about its spiritual support system.

An even more dubious impression is conveyed to the present-day reader in a scene following the great victory of the English army. William of Warwick's young son has followed him into battle, over the objections of his mother. William decides the boy should be given the chance to execute a giant Saracen prisoner:

> His men had captured a Saracen so huge he might have been a giant. Having knighted the countess's son, His Majesty decided the boy should slay that Saracen. The lad drew his sword and stabbed him again and again till he was dead. Then the king seized the boy's hair and flung him on the infidel. He kept him there until the boy's face was covered with gore and made him stick his hands inside the wounds, thus baptizing his son in infidel blood. The child grew up to be a valiant knight and most fearless in battle. So great was he in his day that in much of the world one could not find his equal.[106]

106 *Tirant*, trans. Rosenthal, p. 33.

The immediate hunting association lies in the tradition of "blooding" a new member of the hunt who has performed with credit for the first time. William initiates his son as a crusader in a new ritual with primitive affinities to all too many ancient ceremonials of blood sacrifice.

Martorell's initial hero, William of Warwick, bears witness that the hermit-knight continued to be admired as late as 1460. William is modeled explicitly after Guy of Warwick, a thirteenth-century hero of fiction who wins his proud bride through seven years of exploits as far afield as Constantinople, only to renounce her to become a pilgrim and then a hermit. Guy emerges from his hermitage later, as William does here, to save his country from the Danes in single combat against an African giant much like the one William's son kills in *Tirant*. Martorell later conflates the Anglo-Norman Guy with Ramon Lull's hermit knight who instructs his squire in the *Libre del orde de cavayleria*, repeating much of Lull's instruction in the process. What Martorell does not introduce in this section of his romance is the idea of the knight as missionary, though he will return to it later.[107] This is still a religious chivalry that gives no quarter to the Saracen invader. Instead, the exemplary William inflicts a savage revenge for English losses, much like the reaction of Gadifer to the loss of his men.[108] In cases like this there is no effort directed to saving souls. Gadifer the missionary knight had to look elsewhere in romance, or to Lull himself and to Philippe de Mézières, for his inspiration. *Le Canarien* and *Tirant* show fifteenth-century knights selecting divergent elements of the Lullian chivalric tradition to incorporate in their own lives or fantasies.

---

[107] E.g. pp. 593–94 where Tirant instructs Pleasure-of-my-life, or the passage where he explains Christianity to King Escariano.

[108] *Le Canarien*, III.83: "Mais euls ont este bien revengiez depuis, car nous en avons tué pour plus de L que de ceuls qui furent à leur mort que d'autrez" ("But they were well avenged later, for we killed more than fifty of those who were present at their deaths or others").

CHAPTER FIVE

The Lady with the Sword: Philippa of Lancaster and the chivalry of Prince Henry the Navigator

We few, we happy few, we band of brothers . . .[1]

ONE OF THE MOST persistent and exuberant medieval literary traditions is that of the woman as an impediment to chivalry.[2] Indeed, in some romances female characters function as an animated obstacle course: *Sir Gawain and the Green Knight* offers a clear example of this effect. Citations supporting this line of thinking go all the way back to that band of brothers, the Germanic *comitatus*. Grendel's mother, Chrétien de Troyes' Enide, Perceval's mother (foundress of the "ignorance is bliss" school of chivalric education), Morgan le Fay, Guinevere – one could go on like this possibly *ad infinitum*, if not *ad nauseam*, and crown it all with Malory's Arthur, as he asserts that he regrets the loss of his knights more than the loss of Guinevere, "for quenys I myght have inow, but such a felyship of good knyghtes shall never be togydirs in no company."[3]

---

1   William Shakespeare, *Henry V*, IV.iii.60.
2   An earlier version of this chapter was first published in the volume *Queens, Regents and Potentates*, ed. Theresa M. Vann, *Women of Power I* (Sawston, 1993), pp. 149–65. It is reproduced here by permission of the Executive Editor, Derek Baker. I am grateful to Professor Baker for his permission to reproduce this essay. The initial research for this paper was presented to the Old and Middle English Doctoral Colloquium of the Department of English at Harvard University in March 1990, as part of a larger paper on chivalry in the age of discovery. It was further developed during a period of summer study in Spain and Britain supported by an NEH summer stipend offered under the Columbian Quincentenary Initiative. The revised version of the paper was presented in February 1992 at the TEMA-MAMA joint conference in Denton, Texas. I am grateful for all the assistance and good counsel I received in the course of these dialogues and investigations.
3   Sir Thomas Malory, *Works*, ed. Eugène Vinaver (2nd edn, 1967; rpt. with additions and corrections, Oxford, 1973), III.1184. The antifeminist element in chivalric literature contrasts strikingly with the element of *fin'amors* and the role of the knight as a supporter of women. Antifeminist material in chivalric works can be subdivided into a number of strands. Most relevant to this paper are the following: a stress on knighthood as a purely masculine enterprise, for which see Ramon Lull's *Libre del orde de cavayleria* of c.1284, ch. 2, as translated by Sir Gilbert Haye, *The Buke of Knyghthede* (1456), 13: "And allsua, in samekle as man is mare worthy, mare curageus, and vertuous, and mare wit and understanding has na womman, and of mare stark nature, in samekle is he better na womman – or ellis nature war contrary till it self . . . and thus sen a man is mare hable till

Perhaps nowhere does chivalry appear more exclusively masculine than in the knighting ceremony. The pictorial records of such scenes rarely depict any female assistance, whether the dubbing takes place in a courtly setting, in church, or on the battlefield.[4] This is, after all, one of the great male initiation rituals of the Middle Ages.[5]

There is a familiar counter-tradition, that of the woman who is chivalrous herself and a cause of chivalry in others. This positive evaluation of the woman's relationship to the knight stretches far beyond the courtly ideal of the lady as the knight's beloved, the essential audience and ultimate reward of his military prowess. Throughout the history of chivalric literature, ladies take on the role of guides and instructors of knights, as well as victims to be rescued. On occasion they can create knights, or even become knights themselves. As a significant instance of feminine chivalric activity, this chapter re-examines a key scene from a notable Portuguese historical work of the 1440s, Gomes Eanes de Zurara's *Crónica da Tomada de Ceuta* (*The Chronicle of the Conquest of Ceuta*, composed in the 1440s). Zurara's work is important to exploration history as a depiction of the initial fifteenth-century Portuguese military expedition to North Africa, and as a history of the youthful deeds (the *enfance*) of the Infante

have mare noble curage, and tobe better na womman, insamekle is he mare enclynit tobe tempit to vice na is the womman, for he is mare hardy undertakare, bathe in gude and evill, opynly . . ." A number of texts discuss the conflict between knighthood and marriage: Cf. Chrétien de Troyes, *Erec et Enide*, lines 2430–502, 2536–71 and Malory's *Lancelot*, *Works*, ed. Vinaver, I.270–71, where "love paramours" is also identified as damaging to the knight. Male virginity is identified in the *Queste del Saint Graal* as essential to chivalric pre-eminence, at least that of Galahad and the Grail knights. The Portuguese Constable Nun'Alvares Pereira was reported to have adopted this viewpoint early in his career. The tradition apparently survived in Portugal into the sixteenth century, as the chivalric career of King Sebastian would seem to indicate. The over-protective mother as a deterrent to her sons' chivalric training appears in Chrétien's *Perceval*, lines 319–22, 401–88. Other chivalric texts berate women as destroyers of men in general and knights in particular, drawing on a broad range of medieval antifeminist texts. C. Batt's recent article "Gawain's Antifeminist Rant, the Pentangle, and Narrative Space," *Yearbook of English Studies* 22 (1992), pp. 117–39 elucidates Gawain's antifeminist outburst towards the end of *Sir Gawain and the Green Knight* and provides useful references to other recent studies of the problem. In Malory Arthur's knights debate whether Guinevere is an enemy of knighthood: "but as for quene Gwenyvere, we love hir nat, because she ys a destroyer of good knyghtes" (Malory, *Works*, ed. Vinaver, II.1054). Bors defends Guinevere on the grounds of her generosity: "ever she hath bene large and fre of hir goodis to all good knyghtes." For more historical and literary background, see R. W. Ackerman, "The Knighting Ceremonies in Middle English Romances," *Speculum* 19 (1945), pp. 285–313; Richard Barber, *The Knight and Chivalry* (1970; revised edn, Woodbridge, 1996); Richard Barber, *The Reign of Chivalry* (New York, 1980).

4   Maurice Keen, *Chivalry* (New Haven, 1984), plates 11–15; Barber, *The Knight and Chivalry*, plates 2–4 and II.

5   One might allude here to Robert Bly's *Iron John*, a work which recently inspired a variety of forest retreats for groups of men and contemporary male initiation rituals in the United States. These events were inevitably criticized for their exclusion of women.

dom Henrique (the English-speaking reader's "Henry the Navigator") as he wanted them to be written. But this chapter will center its attention on that remarkable Englishwoman, Philippa of Lancaster, queen of Portugal, Henry's mother.[6]

Philippa of Lancaster was the elder sister of King Henry IV of England, a daughter of Duchess Blanche of Lancaster (in whose memory Chaucer composed the *Book of the Duchess*) and John of Gaunt. Her marriage to João I of Portugal on 2 February 1387 remained one of the principal achievements of Gaunt's campaign to obtain the throne of Castile in right of his wife, Constance, daughter of Pedro I "the Cruel" (1350–69). Queen Philippa's significance in Portuguese history rests on her maternal role. Henry the Navigator, his four surviving brothers, and their sister Isabel (1397–1471), later duchess of Burgundy, comprised the *inclita geração*, the extraordinary generation of princes to be celebrated by Camões in *The Lusiads*. Twentieth-century scholars have also reconsidered Philippa's political and cultural impact. Philippa's determined assertion of her English identity and its importance has been studied by Russell and Entwistle. We know she kept up her English correspondence, and some letters survive. There she expresses concern for the welfare of her friend, the bishop of Norwich, records her enjoyment of his present of small purses, and makes provision for the comfortable retirement of at least one English attendant. Fernão Lopes comments on her insistence on the Use of Sarum, and her efforts to train Portuguese clergy in its proper performance. Other evidence for this English trait includes Robert Payn's lost Portuguese translation of John Gower's *Confessio Amantis*, the noticeable English contingent among her household staff, and her possible employment of English architectural consultants in the design of the abbey at Batalha where she is buried in a double tomb beside her husband, their effigies holding one another's hands.[7] All of these clues combine to suggest something of Philippa's distinctive individuality. She

---

6   Gomes Eanes de Zurara, *Crónica da Tomada de Ceuta por el rei D. João I*, ed. Francisco Maria Esteves Pereira (Lisbon, n.d.). All citations of the Portuguese text are taken from this edition. The English translation I am citing is Gomes Eanes de Zurara, *Conquests and Discoveries of Henry the Navigator*, ed. Virginia de Castro E. Almeida, trans. Bernard Miall (London, 1936). Cf. P. E. Russell, *Prince Henry the Navigator: The Rise and Fall of a Culture Hero* (Oxford, 1984), and for background in general, P. E. Russell, *The English Intervention in Spain and Portugal in the Time of Edward III and Richard II* (Oxford, 1955). For Philippa, see in addition Fernão Lopes, *The English in Portugal, 1367–87*, ed. and trans. Derek W. Lomax and R. J. Oakley (Westminster, 1988), pp. 219–41 on the circumstances of Philippa's marriage, and her personal character, and W. J. Entwistle and P. E. Russell, "A Rainha D. Felipa e sua côrte," *Congresso do mundo português – publicações*, 11 (Lisbon, 1940), pp. 319–46, on her entourage in Portugal. Several of her letters are reproduced there and in Dominica Legge, ed., *Anglo-Norman Letters and Petitions from All Souls MS. 182*, Anglo-Norman Texts 3 (Oxford, 1941), nos. 28, 287, 307. I am grateful to Lois L. Honeycutt for her recollection of Philippa's tomb at Batalha.

7   Russell, *Intervention*, pp. 541–47.

makes what may be her most dramatic appearance, though, in the narrative of
Zurara.

The entire opening section of Zurara's *Crónica* rewards analysis. It focuses
attention, as P. E. Russell once suggested, on Queen Philippa's role in the
cultivation of a new Portuguese chivalric mentality. The narrative starts with
King João of Portugal's wish "that his sons should be knighted in a splendid
fashion." The year is 1412. The actual conquest of Ceuta did not occur until
August 1415, about the same time Henry V of England, the Portuguese princes'
first cousin, was engaged at Agincourt. The heir to the throne, the Infante Dom
Duarte, was then twenty-one; his more robust brother Dom Pedro was twenty,
Dom Henrique only eighteen. Two other, younger sons, João, twelve, and
Fernando, nine, were not yet involved in chivalric exploits. The king envisions
a great feast, with an aristocratic, international guest list, jousts, banquets and
dancing, a display of magnificence calculated to arouse universal admiration.
The princes object.

> "The fashion in which the King has thought to make us enter the order of
> chivalry is in truth most unworthy of the greatness of such a happening. It is
> not by feasts, even the most splendid, that such a happening may be cele-
> brated. Great exploits, courage, deadly perils, and the spilling of enemy blood,
> these are the things that open the path of chivalry to such as we. It is for the
> sons of citizens and merchants to celebrate the great events of their life by
> feasts, for their honour cannot outstrip their state, and their renown is in
> proportion to their expenses."[8]

This passage suggests that, just as merchants were adopting elements of courtly
culture, aristocrats were struggling to differentiate themselves from their affluent contemporaries. A well-heeled citizen could compete with the king in
holding a banquet, or even a joust, but not a crusade.

It was João Affonso, intendant of the king's finances, who suggested the
capture of the North African port of Ceuta in Morocco as a more appropriate
prelude to knighthood than a mere banquet. There had been at least one prior
expedition, which is noted in P. E. Russell's *English Intervention*. Chaucer's
knight seems to have been in the vicinity, no doubt because one of the models
Chaucer may have used for his knight, Duchess Blanche of Lancaster's father
Henry of Derby, had been there too. After having come to take part in the siege

---

8   Zurara, *Conquests*, trans. Miall, p. 33. Zurara, *Crónica*, ed. Pereira, pp. 25–26: "Ca polla
    maneira que sua senhoria tem vontade de o fazer todo he cousa de pequeno valor pera a
    grandeza de tamanho feito. que por grandes que as festas sejam nunqua seu nome he de
    grande vallia pera semelhante caso. por que semelhantes pessoas nos grandes feitos de
    fortaleza com grandes trabalhos e perigos vendo o sangue dos seus jmigos espargido ante
    seus pees soo he de rreçeber o grado de sua caualaria. E os filhos dos çidadãos e dos
    mercadores cuja honrra *nom se pode mais estender que a semelhante estado .ss. de
    serem caualeiros. a estes he cousa conuinhauel de se fazerem festas e jogos. porque toda
    a força de sua honrra esta na fama de sua despesa."

of Algeciras (the Middle English "Algezir"), Derby joined the Castilian *almirante mayor de la mar* Egidio Boccanegra in his galley of war for an attack against the Moorish fleet at Ceuta. Evidently Henry of Derby and his colleague Salisbury made full reports on their return; Russell credits them with stimulating English interest in Spain. "It is not without significance that it was John of Gaunt's father-in-law, Henry of Derby, to whom most credit must be given for the Anglo-Castilian *rapprochement* during the last years of Alfonso's reign."[9]

The importance of Henry as a chivalric model for his descendants, in the choice of specific knightly exploits and in their combination of knighthood and authorship, needs to be better appreciated. Henry's spiritual autobiography, the Anglo-Norman *Livre de Seyntz Medicines*, should probably be related to his great-grandson Duarte's equally didactic and personal *Leal Conselheiro* and Pedro's *Virtuosa Bemfeitoria*. In the case of the Portuguese princes of the House of Aviz, models of royal authorship were available on both sides of the family, since João I was the author of a treatise on hunting.[10] For whatever reason, ancestral, literary, or otherwise, the Princes were immediately attracted to the idea of persuading their father to mount a crusade for them, rather than hosting a party.

In Zurara's twentieth chapter the princely enterprise is divulged, hesitantly, to two influential "obstacles," Queen Philippa and the Constable, Nun'Alvares Pereira, famed for his "holy life and high exploits," long recognized as a preeminent military and chivalric figure in Portugal.[11] The princes ask their

---

9   Russell, *Intervention*, pp. 7–9.
10 Henry of Derby, *Livre de Seyntz Medicines*, ed. Emile J. Arnould. Anglo-Norman Texts 2 (Oxford, 1940). For excerpts and discussion of the works of João, Duarte and Pedro of Portugal, see Rodrigues Lapa, ed., *Dom duarte e os prosadores da Casa de Avis* (3rd edn, Lisbon, 1972). Duarte's manual of horsemanship, the *Libro da Ensinança Cavalgar toda sela* of c.1434 (*Book of Training in Riding in all kinds of saddles*), was admired and translated in part in Richard Barber and Juliet Barker, *Tournaments: Jousts, Chivalry, and Pageants in the Middle Ages* (Woodbridge, 1989), pp. 197–205, as the only surviving practical handbook of equestrian technique for the medieval knight, and apparently the first manual of horsemanship in any European vernacular. As another influential factor operating on the princes, one might cite the mass knighting João I conducted before his surprising victory over Juan I of Castile in the battle of Aljubarrota of 14 August 1385 (for this see the *Chronicle* of Fernão Lopes, Parte Segunda, XXX–XLIII).
11 Pereira has long been recognized as the military genius behind João of Aviz's success against Castile. "On 6 April [1384], at Os Atoleiros in Alemtejo, the earnest young student of the Round Table, Nun'Alvares Pereira – whose decision to break his family ties and join Dom João had given the latter the services of a military commander of real distinction – had severely defeated a superior Castilian force by employing new tactics on the English model against the mounted Castilian men-at-arms" (Russell, *Intervention*, pp. 365–66). He needs also to be seen as a powerful and rather uncommon chivalric influence in his own right. This is the Nun'Alvares Pereira who at sixteen is supposed to have resisted marriage because, as an enthusiastic reader of the Quest of the Holy Grail, he believed that Galahad's military success was due to his virginity. This occurs in a story Fernão Lopes tells: "liia ameude per livros destorias, especiallmente da estoria de Gallaz

mother first. The queen replies by approaching the king with an "unmotherly request," "for in general the mother asks of the father that he will keep their sons from following any dangerous courses, fearing always the harm that might befall them. As for me, I ask you to keep them from sports and pleasures and to expose them to perils and fatigues." Let them be given every chance to emulate their chivalrous ancestors.

> "For myself, Sire, considering the line from which they are descended, a line of very great and excellent emperors and kings and other princes, whose name and renown are broadcast in the whole world, I would not by any means – since God has pleased to make them perfect in body and mind – that they should lack opportunities of accomplishing, by their fatigues, their valour, and their skill, the like high feats as were accomplished by their ancestors."[12]

Zurara underlines the support offered by an earlier generation for the chivalric goals of the young princes. Any apparent conflict of generations collapses at this point in the chronicle. The tension the historian had attempted

---

que falla da Tavolla Redonda. E porque em ellas achava, que per virtude de virgiidade Gallaaz acabara gramdes e notavees feitos, que outros acabar nom podiam, desejava muito de o semelhar em alguua guisa; e muita vzes cuidava em sssi, de seer virgem se lho Deos guisasse" (Fernão Lopes, *Crónica del Rei Dom João I, Parte I*, ed. Anselmo Braamcamp Freire (1915; facsimile: Lisbon, 1973) cited in Russell, *Prince Henry*, p. 28, n. 11). Russell suggests that Henry the Navigator's insistence on his own virginity indicates he subscribed to the same view. This fifteenth-century Portuguese chivalric vision – masculine, monastic, austere, with its clear affinity for Galahad as a model – may derive to some extent from the religious orders of knighthood. João I (1357–1433), illegitimate son of Pedro I of Portugal, was Master of the military order of Aviz when he became a somewhat reluctant claimaint to the throne of Portugal, and needed a papal dispensation from his own vow of celibacy before he could marry Philippa. (See Russell, *Intervention*, p. 449 for the difficulties involved; this did not prevent João from siring three illegitimate children of his own in the early 1370s.) The remarkable series of Portuguese Galahads continues through King Sebastian, who died on another North African crusade in 1578. By the time he was consulted regarding the Ceuta expedition, Nun'Alvares Pereira had retired to a life of religion, very much in the manner of the hermit knights of the Arthurian tradition, or Ramon Lull's *Book of the Ordre of Chyualry*. (Charles V in 1556 would resign as emperor in much the same way.)

12 Zurara, *Conquests*, trans. Miall, pp. 52–53. Zurara, *Crónica*, ed. Pereira, p. 63: "Senhor, disse a Rainha, eu uos quero rrequerer huua cousa que he mujto comtrayra pera rrequerer madre pera filhos, porque comuumente as madres rrequerem * aos padres que arredem seus filhos dos trabalhos perijgosos, teemdo sempre gramde arreeo de quaaesquer danos que lhe possam acomteçer. eu tenho teemçom de uos rrequerer que os arredees dos jogos e das follgamças, e os metaaes nos trabalhos e perijgos ... E eu senhor esguardamdo como elles ueem de linhagem demperadores e rrex e doutros muy notauees e gramdes primçipes, cujo gramde nome e boa fama he oje per as partes do mundo muy nomeada, nom queria per neuua guisa, pois lhe Deus por sua merçee quis dar a desposiçom dos corpos e do emtemder, que elles per seu trabalho falleçessem de comsseguir os feitos daquelles que disse."

to develop did not reflect any substantive disagreement between parents and sons. The historian had questioned whether the sons would share the chivalric enthusiasm of their fathers. The question is here answered in the affirmative. Far from losing interest in chivalry, the young princes have turned out to be chivalric perfectionists.

A series of attempts by the suspicious Moors to obtain promises of immunity from the House of Aviz include an attempt to bribe Philippa with a fabulous trousseau for her daughter Isabel. This initiative is ascribed to the chief wife of the king of Granada, Rica Forma. Her appeal to Philippa, woman to woman, asserts the importance of feminine influence behind the scenes. "Rica Forma knew well, they said, that the prayers of women had much power over the hearts of husbands . . ." Philippa is represented as retorting:

> "I do not know . . . what may be the manners of your kings with their wives. Among Christians it is not the custom for a queen or a princess to meddle with the affairs of her husband in such cases, since for this they have their councillors, and their wives are the wiser the more they hold themselves aloof from matters which do not concern them, and avoid knowing what they cannot understand. . . ."

Here Queen Philippa beats a tactical retreat into stereotype. The ideal Christian princess she depicts is not entirely believable, but she is useful in this particular diplomatic predicament. "As to the outfit of which you speak, she must do as she pleases, for, with God's grace, my daughter will have all that she needs for her marriage. . . ." Of course, Philippa is really trying to avoid either an outright lie or any confirmation that an attack is being planned.[13]

As the fleet approaches completion, Zurara stresses the unity of Portugal, especially the unity of purpose of the older knights and their untried sons.[14] Again Prince Henry distinguishes himself by the superior preparation of his own fleet. The plague, possibly spread from foreign ships, does not halt preparations. Volunteers turn up. Among them, a ninety-year-old knight, Ayres de

---

[13] Zurara, *Conquests*, trans. Miall, pp. 66–67. Zurara, *Crónica*, ed. Pereira, pp. 107–08: "E por quamto ella sabia quamto os boõs rrequerimentos das molheres mouiam os coraçõoes dos maridos . . ." "Eu nom sei rrespomdeo ella, a maneyra que os uossos rrex teem com suas molheres. mas amtre os christaãos nom he bem comtado a nehha rraínha nem a outra nehuua gramde prímçesa de sse tremeter nos feitos de seu marido, quamto em semelhamtes casos, pera os quaaes elles teem seus comsselhos, homde determinam seus feitos segumdo entemdem. e as suas molheres quamto melhores ssam, tamto com mayor dilligemçia se guardam de quererem saber o que a ellas nom perteeçe . . . [Verdade he que * ellas nom som assy afastadas de todo, que lhe nom fique poder de rrequerer o que lhes praz. mas estes rrequerimentos ssom taaes, que os maridos nom ham rrezam de lhos neguar. e alguuas que o comtrairo fazem, nom ssom auidas por emsinadas nem discretas.] Porem uos direes aa rrainha uossa senhora, que eu lhe agradeço sua boa voomtade. mas que ella podera de seu emxouall fazer o que lhe prouuer. ca com a graça de Deos a minha filha nom falleçera emxouall pera seu casamento."

[14] Zurara, *Conquests*, trans. Miall, p. 69.

140

Figuereido, presents himself to Henry, who laughs at him. The nonagenarian is immediately joined by two squires from Bayonne of similar age.[15] Zurara tells us the dead themselves wished to be resurrected in order to join the fleet. He also records a vision of a Dominican at Porto. The friar reported seeing King João, armed, kneeling before the Virgin Mary: "armed at all points, on his knees, his hands being folded and lifted toward the heavens, whence was presented to him a sword, whose brilliance could not be likened to any earthly thing; but the good monk could not see who held the sword, for his eyes could not endure this divine splendour."[16] This scene sets the stage for the later arming of his three sons by their mother. It gives João his own moment of mystical chivalric exaltation. Zurara's account of the reverent king, receiving a heavenly sword in the presence of the Virgin Mary from a splendid, invisible but presumably divine source, echoes Arthur's reception of Excalibur from the arm clad in white samite, only with enhanced supernatural authority.

Zurara describes the final preparations of Henry's fleet, its magnificent provision of flags, glittering devices, canopies, and the prince's own motto: "Talent de Bien faire," translated by Miall as the "power to do well."

> The ordering of this fleet was glorious; all the ships of war, galleys, and other vessels were adorned with the great standards of the chevaliers of Christ and little flags with the colours and the device of the Infante; and as they were new and richly adorned with gold, men marvelled to behold them. Tilts and canopies of rich stuffs in the colours of the Infante, and bearing his written device, covered the decks of the galleys . . .[17]

The crew, needless to say, were completely outfitted in the prince's livery, "garlands of holm oak overlaid with silver, surrounding the device *Power to do well*; and the colours were white, blue, and black."[18] As in contemporaneous tournament records, the chronicler is intent on recording visual effects, individual presences, and the magnificence of the total event. Zurara describes the meeting of the fleets, dwelling with particular insistence on the affectionate reunion of Henry and Pedro, and on the unparalleled closeness of the relation-

---

15 Ibid., pp. 70–71.
16 Ibid., p. 72. Zurara, *Crónica*, ed. Pereira, p. 112: ". . . amtre as quaaes lhe pareçeo que uija amte a uirgem Maria elRey Dom Joham, estamdo armado com os jeolhos em terra e as maãos aleuamtadas comtra o çeeo, homde lhe apresemtauam huua espada, cujo rresplamdor pareçia aaquelle boom homem que nom tijnha comparaçam. mas o portador daquella espada nom conheçeo elle, como quer que a sua uista quamto ao seu conheçimento lhe pareçia cousa diuinall."
17 Zurara, *Conquests*, trans. Miall, p. 73. Zurara, *Crónica*, ed. Pereira, pp. 113–14: "e era fremosa cousa de ueer o corregimento daquella frota, porque todallas naaos e gallees e outros nauios eram nobremente apemdoadas com balssoões e pemdoões pequenos das coores motos e deuisa do Iffamte. e porque eram todos nouos e bem acompanhados douro, dauam mujto gramde uista. e as gallees eram tolldadas de finos panos daquelles motos e deuisa que ja disse."
18 Zurara, *Conquests*, trans. Miall, p. 74.

ship between all five of the brothers and their father. Zurara emphasizes this fraternal amity as a marvel unprecedented in literature. "There is no writing which could make us believe that ever the like was seen."[19]

At this joyous moment, a squire of Henry's brings news that Queen Philippa has contracted the plague, and her family rush to her bedside. She, too, had been making her preparations for the fleet's departure. Zurara describes the three swords, with scabbards and guards adorned with gold, pearls, and cut stones, that she had ordered for the knighting ceremony of her sons. The reversal of mood, from joyous anticipation to the sombre apprehension of the queen's death, is stressed through the medium of Zurara's heightened language. This scene, in which the queen takes leave of her sons and confers a sword upon each of them, is remarkable for its chivalric implications. The princes are not knighted in her presence before their departure, as she had hoped they would be. Instead, the scene serves as a prelude to the actual knighting ceremony, with the queen offering each son his sword and charging him with an office suited to his position and character. Philippa asks the king to knight her sons with the swords she has given them. "It is said that arms offered by women weaken the hearts of chevaliers; but I believe that, having regard to the line from which I am descended, the swords which the Infantes receive from my hand will by no means enfeeble their hearts."[20] Clearly, Philippa is alert to more than one aspect of the complex tradition of chivalric antifeminism.

Philippa evokes a different chivalry. Notice in the queen's remarks her stress, now explicit, on her own lineage: "I require you to accept this sword from my hand with my blessing and that of your forefathers from whom I am descended."[21]

So far, I have found no other case where the mother gives the sword in preparation for a knighting ceremony, though fathers regularly elevate their own sons to knighthood, as in the case of Lancelot and Galahad. There is one loose parallel in earlier French literature. When the lady gives the sword to her son Yonec in Marie de France's lay of that name, the story seems to be caught between the idea of the woman as an inciter to violence and the idea of the woman passing on the father's chivalry to the son, here also immediately prior

---

[19] Zurara, *Crónica*, ed. Pereira, p. 114: "Mas porque eria gramde prolixidade escpreuermos a deuisa de cada huu, abasta soomente que a do Iffamte eram huuas capellas de carrasco bem acompanhadas de chaparia, e por meyo huus motos que deziam uoomtade de bem fazer, e as suas coores eram bramco e preto e uijs." Zurara, p. 115: "numca sse achou em espcrituras que os alguu primçipe teuesse."

[20] Zurara, *Conquests*, trans. Miall, p. 76; Zurara, *Crónica*, ed. Pereira, p. 121: "ca posto que seia dito, que as armas das molheres emfraqueçem os corações dos caualleiros, bem creeo que segumdo a geeraçom de que eu uenho, numca seram emfraqueçidos por as rreçeberem de minha maão."

[21] Zurara, *Conquests*, trans. Miall, p. 77. Zurara, *Crónica*, ed. Pereira, p. 128: "Porem uos rroguo que sem empacho uos queyraaes filhar esta de minha maão, a quall uos eu dou com a minha beemçom e de uossos auoos, de que eu deçemdo."

to her own death. (Several versions of the Perceval story make powerful use of the motif of the mother's death, but in that case the mother is vehemently opposed to her son's knighthood and, in a way, its victim. The loss of her one remaining son to chivalry contributes to her death.) For the moment it appears that this ceremony represents a creative reworking of chivalric tradition. Philippa and her sons, or perhaps only their chronicler, consider her so essential to their chivalric identity that she must be made to play a role in their accession to knighthood, even on her deathbed. Or should we interpret the episode as Queen Philippa insisting on taking part, creating a role for herself?

In presenting these swords Philippa also presents her sons with chivalric fields of specialization. This aspect of the ceremony might be interpreted as a pragmatic effort to prevent sibling rivalry among the princes by pointing them in different directions.

In a rite with biblical and feudal overtones, each son kneels, kisses Philippa's hand, promises to obey her, and receives a sword, as Philippa blesses him with hand raised. This innovative family event testifies to the creative vigor of chivalric life at the Portuguese court rather than its decadence, in my opinion at least. Another reader might adopt the opposite view, and argue that this is merely the classic knighting ceremony going downhill fast through the intrusion of an impertinent female.

To Duarte, as heir to the throne, Philippa offers a sword of justice – justice with mercy. Does this sound like a prelude to coronation as well as a prelude to knighthood? "And note well, my son, that whereas I say justice I mean justice with compassion, for justice without mercy is no longer to be called justice but cruelty."[22] Duarte, as king, is to care for the populace at large. The second son, Dom Pedro (who was to play a problematic role in Portuguese history, to travel and crusade in Transylvania, and become a special object of study of the late Francis M. Rogers), is, like another problematic character, Gawain, dedicated by the queen to the service of ladies.

> "My son, since your childhood I have ever seen how greatly you are con-
> cerned respecting the honour and service of ladies and damozels, which is
> one of the things that are especially to be commended to knights . . . for you,
> I recommend you to have always in mind the care of defending and protect-
> ing the honour and happiness of ladies and damozels."[23]

---

22 Zurara, *Conquests*, trans. Miall, pp. 76–77; Zurara, *Crónica*, ed. Pereira, p. 127: "E ueedes filho, como diguo justiça, justiça com piedade. ca a justiça, que em alguua parte nom he piedosa, nom he chamada justiça mas cruelldade."

23 Zurara, *Conquests*, trans. Miall, p. 77; Zurara, *Crónica*, ed. Pereira, p. 128: "Meu filho, porque sempre des o tempo de upssa mininiçe uos ui mujto chegado aa homrra e seruiço das donas e domzellas, que he huua cousa que espiçiallmente deue seer emcomemdada aos caualleiros, e porque a uosso jrmaão emcomemdei os pouoos, emcomemdo ellas a uos. as quaaes uos rroguo que sempre ajaaes em uossa emcomemda." For Pedro's future career, see Francis M. Rogers, *The Travels of the Infante Dom Pedro of Portugal* (Cambridge, 1961).

I remain uncertain about the precise effect of this recommendation on Pedro's future career.

Zurara heightens the emotional pitch still further before his hero, Henry, approaches his mother. Queen Philippa smiles at the youngest of the three princes "for he was yet all but a child." She commends his strength:

> "This third sword I have kept for you, for as you are strong, so also it is strong. . . . To you I wish to commend all the seigneurs, chivaliers, *fidalgos*, and squires of this realm, for albeit they all belong to the King . . . yet they will often have need of your aid in order to maintain their rights and receive the benefits and rewards which they may deserve; for often, by reason of the false witness and abusive requests of the people, the kings take action against them, which thing they should never do."[24]

By making Henry the protector of lords and knights, and their representative before the king, Philippa gives her third son a special chivalric status. He is to be a secular head and protector of the chivalric classes of Portugal.

These three charges – to administer justice, with mercy, to the people, to serve women, and to honor the knightly classes, appear among the key duties of knights and princes in Ramon Lull's Catalan *Libre del orde de cavayleria* of about 1280, still a widely circulating, popular chivalric manual in the fifteenth century. The scene closes with the queen fortelling the precise moment of the fleet's departure, and that of her own death. At the last she experiences a vision of the Virgin Mary. King João is only persuaded to leave Philippa's bedside when his advisors warn him that the sight of her corpse might diminish his courage for the coming expedition.

There are parallels to this scene in the annals of medieval romance. Any number of ladies finance their knights and supply them with armor. In some cases they do provide a first sword. Closer involvement with the knighting ceremony itself are less common. Maurice Keen does note that Orderic Vitalis tells of Cicely, the wife of Tancred of Antioch, knighting a group of squires

---

[24] Zurara, *Conquests*, trans. Miall, p. 78. Zurara, *Crónica*, ed. Pereira, pp. 128–29: "Meu filho, chegaiuos pera ca, uistimdo ella sua comtenemça de nova lediçe, e emchemdo sua boca de rriso muy honestamente, e disse. Bem uistes a rrepartiçom, que fiz das outras espadas que dey a uossos jrmaãos. e esta terçeira guardey pera uos, a quall eu tenho que assy como uos sooes forte, assy he ella. (E porque ahuu de uossos jrmaãos emcmemdei os pouoos, e a outro as donas e domzellas,) a uos quero emcomemdar todollos sehores, *caualleiros fidallgos e escudeiros destes rregnos, os quaaes uos emcomemdo que ajaaes em uosso espiçall emcarreguo. Ca pero todos seiam delRey, e elle delles tenha espiçall cuidado, cada huu em seu estado, elles porem aueram mester uossa ajuda pera seerem mamteudos em dreito, e lhe seerem feitas aquellas merçees que esteuer em rrezom. ca mujtas uezes acomteçe, que per emformaçoões fallsas e rrequimentos sobeios dos pouoos os rrex fazem comtra elles o que nom deuem." Cf. Ramon Lull, *Libro del orde de Cauayleria*, in vol. 1 of his *Obres Essencials*, ed. Miguel Batllori, Joaquim Carreras i Artau, and Martí de Riquer (Barcelona, 1957).

before combat in 1119.[25] In the Middle English *King Horn* Princess Rymenild helps arrange for Horn to be made a knight by her father, but at Horn's own request: she remains discreetly backstage. *Partonope of Blois* may be the only romance in English in which a lady dubs a knight: in this case the fairy Melior takes the sword hung round her beloved's neck and girds it around his waist.[26]

The idea of receiving a sword from a lady is especially prominent in Arthurian narrative, much more so, I believe, than in any other cycle of romances I know, or in the non-cyclic works of my acquaintance. It might even be identified as an Arthurian motif. English-speaking readers may be most familiar with the instances represented in Malory. In one of the two versions of the story Malory presents, Arthur receives his sword Excalibur from the Lady of the Lake, by way of the Arm Clad in White Samite that rises mysteriously from the lake.[27] Excalibur is stolen from him by another woman, Morgan le Fay, who provides him with a most inadequate substitute, and still another, Nynyve, the Damsel of the Lake, helps him to recover it.[28] In "The Knight of the Two Swords" Balin obtains the ominous sword that dooms him from the damsel sent by Lady Lyle of Avilion, and refuses to give it back to her – it will become Galahad's sword.[29] Later still, at a strategic point Lancelot states that he received his mislaid sword as a new knight not from Arthur but from Guinevere, and that this incident inspired him with devotion to her. This is the story told with circumstantial detail in the French *Lancelot*.[30] This giving and taking of swords has multiple Freudian possibilities, which the twentieth-century reader can develop without authorial assistance.

In the *Quest of the Holy Grail* Percival's sister helps Galahad to claim the ancient and mystical sword he finds in the ship, and she supplies it with girdles she has braided from her own hair. As she girds it on him, she remarks: " 'Now recke I nat though I dye, for now I holde me one of the beste blyssed maydyns of the worlds, whych hath made the worthyest knyght of the worlde.' 'Damesel,' seyde sir Galahad, 'ye have done so muche that I shall be your knight all the dayes of my lyff.' "[31] This may be the most pertinent Arthurian parallel. If so, it may underline again the special appeal of the Grail story for Portuguese chivalry of this period.

This material all became accessible to English-speaking readers of the final decades of the fifteenth century in the version of Sir Thomas Malory. However, Malory does not present the prose *Lancelot*'s thirteenth-century account of young Lancelot's education by the Lady of the Lake (*la dame del lac*). That lady gives Lancelot a famous lecture on the true nature of knighthood before

25 Keen, *Chivalry*, p. 80.
26 Ackerman, "Knighting Ceremonies," p. 297.
27 Malory, *Works*, ed. Vinaver, I.41.
28 Malory, "Arthur and Accolon," ibid., I.105.
29 Ibid., I.68.
30 Ibid., III.1058; for the French scene, see the following pages.
31 For the whole episode, see ibid., II.706–15.

delivering him to King Arthur to be made knight. Arthur knights him, but Lancelot evades the crucial act, the giving of the sword, so that he can receive his sword from Guinevere. The author stresses that Lancelot is not a knight until he receives this sword. In a subsequent scene, when Guinevere asks her young admirer who knighted him, he is able to reply, "Lady, you did. . . . For it has been the custom in the kingdom of Logres that a knight cannot be made unless he is girded with his sword, and the one from whom he receives the sword makes him a knight, and from you I have mine, which the king never gave me."[32] Nothing here is exactly like Philippa of Lancaster's ceremony, but perhaps it should be seen as a distinctive recombination of the Lady of the Lake's parting instruction and Guinevere's gift of the sword.

Zurara's scene sheds light in other directions as well. It underlines the importance of maternal ancestry – a matrilineal chivalry – for these Lancastrians of England and Portugal. Henry of Derby left his daughters great wealth, but also a high international chivalric reputation as crusader and jouster. One should note as well that Edward III of England claimed the throne of France through his mother Isabel: Edward's son John of Gaunt became duke of Lancaster through his first wife, Blanche, and claimed the throne of Castile through his second wife, Constance, the daughter of King Pedro the Cruel. This is, then, a family specially preoccupied with its maternal lineage.[33]

Zurara's text displays a particular sensitivity to the queen's dual role as mother and wife. As Philippa responds to her sons' initial request, and later to

---

[32] H. Oskar Sommer, ed., *The Vulgate Version of The Arthurian Romances*, III: *Le Livre de Lancelot del lac* (Washington, 1910), p. 131: "Et mesire ye[u]ains len remaine parmi la sale. & quant il vint a son ostel. si li a arme son chief & ses mains. Et quant il li volt lespee chaindre si li menbre de chou que li rois ne li auoit onques chainte si li dist. Sire par mon chief [R 26 a] vous nestes mie cheualiers. porcoi fait li valles por chou fait mesires ye[v]vains que li rois ne vous a pas lespee chainte." Later, at p. 259 (in a meeting of Guinevere and Lancelot, arranged by Galehot): "Or me dites fait ele. qui vous fist cheualier. Dame fait il vous. Ie fait ele quant. dame fait il menbre vous il que vns cheualiers vint a monseignor le roi artu a camaalot qui estoit naures parmi le cors. & dune espee parmi le teste. & que vns valles vint a lui le vendredi au soir. & si fu cheualier le diemenche. de che fait ele me souient il bien. Et se diex vous ait fait ele fuste vous cil qui la damoisele amena au roi. vestue de robe blance. Dame fait il oil. porcoi dites vous dont que ie vous fis cheualier. Dame por ce que il est voirs. Car la coustume estoit el roialme de logres que cheualiers ne pooit estre fais sans espee chaindre. & chil de qui il tient lespee le fait cheualier & de vous le tieng ie. que le rois ne men douna point. por ce di ie que vous me feistes cheualier. Chertes fait ele de che sui ie moult lie . . ." Cf. Harvey L. Sharrer, *A Critical Bibliography of Hispanic Arthurian Material*, I: *Texts: The Prose Romance Cycles* (London, 1977) on surviving Portuguese Arthurian works. As her letters demonstrate, Philippa of Lancaster read and wrote French.

[33] Here one should also take into account the view of Philippa and her ancestry developed in Portuguese chronicles like that of Fernão Lopes. Cf. Fernão Lopes, *The English in Portugal*, ed. and trans. Lomax and Oakley (Westminster, 1988), p. xxxi. There, the impressive success of Philippa and her offspring vindicates the English intervention in Iberia.

the Moorish queen's message, we see her define herself against long-established stereotypes. She is not one of these clinging mothers like Perceval's: she encourages her sons' military ambitions. Neither is she a wife who makes private diplomatic arrangements or takes bribes to influence her royal husband. It seems notable, or at any rate, symmetrical, that the bribe attempt focuses on Philippa's daughter's wedding – the primary female rite of initiation in many societies, and in that respect the feminine counterpart of the knighting ritual.

The powerful feminine presence in fifteenth-century chivalric life and literature deserves more attention than it has yet received. Christine de Pizan stands out from among her contemporaries as a female author who ventured to write a chivalric manual, *Le Livre des Fais d'Armes et de Chevalerie* (*The Book of Feats of Arms and of Chivalry*) around the first decade of the fifteenth century.[34] In a well-known opening passage Christine invokes Minerva, "goddess of arms and of chivalry," credited with the invention of armor, like herself "an Italian woman."[35] It is also the era of Joan of Arc (1412–31). Women, as well as men, showed increasing tendencies to act out fantasies inspired by chivalric romance, as a series of startling aristocratic love-matches of the mid-fifteenth century may testify.[36] By the end of the century Italian and Spanish authors would add notable new women warriors to the world of romance, as in Boiardo's *Orlando Innamorato* and the Californian Amazons of *Las Sergas de Esplandián*.[37] To appreciate the magnitude of the change we have only to look back at Lull's *Libre del orde de cavayleria*, where the woman is presented as the antithesis of the knight, and where her sole duty is identified as sexual fidelity to her husband. Whether this alteration of the tradition represents abject decadence or maturity remains for the reader to decide: like Caxton's readers, "ye been at your liberté."

---

[34] Charity Cannon Willard, *Christine de Pizan: Her Life and Works* (New York, 1984), pp. 83–84.

[35] Willard, *Christine de Pizan*, pp. 180, 183–86.

[36] Among the more startling *mésalliances* of the fifteenth century should be included that of Catherine de Valois, widow of Henry V, and Owen Tudor (c.1425?), of Jacquetta de St Pol, widow of Henry's brother John, duke of Bedford, and Sir Richard Woodville (c.1436), and that of Jacquetta's daughter Elizabeth Grey and Edward IV in 1464. These should probably be regarded as a series. Ian Michael regards Isabel of Castile's elopement as a deed perhaps inspired by the reading of romances. See I. Michael, " 'From Her Shall Read the Perfect Ways of Honour': Isabel of Castile and Chivalric Romance," in *The Age of the Catholic Monarchs, 1474–1516: Literary Studies in Memory of Keith Whinnom*, ed. Alan Deyermond and Ian MacPherson, *Bulletin of Hispanic Studies*, Special Issue (Liverpool, 1989).

[37] Boiardo, *Orlando Innamorato*, trans. Charles Stanley Ross (Italian text rpt. from the edition of Aldo Scaglione) (Berkeley, Los Angeles, and Oxford, 1989). Notice also the rise of works cataloguing women of accomplishment to parallel the masculine pantheon of the *Neuf Preux* (The Nine Worthies): the *Neuf Preuses* (Nine Women Worthies). Boccacio's *De Feminis Illustribus*, Christine de Pizan's *Livre de la Cité des Dames* (*The Book of the City of Ladies*). See Horst Schroeder, *Der Topos der Nine Worthies in Literatur und bildender Kunst* (Göttingen, 1971), pp. 168ff.

But I might add that one of my hopes for this chapter is that it may serve as a gateway into the larger subject of the woman's experience of chivalric literature.

Queen Philippa's deathbed presentation of swords to her three sons, as portrayed in Zurara's work, gives ceremonial form to their maternal chivalric inheritance. Philippa here creates a powerful role for herself. If she does not knight her sons, she comes close, by instructing them, identifying their fields of specialization, and supplying them with the essential emblem of knighthood and of masculine identity, the sword itself.

CHAPTER SIX

The Quest for Montezuma:
rereading the *cartas de relacíon*

"God give us the same good fortune in fighting . . . as he gave to the Paladin Roland."[1]

HERNAN CORTES, the conqueror of what is now called the Mexica "empire," was recognized from the first as the very model of a conquistador.[2] As Anthony J. Pagden points out in the introduction to his translation of Cortes' letters, his conquest established a precedent. Pizarro in Peru, Coronado in New Mexico, and any number of later adventurers in the Americas were to pattern themselves upon him.

Pagden also notes that Cortes is the only conquistador who wrote at any length about his own deeds. In effect, he wrote his own press releases. In his four surviving letters, the *cartas de relacion* ("letters of relation") dated between 1520 and 1526, Cortes invents his own legend. These letters have often been explored as historical documents and in some instances found wanting. Cortes' account of his own exploits was indeed challenged by other contemporary witnesses. Bernal Diaz and Bartolomé de las Casas were to supplement and censure him. In spite of this, Cortes stands preeminent as the chief mythographer of the enterprise of conquest. He may have had greater influence as a writer than as a soldier. What Cortes wrote of his adventures among the Aztecs proved so intoxicating that in 1527 their publication in Spanish was banned by royal command.[3] Closer analysis of the literary context of his letters can help to explain their outlook and effectiveness. Such an analysis inexorably draws the student into the chivalric literature of the fifteenth and sixteenth centuries.

In his *cartas de relacíon*, Cortes practices the difficult art of the chivalric

---

[1] Hernan Cortes, in Bernal Diaz del Castillo, *The Conquest of New Spain*, trans. J. M. Cohen (1963; rpt. Harmondsworth, 1981), p. 84.

[2] Hernan Cortes, *Letters from Mexico*, ed. and trans. Anthony Pagden (New Haven, 1986), p. xxxix. Pagden notes (p. xl, n. 3) that *cartas de relacíon* is not Cortes' term. The title page of the second letter, printed at Seville in 1522, describes it as "*carta de relacion enbiada a su. S. Majestad del emperador nuestro señor*" (Cortes, *Letters*, ed. and trans. Pagden, pp. 47, 50).

[3] Cf. Marcel Bataillon, "Hernán Cortés, autor prohibido," in *Libro Jubilar de Alfonso Reyes* (Mexico, 1956), pp. 77–82.

autobiography. The chivalric biography proper has attained some recognition at least among students of chivalry.[4] Chivalric autobiography is barely accorded recognition as a subgenre.[5] Of the two, it proves much less respectable. William Marshal, St Louis, Bertrand du Guesclin, the Black Prince, Boucicaut, Jacques de Lalaing, Don Pero Niño, and the Chevalier Bayard could all enlist their faithful servants to chronicle their deeds of prowess. One imagines the *loyal serviteur* or Chandos Herald riding along behind the great man taking notes, like a literary Sancho Panza or Boswell errant. On a personal level, such authors duplicate the activity of the historian writing for a noble patron. They do for the individual knight what Zurara did for the Portuguese royal family at Ceuta. The knight who lacks his own herald finds himself at a considerable disadvantage. In such a case there may be nothing for it but to recount his own exploits, as Gadifer de la Salle seems to be doing from time to time. The risks of encountering a sceptical response are great: Thomas Fuller objected to Captain John Smith's account of his own adventures, "It soundeth much to the diminution of his deeds that he alone is the herald to publish and proclaim them."[6] He was by no means the first to do so. Still, disbelief is preferable to oblivion. With the rise of literacy among the knightly classes, it became more feasible for knights to write about themselves. Cortes, who had worked as a notary, brought both legal and chivalric expertise to his narratives.

To trace the origins of the chivalric autobiography would involve a study of the ancient military memoir, as practiced by Xenophon or Julius Caesar. The chivalric autobiography of the Middle Ages might perhaps spring in part from this source, in part from the eyewitness chronicles of crusaders like Villehardouin and Robert de Clari. These, however, are accounts of group expeditions

---

4 For some discussion of the chivalric biography, see, first, Barber, *The Knight and Chivalry* (1970; rev. edn Woodbridge, 1996), pp. 141–51; Larry D. Benson, *Malory's Morte Darthur* (Cambridge, Mass. and London, 1976), pp. 186–89; S. Ferris, "Chronicle, Chivalric Biography, and Family Tradition in Fourteenth-century England," in *Chivalric Literature*, ed. Larry D. Benson and John Leyerle, Studies in Medieval Culture XIV (Kalamazoo, 1980), pp. 25–38.

5 For contrasting instances of chivalric autobiography, see Ulrich von Lichtenstein, *Frauendienst*, ed. Reinhold Bechstein, Deutsche Dichtungen des Mittelalters 6–7 (Leipzig, 1888); Henry, duke of Lancaster, *Le Livre de Seyntz Medicines*, ed. Emile J. Arnould, Anglo-Norman Texts 2 (Oxford, 1940); Georg von Ehingen, *Diary*, trans. Malcolm Letts (London, 1929); *The Life of Lord Herbert of Cherbury, Written by himself*, ed. Horace Walpole (London, 1770). A list of fifteenth-century practitioners in the genre might be stretched to include Henry the Navigator's brother King Duarte of Portugal, who wrote a kind of spiritual autobiography as well as a separate manual of horsemanship, Oswald von Wolkenstein, who wrote autobiographical poetry, and Olivier de la Marche, who wrote both his *Mémoires* and *Le Chevalier Delibéré* (in Spanish, *El Caballero determinado*), an allegory of the life of the knight that became one of Charles V's favorite volumes. For comments, see Benson, *Malory's Morte Darthur*, p. 177.

6 Thomas Fuller, *The Worthies of England* (1660), cited in the introductory essay to Henry Wharton, *The Life of John Smith, English Soldier*, trans. Laura Polanyi Striker (Chapel Hill, 1957), p. 25.

by a member, not by the leader himself, and they are written in the third person. Closer to a chivalric autobiography is Ulrich von Lichtenstein's flamboyant account of his jousting expeditions, the *Venusfahrt* of 1227 and the *Artusfahrt* of 1240, which Ruth Harvey calls a "pseudo-autobiography." In this case the elements of parody and fantasy dominate the biography for later readers.[7] Duke Henry of Lancaster's *Livre de seyntz medicines* ranks as a sort of spiritual autobiography rather than a chivalric one, but he does discuss his knightly enterprises there to some degree. At the end of the fifteenth century Maximilian I cast his chivalric autobiography in the form of three romances, *Der Weisskunig*, *Theuerdank*, and *Freydal*. The Renaissance revival of interest in classical military writing offered an alternative to be followed by Blaise de Monluc and others.

It is tempting to see *Mandeville's Travels* as a spur to the composition of chivalric autobiographies. We now read it as a most persuasive literary hoax. To its medieval and Renaissance readers, though, the book presented itself as the first-person account of the wideranging journeys of one Sir John Mandeville. In fact, most chivalric autobiographies are also travel books. The need to report to a royal patron on his travels to the Canary Islands would provide the opening for Gadifer de la Salle to publicize his own exploits. The wandering knights of the Round Table are required to report on their peregrinations when they return to court, just as Bertrand de la Broquière had to report to Duke Philip the Good on his discoveries in the Islamic East. Hernan Cortes, Lord Herbert of Cherbury, and Captain John Smith all draw on this tradition of the knight's report of his travels in their autobiographical writings. They all run the same risk of exposing themselves to criticism both as knights and as writers.

All of these works reflect the delicacy of the problem that faces the knight writing about himself. The code of chivalry demands truthfulness and modesty. At the same time, it rewards the public display of prowess. All of these knights are trying to find ways of writing about themselves without infringing on the modesty demanded by chivalric convention.

A handful of specific allusions to chivalric literature has been identified in the narratives of the conquest of Mexico. Bernal Diaz' comparison of the great city of Tenochtitlan to "the enchanted things related in the book of Amadís" may be the best known.[8] Cortes' persistent interest in finding an Amazon island can be traced back to the original instructions supplied to him by Diego Velázquez, the governor of Cuba, when he first set out for Yucatán in October 1518.[9] This quest for the island of women warriors has also been related to the Amadís tradition. In 1510, if not earlier, Montalvo's *Las Sergas de Esplandián* had introduced the black Amazon queen Calafia and her island stronghold,

---

7 See Barber, *The Knight and Chivalry*, pp. 150–51; Maurice Keen, *Chivalry* (New Haven, 1984), p. 92.

8 Irving A. Leonard, *Books of the Brave* (1949; rpt. Berkeley and Los Angeles, 1992), p. 43.

9 Cortes, *Letters*, ed. and trans. Pagden, pp. 299–300; 502, note 21.

California, to European audiences. She remains, arguably, the most flamboyant infidel princess in a long series. For Velázquez, Cortes, and Sir Walter Ralegh, the Amazons were always just around the corner.[10]

These allusions suggest that Cortes and his men were *au courant* with the most fashionable books of chivalry. Conceivably, it might have been socially and intellectually more acceptable to admit to reading the fashionable *Amadís* than the *Historia del Carlo Magno y de los doce pares de Francia*. Other aspects of the letters should focus the reader's attention on earlier, perhaps deeper chivalric influences, since Cortes' portrayal of his deeds conforms to older models. The heroes Cortes and his men identify themselves with most closely are those of the Matter of France – the twelve Peers of Charlemagne. The work that parallels Cortes' letters most closely may be Jean Bagnyon's *Fierabras*. To understand Cortes' *cartas de relacíon*, we need to revert to older patterns of knighthood, and acknowledge the continuing influence of medieval imaginative literature in the sixteenth century.

The accession of Charles V (1500–58) to the throne of Castile would naturally encourage Spanish soldiers to identify with the Peers of Charlemagne. Both the emperor's friends and his enemies portrayed him throughout his reign as a second Charles the Great who might well be the "world emperor" of medieval prophecy. In Spain the effort to depict Charles in this manner was encouraged by that august personage, Queen Isabella's confessor and bishop of Toledo, Cisneros.[11] His ventures against Tunis and Algiers, and against the Turks to the east, accorded with Charlemagne's legendary image as the

---

10 On this Amazon obsession, see Cortes' fourth letter in Pagden, pp. 298–300. "I tell you that on the right-hand side of the Indies there was an island called California, which was very close to the region of the Earthly Paradise. This island was inhabited by black women, and there were no males among them at all, for their life style was similar to that of the Amazons." Garci Rodriguez de Montalvo, *The Labors of the Very Brave Knight Esplandián*, trans. William Thomas Little (Binghamton, 1992), pp. 456–57. See Little's extensive notes on the Arabic roots of the name California, and on the classical background of the Amazon myth. The only metal to be found on the island is gold, so the Amazons wear golden armor. For Calafia herself, and her motivation in undertaking a voyage of exploration and conquest, see her description (Little, pp. 459–60). At the siege of Constantinople she fights the Christians, falls in love with Esplandián, but in the end is converted to Christianity and married to Esplandián's cousin Talanque.

11 Peggy K. Liss, *Isabel the Queen: Life and Times* (Oxford and New York, 1992), p. 357. For the cult of Charles V as world emperor and second Charlemagne, see also Stephen Ozment, *The Age of Reform, 1250–1550: An Intellectual and Religious History of Late Medieval and Reformation Europe* (New Haven, 1980), p. 253. In the words of Mercurio Gattinara, Charles's tutor, congratulating the nineteen-year-old emperor upon his election: "Sire, God has been very merciful to you: he has raised you above all the kings and princes of Christendom to a power such as no sovereign has enjoyed since your ancestor Charles the Great. He has set you on the way towards world monarchy, towards the uniting of all Christendom under a single shepherd." Ozment cites Frances A. Yates, *Astraea: The Imperial Theme in the Sixteenth Century* (London, 1975), p. 26. Ozment traces the idea of a world emperor as the true bringer of peace back to Dante's *Monarchia*.

reconqueror of Europe for Christendom. Charles V's territorial interests in the Burgundian Netherlands, Italy and Germany made his critics suspect him of a desire to revive the Carolingian empire. His recognized expertise as a horseman commanded the respect of his officers. Throughout the period between 1516 and 1555, his use of his great-great-grandfather's Burgundian Order of the Golden Fleece as the ultimate reward of chivalric distinction attempted to bring together the aristocrats of his far-flung empire in a single brotherhood. According to Boulton, "By 1520 the Order had thus succeeded in becoming élite in the highest possible sense – a society, not of mere knights, but of lords and princes, drawn from all over Western Christendom."[12] The young emperor would prove to be an avid chivalric enthusiast. His cultivation of his own image as a knightly emperor would arouse the chivalric ambitions of his subjects.

J. H. Elliott remarks that "success in arms, and resort to the highest authority of all, that of the king himself – these were the aims of Cortes and his fellow conspirators."[13] If Charles V was to be a new Charlemagne, they would appoint themselves as his Peers. Cortes, landing in Mexico, evoked the example of Roland in the quotation that heads this chapter: "God give us the same good fortune in fighting . . . as he gave to the Paladin Roland."[14] Elliott, following Frankl, identifies this as "a quotation from another ballad." The allusion seems to me rather more general; it might evoke a wide range of Charlemagne material. Cortes was not the only member of the expedition to express Carolingian aspirations. According to Irving Leonard, "one of the foremost commentators of Cervantes' writings inserted an interesting footnote to the effect that twelve of Cortes' lieutenants banded together like the 'Twelve peers' of chivalry, solemnly pledging themselves with the vows of knights-errant, 'to defend the Holy Catholic Faith, to right wrongs, and to aid Spaniards and friendly natives!' "[15] Leonard also cites the desperate outcry of a member of Pedro de Mendoza's expedition of 1536 to the River Plate, before his execution for insubordinate conduct, " 'some day things will be as God wills and the Twelve Peers will rule!' "[16]

The urge to mythologize Charles V, and therefore the Americas also, only

---

12 D'A. J. D. Boulton, *The Knights of the Crown: The Monarchical Orders of Knighthood in Later Medieval Europe, 1325–1520* (Woodbridge, 1987), p. 380.

13 J. H. Elliott, "Cortés, Velázquez and Charles V," introduction to Hernan Cortes, *Letters from Mexico*, ed. and trans. Anthony Pagden (New Haven, 1986), p. xvi.

14 Bernal Diaz, *The Conquest of New Spain*, p. 36. Cited in Elliot's introduction, *Letters*, ed. and trans. Pagden, p. xvi.

15 Leonard, *Books of the Brave*, p. 42, and p. 411, n. 13, citing Diego Clemencín, ed., Miguel de Cervantes, *El ingenioso hidalgo don Quijote de La Mancha* (Madrid, 1833), IV.274.

16 Peter Burke traces an extensive later history of allusions to the *Historia del Emperador Carlo Magno* in Latin America, as does André de Mandach. See Leonard, *Books of the Brave*, p. 55; P. Burke, "Chivalry in the New World," in Sydney Anglo, ed., *Chivalry in the Renaissance* (Woodbridge, 1990), pp. 257–62. Burke describes the *Historia del Emperador Carlo Magno* as "the key text in the Brazilian reception of the romances of chivalry" (p. 257). Cf. André de Mandach, *Naissance et développement de la chanson de geste en europe*.

partially accounts for the longterm vogue of the *Historia del Emperador Carlo Magno* in the Americas. Bagnyon's romance was by 1500 the principal authority on the deeds of Charlemagne. This too often neglected volume depicts the Charlemagne of the conquistadores. Charles V would most likely have encountered it first as a French book, one in print since 1478. French had been his first language, the one he claimed to speak in his dealings with men: "I speak Spanish to God, Italian to the ladies, French to men and German to my horse."[17] The earliest surviving complete edition of Nicolás de Piemonte's Spanish translation is that of 1521, published by Jacobo Cromberger at Seville, and reprinted by that printer and his descendants in 1525, 1534, and 1549. A fragment of what appears to be an edition of around 1500–03 published by Peter Hagembach in Toledo is preserved in the Biblioteca de Catalunya. As in the case of *Amadís*, it seems probable that earlier editions than those we possess today may have existed. In that case, Cortes could have encountered Jean Bagnyon's work before his departure from Spain in 1504. Charles V was even more likely to be familiar with it. The probability that he did not know it is small, since this was the most widely disseminated book about Charlemagne of the age of printing, and indeed perhaps of any era. The publisher of both the *Historia del Emperador Carlo Magno* and Cortes, Jacobo Cromberger, ensured that these volumes could appear on the same bookstall. He printed Cortes' second letter in November 1522, his third in March of 1523, while his printings of the *Historia* are dated April 1521 and April 1525. Nothing could be easier than to read these works alongside one another.[18] This evidence suggests that Bagnyon's *Historia del Emperador Carlo Magno* could indeed have helped to inspire Cortes and his men. It unquestionably provided the context into which Cortes' *cartas de relación* slipped on their publication. A familiarity with the *Historia* would help to prepare Cortes' readers and condition their response to his texts.

The association of Cortes and Charlemagne goes beyond coincidences of printing history. In theme and content Cortes parallels the *Historia del Emperador Carlo Magno* to a surprising extent. The worlds of Charlemagne's peers and of Cortes' companions intermesh on many levels. His narrative begins by

---

V. *La geste de Fierabras: Le jeu du réel et de l'invraisemblable, avec des textes inédits*, publications romances et françaises CLXXVII (Geneva, 1987).

17 "Je parle expagnol à Dieu, italien aux femmes, français aux hommes, et allemand à mon cheval." The line is ascribed to Charles V, and rather overestimates his linguistic abilities, according to Ozment, *The Age of Reform*, p. 248: "Linguistic as well as geographical and political barriers handicapped the emperor, whose native language was French. He never became fluent in Flemish, and he learned Spanish only after he had become king. He could speak no German, and his Latin was poor."

18 For the publication history of the Cromberger editions of the *Historia del Emperador Carlo Magno* see Clive Griffin, *The Crombergers of Seville: The History of a Printing and Merchant Dynasty* (Oxford, 1988), p. 236 and appendix 1, nos. 231, 249, 360, and 531. For the Cromberger editions of Cortes, see Griffin, *The Crombergers of Seville*, p. 237, and appendix 1, nos. 239 and 242. For the citation of the Biblioteca de Catalunya edition of Bagnyon, I am grateful to Dr Lotte Hellinga of the British Library and her staff.

evoking the widespread organizing conventions of the quest and the chivalric vow:

> Most excellent Prince, in the other report . . . I also spoke of a great lord called Mutezuma, whom the natives of these lands had spoken to me about. . . . And, trusting in God's greatness and in the might of Your Highness's Royal name, I decided to go and see him wherever he might be. Indeed, I remember that, with respect to the quest of this lord, I undertook more than I was able, for I assured Your Highness that I would take him alive in chains or make him subject to Your Majesty's Royal Crown.[19]

Maurice Keen discusses the phenomenon of the chivalric vow in the later Middle Ages.[20] In his third letter Cortes reports another instance when he and his men bind themselves through a solemn oath, as they look down towards "the province of Mexico and Temixtitian" on their return to the Mexica capital: "all swore never to leave that province alive if we did not do so victorious. And with this resolution we moved on as joyfully as if we were on an outing."[21] The theme of the quest for the distant, all-powerful ruler would call to mind the search for Prester John, or the Grail city, or Jerusalem or Constantinople, all objects of great chivalrous journeys. In the course of his quest, Tenochtitlan in fact becomes a second Jerusalem, though only the ruined Jerusalem of Vespasian. The appeal of the subject peoples for Cortes to free them from the yoke of Montezuma "who held them by tyranny and by force, and took their children to sacrifice to his idols" is a feature that can also be found throughout a broad range of chivalric works.[22] The knight-errant's duty to destroy evil customs bolsters Cortes as he reports on the shocking incidence of cannibalism, sodomy, and human sacrifice among the benighted peoples of New Spain. "They have a most horrid and abominable custom which truly ought to be punished and which until now we have seen in no other part . . ."[23] Cortes stresses these chivalric motivations for action all through his letters. On beyond these generalized chivalric elements, the world of the *Historia del Emperador Carlo Magno* best explains the world of Cortes' *cartas de relacion.*

The specific character of the conflict of the small band of Christian invaders against the massed forces of a mighty infidel empire immediately evokes the predicament of Bagynon's twelve peers, imprisoned and besieged in a Saracen palace, far from their own emperor. The repeated sieges of the *cartas*, alternating with desperate dashes for freedom, recall the action of the central book of Bagnyon's work, as well as the tactics of the Spanish reconquest. The pattern of conquest, loss, and recuperation in Mexico, as Cortes wins, loses, and regains

---

[19] Cortes, *Letters*, ed. and trans. Pagden, p. 50.
[20] *Chivalry*, pp. 212–16; see also Larry D. Benson, *Malory's Morte Darthur*, pp. 189–90.
[21] Cortes, *Letters*, ed. and trans. Pagden, p. 169.
[22] Ibid., pp. 50–51.
[23] Ibid., p. 35.

Tenochtitlan, might also be seen as a parallel to Bagynon. Cortes' Mexican scenery would likewise have struck a chord with readers of the *Historia*. The effort to escape the besieged fortress and the surrounding city is quite reminiscent of the central confrontation in the *Historia* between Charlemagne's knights in their tower and the Saracen army surrounding it. The many combats on bridges echo the *Historia*'s series of struggles at the legendary Bridge of Mantrible. The difficult passes through the mountains hint at Roncesvalles. Cortes' letters portray a Carolingian landscape. Even the marvels of Aztec workmanship find a parallel in the romance's admiration for the wondrous decor of the Saracen palace, "wondrously rich . . . painted by the hand of a great artist . . . The knights were awestruck at the great riches and could never be sated with gazing at the diversity of the artifacts of the chamber."[24]

When he describes the Mexica religion Cortes adopts the viewpoint of Bagnyon's Roland. He presents himself as a religious instructor, explaining Christianity in simplified terms to the natives, much as his hero Roland explained it to Princess Floripas, or Oliver explained it to her brother Fierabras. The knight in the factual text, as in fiction, takes on the role of the missionary, shouldering aside any cleric who may be in attendance. While this feature surfaces in other chivalric traditions, it seems especially strong in Carolingian romance.

Like Roland in the *Historia del Emperador Carlo Magno*, Cortes becomes a destroyer of idols.

> The most important of these idols, and the ones in whom they have most faith, I had taken from their places and thrown down the steps; and I had those chapels where they were cleaned, for they were full of the blood of sacrifices; and I had images of Our Lady and of other saints put there, which caused Mutezuma and the other natives some sorrow . . . for they believed that these idols gave them all their worldly goods, and that if they were allowed to be ill treated, they would become angry and give them nothing and take the fruit from the earth leaving the people to die of hunger. I made them understand through the interpreters how deceived they were in placing their trust in those idols which they had made with their hands from unclean things.[25]

Princess Floripas, under siege, had expressed a similar faith in her idols' power to provide food: "if you had believed in my gods and (sic) without question they would have offered mercy to you, and will provide you with food."[26] The aversion that Cortes expresses in his letter does not differ greatly from the

---

[24] Jean Bagnyon, *Hystoria del emperador Carlo Magno y de los doce pares de Francia . . .*, trans. Nicolàs de Piemonte (Salamanca, 1544), ch. xxx, fol. xv, British Library copy: "rica a maravilla . . . pintado . . . de mano de gran maestro . . . los caualleros fueron marauillados delas grandes riquezas y no se hartauan de mirar la diuersidad de las lauores dela sala."

[25] Cortes, *Letters*, ed. and trans. Pagden, p. 106.

[26] Bagnyon, *Historia del Emperador Carlo Magno*, trans. N. de Piemonte, "si vos creyessedes

viewpoint of Roland and his comrades when confronted by four golden "Saracen idols." One might even venture to suggest that the religious cultures Cortes found in Mexico better resembled the romance's concept of Islam than did Islam itself. In the original French text, the peers remark with glee on the monetary value of the statues, and wish that Charlemagne had them in France, where he could use them to rebuild churches and reward his men. At least by the 1544 Spanish edition this had evidently become a sore point. The Spanish text eliminates any hint of Christian greed.

> She took them all into an underground cave; and in the end of the cave they found a chamber, wondrously fashioned; and in the center of the cave they found a very rich dais; and thereupon there were four idols the size of a man, and all four [were] of pure gold; and one was called Apolin, the next Taualgante, the next one Margot, and the last Jupin . . . And Guy of Burgundy said to Floripes, "Madam, who made these gods?" And she said, "Two goldsmiths, the greatest experts to be found in all the world." . . . and he said "Then men have greater power than your gods; look and see that they have no might at all." And then he drew his sword and struck one of them in the head with it and knocked it to the ground; and Roland with a battle-axe flung the others to earth, and said to Floripes, "Watch, lady, the power of your gods!" Then Floripes, realizing the truth, seeing that her gods did not budge, said "Now I recognize and confess that there is no other god except the God of the Christians."[27]

Smashing the idols accorded with biblical precept and chivalric example, not to mention the iconoclastic temper of the age. Protestant iconoclasm in northern Europe grew from the same roots.

In their frank admission of their interest in the wealth of the Mexica empire, Cortes and his lieutenants also echo Bagnyon's twelve peers. In both cases the emperor must be given his due. It is Charlemagne who should receive the Saracen treasure – and of course, redistribute it to his faithful peers and the church. In the first letter, sent on 10 July 1519, ostensibly by the officers of the

en mis dioses / & sin dubda ya ouieran vsado de misericordia con vos: y vos proueyeran de vitualla." (fol. xx).

[27] Ibid.: ". . . los lleuo todos por vna cueua debaxo de tierra: y en cabo de la cueua hallaron vna sala marauillosamente labrada: y enmedio della estaua vn tablado muy rico: y enel estauan quatro ydolos del grandor de vn hombre y todos quatro de oro fino: y el vno se llamaua apolin / y el otro taualgante: y el otro margot: y el otro iupin: y olia todo la sala tan suauamente que los cauelleros estauan marrauillados: & guy de borgoña dixo a floripes: señora quien hizo estos dioses: y ella le dixo dos plateros los mayores maestros que en todo el mundo se pudieron hallar . . . el le dixo: luego mas poder tienen los hombres que tus dioses: y mira como no tienen poder alguno: & luego saco el espada y dio al vno con ella enla cabeça y lo derribo enel suelo: & roldan con la hacha darmas echo a tierra los otros: y dixo a floripes: mira señora el poder de tus dioses: entonces floripes venida a conoscimiento dela verdad / viendo que sus dioses no se mouian dixo: agora conozco y confiesso no auer otro dios sino el dios de los christianos."

newly founded City of Vera Cruz, Cortes and his men enumerate the treasures they have collected for Charles V, though Bernal Diaz would complain later about Cortes system of distribution and his retention of a "royal fifth" for himself. The conquistadores follow the peers in assessing their own motives. Both chivalric fellowships are in it to advance Christianity, but they are also in it for the money and the land.

As in the *Historia del Emperador Carlo Magno*, the embattled Christians are aided, and even rescued from certain death, by an infidel princess. Cortes and his men are presented with any number of exotic and aristocratic women throughout their foray into the Mexica empire. Pagden documents the fates of Montezuma's daughters, whom the conquistadores baptized, and in some cases married, coming by this means into possession of their lands.[28] In the same way Guy of Burgundy marries Floripas and becomes king of a portion of her father's lands. The principal embodiment of the role of the Saracen Princess, however, is Cortes celebrated, or notorious, interpreter, Doña Marina. She is described in more detail by Bernal Diaz, who helps to bring out the affinities that link her to the traditional Saracen Princess of romance, and to Princess Floripas of the *Historia del Emperador Carlo Magno* in particular. "One of the Indian ladies was christened Doña Marina. She was a truly great princess, the daughter of *Caciques* and the mistress of vassals, as was very evident in her appearance . . . good-looking, intelligent, and self-assured . . ."[29]

> When Doña Marina saw her mother and half-brother in tears, she comforted them, saying that they need have no fear . . . God had been very gracious to her in freeing her from the worship of idols and making her a Christian, and giving her a son by her lord and master Cortes, also in marrying her to such a gentleman as her husband Juan Jaramillo. Even if they were to make her mistress of all the provinces of New Spain, she said, she would refuse the honour, for she would rather serve her husband and Cortes than anything else in the world.[30]

Cortes does record her astuteness in detecting a plot against the Spaniards. In this incident, Doña Marina receives the confidence of a garrulous old woman, and betrays it to save the band of Christian warriors. Floripas of the romance goes farther; she shoves the old woman out of the window to keep her quiet. Both scenes show a young woman rejecting her own culture, and the control of a maternal figure – in Floripas' case her governess (*aya* in the Spanish), in Doña Marina's, her would-be mother-in-law – for her new faith and her male companions. Las Casas regarded this plot as a mere fabrication to justify Cortes' massacre of the innocent chieftains and tradesmen of Cholula, as an act of terrorism designed to intimidate Montezuma (Mocteçucoma). If this should

[28] Cortes, *Letters*, ed. and trans. Pagden, p. 479, n. 94.
[29] Bernal Diaz, *The Conquest*, p. 82.
[30] Ibid., p. 86.

have been the case, the conquistadores patterned their story on a recognizable model from the romance tradition.[31]

Some of Cortes' reticence might stem from the fact, acknowledged by Bernal Diaz long after the fact, that Cortes, a man with a wife back in Cuba, had taken Doña Marina as his mistress. Like Floripas, she is later married off to a subordinate member of the expedition.

Also like the energetic and sometimes violent Floripas, Marina is described as a virago.

> But let me say that Doña Marina, although a native woman, possessed such manly valour that though she heard every day that the Indians were going to kill us and eat our flesh with *chillis*, and though she had seen us surrounded in recent battles and knew that we were all wounded and sick, yet she betrayed no weakness but a courage greater than that of a woman. She and Jeronimo de Aguilar spoke to the messengers we were now sending, telling them that the Tlascalans must make peace at once, and that if they did not come to us within two days we would go and kill them in their own city and destroy the country. With these brave words the prisoners were dispatched to the capital . . .[32]

Jean Bagnyon considered that his heroine's deed in saving the Twelve Peers from her father's prison and the old woman's treachery was *euvre d'omme bien approuvee,* which I take to mean something like "the worthy act of a man."[33] Again, the Spanish translator does not consider this altogether complimentary, and it has disappeared from the 1544 version of the text. The presence of this powerful, romantic figure links the exploration narrative to chivalric fiction still more explicitly.

Doña Marina parallels Floripas in another way – the dubious nature of her position between two cultures. This aspect of the Saracen princess is appreciated more by the Spanish translator of Bagnyon than by Bagnyon himself. A

---

[31] Cortes, second letter, ed. and trans. Pagden, p. 73 (a more circumstantial account appears in Diaz, *The Conquest,* pp. 196–97). Pagden discusses Las Casas' and Vázquez de Tapia's discordant accounts of the events at Cholula (pp. 465–66. n. 27).

[32] Diaz, *The Conquest,* p. 153.

[33] Jehan Bagnyon, *L'Histoire de Charlemagne (parfois dite Roman de Fierabras),* ed. Hans-Erich Keller, Textes littéraires français (Geneva, 1992), p. 79. The propensity to describe an especially energetic or courageous female in masculine terms has persisted in European literature for a long time, as witness Karl Brandi's assessment of Charles V's aunt, Margaret of Savoy, in *The Emperor Charles V,* trans. C. V. Wedgwood (1939; rpt. London, 1963), p. 46: "one of the greatest rulers of the century, firm in her judgements, shrewd in her knowledge of men, and endowed with almost virile energy." A capable woman is almost as good as a man. The censorship of Bagnyon's praise of Floripas by his later editors and translators makes it clear that this compliment was not universally appreciated – though the reasons behind the objection differ considerably from those that would be raised today. See also Liss, *Isabel the Queen,* p. 3, where she cites Pedro Mártir praising Isabella in 1502 as a woman "stronger than a strong man."

heroine to the Peers, the Spanish Floripas admits she can only be seen as a traitress by her own people. "since I purpose, forgetting my gods and the love of my father, of my family and my entire country, to save your lives, even at the risk of my own."[34] This Saracen princess has a sense of herself as a traitor-heroine that does not come across to this reader at least in any other version of the text. Doña Marina would go on to become a villainess of Mexican folk-play and dance down to the present day.[35]

The *Historia del Emperador Carlo Magno* supplied ready-made roles to the principal male inhabitants of Mexico that Cortes encountered as well. The chivalrous young Saracen who accepts baptism and fights alongside Charlemagne's knights, Bagnyon's Fierabras, reappears in Cortes' third letter. Don Fernando of Tesuico is too young for the part, but his brother Istlisuchil (Ixtlilxóchitl), "a very valiant youth of twenty-three or twenty-four years, loved and respected by all," takes over the part.[36] The role of Fierabras' and Floripas' father Balan, the Saracen emir who is executed rather than accept baptism in the *Historia*, belongs by right to Montezuma. Cortes claims to have vowed to capture that tyrannical ruler alive and bind him in chains; in the *Historia*, Balan is dragged into the presence of Charlemagne in this way. The scene cannot be re-enacted before Charles V, although Cortes does hold Montezuma captive in Tenochtitlan, and at one point does order him "to be put in irons, from which he received no small fright."[37] The crisis of the *noche triste* condemns Montezuma to an earlier and less ceremonious death. The testimony of Montezuma's subjects depicts him as a gory tyrant, though in person he proves unexpectedly conciliatory in his speeches as they are reported, or confected, by Cortes. There he conveniently acknowledges the prior sovereignty of Spain:

> For a long time we have known from the writings of our ancestors that neither I, nor any of those who dwell in this land, are natives of it, but foreigners who came from very distant parts; and likewise we know that a chieftain, of whom they were all vassals, brought our people to this region. . . . And we have always held that those who descended from him would come and conquer this land and take us as their vassals. So because of the place from which you claim to come, namely, from where the sun rises, and the things you tell us of the great lord or king who sent you here, we believe and are certain that he is our natural lord . . .[38]

---

34 In the text of the 1544 edition, fol. xix): ". . . por quanto tengo propuesto / oluidando mis dioses y el amor del padre: de los parientes & de toda la tierra / deslavuar vuestras vidas / aun que supiesse por ello perder la mia."

35 See Donald Cordry, *Mexican Masks* (Austin, 1980). André de Mandach has documented the dramatization of *Fierabras* in Spain and Latin America; there too, Marina and Floripas may be parallel figures.

36 Cortes, *Letters*, ed. and trans. Pagden, pp. 220–21 and 488, n. 52.

37 Ibid., p. 91.

38 Ibid., pp. 86–87; cf. pp. 467–68.

This speech puts Montezuma in the same position as a monarch as that occupied by Balan, the fictional Saracen invader of Italy. In spite of his apparent co-operation, the script, as laid down in the *Historia del Emperador Carlo Magno*, dictates that Montezuma must die. As in the case of Balan, Montezuma's continuing existence impedes the orderly succession of Charles V and his men to his throne. Like Balan, Montezuma dies ignominiously, and some literary effort is directed towards absolving the Christians of any desire to do him in. Their intentions were all for the best. Only the fatal contumacy of the Saracens, or the Aztecs, frustrated them.

Another theme that links Cortes' letters to the world of Bagnyon's Roland is that of treachery within the Christian camp. At the time of his departure from Cuba, Cortes already recognized that he was committing himself to a power struggle with the governor who issued his instructions, Diego Velázquez. The literary figures that leap to the conquistadores' minds as their fleet nears San Juan de Ulua, the Conde Montesinos and Roland, are both heroes estranged from their liege lords through treachery. By identifying himself with Roland, Cortes casts Diego Velázquez in the unpalatable role of the jealous arch-traitor Ganelon. In some ways like a Ganelon, Velázquez attempts to obtain Charles V's favor for his own scheme, with the object of frustrating his younger rival, Cortes. The competition for the ear of the monarch leads, in fiction and reality, to armed conflict within the Christian camp. Ganelon, in the *Historia del Emperador Carlo Magno*, eventually succeeds in engineering the death of Roland and his comrades. Cortes must interrupt his occupation of Tenochtitlan to counter the invasion of Velázquez' emissary Pánfilo de Narvaez. According to Cortes' letters, his Spanish enemies are no less deadly than his infidel opponents. ". . . they told me he had powerful forces with him, and brought a decree from Diego Velázquez that as soon as I and certain of my companions, whom he had singled out, were taken we should be hanged . . ."[39] The distraction of coping with Narvaez gives the Mexica time to plot their attack for the *noche triste* that nearly becomes Cortes' Roncesvalles. Nor is this the last time that Velázquez appears as the inspirer of a plot to murder Cortes. At the end of the Third Letter, Cortes describes a conspiracy of Velázquez' friends to kill Cortes and his officers before they leave to attack Tenochtitlan.[40] This new attempt only underlines the governor's role as Cortes' Ganelon.

Are there any shreds of medieval chivalric morality to be detected in the letters of Cortes? Theorists of the decline of chivalry might well imagine not. In fact, the *cartas de relación* are much preoccupied with standard questions of the ethics of combat. Cortes devotes a good deal of space to self-justification in traditional chivalric terms. His tactics may parallel those of contemporary commanders all across Europe in their antichivalric brutality. Burning down houses and towns, the use of mounted troops against enemies on foot, rape,

[39] Ibid., p. 123.
[40] Ibid., pp. 277–78 and 497–98, n. 96.

pillage, and the killing of unarmed civilians and unarmed captives had been frequent enough in the heyday of the chivalric manuals; neither the romancers nor the theorists succeeded in stamping them out. While he takes full advantage of his artillery and his horses, Cortes does recognize that he will be judged to some extent according to chivalric standards of conduct. He takes pains to represent himself as seeking negotiated settlements, offering mercy to the downtrodden, and expressing his horror at the scale of the destruction that his enterprise unleashed.

All of these parallels of name, character, incident, situation, and theme tend to reinforce Cortes' initial vision of himself as a Roland of the Americas. It is tempting to interpret the operation as a fulfillment of a young man's chivalric fantasies on both sides of the Atlantic, of a kind common in the tournaments, royal entries, and courtly entertainments of the period.[41] It would be possible to compile a formidable list of occasions on which Charles V was assured that he embodied the virtues of his great ancestor Charlemagne. The vogue of the *Historia del Emperador Carlo Magno* in Spain can reasonably be related to Charles V, though the book continued to be reprinted and read long after that emperor's death, as it did in France. Writing from New Spain, it might seem plausible enough to imagine Charles V as the second Charlemagne, a chivalrous defender of the faith, presiding over the most prestigious chivalric order in Europe, but as in the *Historia del Emperador Carlo Magno*, a far-off figure of authority.

What, however, was Charlemagne without his twelve peers? When Cortes rashly associates himself with Roland and his lieutenants aspire to emulate the twelve peers, they take on well-established chivalric *personae*. Cortes expresses hope for the same success in battle God granted to Roland. Other aspects of Roland's identity could have attracted Cortes as well. Bagnyon depicts Charlemagne's nephew as a spirited young man, impetuous and even disrespectful towards his uncle's authority. At the beginning of the romance, Charlemagne has occasion to punch him in the nose.[42] In the end, Roland proves loyal to the death, a martyred victim of Christian treachery at court and overwhelming legions of Moors. Roland's rebellious streak might well appeal to Cortes as he set out in defiance of Velázquez, but in his communications he underlines his loyalty. Like Roland, he is prepared to die for his faith and the Emperor Charles.

Similarly, the predicament of the twelve peers as described in the *Historia del Emperador Carlo Magno* seems to have appealed to Cortes' lieutenants. They see themselves as an embattled chivalric brotherhood, far from home, surrounded

---

[41] For references to Charlemagne in the 1522 pageant welcoming Charles V to London, see Alan Young, *Tudor and Jacobean Tournaments* (London, 1987), p. 218, n. 4; Sydney Anglo, *Spectacle, Pageantry, and Early Tudor Policy* (Oxford, 1969), pp. 192–96.

[42] Bagnyon, *Historia del Emperador Carlo Magno*, ch. xiv, fol. vi(v): "Quando Carlomagno oyo a roldan con grande enojo que ouo le arrojo vna manopla de azero & le dio enlas narizes" ("When Charlemagne heard Roland in great anger he flung a gauntlet of steel and struck him in the nose").

by vast alien forces. The local infidel princesses offer some consolation, as does the prospect of booty. As they fought on the bridges and towers of Tenochtitlan, even as they contemplated their fate as potential human sacrifices, Cortes' men could see themselves as heroes in the mould of Charlemagne's Peers. Guy of Burgundy, after all, was nearly executed by the Saracens before his comrades' eyes. The great Oliver was found tortured to death after the Peers' last stand at Roncesvalles.[43] Their feats of arms in New Spain must surely raise them to the same heroic status as that of their counterparts of the days of Charlemagne.

This Carolingian association is of special value for Cortes' second and third letters, though it never altogether fades from the scene. With the destruction of Tenochtitlan, though, the sky darkens. The parallel Cortes evokes also draws on a medieval chivalric tradition – the literature of the destruction of Jerusalem, which in Spanish and Portuguese was sometimes linked to the Quest of the Holy Grail.[44] Only recently have scholars begun to appreciate the widespread influence of such works all across medieval Europe. They remain repellent to most twentieth-century readers for the gleeful attitude with which the Christian authors cheer on the Romans to massacre the Jews, all in the name of the "vengeance of Jesus Christ." The destruction of the Mexica capital, whose wonders Cortes himself recounted in his second letter, falls outside the province of Carolingian history. The parallel that leaps to his mind is, instead, the fall of Jerusalem to Rome. It also occurred to his publisher, Jacobo Cromberger, who notes at the end of his 1522 printing of the second letter: "After this, there came on the first of the month of the March past news from new Spain, of how the Spaniards had taken by storm the great city of Temixtitian, in which there had died more Indians than Jews in Jerusalem during the destruction of that city by Vespasian . . ."[45] This model places responsibility for the utter ruin of the great city first on the insane obstinacy of the inhabitants, then on the wrath of a God determined to punish them for their sins.[46] Cortes and his men are only the

---

43 *Historia del Emperador Carlo Magno*, ch. xlvi, fol. xliii(r): "y hallaron al noble cauallero oliueros aspado cn dos palos y puesto a manera de cruz; y delos dedos delas manos hastalos dedos delos pies estaua dessollado: y tenia doze dardos metidos por el cuerpo que le passauan de vna parte a otra" ("and they found the noble knight Oliver with his arms extended like a cross upon two poles and set up like a cross, and from his fingers to his toes he was flayed, and he had twelve darts thrust through his body that pierced him from one side to the other").

44 According to Harvey L. Sharrer, "Elements from the early Grail history as found in the Vulgate or Post-Vulgate *Estoire del Saint Graal* are included in Spanish and Portuguese incunabula adaptations of the French prose romance *Destruction de Jerusalem*, titled *La estoria del noble Vespasiano* (Toledo, c.1490; Seville, 1499) and *Estória do mui nobre Vespasiano, emperador de Roma* (Lisbon, 1496)." See *The New Arthurian Encyclopedia*, ed. Norris J. Lacy et al. (New York, 1991), p. 427.

45 Cortes, *Letters*, ed. and trans. Pagden, p. 159. See also p. 482, n. 119 where Pagden notes that the author of this passage must have seen a lost letter from Cortes describing the fall of Mexico, written in August 1521.

46 Ibid., pp. 258, 263.

agents of an angry God, as Vespasian was before them. By the end of the third letter, Cortes reports on the rebuilding of Tenochtitlan, "for it was completely destroyed."[47] Cortes struck the note of the crusade in the service of Christ and his emperor early in the second letter, well before his first entry into Tenochtitlan. "As we were carrying the banner of the Cross and were fighting for our Faith and in the service of Your Sacred Majesty in this Your Royal enterprise, God gave us such a victory that we killed many of them, without ourselves receiving any hurt."[48] Cortes and his allies at long last attained the city of their fantasies only to reduce it to a heap of rubble. In the circumstances, their best precedent was that of Vespasian.

This change of paradigm signals a turn towards mysticism on Cortes' part, paralleling Columbus' late prophetic phase. Their astonishing success, the magnitude of their achievement against all odds, might well make an explorer or a conquistador turn Franciscan visionary. This comes out at the end of the fifth letter, when Cortes recalls to Charles V his services in the suppression of idolatry, and his hope that "there will, in a very short time, arise in these parts a new Church, where God, Our Lord, may be better served and worshipped than in all the rest of the world."[49] Such a viewpoint was entirely compatible with a chivalric view of the world. Cortes maintains his interest in deeds of prowess. He begins the fifth letter by complaining that "it seemed to me that I had for a long time now lain idle and attempted no new thing in Your Majesty's service on account of the wound in my arm; and although that was not yet healed, I determined to engage in some undertaking."[50] The voice here could easily be that of Lancelot or Tristram in its insistent desire to perform a new exploit and its impatience with injury. (The idea of "playing with pain" in modern sporting competitions can easily be traced back as far as the Arthurian prose romances.) When Cortes sends out his captains in all directions with instructions to search for various actual or fabled places, as at the end of the fifth letter, his action recalls the outset of the Quest of the Holy Grail, or, indeed, the opening of any Arthurian romance that interlaces the separate journeys of the Knights of the Round Table. He himself projects a voyage to "the Spice Islands and many others, if there be any between Maluco, Malaca, and China," complete with a fresh chivalric vow: "for I pledge myself . . . to go in person or to send thither such a fleet as will subdue those islands, and to settle them with Spaniards and to build fortresses . . ."[51] The form of Cortes' pledge is recognizably that of a crusader's vow, pledging the speaker's participation.

Later conquistadores had the model of Cortes to follow, as well as a rapidly expanding matrix of chivalric fiction on which to draw. Pizarro, in particular,

---

[47] Ibid., p. 270; see also p. 266: "we had destroyed and razed it to the ground."
[48] Ibid., p. 60.
[49] Ibid., pp. 442–43 and p. 525, n. 114.
[50] Ibid., p. 339.
[51] Ibid., p. 445.

has been described as a dogged imitator of Cortes in his invasion of Peru, with parallels extending to the death of Atahualpa. Inca princesses figure prominently in the action, as their counterparts did in Mexico. The dominant pattern still seems to be that of the *Historia del Emperador Carlo Magno*; indeed, that work has endured longer in South America than perhaps anywhere else in the world, retaining its readership and inspiring later authors.[52]

One powerful aspect of the Charlemagne tradition that was downplayed in Cortes' letters, for obvious reasons, is the motif of the rebellious vassal. Roland had his moments of contention with Charlemagne, one of which at least is depicted in the *Historia del Emperador Carlo Magno*. Other knights went further. In other successful narratives, the irascible old emperor was often at odds with his men; at one time or another Ogier the Dane, Huon of Bordeaux, and Renaut de Montauban and his family all took on the emperor. In most cases the writer's and audience's sympathies remain with the rebel. The complication is not limited to Carolingian narratives. In Arthurian romance, Lancelot and Tristan both find themselves at odds with their respective liege lords, and Amadís contends at some length with King Lisuarte, the father of his beloved Oriana. Cortes' decision to invade the Mexica empire was an act of calculated insubordination. He cloaked his disobedience in the language of chivalric ardor and personal devotion to Charles V. His successors found the temptation to set up their own kingdoms irresistible, especially as it became clear that the crown did not mean to allow the conquerors free rein to rule their own conquests. The maverick conquistador could bolster his spirits with elements of the same chivalric legacy that tied him to the emperor.[53]

Neglected chivalric elements also surface in those narratives that recount the conquistadores' failures. Contrary to some current theories, the knights of the romances were no strangers to failure, shame, and death. Their lot is not invariably a happy one. The tale of Alvar Nuñez Cabeza de Vaca's wanderings from Florida through Texas between 1527 and 1536, as captive, slave, wild man, and wonderworker among the Native American tribes of those parts, displays many affinities with chivalric fiction. Indeed, the conventions of that fiction made it possible for Cabeza de Vaca to present his ignominious failure as, in some sense, heroic. He has suffered, and survived, the ultimate loss of identity, in the service of his prince. Like the mad Tristan, like Lancelot, or Orson, he is stripped of all signs of his prior knightly status to become a new subspecies of that old and potent European figure, the Wild Man. In the miracles of healing that he and his band are able to perform amongst the natives, Cabeza de Vaca reaches out for a different form of prestige, a sign of divine mercy and grace. A parallel effect in fiction occurs in Sir Thomas Malory's "The Healing of Sir

52 For Pizarro's imitation of Cortes, see Pagden's introduction, p. xxxix; on the fortune of the *Historia*, see Burke, n. 16 above.
53 For a few instances of rebellious conquistadores, see Cortes, *Letters*, ed. and trans. Pagden, p. xli.

Urry." Having lost his pretensions to military prowess, Cabeza de Vaca struggles to regain some social status by detailing his endurance and religious experiences.[54]

It is notable that in many cases the Spaniards confronted societies with equally well-defined and elaborate warrior cults of honor. Analogies are hazardous; they should really await in-depth comparative studies. Did the Eagle and Jaguar Warriors, for instance, enjoy the same prestige at the court of Montezuma as did the Order of the Golden Fleece among the courtiers of Charles V? These systems sometimes acknowledge one another, as when "El Inca" Garcilaso de la Vega explains the Inca system of military initiation as an initiation to knighthood.[55] On other occasions they refuse to recognize any parallel; neither Atahualpa nor Pizarro considered his opponent worthy of respect in chivalric terms, a "foeman worthy of his steel." Both the recognition and the refusal had their uses. Recognition of a noble enemy enhanced the glory of the enterprise. The refusal to accord him chivalric status freed the warrior to employ the least prestigious modes of combat. As circumstances dictated, both sides would shift their approaches for pragmatic reasons.

This study is a preliminary exploration, or perhaps a letter of challenge. The whole matter would repay more detailed inspection by a specialist in the Spanish literature of this period. It does demonstrate that the still unedited *Historia del Emperador Carlo Magno* should be considered a useful and under-utilized resource for the student of the annals of the conquistadores. The language of European chivalric tradition offered Cortes a code in which to communicate with Charles V. The legend of Charlemagne, as modified by Jean Bagnyon, provided a persuasive context in which Cortes and his lieutenants conquered a second empire for the second Charles the Great. It is likely that they themselves knew this most basic and ubiquitous fifteenth-century volume.

---

[54] Malory's tale of Lancelot's healing of the wounded Hungarian knight Sir Urry has never been securely attached to any French source. For Cabeza de Vaca, see *The Narrative of Alvar Nuñez Cabeça de Vaca*, ed. Frederick W. Hodge, in *Spanish Explorers in the Southern United States, 1528–1543*, ed. Frederick W. Hodge and Theodore H. Lewis (1907; rpt. Austin, 1990), pp. 12–126.

[55] Cf. "El Inca" Garcilaso de la Vega, *The Incas: The Royal Commentaries of the Inca Garcilaso de la Vega*, trans. Maria Jolas (New York, 1961), pp. 185–91. Here, in chapters 22 through 26 of his sixth book, the Inca Garcilaso describes the training of a young Peruvian warrior, and his initiation ceremony, the *huaracu*, which is compared in some detail to a European knighting ritual. For the Jaguar and Eagle Warriors of Mexico, see Jane S. Day, *Aztec: The World of Moctezuma* (Denver, 1992), pp. 35–37, 51. These two military orders were restricted to noblemen. Their special quarters in the precincts of the Templo Mayor at Tenochtitlan were sites for military banquets and ceremonies. Rites associated with the fertility cult of Xipe Totec pitted a captive warrior against Eagle and Jaguar Warriors. Plate 51 (p. 37) reproduces a page of the Codex Mendoza that depicts the increasingly elaborate costumes awarded to a warrior based on the number of prisoners he had captured in battle; they are the Mexica version of the visual emblems of valor Charles V might bestow – like the collar of the Order of the Golden Fleece.

It is even more likely that it was familiar to Charles V himself, from childhood, as a French book. Neither party would need a scholarly interpreter to point out the many parallels that connect the two narratives. Without question, the publication history of the *Historia* and Cortes' second and third letters made these complementary works accessible to sixteenth-century readers alongside one another, from the first. In Spanish, at least, it would be the *Historia del Emperador Carlo Magno* that would survive the longest. The ban of 1527 on the Spanish-language publication of Cortes' *cartas* removed these inflammatory documents from the bookstalls. It did not touch the work that might have inspired Cortes in the first place.[56] Charlemagne and Roland remained free to fire the imaginations of new generations of aspiring Paladins.

[56] Irving Leonard discusses the largely ineffective efforts of a succession of sixteenth-century Spanish monarchs to exclude romances of chivalry from their colonies. Leonard, *Books of the Brave*, pp. 75–90.

CHAPTER SEVEN

The Matter of England: Ralegh among the Amazons

> *But let that man with better sense advize,*
> *That of the world least part to us is red:*
> *And dayly how through hardy enterprize,*
> *Many great Regions are discoveréd,*
> *Which to late age were never mentionéd.*
> *Who ever heard of th'Indian Peru?*
> *Or who in venturous vessel measuréd*
> *The Amazons huge river now found trew?*
> *Or fruitfullest Virginia who did ever view?*[1]

> *But it shall be found a weake pollicie in mee, eyther to betray my selfe, or my Countrey with imaginations, neyther am I so farrre in loue with that lodging, watching, care, perill, diseases, ill savoures, bad fare, and many other mischiefes that accompany these voyages, as to woo my selfe again into any of them, were I not assured that the sunne couereth not so much riches in any part of the earth.*[2]

THE ENGLISH RESPONSE to the Spanish experience of exploration and conquest materialized in the course of the 1590s. In part, it was shaped by England's own temporary union and subsequent conflict with Spain. In part, too, it was an imitation of the Spanish and Portuguese enterprises as described in exploration narratives. A rereading of the major English exploration accounts makes it clear how large the exploits of Columbus, Cortes, and Pizarro loomed in their English contemporaries' consciousness. To some extent their deeds mirror the established Hispanic model. The goal of the English adventurer was, as Ralegh put it, to offer Elizabeth I and her successors, "a better Indies for her maiestie then the King of Spain now hath any."[3] The English, as befitted a hostile, now-Protestant nation, both admired and criticized the deeds of Spain. English explorers hoped to outdo their Spanish models. They also objected to their

---

[1] Edmund Spenser, *Faerie Queene*, bk II, lines 9–18.
[2] Sir Walter Ralegh, *The Discoverie of Guiana* (London, 1595), p. 68. All citations are taken from this edition.
[3] Ralegh, Epistle Dedicatory, *Discoverie*, f. A5.

proceedings. For critical ammunition and guidance it is no surprise to find writers as different as Hakluyt, Ralegh, and Captain John Smith looking to the native English chivalric tradition.

The English encountered their Spanish counterparts as adversaries in the Netherlands, where English volunteers supported the Dutch in their war of independence against Spain. They met them in conflict at sea and sometimes on land in a long series of engagements, the most famous being the great Armada of 1588, conceived by Philip as an *empresa*, a formal chivalric undertaking. Further afield, in eastern Europe, individual English and Spanish soldiers might still meet one another as allies against the Turks, but for the most part the two nations remained opponents. Spain encouraged the rebellious Irish in their defiance, and, as James Muldoon points out, the "savages of Ireland conditioned the English to deal similarly with the natives of North America."[4] Accounts of Spanish survivors of the Armada, cast ashore in Ireland, reveal a similar viewpoint, and at times recall the misfortunes of Arthur of Algarbe in his Irish forest.[5]

As they confronted the Catholic imperial chivalry of Spain, the English gentlemen of the age of Elizabeth were formulating their own Protestant chivalry. Sir Philip Sidney, the earl of Essex, Sir Henry Lee, Sir Walter Ralegh and their contemporaries who fought in the lists in Elizabeth's Accession Day tournaments every year were all committed to this project. Their own careers at court depended on it.

The fascination of the enterprise for the historian of chivalric culture is to see how new Hispanic and Italian courtly ideas were challenged by entrenched English approaches to knighthood. In the English exploration literature of this period, King Arthur confronts Cortes, and the Redcrosse Knight counters Amadís. The English adventurer must in the end choose between ancient and modern, national and international patterns of heroic behavior.

It is important to recognize that the war between Spain and England was also a conflict of chivalries. Each side deployed all the resources of its native heroic tradition to bolster its forces. Displays of knightly panache still had definite

---

4 J. Muldoon, "The Indian as Irishman," *Essex Institute Historical Collections* 111 (1975), pp. 267–89. Edmund Spenser's *View of the State of Ireland* (completed c.1596 but first printed in 1633) catalogues the "evil usages" of the rebellious natives and recommends that they be hunted down in winter and starved into submission.

5 Winston Graham, *The Spanish Armadas* (New York, 1972), pp. 152–65. Captain Francisco de Cuellar of the *San Pedro* describes his rescue by a "beautiful girl of about twenty," a "young savage woman" who demanded as a reward the relics he wore round his neck, "telling me that she was a Christian, though she was no more a Christian than Mahomet was" (p. 162). For this Graham cites the letter, translated by Frances Partridge, and printed in E. Hardy, *Survivors of the Armada* (London, 1966). The chivalric imagination sees Saracen princesses in all quarters of the globe. For Arthur of Algarbe's Irish experiences, see Gail Orgelfinger, ed., *The Hystorye of Olyuer of Castylle*, trans. Henry Watson (New York and London, 1988), pp. 149–57.

publicity value in the 1580s and 1590s. This, too, needs to be viewed in its medieval context. The Iberian peninsula had attracted English knights in search of adventure – crusades or crowns – since the early fourteenth century. The Black Prince and John of Gaunt had meddled in Iberian dynastic affairs in the wake of Duke Henry of Lancaster's expedition of 1343.[6] Individual Spanish and Portuguese knights had reciprocated, perhaps encouraged by new courtly connections between royal courts, in the wake of the marital alliances that made John of Gaunt's daughters Catherine and Philippa queens of Castile and Portugal. Don Pero Niño counted among his early exploits a raid on English seaports from Cornwall to Southampton. Joanot Martorell visited England in 1438-39, hoping to arrange a duel with his sister's lover Joan de Montpalau to be fought before Henry VI. Martí de Riquer and William Entwistle suggest that he traveled to England again around 1450. Philip Boyle of Aragon fought Sir John Astley at Smithfield in 1442; later Boyle would return to England as an ambassador. Pedro Vasquez (d. 1477) should also be mentioned as a notable Spanish knight who made his way to England.[7] Englishmen appear on occasion in the annals of the Spanish conquest of Granada; Mosen Diego de Valera records the *conde inglés* Earl Rivers' philosophical reaction to the loss of three teeth in the service of Ferdinand and Isabella. The marriages of Henry VIII and Mary Tudor were to bring many more Spaniards to England for courtly and chivalric pastimes.[8]

Both Spain and England admired and adopted the Burgundian chivalric ceremonies of Duke Philip the Good, and both became in some respects heirs to fifteenth-century Burgundian chivalry. Charles V, raised in the Burgundian Netherlands, brought the Order of the Golden Fleece to Spain. Edward IV, who had spent some time in exile at the court of Philip the Good, and his brother-in-law Anthony Woodville, Caxton's patron, adapted Burgundian pageantry to revive the English Order of the Garter and elaborate the English tournament. Gordon Kipling has argued for an even more enthusiastic emulation of things Burgundian at the court of Henry VII, who also recognized the value of the

---

6   See P. E. Russell, *The English Intervention in Spain and Portugal in the Time of Edward III and Richard II* (Oxford, 1955).

7   See Guitierre Diaz da Gamez, *The Unconquered Knight: A Chronicle of the Deeds of Don Pero Niño*, trans. J. Evans (London, 1928); Larry D. Benson, *Malory's Morte Darthur* (Cambridge, Mass. and London, 1976), pp. 175, 178; Joanot Martorell and Martí Joan de Galba, *Tirant lo Blanc*, trans. David H. Rosenthal (London and New York, 1984), Intro-duction, pp. viii–xiii. For the Spanish knights errant see Martí de Riquer, *Caballeros andantes españoles* (Madrid, 1967) and *Cavalleria fra realtà e litteratura nel quattrocento* (Bari, 1970).

8   *Crónica de los Reyes Católicos*, VIII.201, cited in E. Prestage, "The Chivalry of Spain," *Chivalry*, p. 139. Rivers is represented among other participants in the conquest on the choir stalls of the cathedral of Toledo (Prestage, "Chivalry," pp. 138–39). On pp. 134–36, Prestage gives a useful overview of the chivalric associations of England and Spain. For later events see also Alan Young, *Tudor and Jacobean Tournaments* (London, 1987), and Sydney Anglo, *Spectacle, Pageantry, and Early Tudor Policy* (Oxford 1969).

judicious use of display. The marriages of Henry VIII and Catherine of Aragon, Philip of Spain and Mary Tudor reinforced the connection. The dynastic links were further emphasized through chivalric ceremony.[9]

Spanish chivalric literature had already identified the British Isles as a romantic locale. *Amadís de Gaula* offers the most famous instance of an Iberian romance in a British setting, but *Tirant lo Blanch* was first on the ground. In *Olivier de Castille* Castilian and Portuguese princes find adventure in Britain. Concurrently, the English translations of Charlemagne romances gave British readers an image of Spain as a battleground of Christians and Saracens. They might also "rede Froissart," in Caxton's phrase, and after 1525 in Lord Berners' celebrated translation, and find a detailed account of the Black Prince's Spanish expedition. Lord Berners, who traveled to Spain as an ambassador in 1518 and translated Guevara's *Golden Book of Marcus Aurelius* and Diego de San Pedro's *Carcel de amor* (*The Prison of Love*), should be included among the chivalrous Englishmen of the period who helped to foster courtly ties with Iberia.

In the contention that followed between Elizabeth's England and Philip's Spain, chivalry was enlisted by both contenders. The English raiders who went out against Spain from the English court, with or without Elizabeth's approval, operated in the tradition of the individual knight errant. They left the court in search of martial adventure, glory, and loot, much as Arthur's knights did, and reported to their royal patron for an appropriate accolade in the traditional manner. (They also gave her a cut of their takings, on occasion, also in the traditional manner.) Some were as conventional in their chivalric exploits as the earl of Essex, a descendant of Edward III who would later make his own attempt on the English throne. In 1589, as the English were lifting their siege of Lisbon, the earl presented himself at the city gate, thrust in his sword, and challenged any "Spaniard mewed therein [who] durst adventure forth in favour of my mistress to break a lance." No one ventured out.[10]

On the Spanish side, Philip had envisioned his Armada of 1588 as an *empresa*, a formal chivalric undertaking.[11] It was also to be a crusade, in which knights of the Order of Santiago, like the eminent Spanish Admiral Juan Martinez de Recalde, or of the Order of the Golden Fleece, like the Duke of Medina Sidonia, pitted themselves against Knights of the Garter like Lord Howard of Effingham, Elizabeth's Lord Admiral in command of the English

---

9   For the history of the Order of the Golden Fleece under Charles V, see D'A. J. D. Boulton, *The Knights of the Crown: The Monarchical Orders of Knighthood in Later Medieval Europe, 1325–1520* (Woodbridge, 1987), pp. 380, 389, 449–50; for the Order of the Garter, and Edward IV's Burgundian connection, see Boulton, *Knights of the Crown*, pp. 133–34, 145–47, and 379; Gordon Kipling, *The Triumph of Honour: Burgundian Origins of the Elizabethan Renaissance* (The Hague, 1977); Anglo, *Spectacle, Pageantry*, and Young, *Tudor and Jacobean Tournaments*, discuss the relevant chivalric events.

10   Graham, *The Spanish Armadas*, pp. 182; 200; Alan Young, *Tudor and Jacobean Tournaments*, p. 170.

11   Graham, *The Spanish Armadas*, p. 62.

fleet. The Armada sailed under a banner blessed by the Pope, portraying the Crucifixion, with the Virgin Mary and Mary Magdalene. On the failure of this expedition, the English spy Anthony Copley reported that Philip responded by swearing "a great oath, that he would waste and consume his Crown, even to the value of a [last] Candlestick (which he pointed to standing upon the Altar) but either he would utterly ruin her Majesty and England, or else himself, and all Spaine become tributary to her."[12] Philip made two further attempts, sending a fleet in 1596 under Martin de Padilla, a knight of the Order of Alcantara, and another in 1597.

The appearance of King Arthur in the role of a conquistador at the head of Richard Hakluyt's *Second Part of the Principall Nauigations, Voyages and Discoueries of the English Nation, made to the North and Northeast Quarters of the World* may come as a shock to modern readers. Indeed, this is not a phase of his legend familiar to most Arthurian specialists. The eminent Elizabethan compiler of exploration accounts refers here to book nine, chapters ten and twelve of Geoffrey of Monmouth's *Historia Regum Britanniae* of 1136 (in a Heidelberg edition of 1581). For greater authority he cites both Latin and English passages, though I only reproduce the English:

> In the yeere of Christ, 517, king Arthur in the second yeere of his raigne, hauing subdued all partes of Ireland, sayled with his fleete into Island, and brought it and the people thereof vnder his subiection. The rumor afterwards being spred throughout all the other Islands, that no countrey was able to withstand him, Doldauius the king of Gotland, and Gunfacius the king of Orkney, came voluntarily vnto him and yelded him their obedience, promising to pay him tribute.[13]

In 1589 the reference to Arthur still offered the English writer a chance to assert his nation's historical priority, along with international chivalric prestige. Elizabeth I's physician Dr John Caius evoked Arthur in 1568 as a fictional founder of Cambridge University, in an attempt to trump Oxford's claim that it had been founded by Alfred and was therefore the senior institution. Edward I had trotted Arthur out to the same effect around 1300 to argue for English precedence over her Continental rivals at an international conference.

Hakluyt's Arthur addresses English concerns of the 1590s with notable accuracy. He disposes at once of the pestiferous Irish problem, this in mortifying contrast to the painful experiences that Tyrone and his allies were inflicting on the current administration. He then sails to Iceland and subjugates that isle, an imaginative development that might well surprise any Icelandic reader. At this, other monarchs submit without a struggle and offer tribute. England then basks in "perfect peace," a *pax arthuriana*, for twelve years. Hakluyt's excerpts

---

12 Ibid., p. 166.
13 Richard Hakluyt, *Principall Voyages* (London, 1589), p. 243. See John Caius, *De Antiquitate Cantabrigiensis Academiae Libri duo* (London, 1568).

from the Arthurian chronicle tradition stress Arthur's dominant position in northern Europe: Ireland, Iceland, Gotland, Orkney, Norway and Denmark become subject to him, and supply him with soldiers. This item of Arthurian lore had already proven useful for Tudor propagandists. On Charles V's visit to London in 1522 a pageant showed King Arthur attended by kings of Wales, Scotland, Ireland, Norway, Denmark, and Iceland.[14] While these conquests were lost after Arthur's fall, later in Geoffrey of Monmouth, one Malgo is reported to have recovered Arthur's lost northern empire, this time by "most sharpe battailes."[15]

Hakluyt concludes by citing "Master Lambarde's" description of Arthur, again in both Latin and English. Lambarde extends Arthur's empire as far east as Russia and northward to the North Pole. Arthur emerges here as he did in medieval sources like Geoffrey of Monmouth, Layamon's *Brut*, and the *Alliterative Morte Darthur*, as an Alexander or perhaps a Charlemagne of the north: "a mightie, and valiant man, and a famous warrior. This kingdom was too litle for him, and his mind was not contented with it."[16] This conqueror's mentality recalls the Alexander romances, although his Arthur's urge to spread Christianity is more reminiscent of the Matter of France:

> These people were wild and sauage, and had not in them the loue of God nor of their neighbors, because all euill commeth from the North, yet there were among them certaine Christians liuing in secret. But King Arthur was an exceeding good Christian, and caused them to be baptized, and throughout all Norway to worship one God, and to receiue and keepe inviolably for euer, faith in Christ onely.[17]

This portrait, too, reflects current British interest in a northern sphere of influence, reciprocated with a vengeance by the Norsemen described in Hakluyt. "For this cause the Norses say, that they ought to dwell with vs in this kingdome ... for they had rather dwell here then in their owne natiue countrey, which is drie and full of mountaines ... "[18] The long search for the "North-West and North-East passages" by Frobisher, Willoughby, and their successors, grew out of this kind of geographical speculation.

By the time Captain John Smith published the *Generall Historie of Virginia* in 1624, Arthur's claims to priority as a conqueror of the north could only be assserted with hesitation. "For the Stories of *Arthur*, *Malgo*, and *Brandon*, that say a thousand yeares agoe they were in the North of America; or the Fryer of *Linn* that by his blacke Art went to the North pole in the yeare 1360, in that I

---

14 Young, *Tudor and Jacobean Tournaments*, p. 168.
15 Hakluyt, *Principall Voyages*, p. 244.
16 Ibid., p. 245.
17 Ibid.
18 Ibid.

know them not. Let this suffice."[19] Arthur clings to his position by his fingernails, but Smith is not quite ready to relinquish him altogether. He seems to represent, for these writers, an ancient British heroic presence. This element of historical priority was important in a legal sense, too, with reference to the title of the English crown to any newly discovered lands. In 1580 Elizabeth had set Dr John Dee to researching this matter, in the intervals between his more occult studies.[20] It held some psychological importance, too, since the English were all too conscious of their own tardiness in entering the field of overseas exploration and conquest. Columbus had offered his services to Henry VII, but Henry had failed to grasp the opportunity. Now his countrymen were left to harass the rear of Spain's treasure fleets.

Some stress should also be placed on the adjective "heroic." For all the effort to remodel him as a conqueror in the classical tradition, or the Carolingian mode, Arthur still carried strong chivalric associations for sixteenth-century English readers brought up on Malory's *Morte Darthur*. Hakluyt does not mention the Round Table, or any of Arthur's knights. Fiction is shut out in order to present a historical Arthur. Chivalry can only be implicit.

In 1596, between the two editions of Hakluyt's *Principal Voyages*, Sir Walter Ralegh's *Discoverie of the Large, Rich and Bewtiful Empire of Guiana, with a Relation of the Great and Golden Citie of Manoa (which the Spaniards call El dorado) . . . Performed in the yeare 1595 by sir W. Ralegh Knight, Captaine of her Maiesties Guard, Lo. Warden of the Stanneries, and her Highesse Lieutenant generall of the Countie of Cornewall* appeared. This characteristic work ranks among the most flamboyant of the English exploration narratives. Its distinction of style sets it apart from the rest. This is the military plain style as interpreted by one of Elizabeth's most judicious court poets. Ralegh's account of his expedition of 1594 to the Orinoco, an event that does not loom large in the annals of Latin America, stands by itself, as well, as a landmark in the English chivalric tradition. It is this aspect of Ralegh's writing that must be emphasized here.[21]

Ralegh's *Discoverie* combines three forms of writing about travel that are often found separately – narration, description, and persuasion. Each one involves chivalry in a different way. The traveler, first of all, narrates his own

---

[19] Captain John Smith, ed., *The Generall Historie of Virginia, New England, & the Summer Isles* (London, 1624), reprinted in Captain John Smith, *Works*, ed. Edward Arber (Birmingham, 1884), p. 303.

[20] "John Dee," in *Encyclopedia Britannica* (11th edn, New York, 1910–11). See also the entry on Dee in Sir Leslie Stephen and Sir Sidney Lee, ed., *Dictionary of National Biography* (1921–22; rev. edn, London, 1973), V.724.

[21] Cf. John Hemming, *Red Gold: The Conquest of the Brazilian Indians, 1500–1760* (Cambridge, Mass., 1978), pp. 223–24. For discussions of the *Discoverie* emphasizing different aspects of the text, see Mary Campbell, *The Witness and the Other World: Exotic European Travel Writing, 400–1600* (Ithaca, 1988), ch. 6, pp. 211–54; Stephen Greenblatt, *Sir Walter Ralegh* (New Haven, 1973), ch. 4, pp. 99–112.

adventures. As he does this, Ralegh, a supremely self-conscious narrator, sees himself momentarily in the position of an Elizabethan Mandeville. "Such a nation was written of by Maundevile, whose reportes were held for fables, many yeares, and yet since the East Indies were discovered, wee find his relations true of such thinges as heretofore were held incredible."[22] Ralegh places himself in competition with Columbus and Cortes as well, but the citation of Mandeville reasserts English priority. We were there first. Ralegh recognizes obliquely here that he faces the same problem of credibility. The difficulty will be all the greater since Ralegh, that notorious sceptic, does not intend to demythologize the New World. On the contrary.

As a story of the voyage of 1595, the *Discoverie* may usefully be seen as Ralegh's chief formal contribution to chivalric autobiography, just as his account of his cousin Richard Greville's exploits in the *Revenge* might be read as chivalric biography, as it was read by generations of English schoolboys. In fact, the self Ralegh presents in the *Discoverie* proves to be much preoccupied with his chivalric image and principles. Ralegh the intelligent and learned eyewitness, Ralegh the sophisticated political operator and Ralegh the chivalrous English gentleman all surface by turns in his *Discoverie*. Not at all a conventional swashbuckler, he does not depict himself in combat after the first episode, the capture of the Spanish town of St Joseph on the island of Trinidado. Ralegh justifies this action in both chivalric and pragmatic terms, but he describes his chivalric justification for action at much greater length. The pragmatist recognizes that "to enter Guiana by small boats, to depart 400 or 500 miles from my ships, and to leave a garrison in my backe interested in the same enterprize . . . I should haue sauored very much of the Asse."[23] This sensible observation is preceded by detailed accounts of the Spanish governor Berreo's treachery to an earlier English party: Berreo "the yeare before betraied 8 of Captaine Whiddons men, & tooke them . . . notwithstanding that he had giuen his worde . . ."[24] Berreo is not only a man whose word cannot be trusted, he is also a cruel tyrant. He threatens the natives with hanging and quartering merely for trading with the English, "having executed two of them for the same which I afterwardes found."[25] Ralegh records "most lamentable complaints of his cruelty." Indeed, to lend verisimilitude to his narrative, Ralegh supplies the names of five native chieftains he rescued from Berreo's prison "in one chaine almost dead of famin & wasted with torments."[26] Ralegh only burns the Spanish settlement "at the instance of the Indians."[27] His prisoner, Berreo, he recognizes as a member of his own class: "This *Berreo* is a gent. well descended, and had long serued the

---

[22] Ralegh, *Discoverie*, p. 70.
[23] Ibid., p. 6.
[24] Ibid., p. 5.
[25] Ibid., p. 6.
[26] Ibid., p. 6.
[27] Ibid., p. 7.

Spanish king in *Millan, Naples,* the lowe Countries and elsewhere, verie valiant & liberal, and a Gent. of great assurednes, and of great heart."[28]

This initial event establishes Ralegh's characteristic manner of proceeding, together with the quality and limits of his chivalry. His actions can be defended in both medieval chivalric and modern Machiavellian terms. He is at once removing a cruel tyrant, rescuing captive princes, restoring the isle to its rightful rulers, avenging his countryman's wrongs, and protecting his rear. The last may seem to cynical twentieth-century readers the only true motive, and all the rest merely another form of self-protection. The fact remains that Ralegh is by no means content to present himself in the character of a grim realist. He wants, and perhaps needs, the rationale offered by chivalric precedent. This elevates the inglorious tale of the burning of one Spanish outpost surrendered with little resistance: "They abode not any fight after a few shot."[29] This is, after all, as close as Ralegh comes to a conventional military action. It can at least be invested with the trappings of a noble deed of errantry. What we see here may be the emergence of a familiar modern heroic mentality – a masculine acrobat who must display the physical prowess of a Tristram, the moral rectitude of a Galahad, and undercut it all with the sardonic Renaissance pragmatism of *The Prince.* Ralegh sets himself the task of conforming to chivalric expectations while never permitting himself to admit he believes in them wholeheartedly. This is more like the sensibility of Humphrey Bogart's Rick in *Casablanca* than like anything encountered so far. The "hardboiled detective" who performs all the most conventional deeds of prowess while refusing to confess a belief in any ideal except self-preservation lurks only a few steps away.

Ralegh is not a critic of chivalry here. He does not even mock chivalric ideals from within, as Sir Dinadan does in the prose *Tristan* or Malory's *Boke of Sir Tristram de Lyonesse.* In fact, he defends it – not an unexpected tactic from a man whose public image was founded on his mastery of the grand chivalrous gesture. While a good many sixteenth-century soldiers had deplored chivalric literature as impractical idiocy – Blaise de Monluc, for one – Ralegh makes chivalry and pragmatic self-interest prescribe one and the same course of action. Chivalry and down-to-earth realism are harmonized in the *Discoverie* as they rarely are elsewhere in the sixteenth-century debate over the continuing usefulness of medieval chivalric ideals. Ralegh has much in common here with the attitude expressed in Sir Philip Sidney's famous remark "Honest king Arthure will never displease a souldier."[30] In the course of his venture into the maze of the Orinoco, Ralegh explores a new pathway for the preservation of chivalric fantasy in a cynical world.

---

28 Ibid., p. 8.
29 Ibid., p. 6.
30 Sir Philip Sidney, *The Defence of Poesie,* in his *Works* (Cambridge, 1923), III.32. Incidentally, Sidney displays familiarity with a variety of romances in addition to "honest king Arthure," from *Theagenes and Chariclea* to *Orlando Furioso* and *Valentine and Orson.*

The confrontation on Trinidado underlines a second key aspect of Ralegh's chivalry. It is a competitive business. Ralegh pits himself against Berreo as Elizabeth faces off the king of Spain. Here Ralegh interrupts the tale of his own expedition up the Orinoco to relate the history of Spanish ventures in the same region. This section of the *Discoverie* might perhaps be classified as an antichivalric biography. This is Berreo's own report as told to Ralegh, who undercuts his confiding rival's chivalric pretensions at every turn. Berreo and his fellows struggle towards the goal of their enterprise – the fabled golden city of El Dorado. Their own ferocity, gross ignorance, and greed defeat them. Berreo's losses and frustrations are perhaps eclipsed by the tragedy of "Agiri" (Lope de Aguirre) the mutineer. His career of murder and pillage ends with the killing of his own daughter, a gory finale much to the taste of the Elizabethan theatrical public. The Spaniards massacre one another, are massacred in their turn by the local tribes, egged on by rival Spaniards, execute one chieftain, and hold another to ransom. Moments of chivalrous aspiration do occur; Gonzales gives his daughter to Berreo, "taking his oth and honor, to follow the enterprise to the last of his substance and life."[31] Spanish missionary activities cut little ice with the Elizabethan Protestant audience, especially since they are always allied to schemes of usurpation.[32] As a "fellowship of knights," they prove fatally inept. Ralegh asserts that Berreo "hath spent 100,000 ducates in the same, & yet neuer could enter so farre into the land as my selfe with that poor troupe or rather handful of men, being in all about 100, gentlemen, soldiers, rowers, boies and of all sortes."[33]

The thought is the more consoling since Ralegh admits from the first that his own concrete achievements, whether as conqueror, gold-digger, or missionary were not much to write home about. For their investment Ralegh's London backers are to receive the *Discoverie*, together with a top-secret map of the region, for the eyes of Lord Admiral Howard and Cecil only. In effect, this is the map leading to the treasure, soon to become a cliché of later romances. Ralegh offers many sensible reasons why he was not able to bring back a shipload of Inca gold, and why his deluded followers are embarrassing him by wandering the streets with pathetic samples of "fool's gold." The romance he offers is a tale of physical endurance and narrow escapes from death in a hostile but fantastic environment.

Berreo marks the transition with a warning speech. The English can never hope to succeed:

> it would be labour lost: & that they should suffer manie miseries if they proceeded: And first he deliuered that I could not enter any of the riuers with my barke or pinace, nor hardly with anie ships bote, it was so low, sandie: and

---

[31] Ralegh, *Discoverie*, p. 20.
[32] Ibid., p. 33.
[33] Ibid., pp. 11–12.

full of flats, and that his companies were dailie grounded in their *Canoas* which drew but twelue inches water: hee further saide that none of the countrey would come to speake with vs, but would all flie, and if we followed them to their dwellings, they would burne their owne townes, and besides that the way was long, the winter at hand, and that the riuers beginning once to swel, it was impossible to stem the currant, & that we could not in those smal botes by any means carry victuall for halfe the time, and that (which indeed most discouraged my companie) the Kings and Lords of al the borders and of *Guiana* had decreed, that none of them should trade with anie Christians for gold, because the same would be their owne ouerthrow, and that for the loue of gold the Christians meant to conquer and disposesse them of all together."[34]

The Spanish governor here serves as the human equivalent of the dire inscription that confronts the knight entering any "strong adventure." As we saw earlier, *Gyron le Courtoys* displayed a special fondness for this convention. Malory and his sources provide examples, like the inscription on the cross at the crossroads where Galahad and Melias part. Still, on the whole, they tend to prefer human prophets of triumph or disaster: King Arthur's forebodings after Gawain's vow to seek the Holy Grail, or Gawain's warning to Arthur before his final battle with Mordred.[35] The foreboding speech Ralegh inserts, prompted by Berreo's understandable desire to exclude the English from Guiana, enhances the suspense of the story from the outset in a most traditional manner.

Put on their mettle by this doleful warning, Ralegh and his men make their way into a "labyrinth of rivers."[36] Their prowess consists largely of endurance – endurance of heat, rain, fatigue, and the threat of more exotic dangers like poisoned arrows, upon which Ralegh punctuates his account with "a digression not unnecessary."[37] The elegant Elizabethan courtier's diatribe against life in a small boat on the Orinoco frankly reveals his physical disgust:

being al driuen to lie in the raine & weather, in the open aire, in the burning sun, & vpon the hard bords, and to dresse our meate, and to cary al maner of furniture in them, wherewith they were so pestred & vnsauery, that whatwith victualls being most fish, with the wet clothes of so many men thrust together and the heate of the sunne, I will vndertake there was neuer any prison in England, that coulde be founde more vnsauory and lothsome, especially to my selfe, who had for many yeares before beene dieted and cared for in a sort farre more differing.[38]

---

34 Ibid., pp. 35–36.
35 Malory, *Works*, ed. Eugène Vinaver (2nd edn, 1967; rpt. with additions and corrections, Oxford, 1973), II.867, III.1234.
36 Ralegh, *Discoverie*, p. 39.
37 Ibid., p. 58.
38 Ibid., pp. 8–9.

Clearly Ralegh was not the man to introduce a fashion for camping into Britain. There are also monstrous new creatures like the *lagarto* (Spanish for "alligator." By contrast, Spenser's Duessa is a "cruell craftie crocodile."). This "uglie serpent" devours a crewman before his comrades' eyes. "Poisonfull wormes and serpentes," and deadly red water threaten the English party.[39] Cannibal tribes lurk in forests "full of prickles, thorns and briers."[40] These arduous travels fall short of the goal. Ralegh never reaches El Dorado, for many excellent reasons, as he explains. Nevertheless, the experience serves as a test of character, a chance for Ralegh to display traditional chivalric virtues, as well as certain additional skills requisite to the leader of a Renaissance expeditionary force and a gentleman reader of Machiavelli, Elyot, or even Della Casa's *Galatea*.

The competitive edge comes to the fore again whenever Ralegh compares his practice with that of his Spanish predecessors. Ralegh stresses his own superior intelligence-gathering abilities, as against his Spanish competitor, Berreo: "neither was he curious in those things, being vtterlie vnlearned."[41] Where the Spaniards are much given to raping the native women, he depicts himself as imposing the strictest sexual morality upon the members of his party.

> But I protest before the maiestie of the liuing God, that I neither know nor beleeue, that anie of our companie one or other, by violence or otherwise, euer knew any of their women, and yet we saw many hundreds, and had many in our power, and of thse very yoong, & excellently fauoured which came among vs without deceit, starke naked.[42]

His men were forbidden to take anything without paying for it, though this proved more difficult to enforce. Both of these proceedings make the English party very popular, by Ralegh's account. Ralegh recommended Elizabeth to the inhabitants, similarly, for her conspicuous virtues: her greatness, justice, and charity to the oppressed.

In contrast to his Spanish rivals, Ralegh made no attempt to convert the natives he encounters. His most conspicuous display of faith was the naming of "the riuer of the Red crosse, our selues being the first *Christians* that euer came therein."[43] Any religious confrontation seemed premature to him at this preliminary stage, for politic reasons, especially if it entailed the excavation of native religious sites. "But if we shoulde haue grieued them in their religion at the first, before they had beene taught better, and haue diggged vppe their graues, wee had lost them all."[44]

---

[39] Ibid., pp. 25, 27.
[40] Ibid., p. 52.
[41] Ibid., p. 28.
[42] Ibid., p. 52.
[43] Ibid., p. 39.
[44] Ibid., p. 93 (misnumbered 90).

All of this is in line with the English chivalric tradition, in particular with the principal oath of King Arthur's knights as recorded by Malory:

> never to do outerage nothir mourthir, and allwayes to fle treson, and to gyff mercy unto hym that askith mercy . . . and allwayes to do ladyes, damesels, and jantilwomen and wydowes [socour:] strengthe hem in hir ryghtes, and never to enforce them, uppon payne of dethe. Also, that no man take no batayles in a wrongefull quarell for no love ne for no worldis goodis."[45]

The emphasis on knightly self-restraint, especially from theft and rape, is stressed elsewhere in Malory, as in Sir Lancelot's exclamation: " 'What?' seyde sir Launcelot, 'is he a theff and a knyght? And a ravyssher of women? He doth shame unto the Order of Knyghthode, and contrary unto his oth. Hit is pyté that he lyveth!' "[46]

The name of "Red crosse" given to the river inevitably calls to mind Edmund Spenser and his "Redcrosse Knight," St George, of Book I of the *Faerie Queene*. Redcrosse represents Holiness, the first of the "twelve private morall virtues" Spenser had told Ralegh that he planned to represent in his poem.[47] Spenser claimed to derive these virtues from Aristotle. His annotators point instead to more recent philosophers, Lodowick Bryskett and Piccolomini. In fact, the virtues Spenser tackled first in his project "to fashion a gentleman or noble person in vertuous and gentle discipline" had found a place in earlier "mirrors of knighthood" as well. Alain Chartier's fifteenth-century "Breviaire des nobles" or Lull's *Libre del orde de cavayleria* identify similar qualities of character. Spenser's "holiness" corresponds to Chartier's and Lull's "faith," the first requisite of a knight. His "temperance" is Lull's "attemperaunce," which covers some of the same ground as Chartier's *sobresse* or *necteté*. Chastity as depicted by Spenser recalls the sexual self-restraint practiced by the more successful Grail knights, and by the ideals of the military orders like the Templars and Hospitallers. Chartier recommends *bonne amour*, a virtue represented in Spenser by such loving couples as the Redcrosse Knight and Una, or by Prince Arthur's love for the Faerie Queene. The first three books, with the letter to Ralegh as an explanatory preface, were printed in 1590. Three more appeared in 1596, devoted to the virtues of friendship, justice, and courtesy. The posthumously published "Mutability Cantos" of 1609 were ascribed to an unfinished book "under the legend of Constancie." According to Spenser, Prince Arthur was to signify the royal virtue of Magnificence throughout the romance epic, a virtue traditionally considered appropriate to a monarch rather than to a subject. Otherwise, the virtues Spenser identifies as critical to a gentleman are often

---

[45] Malory, *Works*, ed. Vinaver, I.75.
[46] Ibid., I.160.
[47] Edmund Spenser, explanatory letter of 1589, *The Faerie Queene*, in his *Works*, ed. Edwin Greenlaw, Charles G. Osgood, and Frederick M. Padelford (London and Baltimore, 1932), I.167–69.

identical to the prime chivalric virtues.[48] They are also qualities of character stressed by Ralegh in the *Discoverie*. He praises Elizabeth I as a great queen notable for her justice and charity to the oppressed; the public display of English chastity, temperance (to a certain extent; some social drinking does go on) and justice forms a principal part of Sir Walter Ralegh's enterprise, both in Guiana and in composing this account of his voyage.

The Faerie Queene has been often identified as a courtesy book in the tradition of Castigliano's *Book of the Courtier*. To an even greater extent it inherits the mantle of the chivalric manual. The usefulness of the romance plot as a means of sugaring the pill of knightly moral instruction was recognized by Lull in his preface to the *Libre del orde de cavayleria* and again in *Blanquerna*, the fourteenth-century author of the *Chemin de vaillance*, Olivier de la Marche, William Caxton, in his preface to Malory, if not Malory himself, and a horde of competitors. Ralegh, Spenser's "Shepherd of the Ocean," patron and mentor, draws on the same conservative tradition of chivalric morality in his *Discoverie*.

The celebration of chivalric virtues by these Elizabethan writers can be accompanied by a rather condescending attitude towards beings they regard as less civilized. The cultivation of a higher morality would seem to tempt its adepts towards becoming "holier than thou," the besetting sin of the modern Minnesotan. Spenser's *View of Ireland* details his proposal for the suppression of Irish resistance to English rule in drastic terms. Order can at long last be imposed on these brutish savages by the strictest measures. In Grill, who appears in the second book of the *Faerie Queene*, Spenser depicts a perverse human being who prefers an animal state of existence to his manhood. Ralegh writes with more respect for the natives he encounters. In the *Discoverie* it is usually the Spaniards who treat the local inhabitants like animals, chaining chieftains up "like a dogge."[49] Still, his astonishment at the eloquence of the ancient chief Topiawari hits a discordant note: "This Topiawari is held for the proudest, and wisest of all the Orenoqueponi, and so he behaued himselfe towardes me in all his answers at my returne, as I maruelled to finde a man of that grauity and iudgement, and of so good discourse, that had no helpe of learning nor breed."[50]

Such an analysis can be attacked as a cheap shot at Spenser, Ralegh, and their contemporaries. One of the challenges of their era was the need to figure out

---

[48] Compare Maurice Keen, *Chivalry* (New Haven, 1984), pp. 2–17 on chivalric virtues. Keen stresses *prouesse, loyauté, largesse, courtoisie,* and *franchise.* Alain Chartier's twelve prime virtues from the "Bréviaire des nobles," in *The Poetical Works of Alain Chartier,* ed. J. C. Laidlaw (Cambridge, 1974), pp. 395–409, are *Foy, Loyaulté, Honneur, Droitture, Proesce, Amour, Courtoisie, Diligence, Necteté, Largesce, Sobresse, Perseverance.* In John Skelton's early sixteenth-century political morality play, *Magnyfycence,* the title role is that of the king, perhaps modeled after Henry VIII.

[49] Ralegh, *Discoverie,* p. 100.

[50] Ibid., p. 64.

the place of newly encountered indigenous peoples in the scheme of human affairs. This issue is still with us. Ralegh at least portrays the natives of the regions bordering the Orinoco as worthy potential allies or adversaries, for the most part. But the Elizabethan gentleman's faint sneer is important, too.

A second key goal of Ralegh's enterprise in the *Discoverie* is to describe his findings. He vaunts his own superior powers of observation and interrogation, and displays the fruits of his investigations throughout the account of the voyage. Since he brings back little of immediate value, he can at least "give color" to his report. Much of the "color" he gives is that of the romance landscape. Ralegh's party take to small boats rather than horses; nevertheless, they traverse a forest as treacherous and teeming with marvels as any Huon of Bordeaux ever knew. The branches of the Orinoco become, for Ralegh, a "labyrinth," a classical reference pleasing to the Renaissance imagination, but also an essential underlying form in much medieval literature, as Penelope Doob has established.[51] (The Spaniards whose letters are appended to Ralegh's *Discoverie* call the multiple river mouths "*las siete bocas de drago*," "the seven mouths of the dragon," an even more sinister romantic term, though it also suggests a classical reference, to Hercules' Hydra.) The goal of the quest, the Inca city of Manoa, Ralegh's El Dorado, lies over the mountains. The intervening territory offers monsters, human and animal. In place of St George's dragon, Ralegh offers us the *lagarto*. The armadillo proves a less menacing but potentially more useful marvel:

> which seemeth to bee all barred ouer with small plates somewhat like to a *Renocero*, with a white horne growing in his hinder parts, as big as a great hunting horne, which they vse to winde in steede of a trumpet. *Monardus* writeth that a little of the powder of that horn put into the eare, cureth deafnes. [52]

There are exotic foods, like "Tortugas eggs," "verie wholesome meate" and the pineapple, "the princesse of fruits." Astonishing waterfalls, "every one as high over the other as a church tower," red water only safe to drink at noon, "and in the night strong poison" threaten the unwary traveler.[53] After their struggle upriver through the forest, the English are consoled when they arrive at a *locus amoenus* that reminds them strangely of home, "and all as full of deare, as any forest or parke in England."[54]

> I neuer saw a more beawtifull countrey, nor more liuely prospectes, hils so raised heere and there ouer the vallies, the riuer winding into diuers

---

[51] See Penelope Doob, *The Idea of the Labyrinth from classical antiquity through the Middle Ages* (Ithaca, 1990).

[52] Ralegh, *Discoverie*, p. 61.

[53] Ibid., pp. 60, 67, 75.

[54] Ibid., p. 82 (misnumbered 92).

braunches, the plaines adioyning without bush or stuble, all faire greene grasse, the ground of hard sand easy to march on, eyther for horse or foote, the deare crossing in euery path, the birds towards the euening singing on euery tree with a thousand seueral tunes, cranes & herons of white, crimson, and carnation pearching on the riuers side, the ayre fresh with a gentle easterlie wind, and euery stone that we stooped to take vp, promised either gold or siluer by his complexion.[55]

This is a tropical Eden made more alluring by its resemblance to the traveler's own far-off country. It should be set next to other explorers' reports of earthly paradises, as in Mandeville or *The Book of Marco Polo*, and against those of fiction, as in *Gyron le Courtoys*, or in Spenser. Perhaps not altogether by coincidence, Ralegh reports that several of the native chiefs he met were a hundred years old or more – another marvel suggestive of a return to paradise.

Perhaps the most tantalizing element of scenery Ralegh describes is the mountain of crystal – or could it be sparkling with diamonds? "Wee saw it a farre off and it appeared like a whit Church towre of an exceeding height," with a waterfall rushing over it "with a terryble noyse and clamor, as if 1000 great belles were knockt one against another." Ralegh can only compare this white pinnacle, glimpsed from afar, to a cathedral. This recurrent simile gives his perception of natural beauty a Christian flavor just skirting the fringes of mysticism – or is this an act of imaginative appropriation? Ralegh himself stops short of recognizing the "mountaine of Cristall" as a mystical vision, but he points his readers in that direction. This is as close as Ralegh comes to a Grail city. In a way, it substitutes for the sight of El Dorado, which he fails to attain. Readers who knew Cortes' description of Tenochtitlan, or the accounts of Pizarro's encounter with the Inca empire, might well be dashed at the anticlimax of the *Discoverie*. The "mountaine of Cristall," a long-standing image in European folklore and romance in its own right, is the best Ralegh can do. (In folklore, of course, the mountain would normally have a princess on top, to be won by the hero.)

If he falls short in his exploration of the mysterious terrain of the Orinoco, Ralegh makes up for it in his accounts of the population. Here Ralegh can only disappoint his modern admirers who revere him as a sceptical thinker lightyears ahead of his time. It is no part of his enterprise in the *Discoverie* to debunk the legends of the New World. On the contrary, Ralegh endorses all the rumors. He has not himself seen:

a nation of people whose heads appeare not aboue their shoulders, which though it may be thought a meere fable, yet for mine owne part I am resolued it is true, because euery child in the prouinces of *Arromaia* and *Canuri* affirme the same: they are called *Ewaipanoma*: they are reported to haue their eies in their shoulders, and their mouthes in the middle of their breastes, &

---

[55] Ibid., pp. 67–68.

II. Headless natives and
an armadillo in an
illustration from the
Latin edition of Sir
Walter Ralegh, *Discoverie
of Guiana* (1500).
By permission of the
James Ford Bell Library,
University of Minnesota

that a long train of haire groweth backward between their shoulders.... If I had but spoken one word of it while I was there, I might have brought one of them with me to put the matter out of doubt.[56]

So many people could hardly be lying. After all, Mandeville described such a race, and many contemporary reports, from native and Spanish sources, confirm their existence. Ralegh can even cite that staple of modern journalism, an authoritative but confidential informant: "I may not name him because it may be for his disadvantage."[57] The publisher of the Latin edition of 1599 of Ralegh's work did not hesitate to present depictions of these interesting beings on the title page, next to an Amazon brandishing an arrow.

Ralegh never encountered any Amazons, either, but he includes a full report on their society. He "was verie desirous to vnderstand the trueth of those warlike women, bicause of some it is beleeued, of others not."[58] Irving Leonard and his successors have established that this preoccupation with Amazons was inspired by both classical sources and sixteenth-century romance. Ralegh makes direct reference to such authorities: "The memories of the like women are very ancient as well in *Africa* as in *Asia*: In *Africa* those that had *Medusa* for *Queene*... in many histories they are verified to haue been, and in diuers ages and prouinces."[59] Whether Ralegh included *Las Sergas de Esplandián* among his "histories" may be difficult to establish with any degree of certainty. His Amazons parallel Esplandián's to some extent in their golden trappings, and in their mating customs, though Ralegh's are a good deal less ferocious:

> But they which are not far from *Guiana* do accompany with men but once in a yeeare, and for the time of one moneth, which I gather by their relation to be in Aprill. At that time all the kinges of the borders assemble, and the Queenes of the *Amazones*, and after the Queens haue chosen, the rest cast lottes for their *Valentines*. This one moneth, they feast, dance, & drinke of their wines in abundance, & the Moone being done, they all depart to their owne prouinces. If they conceiue, and be deliuered of a sonne, they returne him to the father, if of a daughter they nourish it, and retaine it, and as many as haue daughters sende vnto the begetters a present, all being desirous to increase their owne sex and kinde ...[60]

By contrast, Montalvo's Amazons kill their male offspring to shift the male-female ratio in their favor. They also kill the men captured in raids, while Ralegh's limit themselves to killing prisoners of war and invaders: "for they are said to be verie cruell and bloodthirsty, especially to such as offer to inuade their

---

[56] Ibid., pp. 69–70.
[57] Ibid., p. 71.
[58] Ibid., p. 23.
[59] Ibid., p. 23.
[60] Ibid., pp. 23–24.

territories."[61] "A nation of inhumane Cannibals" also lurks in the underbrush, intimidating the most intrepid ancient or modern explorers.[62]

Ralegh devotes little attention to destroying earlier reports, though he is not always as exuberant as this in his descriptions of the peoples he meets. He admires the dignity of the local orators: "These *Tiuitiuas* are a very goodlie people and verie valiant, and haue the most manlie speech and most deliberate that euer I heard of what nation soever."[63] (Are these by any chance Hemming's "almost chivalrous" Tupi?) The Aroras "are as blacke as *Negroes*, but haue smooth haire, and these are very valiant, or rather desperate people, and haue the most strong poyson on their arrowes . . ."[64] This descriptive language veers between positive and negative poles according to whether Ralegh envisions the natives as worthy potential allies or fearsome enemies.

One specialized element of the scene Ralegh depicts is the amount of space he devotes to what a twentieth-century academic reader might call "women's issues." The feminist undercurrent of the whole piece is most unusual in this literature. Over and above the myth of the Amazons, a common enough preoccupation of European wanderers, the ordinary women of Guiana and their lives crowd their way into Ralegh's description. This material ranges from outraged reports of Spaniards who take native women by force, or of natives selling their own nieces and daughters into slavery in the Caribbean islands "for 3 or 4 hatchets."[65] The border tribes, Ralegh reports, are likely to ally themselves with the English against the rulers of El Dorado in order to recover their own captured women.

> hee farther complayned very sadly (as it had beene a matter of greate consequence) that wereas they were wont to haue ten or twelue wiues, they were now inforced to content themselues with three or fower, & that the Lords of the *epuremei* had 50 or 100. And in truth they warr more for women then either for gold or dominion.[66]

The women who motivate these wars are portrayed as attractive beings, well worth fighting for. Ralegh describes in detail a chieftain's beautiful and

---

61 Ibid., p. 24. For extensive discussions of the Amazons, see Irving A. Leonard, *Books of the Brave* (1949; rpt. Berkeley and Los Angeles, 1992), pp. 36ff and William Thomas Little's notes to his translation: *The Labors of the Very Brave Knight Esplandián* (Binghamton, 1992), pp. 457–58. Both Ralegh and Montalvo reject the ancient notion that the Amazons cut off their right breasts to improve their skill in archery. Montalvo simply omits it; Ralegh says he does not find it to be true. The earliest known translation of *Las Sergas de Esplandián* into English is Adam Islip's version published in 1598, but this volume had been available in French since 1550, and in Spanish since 1510. See Little's introduction to *Esplandián*, pp. 20–22.

62 Ralegh, *Discoverie*, p. 91.

63 Ibid., p. 42.

64 Ibid., p. 59.

65 Ibid., pp. 52, 34, 72.

66 Ibid., p. 78.

convivial wife he meets along the way who reminds him of an English lady of his acquaintance. "I haue seene a Lady in England so like her, as but for the difference of colour I would haue sworne might haue beene the same."[67]

This preoccupation extends to the landscape. Some of the stones Ralegh picks up are identified by a convenient Spanish expert as being *el madre de oro*, "the mother of gold," and presage a rich mine below the surface.[68] Ralegh concludes his exploration by announcing that "Guiana is a Countrey that hath yet her Maydenhead," an observation that helps to spark Mary Campbell's detailed discussion of this aspect of the *Discoverie*. The long-running topos of the "woman's body as Landscape," or, more properly in this case, "the landscape as woman's body," is without question much in evidence here. In this rash statement, indeed, the Latin American landscape becomes a specific woman's body. Guiana becomes, for a moment, the Virgin Queen, Elizabeth herself.

This strand of Ralegh's discussion supports two goals, one chivalric and the second political. The defence of women had become entrenched as a motive for chivalric action, in theory and fiction. Ralegh represents the tribeswomen of Guiana as much in need of defence, both from tyrannical Spaniards and from the evil customs of their own race. The trade in female slaves, native burial customs that include the live burial of wives alongside the chief and his treasures, and the widespread practice of polygamy all qualify in Ralegh's book as abuses. In life, all native men appear to have many wives, who eat separately after serving their husbands. "Those that are past their yonger yeares, make all their bread and drinke, and worke their cotten beddes, and do all else of seruice and labour, for the men doe nothing but hunte, fish, play, and drinke, when they are out of the wars."[69] The 63-year-old Elizabeth might be expected to sympathize with the old wives of Guiana. Whether this should be read as a paradise for men or a traditional society grinding down its women in time-honored fashion, or a classic combination of both, must depend on the gender and political affinities of the reader. Clearly, though, when approached from a sixteenth-century English chivalric perspective, the women of Guiana languish in need of rescue. Ralegh identifies any number of evil customs of a sort that galvanized the knights of Malory or Spenser to action. The most pertinent reference I can offer from the *Morte Darthur* is Sir Lancelot's liberation of "three score of ladyes and damesels" from a sweatshop maintained by a pair of giants at Tintagel Castle. The imprisoned ladies explain "the moste party of us have bene here this seven yere [theire] presoners, and we haue worched all maner of sylke workys for oure mete, and we ar all grete jentylwomen borne."[70] (Lancelot also intervenes in a domestic dispute, with a much less successful outcome.)

The other purpose that drives Ralegh to supply so much material relating to

[67] Ibid., p. 55.
[68] Ibid., p. 68.
[69] Ibid., p. 92 (misnumbered 98).
[70] Malory, *Works*, ed. Vinaver, I.161–62.

women is that he anticipates an all-important female auditor. In fact, this aspect of the *Discoverie* suggests that Ralegh is writing over the heads of his male dedicatees, Burleigh and Howard, to catch the eye of Queen Elizabeth herself. He goes out of his way to point out that the natives he encounters would be receptive to Elizabeth's rule. After all, they have female chiefs of their own, one of whom interviewed Ralegh herself "and asked me divers questions of her Maiestie."[71] Should Elizabeth fund a return trip, the Amazons themselves will come to hear of her. It seems notable that the one religion Ralegh does make an effort to introduce to the Americas is the cult of Elizabeth. "I shewed them her maiesties picture which they so admired and honoured, as it had beene easie to haue brought them Idolatrous thereof." "I gaue among them manie more pesoes of Golde then I receiued of the new money of 20. shillings with her Maiesties picture to weare, with promise that they would become her seruantes thenceforth."[72] The device of displaying a princess's picture to inspire devotion at a distance was to persist in fairy tales; in the sixteenth century princes such as Henry VIII sent artists to paint the portraits of prospective brides for the most pragmatic reasons, though the attraction such images inspired had been known to prove delusive, as in the case of Anne of Cleves.

Ralegh's narrative and his descriptive sections both labor in the service of persuasion. This report is geared to win Ralegh the financial backing for a second trip. For all his expressed distaste for the rigors of travel in the tropics, Ralegh portrays himself here as keen to go back to seek for El Dorado. The decision rests with Elizabeth. Ralegh attempts to convince her that the enterprise is necessary to the national security of Britain, feasible, and especially suited to her genius as a ruler. Indeed, English intervention is a matter of Inca prophecy, attested by the Spanish conquistadores of Peru "that from *Inglatierra* those *Ingas* should be againe in time to come restored, & deliuered from the seruitude of the said Conquerors."[73] This has the unmistakable ring of the Mexican messianic beliefs that proved so useful to Cortes. It also chimes in well with the European tradition of the prophecies of Merlin, a body of lore that fascinated everyone from Columbus and Ferdinand and Isabella, to sixteenth-century British political propagandists.[74] Undoubtedly Ralegh had been

---

[71] *Discoverie*, p. 91.

[72] Ibid., pp. 7, 81.

[73] Ibid., p. 101.

[74] The fascination can be traced back at least as far as Geoffrey of Monmouth's *Prophetiae Merlini* in the twelfth century; this became bk 7 of the *Historia Regum Britanniae*. For the French prophecies of Merlin (c.1270), see Anne Berthelot, ed., *Les Prophesies de Merlin* (Cologne, 1990); Lucy Allen Paton, ed., *Les Prophécies de Merlin* (2 vols., New York, 1926); Paul Zumthor, *Merlin le prophète: un thème de la littérature polémique, de l'historiographie et des romans* (Lausanne, 1943). The *Baladro del Sabio Merlín* (Seville, 1535) includes prophecies pertaining to late medieval Spain; Columbus refers to some of this material in his *Libro de Profécias*. Peggy K. Liss refers to this prophetic material often in *Isabel the Queen: Life and Times* (Oxford and New York, 1992). For British interest in this material, which continued into the eighteenth century and drew the fire of Jonathan Swift, see

scrutinizing his predecessors' methods. In a more cynical vein, he also notes that dissention between rival tribes furnishes the English with the chance to play one side against the other, as the Spaniards did before them: "For by the dissention between *Guascar* and *Atabolia, Pacaro* conquered *Peru,* and by the hatred that the *Traxcallians* bare to *Mutezuma, Cortez* was victorious ouer *Mexico,* without which both the one and the other had failed of their enterprize . . . ."[75]

Ralegh does not, however, simply present the deeds of Cortes for Elizabeth's emulation. He offers her a choice of two chivalric models for action, one based on ancient English precedents, and one on modern Hispanic experience. His first suggestion is that Elizabeth might send an expeditionary force to ally itself with the natives. "A small army a foote" might easily induce the Inca ruler of El Dorado to agree to pay tribute to Elizabeth and accept her protection.[76] This optimistic notion recalls King Arthur's bloodless subjugation of Scandinavia, as described by Hakluyt, and detailed at the outset of this chapter. Ralegh portrays himself as partial to this approach. He is paving the way for this first, traditionally English, form of domination as he sprinkles the jungle with Elizabeth's portrait and insists on the "good vsage of the people."[77] According to this scenario, the English would win Guiana from Spain by means of their superior chivalric virtues. For this reason Ralegh had to resist the urge to get rich quick. Any revelation that the English were just as avid for gold as the Spaniards would put paid to this golden opportunity. The natives must on no account discover "wee came both for one errant, and that both sought but to sacke and spoyle them."[78] On the other hand, should Elizabeth decline to send such an army, she might permit her loyal vassals to attempt the conquest of El Dorado themselves. "I trust in God, this being true, will suffice, and that he which is king of all kings and Lord of Lords, will put it into her hart which is Lady of Ladies to possesse it, if not, I will iudge those men worthy to be kings therof that by her grace and leaue will vndertake it of themselves."[79] The familiar image of the individual knight who wins an empire with his sword, as Tirant lo Blanch nearly does, and as so many Spaniards were trying to do, comes into focus here. This had become normal operating procedure at the English court, in an era when British adventurers were taking to the sea on privateering expeditions, with Elizabeth's tacit consent, but without her official imprimatur.

The suspicious mind cannot help but infer that Ralegh's hope was for Elizabeth to send him back as the chivalrous leader in charge of the little English army. Once they reached El Dorado the likelihood that the native ruler would settle comfortably into a tributary relationship with England was small. In the

---

Keith Thomas, *Religion and the Decline of Magic: Studies in Popular Beliefs in Sixteenth and Seventeenth Century England* (London, 1971).

[75] Ralegh, *Discoverie,* pp. 28, 65–66.
[76] Ibid., p. 100.
[77] Ibid., p. 50.
[78] Ibid., p. 35.
[79] Ibid., p. 101.

event it would be simple enough to emulate Cortes or Pizarro on his own account. On this point Ralegh is as pragmatic, and as unchivalric, as Gadifer: "if not, he hath neither shotte nor iron weapon in all his Empyre, and therfore may easily be conquered."[80] In both cases, Ralegh minimizes the investment necessary to mount a second expedition. A small band of "gentlemen that are younger brethren" or unemployed captains might do the job.[81] It would hardly be necessary to offer wages: "the common soldier shall here fight for golde and pay himselfe in steede of pence."[82] This advertisement is pitched to allure both the soldier and his employers, though the soldier would naturally be more interested in Ralegh's assurance that the climate is healthful; he is not likely to succumb to some vile tropical disease. At this point Ralegh does not mention the Lagarto.

This presentation is not without an edge to it. Male competition is evoked as a spur to female decision. Ralegh warns his reader that if the king of Spain wins Guiana, he will become "unresistable" in Europe.[83] An equally unpalatable thought, for Elizabeth, would be the notion of allowing Englishmen to make themselves into rival kings in America. Ralegh seems to engage here in the most patent of motivational tactics, dangling the carrot of El Dorado before Elizabeth's nose while goading her from behind.

> Her Maiesty heereby shall confirme and strengthen the opinions of al nations, as touching her great & princely actions. And where the south border of *Guiana* reacheth to the Dominion and Empire of the *Amazones*, those women shall heereby heare the name of a virgin, which is not onely able to defend her owne territories and her neighbors, but also to inuade and conquere so great Empyres and so farre remoued.[84]

A conspicuous element of Ralegh's proposal is its incitement to Elizabeth's own chivalrous ambitions. Ralegh dares his queen to emulate the male European rulers who are her rivals by undertaking a new imperial enterprise. He even dares her to become another Amazon queen, on the model of Montalvo's Calafia. That imperious lady

> conceived a grand design to achieve great deeds . . . and she thought that her great strength and that of her own people would enable her, by means of force or gratitude, to win the largest share of all the spoils. Therefore, she told all her ladies who were skilled in war that it would be a good idea to join the great fleets and sail in the same direction all those grand princes and mighty men were taking.[85]

---

80 Ibid., p. 100.
81 Ibid., p. 99.
82 Ibid., p. 94.
83 Ibid., p. 101.
84 Ibid.
85 Montalvo, *Esplandián*, trans. Little, p. 459. For more about Elizabeth I and the Amadís

Ralegh's *Discoverie* aims squarely for the psyche of the queen who had declared to her troops at Tilbury in 1588 that she had "the body of a weak and feeble woman," but the heart and stomach of a king, "and of a king of England, too." That Elizabeth might well be persuaded to believe, with Calafia, in "the very great fame they could achieve by having their glory bruited throughout the whole world; but, instead, remaining on their island and doing nothing other than what their ancestors did, would be tantamount to being buried alive like the living dead and to living out the rest of their days like dumb animals . . ."[86] Chivalric ambition was by no means confined to the masculine sex in Elizabeth's day, any more than it had been in Isabella's.

Ralegh's peroration is remarkable for the number of chivalric traditions it evokes, and all to no avail. When in doubt, Elizabeth procrastinated. It would be her successor, James I, who would send Ralegh on his last voyage in search of El Dorado, and James I who would order his execution on his return, in the cause of Anglo-Spanish relations. Sir Walter Ralegh would be neither the first nor the last European adventurer to die a human sacrifice.

tradition, see Roy C. Strong, "Queen Elizabeth I as Oriana," *Studies in the Renaissance* VI (1959), pp. 251–60.
[86] Montalvo, *Esplandián*, trans. Little, pp. 459–60.

CHAPTER EIGHT

The Captain's Self-Portrait Revisited

*Many of the most eminent Warriers and others; what their
swords did, their penns writ.*[1]

As MUCH AS ANY personage discussed in this study, Captain John Smith
illustrates the fragility of human reputation. He was hailed by his editor in 1884
as "one of the best and bravest of Englishmen."[2] In 1994 he is summed up racily
as "a soldier of fortune, a vagabond, a castaway, a pirate, a consort with papists
in Rome, a slave who murdered his Muslim master . . ."[3] Smith's multifarious
exploits from Muscovy to Massachusetts, in most cases recorded by himself,
qualify him in the eyes of the twentieth-century academic reader as the ultimate
multicultural villain. Smith pictures himself as the Indiana Jones of the early
seventeenth century, and attains, instead, the status of Jack the Ripper.

Smith's career attracted critics from the start. Smith the historian and
autobiographer has been as often subject to attack as Smith the colonial
administrator. His critics of all eras tend to challenge Smith on two fronts: first,
on his veracity as a writer, and second, on the morality of his conduct, especially
towards the Indians. As I have said before, *The True Travels, Adventures and
Observations of Captaine John Smith in Europe, Asia, and America* of 1629
aroused Thomas Fuller to retort, "It soundeth much to the diminution of his
deeds that he alone is the herald to publish and proclaim them."[4] Henry Adams

---

1 Captain John Smith, Epistle Dedicatory, *The True Travels, Adventures, and Observations
of Captaine John Smith*, in his *Works*, ed. Edward Arber (Birmingham, 1884), p. 809. I first
discussed Captain John Smith's chivalric interests in my article, "The Captain's Self-
Portrait: John Smith as Chivalric Biographer," *Virginia Magazine of History and Biography* 89 (1981), pp. 27–38.
2 Arber's preface to Smith, *Works*, p. ix.
3 Arthur Quinn, *A New World: An Epic of Colonial America From the Founding of Jamestown
to the Fall of Quebec* (Boston, 1994).
4 (London, 1631); Fuller, *Worthies of England* (1662); cited in the introductory essay to
Henry Wharton, *The Life of John Smith, English Soldier*, trans. Laura Polanyi Striker
(Chapel Hill, 1957), p. 25. For a summary of critical views of Smith, see Everett Emerson,
Captain John Smith (New York, 1971), p. 94. See also Philip L. Barbour, *The Three Worlds
of Captain John Smith* (Boston, 1964); and Bradford Smith, *Captain John Smith: His Life
and Legend* (New York, 1953), especially the first appendix, "Captain John Smith's
Hungary and Transylvania," by Laura Polanyi Striker.

and Lewis Kropf expressed similar scepticism towards the end of the nineteenth century. On this score, Smith seems to be finding vindication. As the history of eastern Europe and Asia becomes better known to Western scholars, Smith's exotic experiences appear more and more plausible. By contrast, the level of moral disapprobation shows no signs of subsiding. In his final work, *Advertisements for the Vnexperienced Planters of New-England, or any where. Or the Path-way to experience to erect a Plantation*, Smith conducts a running debate with his English critics, who blame him for his harsh treatment of the natives of Virginia, his failure to convert them to Christianity, and the propriety of English settlement in the Americas.[5]

One might expect that by the time Captain John Smith arrived on the scene there would be little left to link chivalry and exploration, whatever there may have been in the days of Rustichello da Pisa. Few explorers are regarded today as less chivalrous than Smith. Yet, as I suggested in 1981 in "The Captain's Self-Portrait," the conventions of medieval chivalric literature permeate Smith's writings about himself. The *True Travels* of 1629 – written, Smith says, at the request of the celebrated antiquary and book collector Sir Robert Cotton – cries out to be read as a chivalric autobiography, as Larry D. Benson perceived in 1976.[6] The same chivalric concerns percolate through Smith's contributions to the *Generall Historie of Virginia* and his *Advertisements*. A knowledge of romance tradition helps to make sense of Smith's most quixotic adventures, especially his portrayal of his encounters with Pocahontas. A deeper acquaintance with chivalric culture makes Smith the man understandable.

Without going over old ground in too great detail, I shall begin by elaborating on the case for reading the *True Travels* from the perspective of chivalric autobiography. My preliminary study noted that much more could be said about the chivalric element in the *Generall Historie of Virginia*. The second half of this chapter investigates that subject. This discussion, then, takes up Smith's career in chronological order, rather than reviewing his writings in the order in which he wrote them.

John Smith begins his *True Travels* by telling his readers that he was born "in *Willoughby* in *Lincolne-shire*, and a Scholler in the two Free-schooles of *Alford* and *Louth.*"[7] The second of these was probably the grammar school at Louth established by Edward VI, an institution attended by the young Alfred Tennyson two centuries later. In Smith's initial chapter, little touches evoke the world of the chivalric romance. Smith begins by defining himself through his geographical point of origin, his education, and his ancestry, all essential biographical

---

5 Smith, *Works*, ed. Arber, pp. 929, 931, 934.

6 Larry D. Benson, *Malory's Morte Darthur* (Cambridge, Mass. and London, 1976), pp. 177, 270. For Cotton, see Smith, *Works*, ed. Arber, p. 808. It seems altogether appropriate that the man who brought us *Beowulf* and *Sir Gawain and the Green Knight*, not to mention the other Cottonian manuscripts now in the British Library, should also have inspired the *True Travels*.

7 Smith, *Works*, ed. Arber, p. 821.

items. "His father anciently descended from the ancient *Smiths* of *Crudley* in *Lancashire* ; his mother from the *Rickands* at *Great Heck* in *York-shire.*" The double stress on the "ancient" nature of Smith's family reminds us that heredity was still an important element of any claim to the status of a gentleman. Gentlemanly status was still a prerequisite for participants in Elizabethan tournaments, as it had been since the later Middle Ages.[8] Smith's presentation of his pedigree here is a most traditional way to establish his credentials as a gentleman of old family at the start of his chivalric career.

In the process, Smith omits his father's unchivalrous occupation as a prosperous farmer, the source of his "estate." However, his birth at Willoughby associated him with the noble family that would launch his military career by subsidizing his first trip to France, in the entourage of a younger son. His father describes himself in his will of 1596 as Lord Willoughby's "poore tennant." George Smith charged his son "to honoure and love my foresaide good Lord Willoughbie duringe his lyfe."[9] This vestige of feudal patronage did not take Smith far, but it did introduce him to "the life of a souldier." Smith comes as close as he can to Chaucer's Squire, learning his trade in northern France and the Low Countries, "in chyvachie / In Flaundres, in Artoys, and Pycardie."[10]

In the *True Travels*, Smith reports that he was orphaned at thirteen, and denied access to his rightful inheritance by the trustees of his father's estate. This is a heroic predicament familiar from folklore and romance. The dispossessed hero occurs with some frequency in English romances: Havelok, Horn (later renamed Ponthus), Bevis, Gamelyn, Valentine and Orson all begin as boys expelled from their rightful heritage. Smith remembers himself as a thirteen-year-old schoolboy determined upon a life of action: "his minde being even then set upon brave adventures, [he] sould his Satchell, bookes, and all he had, intending secretly to get to Sea."[11] The precocious yearning for adventures beyond the paternal farm and the plot to run away from home in search of them are both familiar motifs, especially of later romance. They turn up in accounts of heroes like Blanchardyn in *Blancandin et l'orgueilleuse d'amours* (Caxton's *Blanchardyn and Eglantine* of 1489–90) or *Les Trois fils du roi* (*The three Kings' Sons*), all of whom run away from home in search of chivalric experiences.

---

8 See Maurice Keen, *Chivalry* (New Haven, 1984), pp. 210–11 and elsewhere. Sir Henry Lee's Ditchley manuscript includes "a speech to Queen Elizabeth by a Hermit on behalf of a 'clowneshly clad' knight and his rustic companions. . . . The countrymen cannot participate in the jousting because they are not of gentle birth; however, they would like to demonstrate their prowess, perhaps at the quintain." Alan Young, *Tudor and Jacobean Tournaments* (London, 1987), p. 160; see also p. 69 on the requirement of gentlemanly status for participation in Elizabethan tournaments.

9 Ed. Arber, *Works*, p. xix.

10 Geoffrey Chaucer, "General Prologue," *The Canterbury Tales*, in *The Riverside Chaucer*, ed. Larry D. Benson (Boston, 1987), p. 24, line 86. Along with Malory, Chaucer needs to be better recognized as a primary source of Elizabethan chivalric lore.

11 Smith, *Works*, ed. Arber, p. 822.

(Oliver of Castile runs away to escape the seductive overtures of his stepmother, so his case is different.) "Such oft is the share of fatherlesse children," Smith remarks.

Smith's first campaigns, like Chaucer's Squire's, took place comparatively close to home. They took him into France, "where he first began to learne the life of a souldier," and back by way of Scotland.[12] At the court of James VI he "failed the means test," lacking the financial ballast and the connections to launch a classic Renaissance career as a courtier. Precedents for this occur in romance, too. The penniless but superlative knight who lurks on the fringes of the court is invariably the hero. Malory's Balin – "the knight with the two swords," Oliver of Castile in England after he is robbed, Boiardo's Ranaldo, described by Charles Ross as "Charlemagne's poorest knight," are all such scruffy figures. These knights test the court's ability to discern true worth. Ramon Lull had warned his readers not to mistake a flashy costume for authentic chivalric virtue. Malory's Balin says much the same thing: "manhode and worship [ys hyd] within a mannes person; and many a worshipfull knyght ys nat knowyn unto all peple. And therefore worhip and hardynesse ys nat in araymente."[13] In the absence of mead or magic, the Grateful Dead, or a friendly sorceress, Smith could only make his way home to Willoughby. Fictional inspiration, it would seem, can only take you so far.

Or can it? To mark the transition between these early attempts and the outset of what Smith regards as his mature career, the autobiographer offers a self-portrait. Here is the future captain as a young man:

> Where within a short time being glutted with too much company, wherein he took small delight; he retired himselfe into a little wooddie pasture, a good way from any towne, invironed with many hundred Acres of other woods: Here by a faire brook he built a Pavillion of boughes, where only in his cloaths he lay. His studie was *Machiavills* Art of warre, and *Marcus Aurelius*; his exercise a good horse, with his lance and Ring . . .[14]

My earlier study noted that other readers tend to stress Smith's up-to-date military reading, at the expense of the larger picture. This image of the solitary hero, encamped in his pavilion by the forest brook, takes the reader back into the wilds of the thirteenth-century romance, to Lancelot and Gyron le

12 Ibid.
13 Matteo Maria Boiardo, *Orlando Innamorato*, trans. Charles Ross, p. 885; see also Ross's introduction, pp. 21–22, and pp. 34–35, I.15–18; Ramon Lull, *Libre del orde de cavayleria*; cf. *Book of the Ordre of Chyualry*, trans. William Caxton, ed. A. T. P. Byles, EETS o.s. 168 (London, 1926), pp. 55–56: "Seche nat noblesse of courage in the mouth / For eueryche mouth sayth not trouthe / Ne seche it not in honourable clothynge / For vnder many a fayr habyte hath ben ofte vyle courage ful of barate and of wyckednesse . . . "; Malory, *Works*, ed. Eugène Vinaver (2nd edn, 1967; rpt. with additions and corrections, Oxford, 1973), I.63.
14 Smith, *Works*, ed. Arber, p. 823.

Courtoys. It is at once reminiscent of the knights of Malory and those of Montalvo. The passage draws on two well-established conventions from the literature of chivalry. The first is the knight of the passage of arms (*pas d'armes*), who plants himself at a bridge, under a tree by his castle, or in any convenient spot, ready to meet any passing knight in a joust. Modern readers of English may be most familiar with Malory's King Pellinor, that dangerous knight, later turned into a comedian by T. H. White. Pellinor is first described as "a knyght in the foreste that hath rered up a pavylon by a welle."[15] He goes on to threaten the lives of young Gryfflet and Arthur himself. The passage of arms reappears persistently elsewhere in romance. It was enacted in real life by such celebrated fifteenth-century knights as the Burgundian Jacques de Lalaing, in his *Pas de la fontaine de pleurs* of 1449. The most celebrated such passage in the annals of Spanish chivalry was the *Passo Honroso* of Suero de Quiñones in 1434, which took place by the bridge at Orbigo, on the road to Compostela.[16] A knight inaugurating a formal *pas d'armes* would need to obtain royal permission. Then he would send out challenges to stimulate potential opponents. Smith's less formal project harks back to the more spontaneous arrangements described in the romances. It also prompts a chivalrous encounter: the earl of Lincoln's riding master turns up to investigate. As a result of their meeting, Smith is translated from his forest encampment to the awesome fifteenth-century splendors of Tattershall Castle.[17] "The countrey wondering at such an Hermite; His friends perswaded one *Seignior Theadora Polaloga*, Rider to *Henry* Earle of *Lincolne*, an excellent Horse-man, and a noble *Italian* Gentleman, to insinuate into his wooddish acquaintances; whose Languages and good discourse, and exercise of riding, drew him to stay with him at *Tattersall*." The drastic alteration of circumstances is itself the stuff of romance, a genre much preoccupied with the business of social climbing.

The second chivalric theme apparent in Smith's picture of himself recalls the opening scene of Lull's *Book of the Ordre of Chyualry*. There the author describes the aged knight, retired to his hermitage in the forest. As Sir Gilbert Haye translates it, he "chesit to mak his habitacion in a thik wod of a wilderness, in a faire haulche, inclosit within wateris . . . sa that he was content to flee the sycht and the repaire of the warld . . ."[18] At the moment when the squire who will become his disciple first catches sight of him, Lull's hermit knight is sitting under a tree, reading a book.

By the mid-fifteenth century this forest encounter of the would-be knight

---

15 Malory, *Works*, ed. Vinaver, I.31.
16 Richard Barber and Juliet Barker, *Tournaments: Jousts, Chivalry, and Pageants in the Middle Ages* (Woodbridge, 1989), pp. 101–03; 107–25 on the *pas d'armes* in general, including some discussion of Jacques de Lalaing.
17 The keep at Tattershall is still pointed out to tourists as one of the finest examples of fifteenth-century brickwork in Britain.
18 Sir Gilbert Haye, trans., *The Buke of Knychthede*, in *Gilbert of the Haye's Prose Manuscript*, vol. 2, Scottish Text Society (Edinburgh, 1914), p. 5.

and his mentor was deeply ingrained in the European chivalric imagination. The Catalan knight and author Joanot Martorell had used it to introduce his hero Tirant lo Blanch to knighthood. The single illustration of Edward IV's manuscript copy of the French text of Lull's manual depicts this scene. The figure of the hermit knight had been long associated with English chivalric spectacles. Caxton's patron and fellow translator Earl Rivers jousted in the guise of a hermit in a tournament of 1477. Elizabeth's champion, Sir Henry Lee, had favored the same device throughout his long career as a jouster, which ran from around 1570 to 1597. He used it perhaps most memorably to announce his retirement from the lists at the Accession Day tournament of 1590. "His helmet now must make a hive for bees / And lovers' sonnets turned to holy psalms / A man-at-arms must now serve on his knees . . . " as the song sung on this occasion ran. "Goddess, allow this aged man his right / To be your bedesman now that was your knight." Lee elaborated the part still further in 1592, when he entertained Queen Elizabeth at Ditchley.[19] Lee's "efforts to create an entire romance mythology, not only for court tournaments but for other court entertainments, too" had been publicized in printed sources like *The Queenes Maiesties Entertainement at Woodstocke* of 1585.[20] Smith might have read of Lee. He might also have heard these events described by participants. The extant heralds' Partition Books, which record customary fees paid by jousters to the officers of arms, note that the Lord Willoughby "gave 6 silk scarves in his colours of watchet and murrey" on his first appearance at a tournament, the Accession Day joust of 17 November 1583. Lee had been present on that occasion.[21]

Smith's language, situation, and attitude come out in his vocabulary: "he retired himselfe"; "the country wondering at such an Hermite." Such pointed allusions might have been enough to suggest Sir Henry Lee's hermit knight to the *cognoscenti* of his own day. Young Smith has updated his reading material, trading the *Book of the Ordre of Chyualry* for Machiavelli and Guevara. His pose seems at once a return to the chivalry of the thirteenth century and an allusion to Elizabethan courtly practice. He manages to be traditional and contemporary at the same time. Part of the fun here is that the "hermit knight" is only twenty years old. Adopting the role of a hoary old mentor is an act of audacity that both demands and receives attention. Elizabethan precedent exists for this irreverent exploit as well. Robert Cecil, when he appeared before Elizabeth in the character of "the hermit of Tybole," was about twenty-eight. He was also campaigning for royal notice and employment, in his case as his father's

---

[19] See Young, *Tudor and Jacobean Tournaments*, pp. 163–64.

[20] Ibid., p. 152. The hermit character also attracted Sir Robert Cecil, who had dressed as a hermit to receive Queen Elizabeth on a visit to Theobalds, the estate of his father, Lord Burghley, in 1591; Cecil and Elizabeth seem to have kept up a running joke about this. See Young, *Tudor and Jacobean Tournaments*, pp. 174–75.

[21] Ibid., pp. 52, 160.

successor. Smith spoke to his neighbors in the language of courtly Elizabethan chivalry, and elicited the desired response when Theadore Polaloga rode out to investigate him. In this case, the professional equestrian found the aspirant to knighthood enacting the authoritative role of the hermit knight.

It is also worth noting Smith's references to exercises of horsemanship and dexterity in the handling of the lance: "his exercise a good horse, with his lance and Ring."[22] "Running at the ring" (the French *course de bague*) was a form of practice widely adopted among European knights of the later Middle Ages and Renaissance. The rider aimed his lance through the center of a ring suspended from above. It required considerable steadiness of aim and control of the horse to carry off the ring on the lance. This test of knightly ability became a form of display in its own right, one that was to be long continued, in the southern United States as late as the end of the nineteenth century.[23]

Smith's biographers have suggested that Seignior Polaloga may have encouraged Smith to turn his sights to combat in eastern Europe against the Turks. The earl of Lincoln's Rider, an Italian of Greek descent, as his name suggests, might be expected to speak with vehemence of the rise of the Ottoman Empire and the loss of Constantinople. A favorite chivalric theme, old as the crusades, reproves Christian knights for fighting among themselves rather than standing together against the infidel. Henry the Navigator argued this point in his day. As John Smith indicates, the ideal came back to haunt the sixteenth and seventeenth centuries, in the throes of the wars of religion. "Thus when *France* and *Netherlands* had taught him to ride a Horse and use his Armes . . . he was desirous to see more of the world, and trie his fortune against the *Turkes*: both lamenting and repenting to have seene so many *Christians* slaughter one another."[24] In a sixteenth-century prose version of *Guy of Warwick*, the hero expresses similar ideas. "He was for seeking out new scenes of action, but would no more employ his arms against Christians; and therefore earnestly entreated them to furnish him with forces to go against the faithless Saracens who had broke in upon the Grecian empire, and besieged Bizantium."[25] The time-tested

---

22 Smith, *Works*, ed. Arber, p. 823.
23 Young, *Tudor and Jacobean Tournaments*, pp. 28, 38, 40, 83, 115. In England Edward VI, James I and his brother-in-law Christian of Denmark, Charles I and his brother Prince Henry all ran at the ring at one time or another. The latest instance mentioned by Alan Young took place at Whitehall in 1613, where James I, Charles, and the Count Palatine all ran at the ring to celebrate the count's wedding to James' daughter Elizabeth. The riders employed at "Medieval Times" (a re-enactment in an arena of late medieval jousting) in Dallas and elsewhere still perform this exercise for the entertainment of paying customers. The ring on the carousel is another vestige of this practice. For "running at ring" in the United States, see James Britton Cranfill, *Dr. J. B. Cranfill's Chronicle* (New York, 1916), which describes "tournaments" held, along with barbecues, in Texas during the 1870s.
24 Smith, *Works*, ed. Arber, p. 823.
25 William J. Thoms and Henry Morley, eds., *Early English Prose Romances* (London, 1907), p. 360.

pattern of progression from regional warfare to enlistment in an international crusade reappears here.

Smith's program for his own military career repeats the sequence of actions described in Chaucer's complementary portraits of his knight and his son the squire.[26] The same idea runs all through Smith's writings: "And truly there is no pleasure comparable to [that of] a generous spirit; as good imploiment in noble actions, especially amongst Turks, Heathens, and Infidels."[27] Or, in a more provocative moment, Smith asserts: "The Warres in *Europe, Asia,* and *Affrica* taught me how to subdue the wilde Salvages in *Virginia* and *New-England,* in *America.*"[28] As late as 1629, Smith continued to insist that combat against non-Christian opponents represented a higher level of chivalry than warfare within Christendom. In seeking out "Turks, Heathens, and Infidels," John Smith aspired to a higher calling.

The same mixture of medieval chivalry and Machiavelli that characterized Smith's portrait of himself as a young man recurs in Smith's experiences in Transylvania. He won promotion to captain by virtue of his skill in signalling and the concoction of newfangled incendiary devices. These Smith names "his fiery Dragons," and supplies a recipe.[29] He received his Majority at the siege of Regall as a reward for his prowess in a series of three single combats against Turkish adversaries. These events of c.1602 call to mind Froissart's description of the young Berber challenger of the siege of al-Mahdiya, discussed above (chapter four). The besieged Turks, bored by a lack of action, and "fearing lest they should depart ere they could assault their Citie, sent this Challenge to any Captaine in the Armie. That to delight the Ladies, who did long to see some court-like pastime, the Lord *Turbashaw* did defie any Captaine, that had the command of a Company, who durst combate with him for his head."[30] Chosen by lot to meet the Turkish champion, Smith encounters an adversary elaborately costumed after the fashion of the Renaissance tournament:

> Truce being made for that time, the Rampiers all beset with faire Dames, and men in Armes, the *Christians* in *Battalio; Turbashaw* with a noise of

---

[26] Geoffrey Chaucer, "General Prologue," *The Canterbury Tales,* in *The Riverside Chaucer,* pp. 24–25, lines 42–100. In some readings the knight, with his missions against infidel opponents in Prussia, Lithuania, Russia, Granada, Algeciras, Morocco and Turkey, stands as a reproach to his son, who has only fought in Flanders and northern France. Other analyses suggest that the Squire can be expected to mature into the image of his father. Still others, like Terry Jones in his *Chaucer's Knight* (Baton Rouge, 1980), reject the Knight himself as a sleazy fourteenth-century mercenary. Nevertheless, it seems evident that the model of chivalric development Chaucer describes in these two portraits was regarded as exemplary when the *Canterbury Tales* were written, and admired by readers in Smith's day and beyond.

[27] Smith, *Works,* ed. Arber, p. 962.

[28] Ibid., p. 925.

[29] Ibid., p. 832.

[30] Ibid., p. 838.

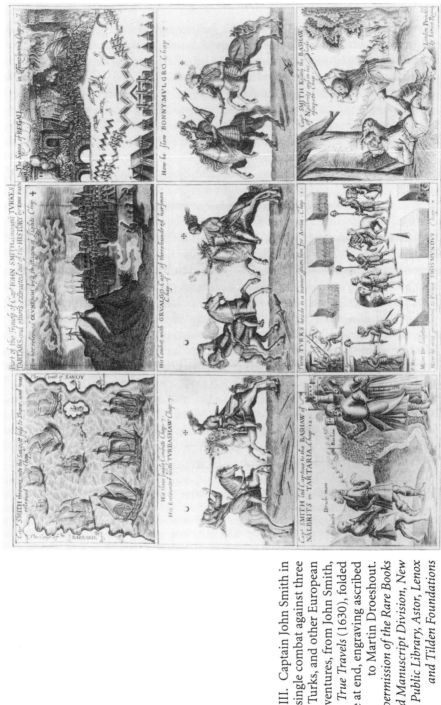

III. Captain John Smith in single combat against three Turks, and other European adventures, from John Smith, *True Travels* (1630), folded plate at end, engraving ascribed to Martin Droeshout. *By permission of the Rare Books and Manuscript Division, New York Public Library, Astor, Lenox and Tilden Foundations*

Howboyes entred the fields well mounted and armed; on his shoulders were fixed a paire of great wings, compacted of Eagles feathers within a ridge of silver, richly garnished with gold and precious stones; a Ianizary before him, bearing his Lance, on each side, another leading his horse.[31]

The English captain can offer no such visual display. He compensates through his superior dexterity with the lance: "Smith with a noise of Trumpets, only a Page bearing his Lance, passing by him with a courteous salute, tooke his ground with such good successe, that . . . he passed the Turke throw the sight of his Beaver, face, head, and all, that he fell dead to the ground."[32] On the next day, Smith is challenged by the defeated Turk's "vowed friend." One could hardly expect so traditional a challenger to manage without a sworn brother, an assistant indispensable to the heroes of many romances.[33] A single course with lances was followed by an exchange of pistol shots, in a way anticipating later developments in the history of the duel. Again, Smith vanquished his opponent. On the third occasion, Smith issued the challenge in his turn, "that the Ladies might know 'he was not so much enamoured of their servants heads, but if any *Turke* of their ranke would come to the place of combate to redeeme them, [he] should have his also upon the like conditions, if he could winne it.' "[34] This mounted duel involved pistols and battleaxes, the choice of the Turkish defendant.

The prose *Guy of Warwick* provides a close analogue to this series of duels between Turk and Christian. The English hero Sir Guy rides into battle to free Byzantium from its Turkish conquerors, and is met by a series of energetic foemen. One falls, only to be replaced by his more ferocious friend:

> This fatal sight being seen by Eskeldort, a bloody and tyrannic Turkish Prince, he straightway vowed revenge, and rides up armed to the place where Guy then stood; "Villain," quoth he, "whom like a dog I hate, I will make thee curse the time that thou wast born: know, therefore, I am come to fetch thy head; for to my mistress I have promised it."[35]

---

[31] Ibid.

[32] Ibid.

[33] For examples of sworn brotherhood between knights in romances, see especially the "romances of friendship," *Amis and Amiloun, Claris and Laris, Oliuer of Castylle,* ed. Gail Orgelfinger (*The Hystorye of Olyuer of Castylle,* trans. Henry Watson (New York and London, 1988)), p. 21: "Than whan they began for to haue knowlege / they loued togyder with so perfyte loue / that [t]hey made alyaunce togyder of fraternall company / in promysynge neuer for to fayle vnto the dethe departed them . . ." Chaucer's Palamon and Arcite are sworn brothers. Such brotherhoods always have dire results in Chaucer. Vows of chivalric brotherhood could also occur in real life. After the joust of Lord Scales and the Bastard of Burgundy at Smithfield in 1467, the two combatants promised to be brothers in arms. In remembrance of this oath the Bastard refused to joust against Lord Scales at his passage of armes in Bruges the following year.

[34] Smith, *Works*, ed. Arber, p. 839.

[35] Cf. Goodman, "The Captain's Self-Portrait," p. 32.

This is not a direct parallel. Guy and his enemies meet in battle, not during a truce, and so the whole scene is less elaborate in its chivalric apparatus. Nevertheless, the combat for the defeated party's head and the motivation of the mistress's regard remain constant.

Smith's victory was rewarded with a triumphal procession to the general's pavilion, with the three Turks' heads paraded on lancepoints. His general presented Smith with a horse, belt, and scimitar, while his commander-in-chief, Meldritch, promoted Smith to sergeant major. Sigismund Bathory, the duke of Transylvania, later granted Smith a coat of arms with three Turks' heads as its principal ornaments, in honor of these exploits.[36] This device recalls the grant to Cortes of seven heads of native kings linked by a chain as a heraldic emblem.[37]

In its basic form, what Smith approximates here is the classic, three-day tournament. Examples in romances known in England are to be found in *Ipomadon* and *Oliver of Castille*, as well as *The Squire of Low Degree*. In all three of these cases, the prize is marriage with a princess. Several three-day tournaments were held in England in the reigns of Henry VII and his son Henry VIII. The last such event Alan Young lists was enacted in 1565. Most appropriately, it took place on the occasion of a wedding.[38] The presence of ladies as spectators colors the Turk's initial challenge and Smith's response.

Smith's series of jousts continues the long medieval tradition of the "jousts of war" between representatives of contending armies. Champions of England and Scotland fought against one another in such events during the fourteenth century.[39] Jousts at sieges, to relieve boredom, appear early in the Middle Ages. An early example recorded by Barber and Barker took place at Valencia in 1238 between Moors and Aragonese knights, with the Moors issuing the challenge. Chaucer's knight counted three formal jousts against Saracen opponents at Tlemcen, near Morocco; he had "foughten for oure feith at Tramyssene / In lystes thries, and ay slayn his foo."[40] In an even more direct parallel, the Squire of Low Degree is told to win advancement to the rank of knight by performing three such duels:

> And yf ye passe the batayles thre,
> Then ar ye worthy a knyght to be,

---

36 Smith, *Works*, ed. Arber, pp. 840–41.
37 Hernan Cortes, *Letters from Mexico*, ed. and trans. Anthony Pagden (New Haven, 1986), p. 492.
38 Young, *Tudor and Jacobean Tournaments*, p. 202. René of Anjou's treatise on the proper conduct of tournaments suggests that such events ran from Tuesday to Thursday, to avoid the fast day on Friday.
39 Barber and Barker, *Tournaments*, pp. 34, 36; see also pp. 125–32 for instances of similar combats *à outrance* on other occasions.
40 Chaucer, "General Prologue," lines 62–63. For the event of 1238, see Barber and Barker, *Tournaments*, pp. 166–68.

And to bere armes then ar ye able,
Of gold and goules sete with sable.[41]

This pattern of three single combats followed by the award of a coat of arms seems to be well on its way to becoming standardized in the English chivalric tradition.

Smith's encounters with the three Turks conform to long-established chivalric practices. The mode of advancement through knightly prowess to the status of a gentleman entitled to bear a coat of arms is also unmistakable here. John Smith is playing by a timeworn set of rules. If he is not knighted, he comes close: he is given a sword by his commanding officer, and a coat of arms by the sovereign he serves. These were internationally recognized symbols of social advancement. Gaining a coat of arms could still do much to enhance a man's status in society; it was one of William Shakespeare's preoccupations around the same time. (The rewards of knightly prowess – personal glory, elevated rank in society, and the acquisition of wealth – all attract Smith to varying degrees. It would be difficult to say which appeals to him most.) At this point in his story, Captain Smith reproduces Sigismund Bathory's Latin letter of 1603, granting the coat of arms, and William Segar's authentication of it in 1625. With this feat and its documentation, John Smith achieves one of the principal goals of knightly enterprise.

Without in any way questioning the factual basis of Smith's autobiography, a reader can observe how often the captain falls into scenes from romance, even when the event contains clear elements of the picaresque. He is robbed of his belongings by a party of confidence men *en route* to France, and fetches up "in a Forest, neere dead with griefe and cold . . . by a faire Fountaine under a tree."[42] Smith, when in trouble, seeks refuge in the landscape of chivalric fiction. More remarkably, perhaps, the landscape of romance never fails to supply some form of relief. The succor can be prosaic, as when a kind farmer offers him room and board. It can also be chivalric in the extreme: in the next forest Smith encounters one of the cheats and obtains satisfaction in a duel.[43] On his passage to Rome, a gang of pilgrims pitch him overboard in a storm, taking him for an English Hugenot Jonah. "Yet God brought him to that little Isle where was no inhabitants, but a few kine and goats."[44] In a page or two Smith moves from the forest fountain setting appropriate to any one of Malory's desolate knights, to a Mediterranean desert island of the sort where Pierre de Provence was marooned – and that would later prove so handy for Dumas' Count of Monte Cristo.

---

[41] *The Squire of Low Degree*, in Walter H. French and Charles B. Hale, *Middle English Metrical Romances* (New York, 1930), p. 782, lines 201–04. See Goodman, "The Captain's Self-Portrait," p. 33.
[42] Smith, *Works*, ed. Arber, p. 825.
[43] Ibid.
[44] Ibid., p. 826.

Smith's notable lament on the desolation of Transylvania is, in some respects, another scene with affinities to the landscape of romance:

> which being one of the fruitfullest and strongest Countries in these parts, was now rather a desart, or the very spectacle of desolation; their fruits and fields overgrowne with weeds, their Churches and battered Palaces and best build-ings, as for feare, hid with Mosse and Ivy: being the very Bulwarke and Rampire of a great part of Europe, most fit by all Christians to have been supplyed and maintained, was thus brought to ruine by them it most con-cerned to support it. [45]

The desolate countryside Smith depicts should remind the twentieth-century reader that the Waste Land comes into twentieth-century literature straight out of chivalric romance. In Malory the land of the Grail King is laid waste by Balin's Dolorous Stroke.[46] This description of the Transylvanian scene rings regretta-bly true once again in the 1990s. It leads Smith to expand upon one of his favorite themes, the woes of the soldier:

> But alas, what is it, when the power of Majestie pampered in all delights of pleasant vanity, neither knowing nor considering the labour of the Plough-man, the hazard of the Merchant, the oppression of Statesmen; nor feeling the piercing torments of broken limbes, and inveterated wounds, the toil-some marches, the bad lodging, the hungry diet, and the extreme misery that Souldiers endure to secure all those estates . . .[47]

The image of the soldier supporting the other estates – king, ploughman, merchant, statesman – echoes Lull's description of the office of the knight as the bulwark of the social order. Once again, Smith's conservative vision brings him into alignment with the *Book of the Ordre of Chyualry*. For Smith, the soldier, not the self-absorbed courtier, inherits the office of the medieval knight. He is by this time no admirer of "The politique Courtier, that commonly aimes more at his owne honors and ends than his Countries good, or his Princes glory, honour, or security . . ."[48] It is tempting here to think of Sir Philip Sidney, Essex, and Ralegh, all elegant presences at Elizabeth's court. The stage is set for a grand debate between the soldier Smith and his courtly contemporaries, as to which of them best embodies the ideals of knighthood. It should also be remembered, though, that these courtiers often preferred to consider themselves soldiers.[49]

---

[45] Ibid., pp. 845–46.

[46] Cf. Malory, *Works*, ed. Vinaver, I.53–54, where Balin's Dolorous Stroke causes the deso-lation of King Pelles' country, though Malory's text stresses the fallen castle and the bodies in the ruins. This is also T. S. Eliot's *Waste Land*.

[47] Smith, *Works*, ed. Arber, p. 846.

[48] Ibid.

[49] E.g., Sir Philip Sidney, "Honest king Arthure may never displease a souldier." At his trial, Sir Walter Ralegh described his upbringing as "wholly gentleman, wholly soldier." He was especially vehement in denying that he had been a law student.

Of all the patterns from chivalric fiction that recur throughout Smith's autobiographical writings, the most persistent may be the story of captivity and rescue by a Saracen princess. In Smith's personal chivalric mythology, just as the wars of Europe and Asia "taught me how to subdue the wilde Salvages of America," so his capture and enslavement in Turkey prefigured his far more famous captivity in Virginia.

John Smith's two accounts of imprisonment, in Asia and America, cry out to be read together. Neither should be dismissed as purely formulaic. At the same time, both draw on a long tradition of stories about imprisoned knights. Each account surrounds its tale of adventure with a protective layer of ethnographic "observations." This alternation of anthropological description and martial action makes Smith read like a new and improved *Book of Marco Polo*. It suggests what Rustichello da Pisa could have done if Marco Polo had been a knight rather than a merchant.

Smith begins the tale of his first episode of captivity with the battle of Rottenton (the pass of Rothenthurm) in Transylvania, which took place on 18 November 1602. He ends his account of that defeat with a list of the English combatants, nine of whom were killed on the field of battle. The others survived to affix complimentary verses to Smith's *Description of New England* of 1616.[50] Smith reports his own capture. Left wounded on the battlefield, he is found by pillagers and marched off to be sold as a slave. "At Axopolis they were all sold for slaves, like beasts in a market place; where everie Merchant, viewing their limbs and wounds, caused other slaves to struggle with them to trie their strength."[51] The Turk who purchases Smith sends him to a young lady in Constantinople, with a letter describing him as "a Bohemian Lord conquered by his hand."[52] Unluckily for her admirer, the lady speaks Italian, so Smith is able to object to this inaccurate label. The Turkish lady, one Charatza Tragabigzanda, lives up to the established role of the Saracen princess of chivalric fiction. She is of noble birth, kindhearted, and apparently susceptible to the charms of the captive captain. She even attempts to extricate him from his difficulties: "but having no use for him, lest her mother should sell him, she sent him to her brother, the *Tymor Bashaw* of *Nalbrits*, in the Countrey of *Cambia*, a province in *Tartaria*."[53]

Like Floripas and Melior before her, the lady seems to have amorous designs on the English prisoner. "To her unkinde brother, this kinde Ladie writ so much for his good usage, that hee halfe suspected, as much as she intended; for shee told him, he should there but sojourne to learne the language, and what it was

---

50 Smith, *Works*, ed. Arber, pp. 230–31.
51 Ibid., p. 853. The comparison of the life of a slave to that of a domesticated animal recurs later, after Smith is sent to Nalbrits: "Among these slavish fortunes there was no great choice; for the best was so bad, a dog could hardly have lived to endure: and yet for all their paines and labours [they were] no more regarded than a beast." (Ibid., p. 855.)
52 Ibid., p. 853.
53 Ibid., p. 854.

to be a *Turke*, till time made her Master of her selfe."[54] The picture of the young Turkish lady scheming to rescue the Christian prisoner so she can marry him herself has a long history in romance. The unsympathetic family members who surround her seem equally familiar. The unworthy suitor who turns out to be that staple of the Renaissance stage, the braggart soldier, the powerful mother who must be outwitted, the cruel brother, all have their fictional precursors.

Smith's narrative offers some insight into the psychological roots of the Saracen princess's story. After describing Tartar society in some detail, he writes: "All the hope he had ever to be delivered from this thralldom was only the love of *Tragabigzanda*, who surely was ignorant of his bad usage."[55] The enslaved prisoner of war clutches at his one remaining straw, the fantasy of escape through the love of a young, beautiful, and powerful woman. As Smith tells the story, he also represents an avenue of escape for Tragabigzanda, who cannot help but prefer him to the braggart Bogall. Her dream is that one day she can choose her own mate, that time will make her "Master of herself." Not surprisingly perhaps, she associates the power of self-determination with the masculine term "Master," not the feminine "Mistress." This is not a mutual fantasy, perhaps, but two reciprocal fantasies of escape through romantic love. These dreams offer hope to both of these powerless individuals. In this case, the Turkish lady's romance is thwarted. The hope proves delusive for both parties. Smith must resort to violence in order to escape. The stock duel with the Saracen princess's brother – Olivier against Fierabras – comes to mind here. This, however, is the world of the slave, not of the Peers of France. Smith, in irons, has to attack his captor with a threshing bat. The Turkish lady, even more securely guarded, never escapes at all, as far as Smith and his readers are concerned. She does receive a dubious consolation prize, in lieu of a romantic conclusion to the story: Smith attempted to name Cape Ann after his benefactress.[56] "Cape Tragabigzanda" appears on Smith's map of New England, but the name was vetoed by Prince Charles, perhaps as an act of mercy to future inhabitants. Smith's narrative transmutes the old story of the Saracen princess into a report of sixteenth-century experience. This rapprochement of art and experience may suggest some reasons behind the tale's persistent appeal to Western audiences.

As in chivalric romance, captivity entails a loss of identity. The Captain becomes a slave:

> for within an houre after his arivall, he caused his *Drub-man* to strip him naked, and shave his head and beard so bare as his hand: a great ring of iron, with a long stalke bowed like a sickle, [was] riveted about his necke, and a

---

54 Ibid., p. 855.
55 Ibid., p. 866.
56 Ibid., p. 232.

coat [put on him] made of Vlgries haire, guarded about with a piece of an undrest skinne.[57]

The change in appearance reflects his degradation to the level of a "beast." Like those knights who lose their identities through insanity or imprisonment, Smith is transformed here into something like a wild man or a fool. Chrétien's *Yvain*, Bevis of Hampton, and the Good Knight without Fear in *Gyron le Courtoys* all are stripped of their knightly status in this way. Malory's *Morte Darthur* includes depictions of Lancelot and Tristram in such altered states. Tristram's condition seems especially evocative of Smith's:

And than was he naked, and waxed leane and poore of fleyshe. And so he felle in the felyshyppe of herdemen and shyperdis, and dayly they wolde gyff hym som of their mete and drynke, and whan he ded ony shrewde dede they wolde beate hym with roddis. And so they clypped hym with sheris and made hym lyke a foole.[58]

Like these heroes, and like their Biblical precursor, Samson, Smith eventually recovers his strength after his physical transformation. He effects his escape through his own prowess, killing his captor, taking his horse and clothes, and riding hell for leather for the Muscovite frontier.

The instinct of the modern reader may be to strip off all the chivalric trappings, so as to read Smith's *True Travels* as the sordid tale of a farmer's son who becomes a soldier of fortune. This would in fact raise the status of Smith's work on the current scale of literary values. At present, the picaresque is rated a great deal higher than the romance. In such a reading chivalric conventions can only be ignored. At best they may be seen as a mask, as they are in *Behind The Mask of Chivalry*, Nancy MacLean's study of 1994 of the Ku Klux Klan. There, chivalry becomes a self-serving disguise, screening the ugliest of realities. As in Johan Huizinga's *Waning of the Middle Ages*, later forms of chivalry have become suspect. They are all too often dismissed as decadent charades, mounted in an effort to disguise the horrid truth.

For this reader at least, the analogy fails when the mask refuses to come off. We are dealing here not with a mask, but with the bones of the narrative. Patterns drawn from the medieval chivalric tradition give the story of Smith's

---

[57] Ibid., p. 855.
[58] Malory, *Works*, ed. Vinaver, I.305. For Lancelot's predicament, see I, pp. 495–99. Such practices cast a long shadow in traditional societies like our own. A spokesman for the administration of the military academy (the Citadel) in South Carolina explained in August of 1994 that students entering the academy have their heads shaven "to take every vestige of individuality away from the members of the corps." See Russell Baker, "It's a Clipping Penalty," *New York Times* vol. CXLIII, no. 49, 780 (6 August 1994), p. 11. Baker remarks that Alexander the Great insisted that his soldiers' hair be trimmed so they could not be seized by the hair in battle – as Captain John Smith was to seize the queues of the native kings he captured in Virginia.

life its shape. When you remove them, the tale collapses. In failing to recognize the structural importance of the romance elements within Smith's autobiography, we also refuse to see how important stories remain as shapers of our own lives. The influence of film, television, and fiction on human behavior continues to run deeper than most of us care to acknowledge.

Chivalry in the *True Travels* proves to be more than a mask, more than the skeleton beneath the Jacobean skin. It also acts as a lens through which Captain John Smith views the world, and through which he prefers his work to be read. This is not to say that every reader, then or now, would agree that Smith appears in a flattering light when viewed in this way. Nevertheless, his chivalry cannot be dismissed as child's play, a fantasy that the pragmatic captain would later outgrow. His chivalric vision of the world accompanies Captain Smith on his voyages to America. Later still, it permeates his advice to the "unexperienced planters" who preferred his writings to his company on the voyage to New England.

This analysis of the *True Travels* as chivalric autobiography should not be allowed to mask the fact that Smith's work is also an account of exploration. As he recounts his own experiences in Europe, Asia, and Africa, Smith details a concrete itinerary. He names towns and prominent citizens, digresses on key features of the terrain or remarkable sights, and brings in others' observations as needed to swell his report. The tale of Smith's captivity is interrupted by a long description of the Crim-Tartars, with special attention to their diet, religion, and military preparedness. "Their best drinke is Coffa"; the Christian slaves got leftover "cuskus" (couscous) "after they have raked it thorow so oft as they please with their foule fists."[59] The final section of the volume of 1629 focuses on Africa. It comprises Smith's own tour of Morocco, with the surprising adventures of an English watchmaker, Master Henry Archer, who might be described as a humble descendant of Chrétien's Knight with the Lion, or of Androcles. There is a chapter of "strange discoveries and adventures of the Portugalls in Africa." Like Ralegh, Smith ekes out his own travels with those of his Hispanic rivals. The book ends with "a brave Sea fight betwixt two Spanish men of warre, and Captaine Merham with Smith" south of the Canary Islands in the vicinity of Cape Bojador. The mixture of genres is again notable; Smith is only carrying Rustichello of Pisa or Gadifer or Cortes to their logical extreme.

The same blend of personal experience, eyewitness description, and the reports of others typifies the *Generall Historie of Virginia*. Book one compiles early reports of the New World, Virginia specifically, from Arthur to Captain George Waymouth in 1605. The verse tags at chapters' ends – this may well be 'rym dogerel' – seem to be another of Smith's rash enterprises. Book two offers Smith's description of Virginia, based on observations that date to the sixth voyage (1606–9). Book three narrates the experiences of the English settlers during the same period. The fourth book supplies a rather less detailed history

[59] Smith, *Works*, ed. Arber, p. 856.

of Virginia from 1609–24, when the Virginia Company was dissolved. The *Generall Historie* offers Smith's self-justification and an apology for the whole enterprise. The interesting feature remains the continuing importance of chivalry to this program of self-defence.

The ceremonial reappearance of King Arthur, propped up at the head of the *Generall Historie of Virginia*, is only the first signal that exploration is still to be defended as a chivalric activity. The first chapter lists the royal patrons and "worthy Knights" involved in early English expeditions to America, not forgetting to specify the rewards such adventures received, when and if the explorer returned. Sebastian Cabot is singled out as the greatest discoverer of his generation, "for which King *Henry* the eight Knighted him and made him grand Pilate of *England.*" Being very aged King *Edward* the sixt gave him a Pention of 166*l.* 13*s.* 4*d.* yearely." Similarly, Martin Frobisher "was knighted, honored, and well rewarded" by Elizabeth I for his voyage of exploration. Sir Hugh Willoughby here represents the perils of the enterprise: after sailing for Russia "the next yeare he was found frozen to death in his Ship, and all his Company."[60] Sir Walter Ralegh, "a noble Gentleman, and then in great esteeme," is also invoked here as the inspirer of the first Virginian voyage. This initial overview of the field establishes exploration as a form of prowess suitable for knights, often qualifying the explorer for elevation to knighthood.

There are some hints that Smith looked to Ralegh, "that noble and industrious knight," as one possible model for his American career. Before his voyage to Virginia, he seems to have made a tour of Ireland and considered joining an expedition to South America, sites associated with Ralegh's enterprises. "The Virginian voyage" shared the connection with Ralegh. The entrepreneur's name shed some chivalric lustre on the strenuous business of founding a settlement. At the same time, Smith emphasizes clear differences between Ralegh's preoccupations and his own. "I promise no Mines of gold," he writes, dilating upon the safer profits to be found in fishing.[61] He is thinking of the *Discoverie of Guiana* and its bitter aftermath.

In Book three John Smith appears first on the Virginian scene, "who all this time from their departure from the Canaries was restrained as a prisoner vpon the scandalous suggestions of some of the chiefe (envying his repute) who fained he intended to vsurpe the government, murther the Councell, and make himselfe King."[62] In his account of "the first planting of the Isle of Mevis," Smith remarks on this episode: "Such factions here we had, as commonly attend such voyages, that a paire of gallowes were made; but Captaine Smith, for whom they were intended, could not be perswaded to use them . . ."[63] This power struggle within the governing council of the colony accords with the old theme

---

[60] Ibid., p. 304.
[61] Ibid., p. 784.
[62] Ibid., p. 388.
[63] Ibid., p. 910.

of the hero's betrayal by his own people. Smith begins his sojourn in Virginia like a Roland, Renaut de Montauban, Ogier or Huon of Bordeaux, at odds with powerful enemies who intend his death or the ruin of his reputation. Once again, the protagonist faces internal and external challenges, in a heroic predicament easily as old as the Homeric epics. Both accounts underline the deadly possibilities, Smith's with an acrid humor as he glances back at the apparatus of execution. He also stresses the reversal that placed his would-be executioners in his power: "but not any one of the inventers but their lives by justice fell into his power to determine of at his pleasure; whom with much mercy he favoured, that most basely and unjustly would have betrayed him."[64] Mercy is one of the great chivalric virtues: "to gyff mercy unto him that askith mercy" was one of the principal tenets of the Round Table oath in Malory. As Captain Smith retells the story, it becomes more dramatic and more chivalric. The subject of murderous contention among the English recurs throughout book three of the *Generall Historie of Virginia*. Attacked for his severity in his dealings with both his companions and the natives, Smith responds by pointing to his own display of mercy.

Another theme not to be overlooked appears here. This is the notion of the European explorer as "the Man who Would be King." This image may be deployed most effectively as an accusation designed to discredit the adventurer in the eyes of his own ruler. The temptation must exist in the mind of the accuser, if not of the accused. As I noted in the two preceding chapters, some of the later Spanish conquistadores were tempted to proclaim themselves sovereigns in their own right. The same thought keeps crossing the minds of their English competitors. In romance the hero wins a kingdom, often an empire, for himself with monotonous regularity.[65] This chivalric fantasy was reinforced by the Renaissance schoolboy's classical curriculum, with its focus on Roman history, and on figures like Caesar and Alexander. In real life the explorer has to resist the urge to declare himself an emperor. John Smith proclaims his loyalty to the crown at the head of the volume, and on the frontispiece. "Nothing but the touch of the King's sacred hand can erect a Monarchy."[66]

The tale of John Smith's capture by Powhatan's men and his rescue by Pocahontas may be the most often discussed section of the *Generall Historie of Virginia*. John Smith's experience as a prisoner of Powhatan looks forward to captivity narratives yet to be penned by the European settlers of the Americas. Without the scope of Cabeza de Vaca's tale of endurance, Smith's story becomes a compressed series of dramatic crises. The captive Englishman engages the

[64] Ibid.
[65] To cite only a few fictional examples here, Martorell's Tirant lo Blanch and Amadís' son Esplandián both win the Eastern Roman empire, though Tirant does not live to marry his princess and rule it. In real life Henry of Trastamara made Bertrand du Guesclin king of Granada in 1369 as a reward for his support, but the French knight never proceeded to conquer his kingdom.
[66] Smith, "Preface of foure Poynts," *Works*, ed. Arber, p. 278.

chivalric imagination of the seventeenth-century reader first as a warrior so indomitable in single combat that he holds off three hundred enemy archers. Only the cold of night induces him to throw down his arms. He then fascinates his captors with his compass and a disquisition on modern European science:

> Much they marvailed at the playing of the Fly and Needle, which they could se so plainely, and yet not touch it, because of the glasse that covered them. But when he demonstrated by that Globe-like Iewell, the roundnesse of the earth, and skies, the spheare of the Sunne, Moone, and Starres, and how the Sunne did chase the night round about the world continually; the greatnesse of the Land and Sea, the diversitie of Nations, varietie of complexions, and how we were to them *Antipodes,* and many other such like matters, they all stood as amazed with admiration.[67]

Like Smith's written message to his compatriots, this instance of English technology is a "marvel" to the "Salvages." Their competing system for interrogating the universe is displayed in its turn before Smith, who regards the ceremony of divination not as a miracle, but as a diabolical rite.[68] The persistent equation of the natives with demons throughout this episode heightens the atmosphere of terror and revulsion. Even when he is offered a feast, Smith is convinced that he is being fattened in order to be eaten himself. The thought may have been prompted by accounts of Latin American religious practices as well as by European folklore.

Smith's reception before Powhatan becomes the latest in a series of such formal scenes of presentation, or confrontation, in which the European traveler faces an alien court. Marco Polo before the Great Khan, or Cortes before Montezuma come to mind. They might well have come to Smith's mind as they would to the minds of his readers. The complement to this scene occurs when Pocahontas and her father's counselor arrive in England and Smith tries to present them to the English court. The royal reception falls short, as far as Vitamacomak was concerned.[69] James I's lack of largesse and majesty find a strange parallel in the legends of Charlemagne. The Saracen princes who visit Charlemagne's court in Bagnyon and Boiardo both express a comparable dissatisfaction. The native of Virginia feels that James failed to display the generosity proper to a king. James has lost one of the primary royal attributes, a quality of character that had been valued as strongly in early English society as it was among the natives of Virginia. The British king fails as a treasure-giver. Bagnyon's Charlemagne was criticized for feasting with the rich while the poor starved on the fringes of his court. In each of these instances, as in Boiardo, the monarch's sense of social justice and true worth is questioned. The foreign

---

[67] Smith, *Works,* ed. Arber, p. 396.
[68] Ibid., pp. 398–99.
[69] "You gave Powhatan a white Dog, which Powhatan fed as himselfe; but your King gaue me nothing, and I am better than your white Dog." (Smith, *Works,* ed. Arber, p. 534.)

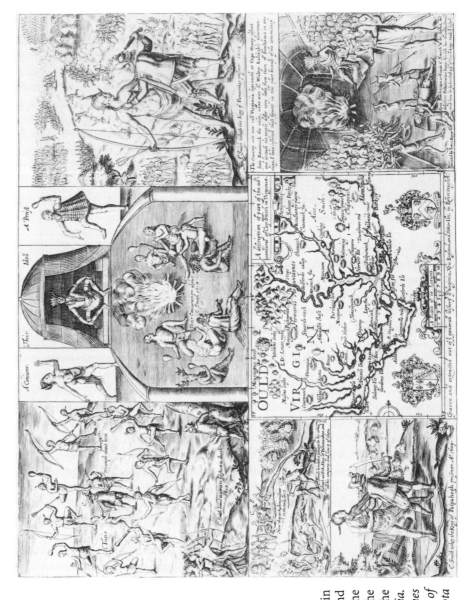

IV. Captain John Smith in Virginia, with his capture and rescue by Pocahontas in the lower righthand corner of the folded plate scenes from the *Generall Historie of Virginia*. By permission of the James Ford Bell Library, University of Minnesota

observer retains his vantage point as social critic. Smith almost certainly shares his views, if he did not invent them. Here, as in many other cases before and since, the stranger criticizes those in power as a spokesman for the native.

In the *Generall Historie of Virginia*'s version, it is possible to interpret the story of Powhatan's attempted execution of Smith and Pocahontas' intervention as part of a well-designed ceremony. The psychological struggle between the English and the natives in this section of the narrative intensifies, through a series of experiments in intimidation. The contest pits European astronomy against Indian divination, with exponents of each system staking their claim to be masters of the universe. Each side hopes to impose its authority upon the other by evoking amazement and terror.

In his "Relation to Queen Anne" of 1616, written to present Pocahontas at court, Smith himself lays the stress on the genuine nature of his peril, at least in his own mind: "at the minute of my execution, she hazarded the beating out of her owne braines to saue mine; and not onely that, but so preuailed with her father, that I was safely conducted to Iames towne."[70] For Smith, Pocahontas functions like a Saracen princess of romance or ballad, snatching the Christian prisoner from the toils of her ferocious father. Francis Jennings points out that from the native perspective Pocahontas is adopting Smith here, and that Smith should properly have accepted assimilation into the tribe.[71]

Pocahontas proceeds to save the English party from starvation. Like Doña Marina, she reveals plans of an attack against them, and in the end she is abducted, accepts baptism, and marries John Rolfe, a gentleman somewhat less respectful than Captain Smith, of her youth and of the social gulf that should separate a king's daughter from an English adventurer. In his letter of 1614 in which he defends his actions, Rolfe protests at length to Sir Thomas Dale that his decision to marry sprang from a burning desire to convert Pocahontas to Christianity, not from any physical attraction whatsoever. Indeed, Pocahontas is repellent to him: "one whose education hath been rude, her manners barbarous, her generation accursed, and so discrepant in all nurture from myself..." "sure if I would and were so sensually inclined, I might satisfy such desire ... with Christians more pleasing to the eye ..."[72] His public display of distress recalls Bevis of Hampton or Guy of Burgundy, shrinking from the caress of an unbaptized female.

The popular success of this dramatic episode, and of Pocahontas herself as a romantic figure for English and American audiences, must rest in part on her combination of familiarity and difference. She is the Saracen princess of romance in a new dress.

---

[70] Ibid., p. 531.
[71] Francis Jennings, *The Invasion of America* (1975; rpt. New York, 1976), p. 152.
[72] John Rolfe's letter, in Louis B. Wright, ed., *The Elizabethans' America* (Cambridge, Mass., 1966), pp. 235, 237.

John Smith's chivalric propensities surface elsewhere in the course of his Virginian experience. The most flamboyant example may be Smith's offer to fight Powhatan's brother Opechancanough in single combat, as a possible way out of a tight corner. Smith and his party, on one of their many foraging expeditions, are surrounded by "at least seven hundred Saluages" supplied with English weapons by their Dutch allies. Still hoping to obtain some provender before resorting to combat, Smith

> in plaine tearmes told the King this. "I see Opechancanough your plot to murder me, but I feare it not. As yet your men and mine haue done no harme, but by our direction. Take therefore your Armes, you see mine, my body shall be as naked as yours: the isle in your riuer is a fit place, if you be contented, and the conqueror (of vs two) shall be Lord and Master ouer al our men."[73]

The contest proposed here might have come straight out of Malory's "Book of Sir Tristram." Young Tristram's initial duel to the death against Sir Marhalt of Ireland for the tribute of Cornwall takes place on such an island, as does Balin's fatal encounter with his brother Balan.[74] In fact, the duel on the island is a chivalric staple. Other examples come readily to hand, notably Lancelot's fictional *pas d'armes* on the Joyus Ile and Jacques de Lalaing's actual *Pas de la fontaine de pleurs* of 1449–50, held on the island of St Laurent near Chalon-sur-Saône.[75] The first of these four passages of arms is a judicial duel over a question of national importance. The other three are sporting events modeled on this form of judicial duel. Bevis of Hampton's Saracen enemy, King Yvor, challenges him in much the same terms that Smith offers the Indian king. The strategic value of the island as a site in chivalric practice seems to be that it isolates the two combatants from outside interference. Smith's offer to fight Opechancanough using the same arms and armor also echoes European chivalric theory and tournament practice. The audacity of the speech, for a contemporaneous reader, might lie in Smith's daring to challenge a king. The disparity of rank between the two adversaries would be a matter of concern to a stickler for knightly protocol. Malory's Marhalt indeed objected that he would "nat fyght with no knyght but he be of blood royall, that is to seye owther kynges son othir quenys son, borne of prynces other of princesses."[76]

The breach of etiquette never occurs, as no duel takes place. Smith's opponent retorts with the even older, pre-chivalric ploy "a great present at the doore, they intreated him to receiue."[77] This "bait" was attended by two hundred archers ready to shoot. As an alternative, Smith takes Opechancanough hostage: he "snatched the King by his long locke in the middest of his men, with his

---

73 Smith, *Works*, ed. Arber, p. 458.
74 Malory, *Works*, ed. Vinaver, II.380, I.88–91.
75 Ibid., II.827–28; Keen, *Chivalry*, pp. 201–03.
76 Malory, *Works*, ed. Vinaver, I.379.
77 Smith, *Works*, ed. Arber, p. 458.

Pistoll readie bent against his brest."[78] This is a shocking affront in the eyes of the king's subjects, as well as the king himself: "little dreaming any durst in that manner haue vsed their King."[79]

Whether such a deed of prowess would have raised Smith's status in Virginia, or lowered it, is difficult to judge. It certainly impressed the illustrator of the *Generall Historie of Virginia*, who represents two such events, one of 1603 and another of 1609. In both images, the Indian king towers over Smith, who is pictured without his armor. The larger map of Virginia that accompanies the third book of the *Generall Historie of Virginia* is embellished with a large-scale picture of a native dressed in skins. Its caption reads, "The Sasquesahanougs are a Gyant-like people thus a-tyred." No such discrepancy in size differentiates Smith from the Turks he fights in the illustrations for his *True Travels*. A change of artist may have made all the difference. For those English draftsmen charged to depict Smith's deeds in visual terms, the combat with the infidel giant was a scene too precious to lose. The images selected for depiction underline precisely the aspects of Smith's actions that most closely resemble the adventures of a hero of romance. In Virginia he is twice represented capturing Indian kings. His own capture, experiences as a captive threatened by death, attendance during mysterious conjurations before an idol, and rescue by Pocahontas at Powhatan's court are all brandished before the least literate viewer. The *True Travels'* illustrator selects Smith's escape at sea after being cast overboard, with small figures of Smith swimming and kneeling in prayer on St Marie's isle, opposite Nice. His "stratagem of lights" and the siege of Regall appear at the top of the page. The three single combats with Turks are drawn with elaborate detail from the account in chapter seven. The final scene in this series shows the three Turks' heads on lances, carried in a procession to the general, while above, before the army drawn up in three divisions, Smith kneels to receive his banner bearing the Turks' heads from Prince Sigismund. The motto "Pro Christo et Patria" ("For Christ and Country") appears here, though whether either figure is meant to be uttering the words is difficult to determine. The two remaining spaces show a bald and barefoot Smith led captive before the Bashaw of Nalbrits, and the same shaven Smith attacking the Bashaw, now bearded more heavily, with a club. In the background, a much smaller figure of Smith rides away on the Bashaw's horse. Smith's coat of arms with the three Turks' heads and the now notorious motto "Vivere est Vincere" ("To Live is to Conquer") recurs in some form on each map of Virginia. (The second coat of arms, with the motto "Accordamus" ("Let us make peace") appears here and again on his epitaph.)[80]

What these pictures promote is the idea of Smith as a chivalric hero in the old style. His story becomes a tale of combat against infidels, in the Americas

[78] Ibid., p. 458.
[79] Ibid., p. 459.
[80] Ibid., p. 971.

against infidel giants. His reward is the traditional emblem of gentlemanly status, the coat of arms.

What is not represented proves equally important. None of Smith's contests against fellow Christians are illustrated, whether in Europe or Virginia. His struggles with the other leaders of the expedition, who imprison him and plot his death on a regular basis, are censored from the pictorial record. (Smith himself considered many of the English settlers "little better, if not worse" than the natives.[81]) Readers of the text learn that Smith is cast overboard by a party of Catholic pilgrims bound for Rome. The caption of the picture of this event reads merely "Capt. SMITH throwne into the SEA gott safe to shore, and was releeued," with all the verbs in passive form. The image of Smith on his knees on "St. Marie's Ile" and the threatening appearance of "the Coast of Barbarie" to the left of the picture might even mislead the viewer into identifying the North African pirates as the agents of Smith's misfortune.

Two inferences seem plausible on the basis of this evidence. The first is that the artists make Smith into even more of a traditional chivalric hero than he does himself. The second is that this conservative visual record of deeds of prowess among Saracens and gigantic Indians seems to have been the kind of thing that sold books.

In the end, as he compiles the annals of his adventures, Smith begins to resemble the hermit knight of the *Boke of the Ordre of Chyualry* even more than he did at twenty. His writings turn into a new kind of chivalric manual. One instance of this is the *Advertisements for the Vnexperienced Planters of New-England, or any where. Or The Path-way to experience to erect a Plantation* (London, 1631). This was Smith's last known publication. According to Arber, it was written in October 1631.[82] Smith died on 21 June 1631, at fifty-two.

Another pertinent item in his list of works is

> An Accidence or the Pathway to Experience Necessary for all Young Sea-men, of those that are desirous to goe to Sea, briefly shewing the Phrases, Offices, and Words of Command, Belonging to the Building, Ridging, and Sayling, a Man of Warre; And how to manage a Fight at Sea. Together with the Charge and Duty of every Officer, and their Shares: Also the Names, Weight, Charge, Shot, and Powder, of all sorts of great Ordnance. With the vse of the Petty Tally.[83]

According to Arber this is "the first printed book on seamanship, naval gunnery, and of nautical terms."[84] It is possible, indeed usual, to read these as Smith's forays into the lively world of the Elizabethan self-help book, a trend in

---

[81] Ibid., p. 929.
[82] Ibid., p. 918.
[83] Ibid., p. 785.
[84] Ibid., p. 786.

publishing that had been notable since the fifteenth century.[85] No one can leaf through either of Smith's pragmatic volumes without recognizing their ancestry. Smith's enumeration of the duties of the ship's officers in *An Accidence* chimes with Lull's discussions of the appointed "offices" of knights, princes, and other orders of society in the *Book of the Ordre of Chyualry* and elsewhere. The Captain's pragmatic account of gunnery, "tearmes of Warre," and "advertisements for yong Commanders, Captaines and Officers" all aim to impart the language, the arithmetic, and the principles of conduct necessary for the correct operation of a ship. As he transmits the language and science of naval warfare, Smith translates chivalric culture into nautical terms.

Smith's *Advertisements* becomes a work of instruction but also of apology. Here, in among his specific advice on planting methods and the clearing of trees, we find Smith's commentary on the theory and practice of European conquest. He emerges as an admirer of Spanish and Portuguese accomplishments, as well as a critic of warfare between Christians. In fact, he here articulates many old chivalric ideals of action, adventure, conquest and conversion of the infidel. Here, too, he sums up his career:

> Having beene a slave to the Turks, prisoner amongst the most barbarous Salvages, after my deliverance commonly discovering and ranging those large rivers and unknowne Nations with such a handfull of ignorant companions that the wiser sort often gave mee [up] for lost, alwayes in mutinies wants and miseries, blowne up with gunpowder; A long time [a] prisoner among the French Pyrats, from whom escaping in a little boat by my selfe . . . and yet to see the fruits of my labours thus well begin to prosper . . .[86]

Smith has not altogether given up hankering for action. At one point he complains that the Puritans preferred his books and maps to the personal assistance of the author. Like the squire of Lull's chivalric manual, they ride off with the book, and leave the hermit knight behind. The pamphlet concludes with an energetic appeal for military preparedness on the part of the colonists and their leaders. "And truly there is no pleasure comparable to [that of] a generous spirit; as good imploiment in noble actions, especially amongst Turks, Heathens, and Infidels; to see daily new Countries, people, fashions, governments, stratagems; [to] releeve the oppressed, comfort his friends, passe miseries, subdue enemies, adventure upon any feazable danger for God and his Country."[87] To counterbalance this ideal, Smith remarks tartly "And there is no worse misery than [to] be conducted by a foole, or commanded by a coward."[88]

The model of advancement that animates Smith here remains that of the

---

85 One of Caxton's last productions was his *Lerne to Die* of 1490. He also published a vocabulary of French and English mercantile terms, a courtesy book for young girls, and two contrasting chivalric manuals.
86 Smith, *Works*, ed. Arber, p. 945.
87 Ibid., p. 962.
88 Ibid., p. 965

medieval knight errant or crusader – dusted off, instructed in the use of gunpowder, but otherwise untarnished by the centuries. His attitude to the "Salvages" differs little from Bevis of Hampton's view of the Saracens. Yet Smith, like Bevis, comes to realize he faces more dangerous foes among his own countrymen. With little effort, Smith can be seen as a monstrous anachronism. Alternatively, one can respect him as a creative adaptor bearing witness to the vitality of the chivalric tradition.

CONCLUSIONS

It is only by studying the minds of men that we shall understand the causes of anything.[1]

Felix qui potuit rerum cognoscere causas.
Happy is the one who can understand the causes of things.[2]

THIS STUDY SUGGESTS that the present day can better understand European explorers and conquistadores by understanding their fantasies. It further proposes that those fantasies remained essentially late medieval. The work of Irving Leonard, Maurice Keen, and others cited earlier points in this direction. However, the contribution of later medieval chivalric romance, discussed in this study, has remained largely unexplored. These books have been closed to most specialists in the early modern period, and indeed to many medievalists, ever since Juan Luis Vives, Roger Ascham and their colleagues tried to slam them shut on the fingers of the sixteenth-century reader. Their hostility has its roots in the revolution of the humanists, who were out to jettison what they considered pernicious baggage in order to remake Western literature in the image of the Ancients. As it happened, the material they worked so hard to discard proves essential to our understanding of our own period, and vital in the ongoing development of vernacular literature. This fundamental misunderstanding has impaired the self-perception of most European cultures. It still warps our understanding of cultural history all across the globe.

This is a study of what European explorers wrote and perhaps how they perceived their actions, not of what we now understand them to have done. Both perspectives call for discussion. The problem becomes more complex when the two observers vary so wildly in their conclusions. One reader's crusade is another's genocide. This study has been constructed on the premise that if we never attempt to plumb the psychology of the crusade, we cannot hope to comprehend the massacre.

A second premise that has been tested here is that it is a mistake to impose strict distinctions between the factual literature of travel and the voyage of imaginative fiction. By enforcing this division, we exclude a valuable body of pertinent material from consideration. Closely related texts, often the work of the same author, are by this means divorced from one another. The distinction becomes all the more meaningless when we recognize that most factual writing

---

[1] Sir James Joll, "1914: The Unspoken Assumptions," inaugural lecture, University of London (1967).
[2] Virgil, *Georgics* II, line 490.

is fictional in some respect, and most fiction draws on factual experience to some degree. All in all, the division of fact from fiction is an anachronism of doubtful validity. They knew better in the Middle Ages. (By the same token, the "unreliability of history" is, as all living scholars have seen, an idea too often abused to support some political agenda.) Imagination plays a far greater role in history than most academics care to admit.

Venturing out in all directions, European explorers encountered peoples with their own highly developed warrior elites, cults of honor, and elaborate codes of conduct in war. This study details how men well versed in these sophisticated, parallel systems still contrived to misunderstand one another on a regular basis. The question remains unanswered: why do these chivalries fail to acknowledge one another? "El Inca" Garcilaso de la Vega deserves better recognition as a pioneer in the still neglected field of comparative chivalry. His work towards reconciling his own Inca and European chivalric ancestry offers us a model for future development. This path is all the more important for present-day scholars because it can lead us to a clearer understanding of the international culture of violence.

Following Huizinga, twentieth-century scholars have tended to assume that late medieval and Renaissance chivalry was merely a decadent pretence. That eminent historian Karl Brandi labeled the elaborate protocol of the court of Philip the Good of Burgundy an "impressive, sumptuous and yet wholly meaningless shell," and asked, "How could the harsh reality of life penetrate into this world of dream?"[3] This pragmatic assumption condescends to the past, as we the living too often condescend to the dead. We run great risks by ascribing sincerity – or insincerity – to our ancestors at this distance. How do we know that certain rituals were meaningless to them? We are the ones who think the duke of Burgundy's rituals ought not to have meant anything. As a rule of thumb, I suggest that if the ceremony had become meaningless, it would have been discarded. If people still engaged in chivalric performances, as they did for a surprisingly long time after the death of Philip the Good, it must be because such rites meant something to them. It is our business as historians of culture to find out the meaning, not to deny the evidence.

Finding out the meaning is perhaps more easily said than done. To do so, we need to reacquaint ourselves with a largely forgotten body of literature, the later medieval chivalric romance. Reading chivalric romances has become a lost art for most practicing scholars. This literature is not easy of access. It reveals its secrets to the practiced, sympathetic eye. Most scholars, including many medievalists, remain prejudiced against these texts, in some cases without giving much evidence of having read them. As often as not, they are also unequipped to cope with them, either because of their language or because of unfamiliarity with the form and its conventions. The academic reader's lack of sympathy with

---

[3]   Karl Brandi, *The Emperor Charles V: The Growth and Destiny of a Man and of a World-Empire*, trans. C. V. Wedgwood (1939; rpt. London, 1963), p. 31.

the chivalric romance is interesting in itself. I have ascribed it in large measure to the legacy of humanism, perhaps augmented by a modern reaction against nineteenth-century romanticism. It will require training and patience to overcome this barrier to understanding.

We should not underestimate how much theology directs our thinking as students of the past. The Christian worldview predisposes the historian to see revivals, rebirths, renaissances and renascences, New Testaments, and broken covenants. The Jewish model is perhaps more receptive to grand continuities. Christian historians see Renaissances, glorious new births, iconoclastic revolutions that discard the immediate past with violent indignation. Jewish historians may be better attuned to the enduring traditions that persist unrecognized beneath more superficial trends in the history of ideas. This project argues against a tidy, compartmental view of history, pecked into fragments of a size suitable for stuffing into the bills of the young. A view that takes into account long vistas, grand intellectual continuities, perhaps even abiding human interests, is needed to redress the balance. Chivalry might be best understood as an ocean in its ebb and flow, advancing and receding, never to be quenched.

In the end, this writer cannot help wondering how much of adult life is truly child's play, enacting fantasies of our earliest years. In *Homo Ludens* Huizinga wondered the same thing.

This book is about principles and how they were put into practice, and about idealism and opportunism. It is also a study of how art evades responsibility. The chivalric fiction discussed in this volume set out to teach behavior. Through its depiction of the knight's infidel opponents, it also channeled Christian violence outward against selected outsiders.

In saying this I am by no means mounting a crusade of my own for the eradication of chivalric literature from Western culture. Such a notion would be doomed from the start. I hope that I have demonstrated that chivalry has always been more deeply embedded in our thought than most twentieth-century thinkers suppose. Instead, we must confront the same problem of interpretation that challenged William Caxton's readers of 1485, as they entered the ambiguous world of the *Morte Darthur*. "For herein may be seen noble chyvalrye, curtosye, humanyté, frendlynesse, hardynesse, love, frendshyp, cowardyse, murdre, hate, vertue, and synne. Doo after the good and leve the evyl, and it shall brynge you to good fame and renommee."

INDEX